THE CUTE GIRL NETWORK

GREG MEANS • MK REED • JOE FLOOD

:01

First Second

NEW YORK

Thanks to Galen Longstreth, Robin Enrico, Hope Larson, Philip Simon, Jeremy Tiedeman, Pete Hallsworth, Colleen AF Venable, Nicole Georges, Nate Beaty, Robin Anderson, Elizabeth Castaldo, and everyone at First Second.

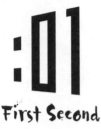

:01
First Second

Published by First Second
First Second is an imprint of Roaring Brook Press, a division of
Holtzbrinck Publishing Holdings Limited Partnership
175 Fifth Avenue, New York, New York 10010

Cataloging-in-Publication Data is on file at the Library of Congress.

ISBN 978-1-59643-751-7

First Second books are available for special promotions and premiums.
For details, contact: Director of Special Markets, Holtzbrinck Publishers.

FIRST
EDITION

First edition 2013
Book design by Colleen AF Venable

Printed in the United States of America
10 9 8 7 6 5 4 3 2 1

BY ART WE LIVE

CHAPTER ONE

"Ass over Teakettle"

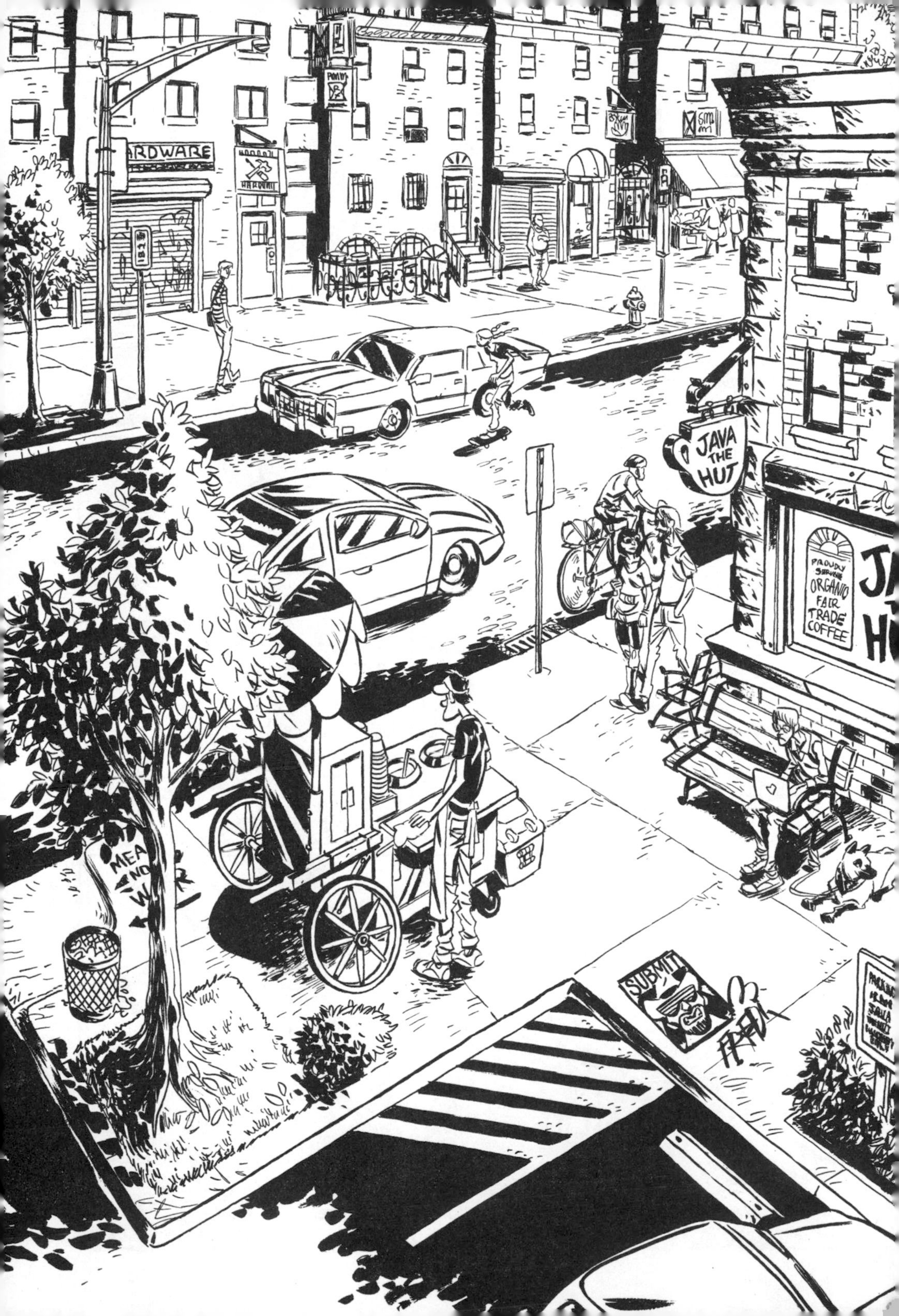
ARDWARE
JAVA THE HUT
PROUDLY SERVING ORGANIC FAIR TRADE COFFEE
SUBMIT

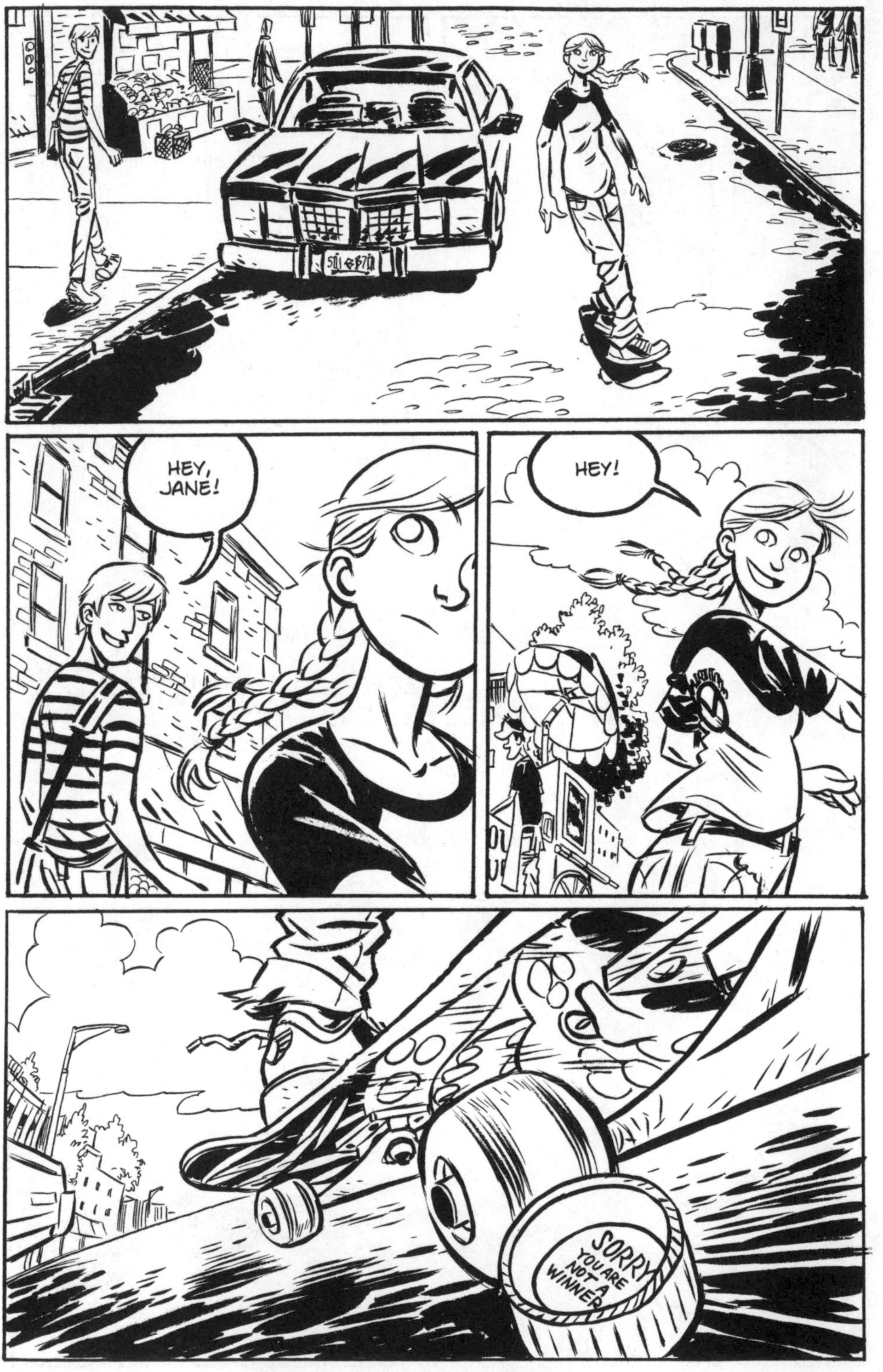
HEY, JANE!
HEY!
SORRY YOU ARE NOT A WINNER

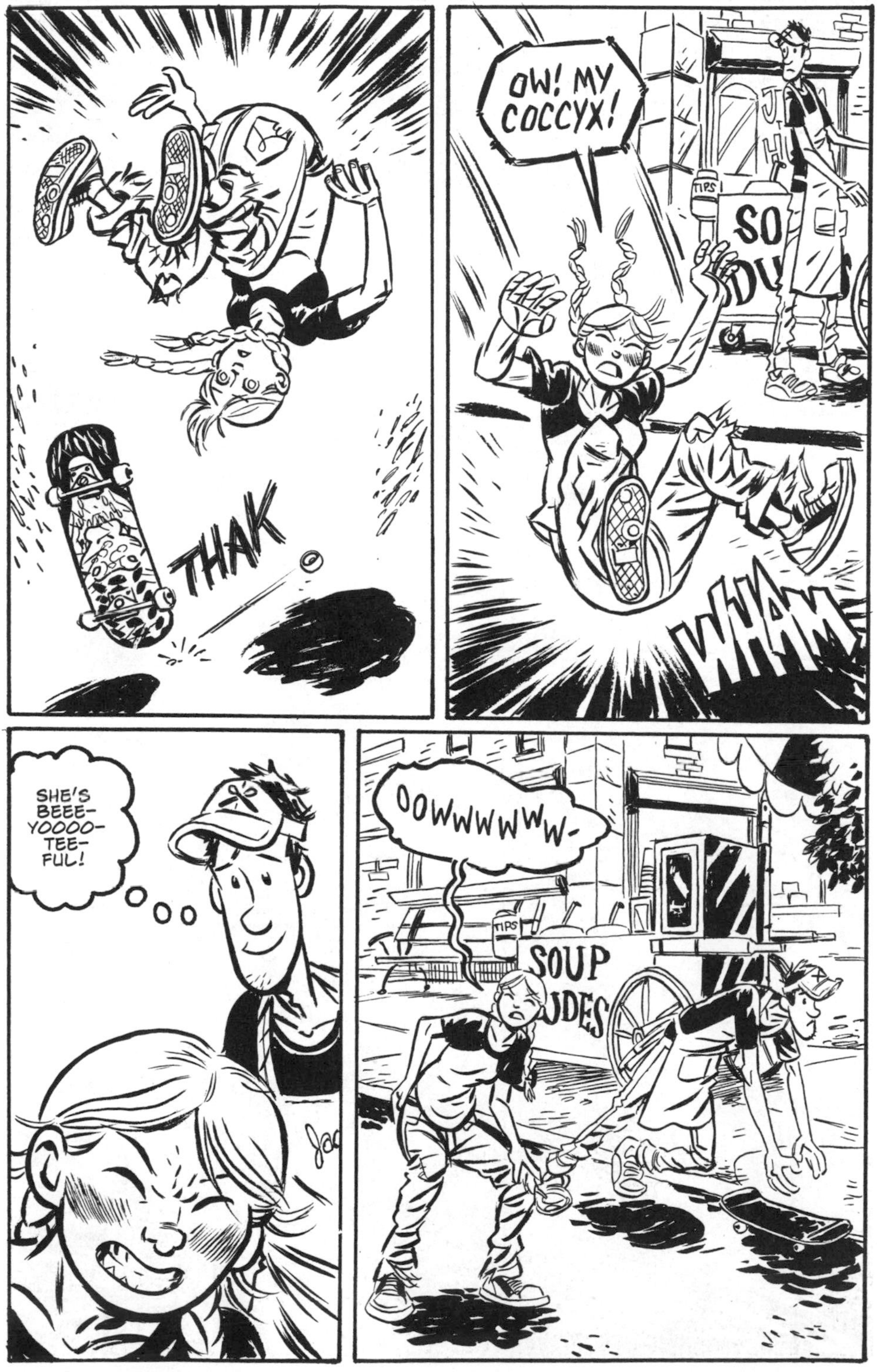
THAK
OW! MY COCCYX!
TIPS
WHAM
SHE'S BEEE-YOOOO-TEE-FUL!
OOWWWWWWW-
TIPS
SOUP

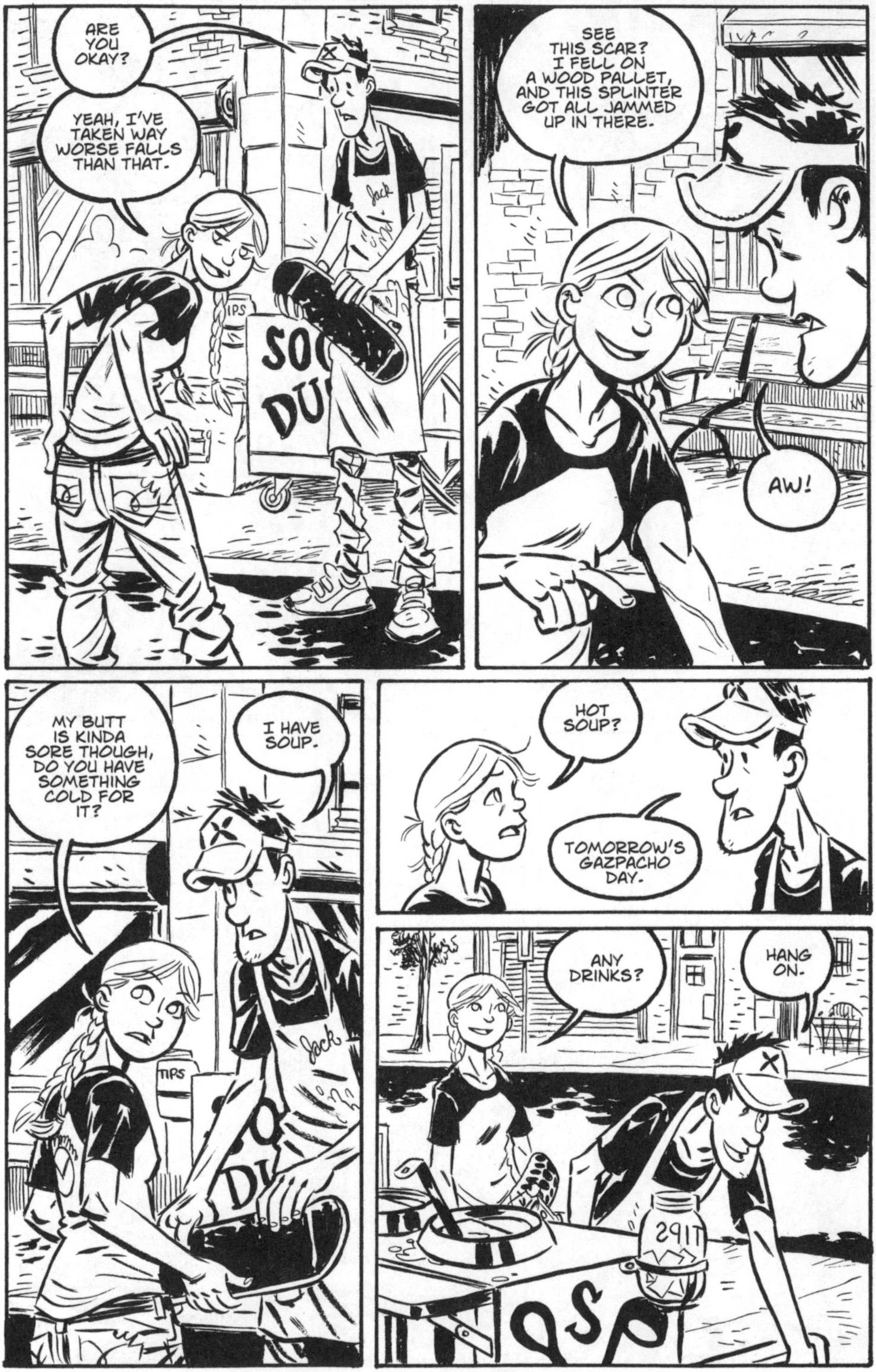
ARE YOU OKAY?
YEAH, I'VE TAKEN WAY WORSE FALLS THAN THAT.
TIPS
SEE THIS SCAR? I FELL ON A WOOD PALLET, AND THIS SPLINTER GOT ALL JAMMED UP IN THERE.
AW!
MY BUTT IS KINDA SORE THOUGH, DO YOU HAVE SOMETHING COLD FOR IT?
I HAVE SOUP.
TIPS
HOT SOUP?
TOMORROW'S GAZPACHO DAY.
ANY DRINKS?
HANG ON.
TIPS

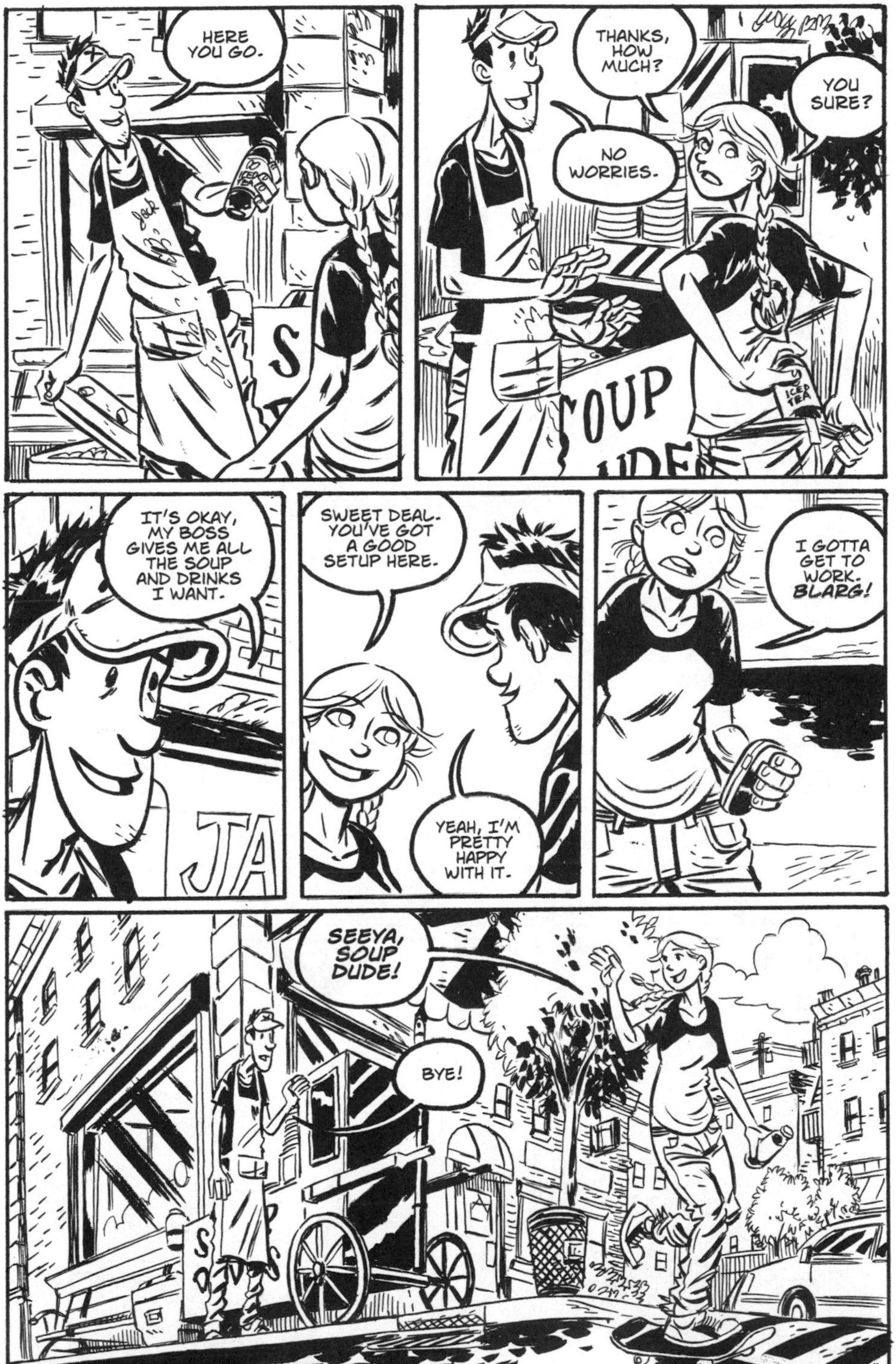
HERE YOU GO.
THANKS, HOW MUCH?
NO WORRIES.
YOU SURE?
IT'S OKAY, MY BOSS GIVES ME ALL THE SOUP AND DRINKS I WANT.
SWEET DEAL. YOU'VE GOT A GOOD SETUP HERE.
YEAH, I'M PRETTY HAPPY WITH IT.
I GOTTA GET TO WORK. BLARG!
SEEYA, SOUP DUDE!
BYE!

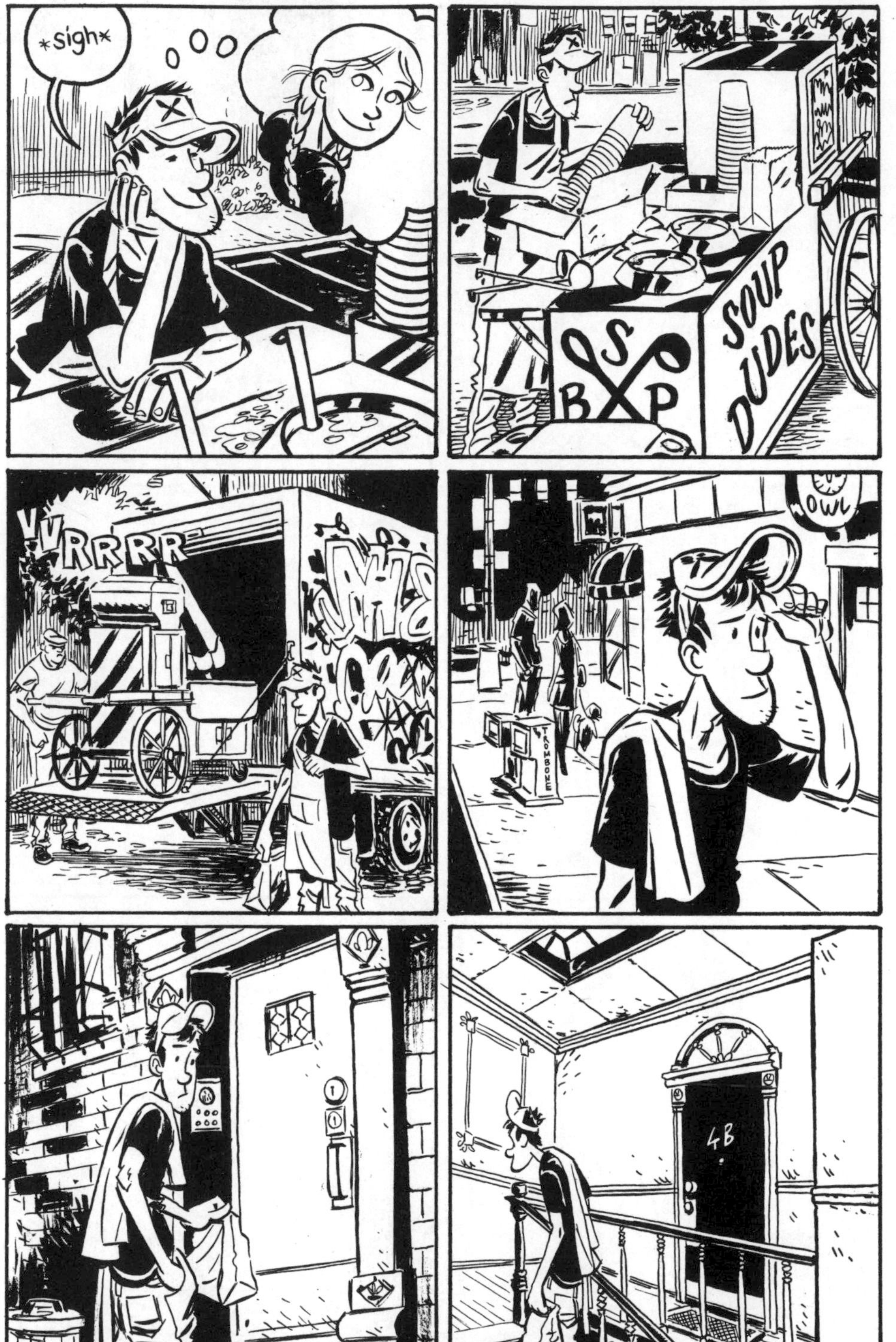
sigh
SOUP DUDES
SBP
VVRRRRR
OWL
TROMBONE
4B

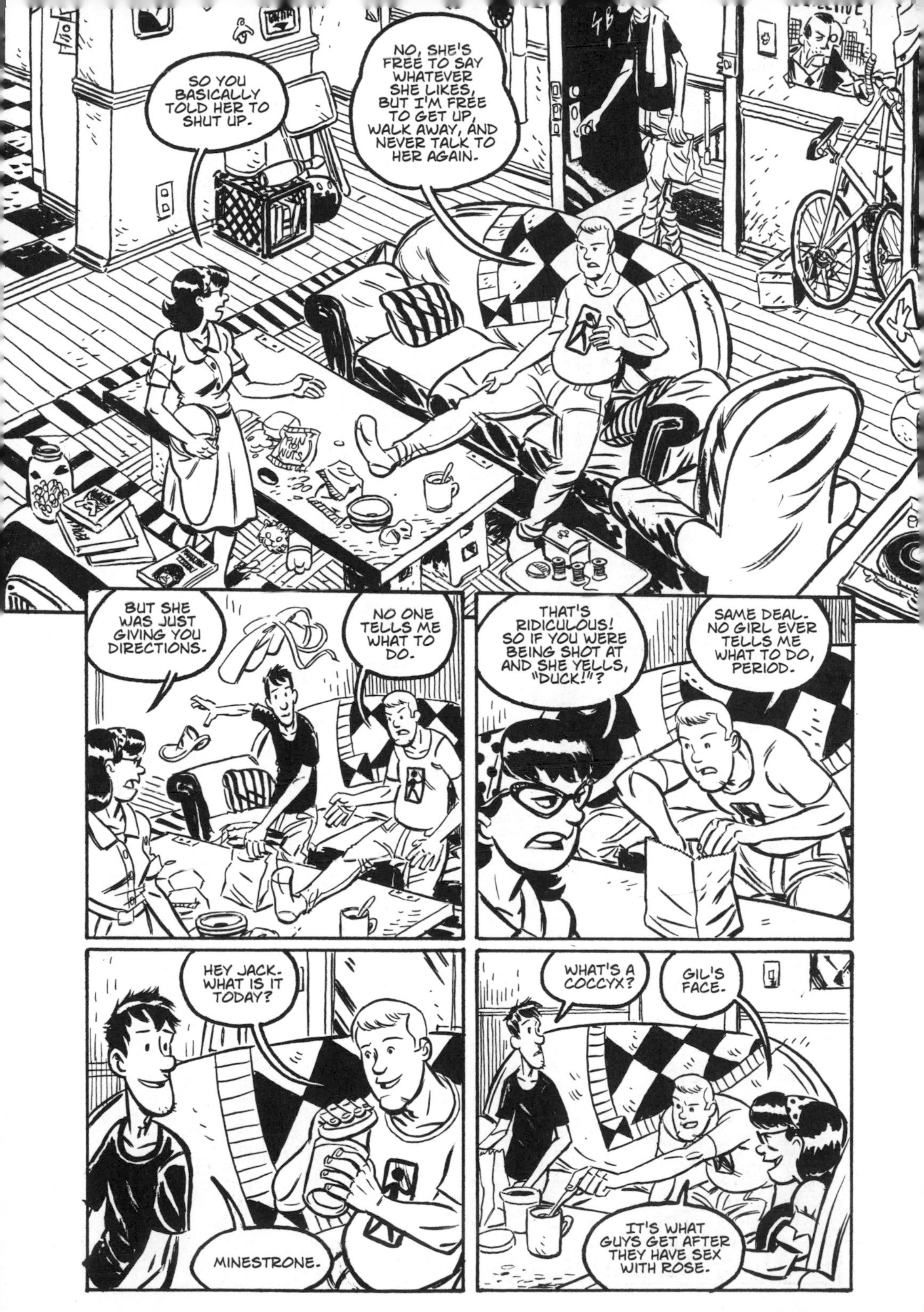
SO YOU BASICALLY TOLD HER TO SHUT UP.
NO, SHE'S FREE TO SAY WHATEVER SHE LIKES, BUT I'M FREE TO GET UP, WALK AWAY, AND NEVER TALK TO HER AGAIN.
FUN NUTS
BUT SHE WAS JUST GIVING YOU DIRECTIONS.
NO ONE TELLS ME WHAT TO DO.
THAT'S RIDICULOUS! SO IF YOU WERE BEING SHOT AT AND SHE YELLS, "DUCK!"?
SAME DEAL. NO GIRL EVER TELLS ME WHAT TO DO, PERIOD.
HEY JACK. WHAT IS IT TODAY?
MINESTRONE.
WHAT'S A COCCYX?
GIL'S FACE.
IT'S WHAT GUYS GET AFTER THEY HAVE SEX WITH ROSE.

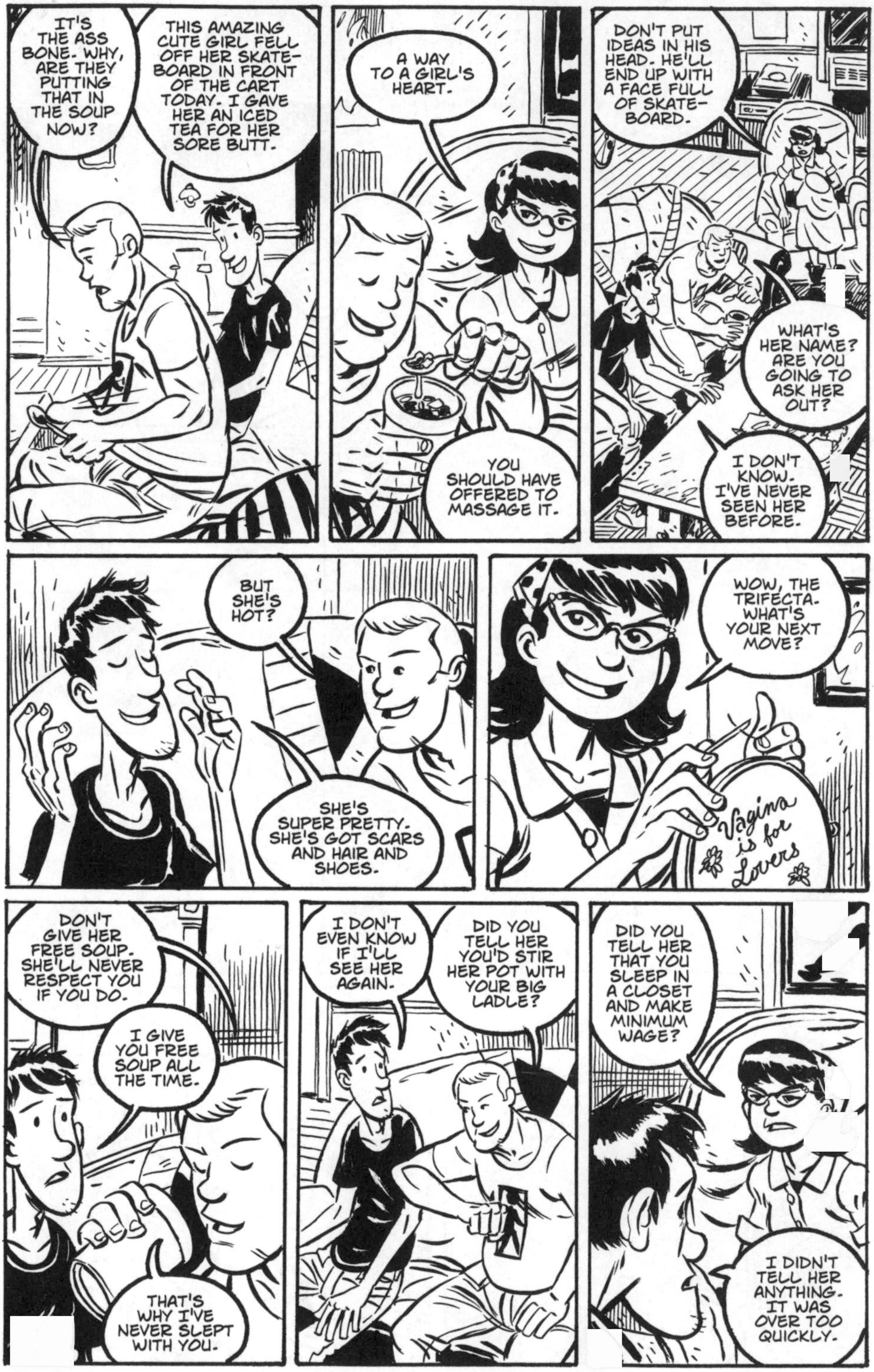
IT'S THE ASS BONE. WHY, ARE THEY PUTTING THAT IN THE SOUP NOW?
THIS AMAZING CUTE GIRL FELL OFF HER SKATE-BOARD IN FRONT OF THE CART TODAY. I GAVE HER AN ICED TEA FOR HER SORE BUTT.
A WAY TO A GIRL'S HEART.
YOU SHOULD HAVE OFFERED TO MASSAGE IT.
DON'T PUT IDEAS IN HIS HEAD. HE'LL END UP WITH A FACE FULL OF SKATE-BOARD.
WHAT'S HER NAME? ARE YOU GOING TO ASK HER OUT?
I DON'T KNOW. I'VE NEVER SEEN HER BEFORE.
BUT SHE'S HOT?
SHE'S SUPER PRETTY. SHE'S GOT SCARS AND HAIR AND SHOES.
WOW, THE TRIFECTA. WHAT'S YOUR NEXT MOVE?
Vagina is for Lovers
DON'T GIVE HER FREE SOUP. SHE'LL NEVER RESPECT YOU IF YOU DO.
I GIVE YOU FREE SOUP ALL THE TIME.
THAT'S WHY I'VE NEVER SLEPT WITH YOU.
I DON'T EVEN KNOW IF I'LL SEE HER AGAIN.
DID YOU TELL HER YOU'D STIR HER POT WITH YOUR BIG LADLE?
DID YOU TELL HER THAT YOU SLEEP IN A CLOSET AND MAKE MINIMUM WAGE?
I DIDN'T TELL HER ANYTHING. IT WAS OVER TOO QUICKLY.

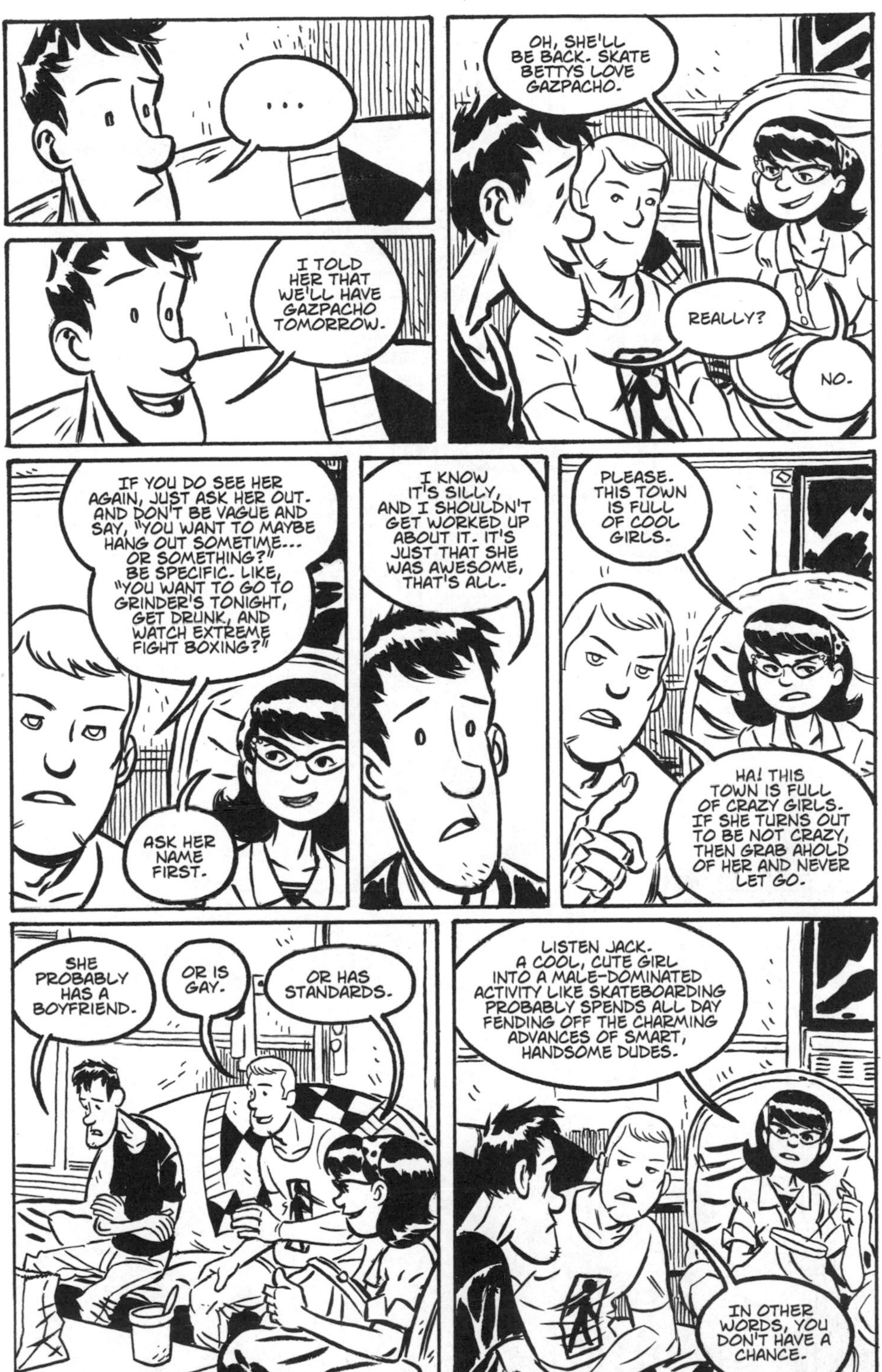
...
OH, SHE'LL BE BACK. SKATE BETTYS LOVE GAZPACHO.
I TOLD HER THAT WE'LL HAVE GAZPACHO TOMORROW.
REALLY?
NO.
IF YOU DO SEE HER AGAIN, JUST ASK HER OUT. AND DON'T BE VAGUE AND SAY, "YOU WANT TO MAYBE HANG OUT SOMETIME... OR SOMETHING?" BE SPECIFIC. LIKE, "YOU WANT TO GO TO GRINDER'S TONIGHT, GET DRUNK, AND WATCH EXTREME FIGHT BOXING?"
ASK HER NAME FIRST.
I KNOW IT'S SILLY, AND I SHOULDN'T GET WORKED UP ABOUT IT. IT'S JUST THAT SHE WAS AWESOME, THAT'S ALL.
PLEASE. THIS TOWN IS FULL OF COOL GIRLS.
HA! THIS TOWN IS FULL OF CRAZY GIRLS. IF SHE TURNS OUT TO BE NOT CRAZY, THEN GRAB AHOLD OF HER AND NEVER LET GO.
SHE PROBABLY HAS A BOYFRIEND.
OR IS GAY.
OR HAS STANDARDS.
LISTEN JACK. A COOL, CUTE GIRL INTO A MALE-DOMINATED ACTIVITY LIKE SKATEBOARDING PROBABLY SPENDS ALL DAY FENDING OFF THE CHARMING ADVANCES OF SMART, HANDSOME DUDES.
IN OTHER WORDS, YOU DON'T HAVE A CHANCE.

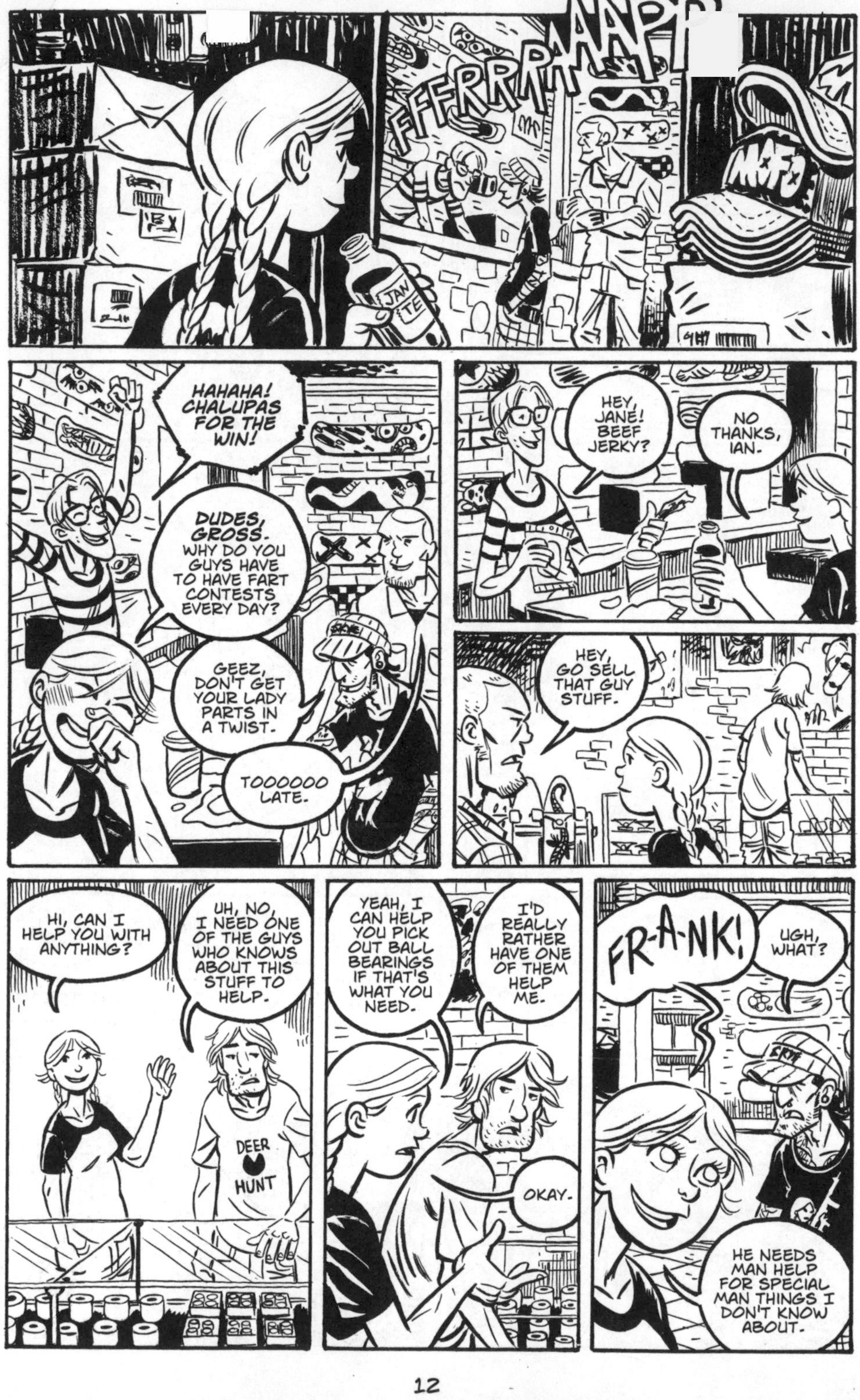
FFFRRRAAAPP
HAHAHA! CHALUPAS FOR THE WIN!
DUDES, GROSS. WHY DO YOU GUYS HAVE TO HAVE FART CONTESTS EVERY DAY?
GEEZ, DON'T GET YOUR LADY PARTS IN A TWIST.
TOOOOOO LATE.
HEY, JANE! BEEF JERKY?
NO THANKS, IAN.
HEY, GO SELL THAT GUY STUFF.
HI, CAN I HELP YOU WITH ANYTHING?
UH, NO, I NEED ONE OF THE GUYS WHO KNOWS ABOUT THIS STUFF TO HELP.
DEER HUNT
YEAH, I CAN HELP YOU PICK OUT BALL BEARINGS IF THAT'S WHAT YOU NEED.
I'D REALLY RATHER HAVE ONE OF THEM HELP ME.
OKAY.
FR-A-NK!
UGH, WHAT?
HE NEEDS MAN HELP FOR SPECIAL MAN THINGS I DON'T KNOW ABOUT.

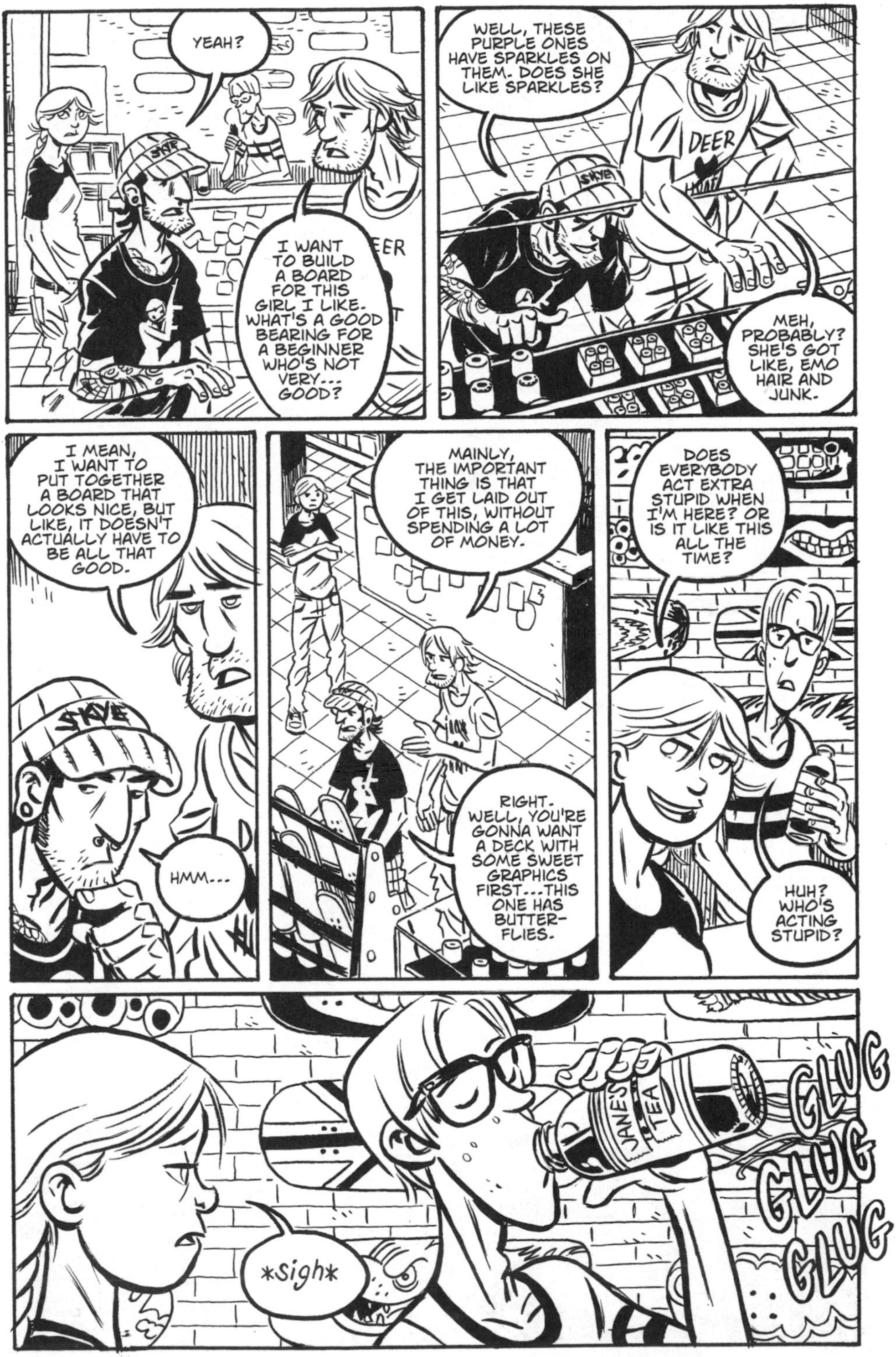
YEAH?
I WANT TO BUILD A BOARD FOR THIS GIRL I LIKE. WHAT'S A GOOD BEARING FOR A BEGINNER WHO'S NOT VERY... GOOD?
WELL, THESE PURPLE ONES HAVE SPARKLES ON THEM. DOES SHE LIKE SPARKLES?
MEH, PROBABLY? SHE'S GOT LIKE, EMO HAIR AND JUNK.
I MEAN, I WANT TO PUT TOGETHER A BOARD THAT LOOKS NICE, BUT LIKE, IT DOESN'T ACTUALLY HAVE TO BE ALL THAT GOOD.
HMM...
MAINLY, THE IMPORTANT THING IS THAT I GET LAID OUT OF THIS, WITHOUT SPENDING A LOT OF MONEY.
RIGHT. WELL, YOU'RE GONNA WANT A DECK WITH SOME SWEET GRAPHICS FIRST...THIS ONE HAS BUTTER-FLIES.
DOES EVERYBODY ACT EXTRA STUPID WHEN I'M HERE? OR IS IT LIKE THIS ALL THE TIME?
HUH? WHO'S ACTING STUPID?
JANE'S TEA
GLUG GLUG GLUG
sigh

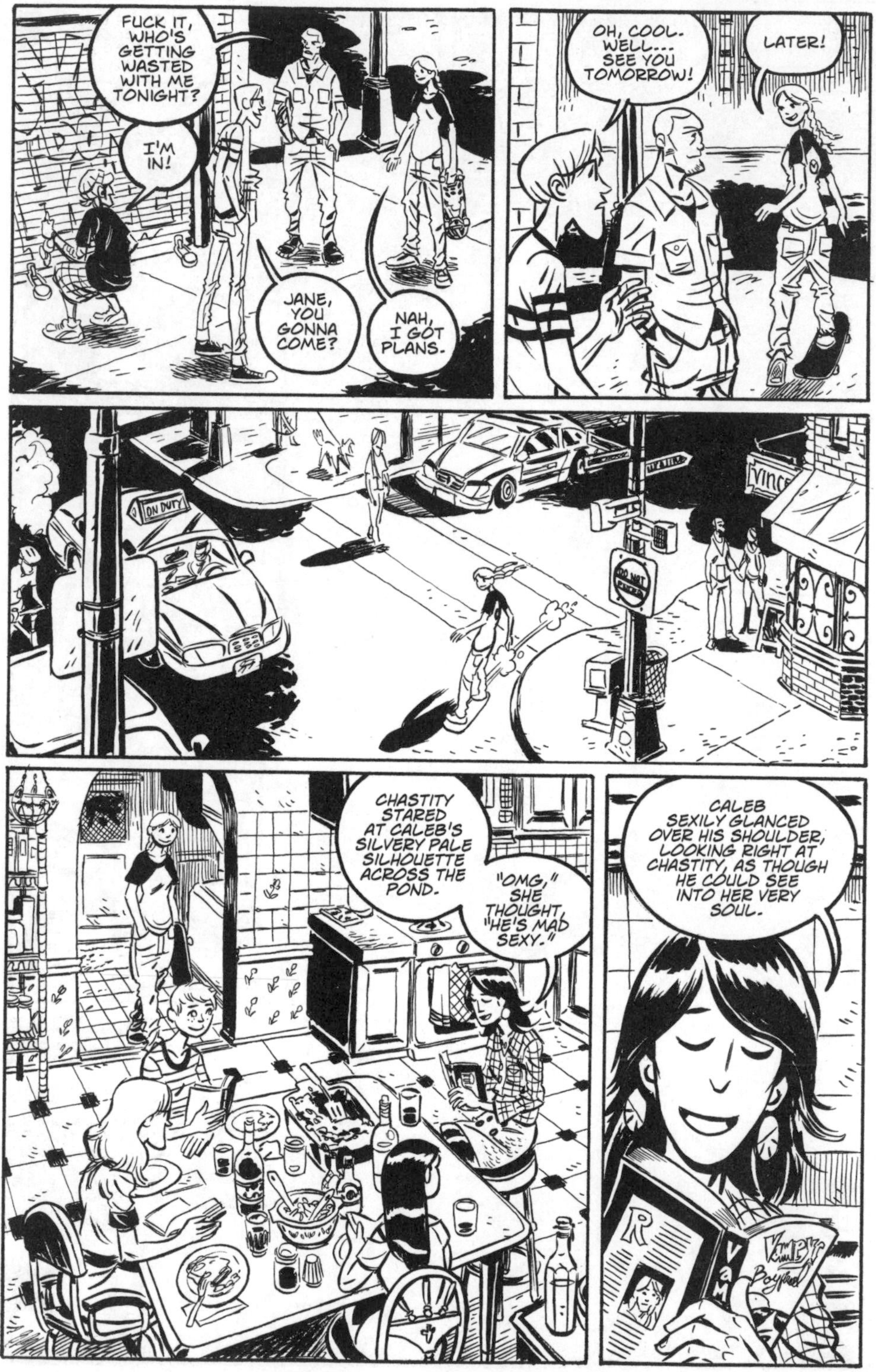

FUCK IT, WHO'S GETTING WASTED WITH ME TONIGHT?
I'M IN!
JANE, YOU GONNA COME?
NAH, I GOT PLANS.
OH, COOL. WELL... SEE YOU TOMORROW!
LATER!
ON DUTY
CHASTITY STARED AT CALEB'S SILVERY PALE SILHOUETTE ACROSS THE POND.
"OMG," SHE THOUGHT, "HE'S MAD SEXY."
CALEB SEXILY GLANCED OVER HIS SHOULDER, LOOKING RIGHT AT CHASTITY, AS THOUGH HE COULD SEE INTO HER VERY SOUL.

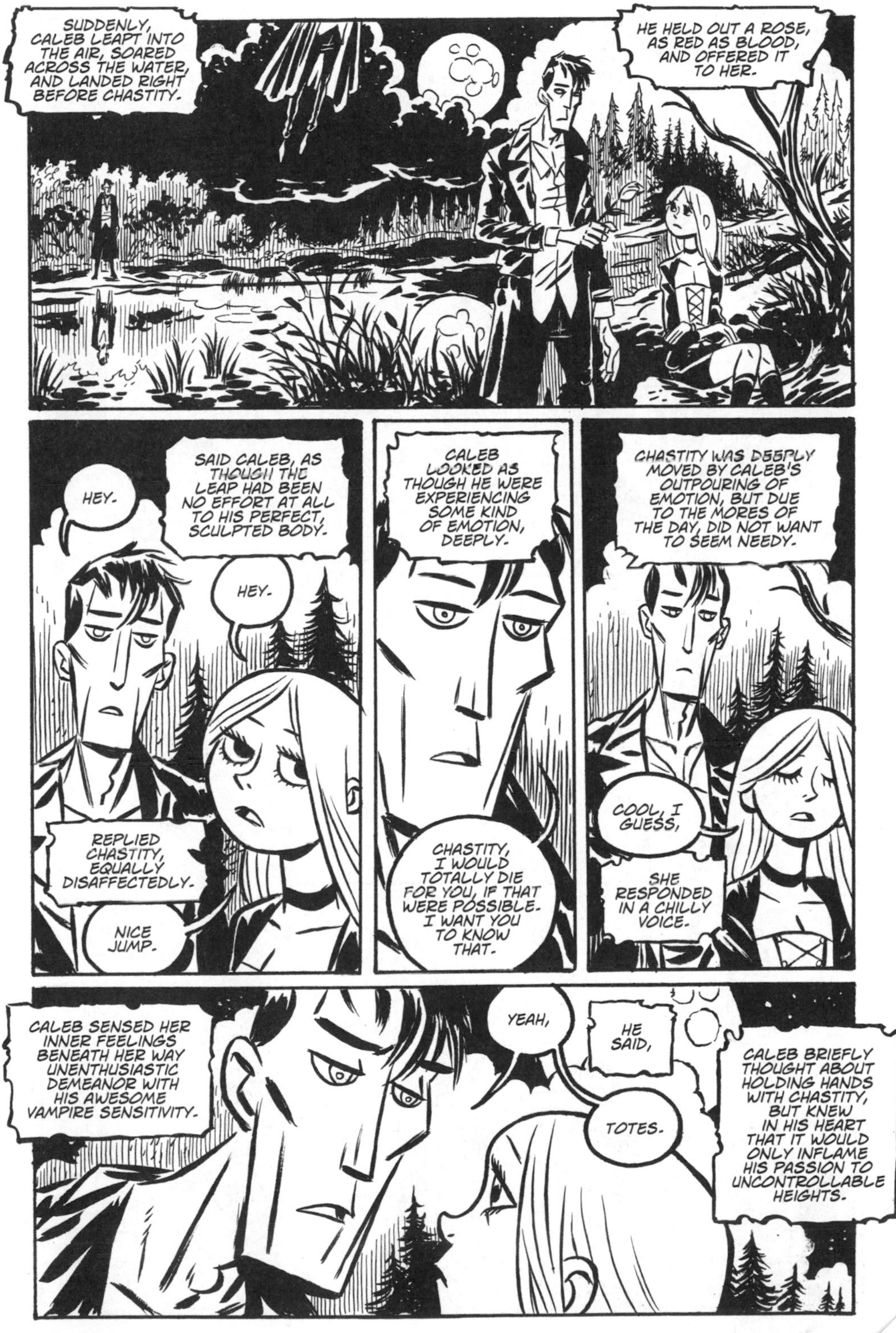
SUDDENLY, CALEB LEAPT INTO THE AIR, SOARED ACROSS THE WATER, AND LANDED RIGHT BEFORE CHASTITY.
HE HELD OUT A ROSE, AS RED AS BLOOD, AND OFFERED IT TO HER.
HEY.
SAID CALEB, AS THOUGH THE LEAP HAD BEEN NO EFFORT AT ALL TO HIS PERFECT, SCULPTED BODY.
HEY.
REPLIED CHASTITY, EQUALLY DISAFFECTEDLY.
NICE JUMP.
CALEB LOOKED AS THOUGH HE WERE EXPERIENCING SOME KIND OF EMOTION, DEEPLY.
CHASTITY, I WOULD TOTALLY DIE FOR YOU, IF THAT WERE POSSIBLE. I WANT YOU TO KNOW THAT.
CHASTITY WAS DEEPLY MOVED BY CALEB'S OUTPOURING OF EMOTION, BUT DUE TO THE MORES OF THE DAY, DID NOT WANT TO SEEM NEEDY.
COOL, I GUESS,
SHE RESPONDED IN A CHILLY VOICE.
CALEB SENSED HER INNER FEELINGS BENEATH HER WAY UNENTHUSIASTIC DEMEANOR WITH HIS AWESOME VAMPIRE SENSITIVITY.
YEAH,
HE SAID,
TOTES.
CALEB BRIEFLY THOUGHT ABOUT HOLDING HANDS WITH CHASTITY, BUT KNEW IN HIS HEART THAT IT WOULD ONLY INFLAME HIS PASSION TO UNCONTROLLABLE HEIGHTS.

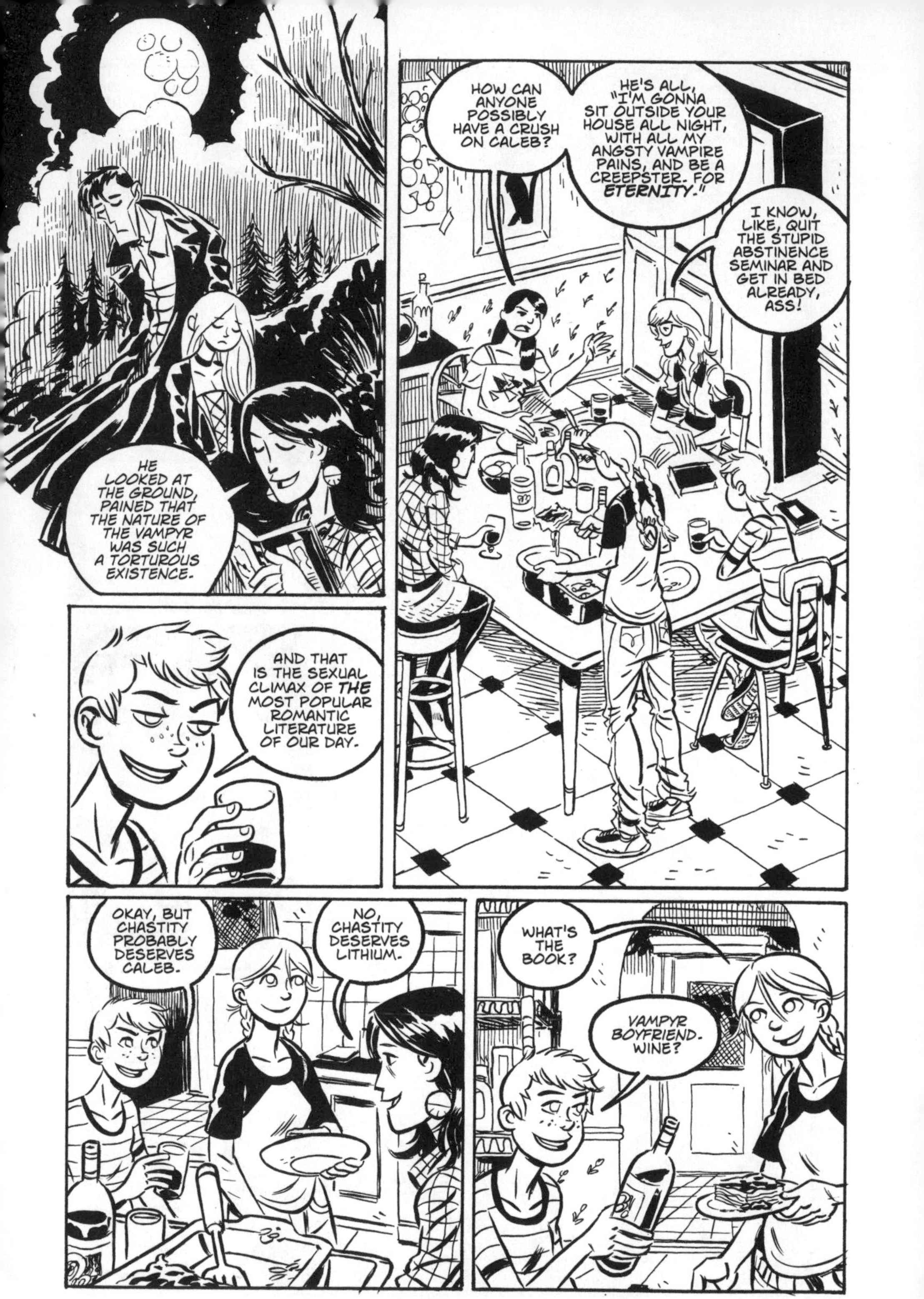
HE LOOKED AT THE GROUND, PAINED THAT THE NATURE OF THE VAMPYR WAS SUCH A TORTUROUS EXISTENCE.
HOW CAN ANYONE POSSIBLY HAVE A CRUSH ON CALEB?
HE'S ALL, "I'M GONNA SIT OUTSIDE YOUR HOUSE ALL NIGHT, WITH ALL MY ANGSTY VAMPIRE PAINS, AND BE A CREEPSTER. FOR ETERNITY."
I KNOW, LIKE, QUIT THE STUPID ABSTINENCE SEMINAR AND GET IN BED ALREADY, ASS!
AND THAT IS THE SEXUAL CLIMAX OF THE MOST POPULAR ROMANTIC LITERATURE OF OUR DAY.
OKAY, BUT CHASTITY PROBABLY DESERVES CALEB.
NO, CHASTITY DESERVES LITHIUM.
WHAT'S THE BOOK?
VAMPYR BOYFRIEND. WINE?

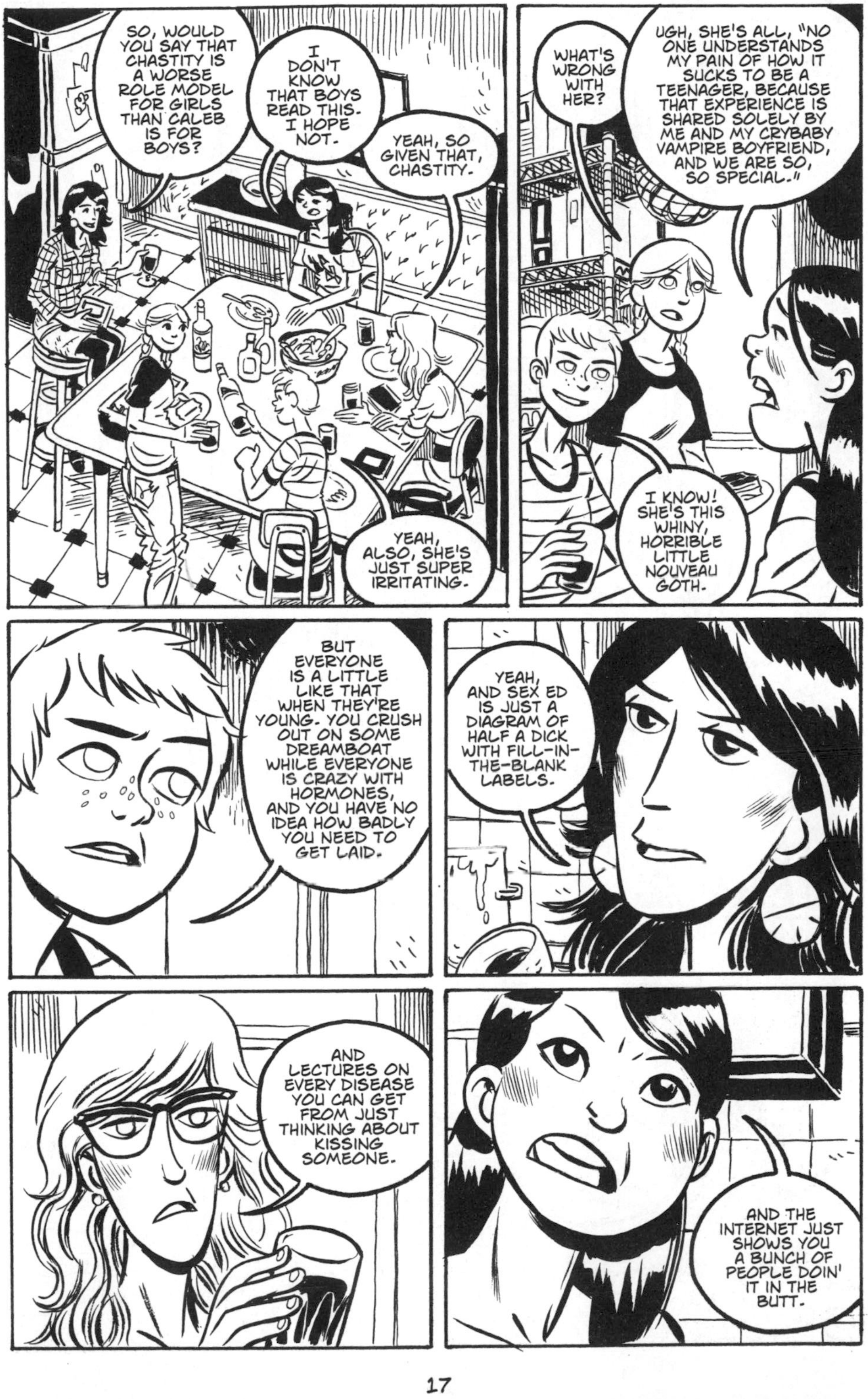
SO, WOULD YOU SAY THAT CHASTITY IS A WORSE ROLE MODEL FOR GIRLS THAN CALEB IS FOR BOYS?
I DON'T KNOW THAT BOYS READ THIS. I HOPE NOT.
YEAH, SO GIVEN THAT, CHASTITY.
YEAH, ALSO, SHE'S JUST SUPER IRRITATING.
WHAT'S WRONG WITH HER?
UGH, SHE'S ALL, "NO ONE UNDERSTANDS MY PAIN OF HOW IT SUCKS TO BE A TEENAGER, BECAUSE THAT EXPERIENCE IS SHARED SOLELY BY ME AND MY CRYBABY VAMPIRE BOYFRIEND, AND WE ARE SO, SO SPECIAL."
I KNOW! SHE'S THIS WHINY, HORRIBLE LITTLE NOUVEAU GOTH.
BUT EVERYONE IS A LITTLE LIKE THAT WHEN THEY'RE YOUNG. YOU CRUSH OUT ON SOME DREAMBOAT WHILE EVERYONE IS CRAZY WITH HORMONES, AND YOU HAVE NO IDEA HOW BADLY YOU NEED TO GET LAID.
YEAH, AND SEX ED IS JUST A DIAGRAM OF HALF A DICK WITH FILL-IN-THE-BLANK LABELS.
AND LECTURES ON EVERY DISEASE YOU CAN GET FROM JUST THINKING ABOUT KISSING SOMEONE.
AND THE INTERNET JUST SHOWS YOU A BUNCH OF PEOPLE DOIN' IT IN THE BUTT.

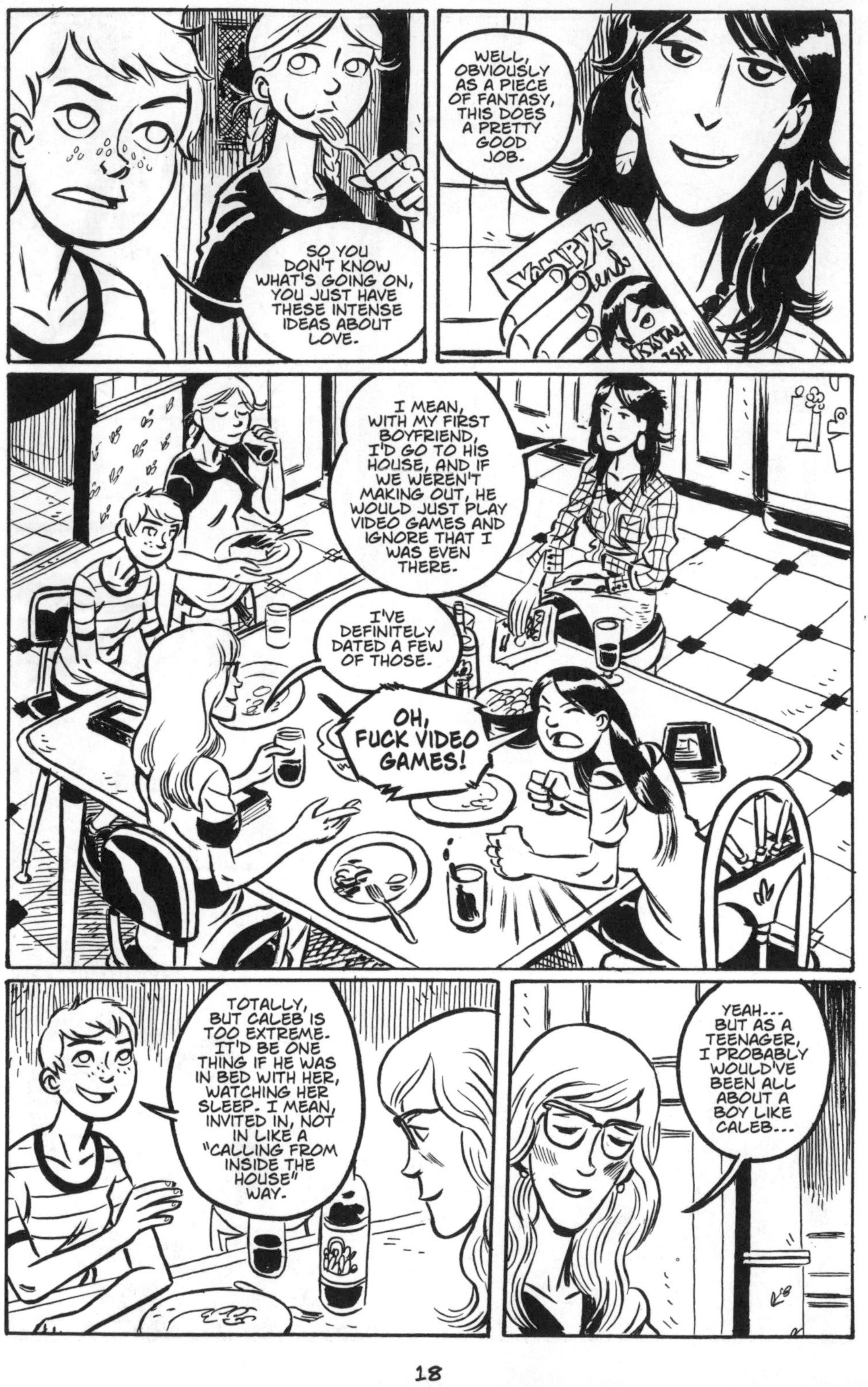
SO YOU DON'T KNOW WHAT'S GOING ON, YOU JUST HAVE THESE INTENSE IDEAS ABOUT LOVE.
WELL, OBVIOUSLY AS A PIECE OF FANTASY, THIS DOES A PRETTY GOOD JOB.
I MEAN, WITH MY FIRST BOYFRIEND, I'D GO TO HIS HOUSE, AND IF WE WEREN'T MAKING OUT, HE WOULD JUST PLAY VIDEO GAMES AND IGNORE THAT I WAS EVEN THERE.
I'VE DEFINITELY DATED A FEW OF THOSE.
OH, FUCK VIDEO GAMES!
TOTALLY, BUT CALEB IS TOO EXTREME. IT'D BE ONE THING IF HE WAS IN BED WITH HER, WATCHING HER SLEEP. I MEAN, INVITED IN, NOT IN LIKE A "CALLING FROM INSIDE THE HOUSE" WAY.
YEAH... BUT AS A TEENAGER, I PROBABLY WOULD'VE BEEN ALL ABOUT A BOY LIKE CALEB...

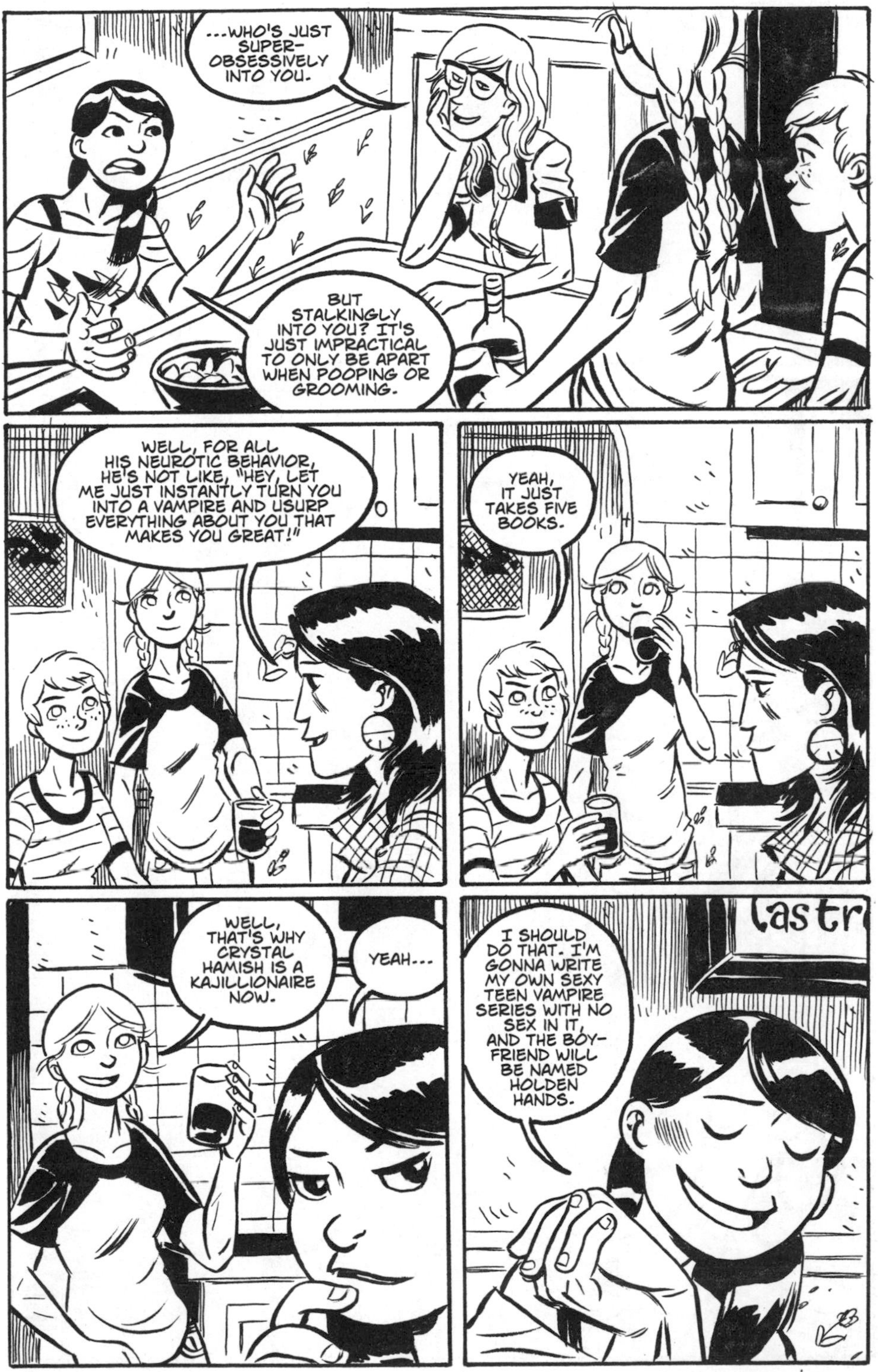
...WHO'S JUST SUPER-OBSESSIVELY INTO YOU.
BUT STALKINGLY INTO YOU? IT'S JUST IMPRACTICAL TO ONLY BE APART WHEN POOPING OR GROOMING.
WELL, FOR ALL HIS NEUROTIC BEHAVIOR, HE'S NOT LIKE, "HEY, LET ME JUST INSTANTLY TURN YOU INTO A VAMPIRE AND USURP EVERYTHING ABOUT YOU THAT MAKES YOU GREAT!"
YEAH, IT JUST TAKES FIVE BOOKS.
WELL, THAT'S WHY CRYSTAL HAMISH IS A KAJILLIONAIRE NOW.
YEAH...
I SHOULD DO THAT. I'M GONNA WRITE MY OWN SEXY TEEN VAMPIRE SERIES WITH NO SEX IN IT, AND THE BOY-FRIEND WILL BE NAMED HOLDEN HANDS.

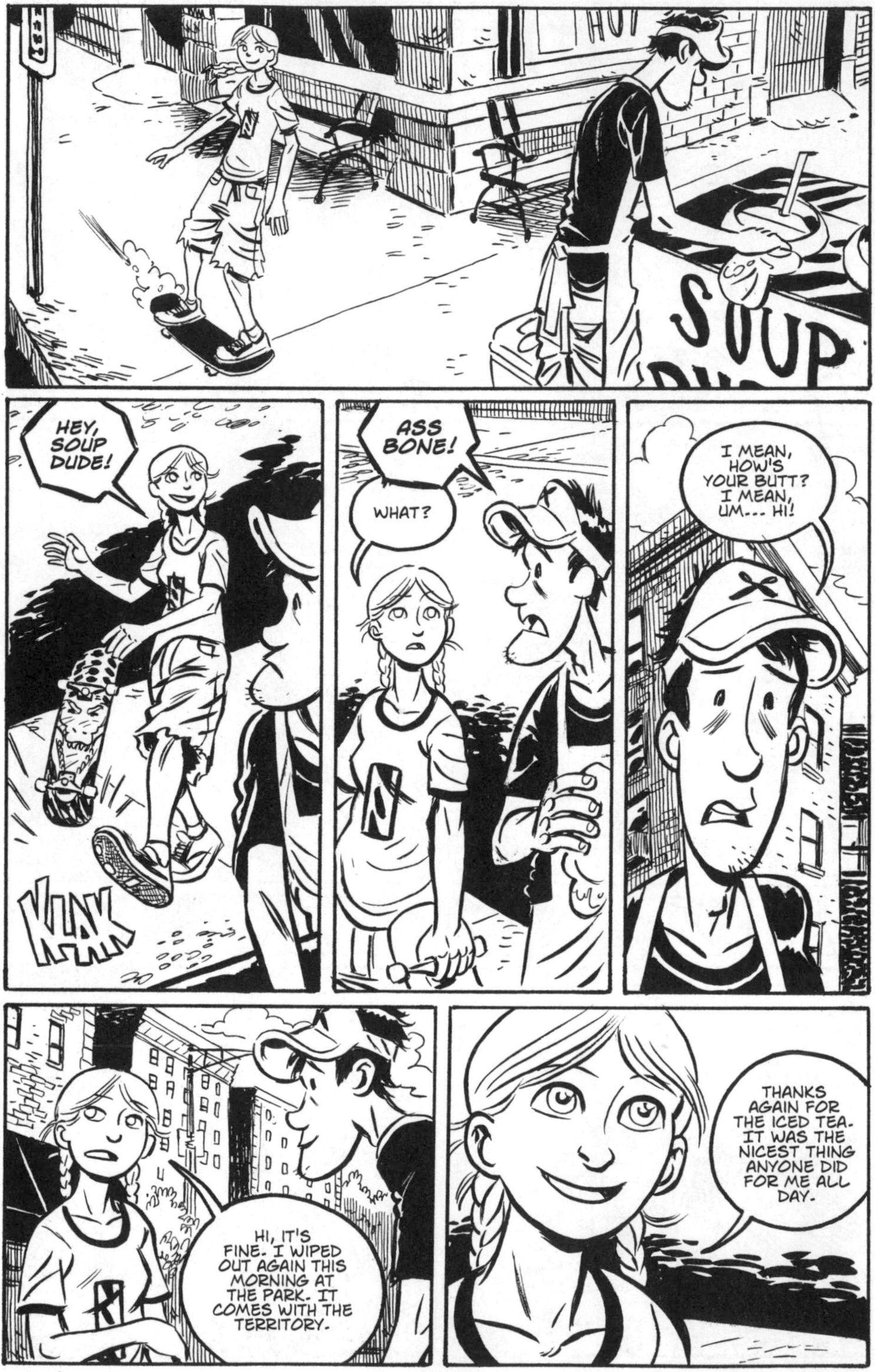
SOUP
HEY, SOUP DUDE!
KLAK
ASS BONE!
WHAT?
I MEAN, HOW'S YOUR BUTT? I MEAN, UM... HI!
HI, IT'S FINE. I WIPED OUT AGAIN THIS MORNING AT THE PARK. IT COMES WITH THE TERRITORY.
THANKS AGAIN FOR THE ICED TEA. IT WAS THE NICEST THING ANYONE DID FOR ME ALL DAY.

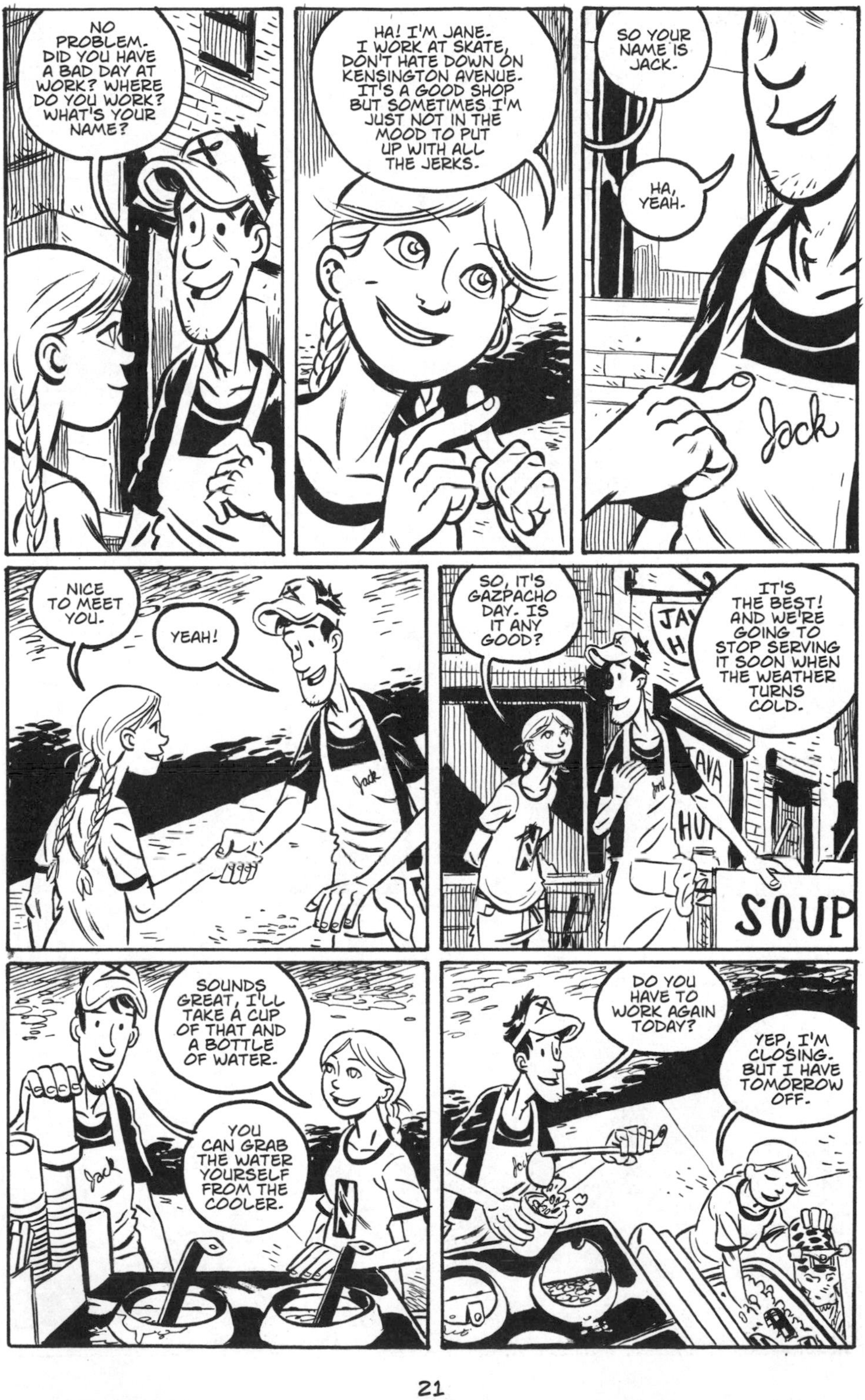
NO PROBLEM. DID YOU HAVE A BAD DAY AT WORK? WHERE DO YOU WORK? WHAT'S YOUR NAME?
HA! I'M JANE. I WORK AT SKATE, DON'T HATE DOWN ON KENSINGTON AVENUE. IT'S A GOOD SHOP BUT SOMETIMES I'M JUST NOT IN THE MOOD TO PUT UP WITH ALL THE JERKS.
SO YOUR NAME IS JACK.
HA, YEAH.
Jack
NICE TO MEET YOU.
YEAH!
SO, IT'S GAZPACHO DAY. IS IT ANY GOOD?
IT'S THE BEST! AND WE'RE GOING TO STOP SERVING IT SOON WHEN THE WEATHER TURNS COLD.
SOUP
SOUNDS GREAT, I'LL TAKE A CUP OF THAT AND A BOTTLE OF WATER.
YOU CAN GRAB THE WATER YOURSELF FROM THE COOLER.
DO YOU HAVE TO WORK AGAIN TODAY?
YEP, I'M CLOSING. BUT I HAVE TOMORROW OFF.

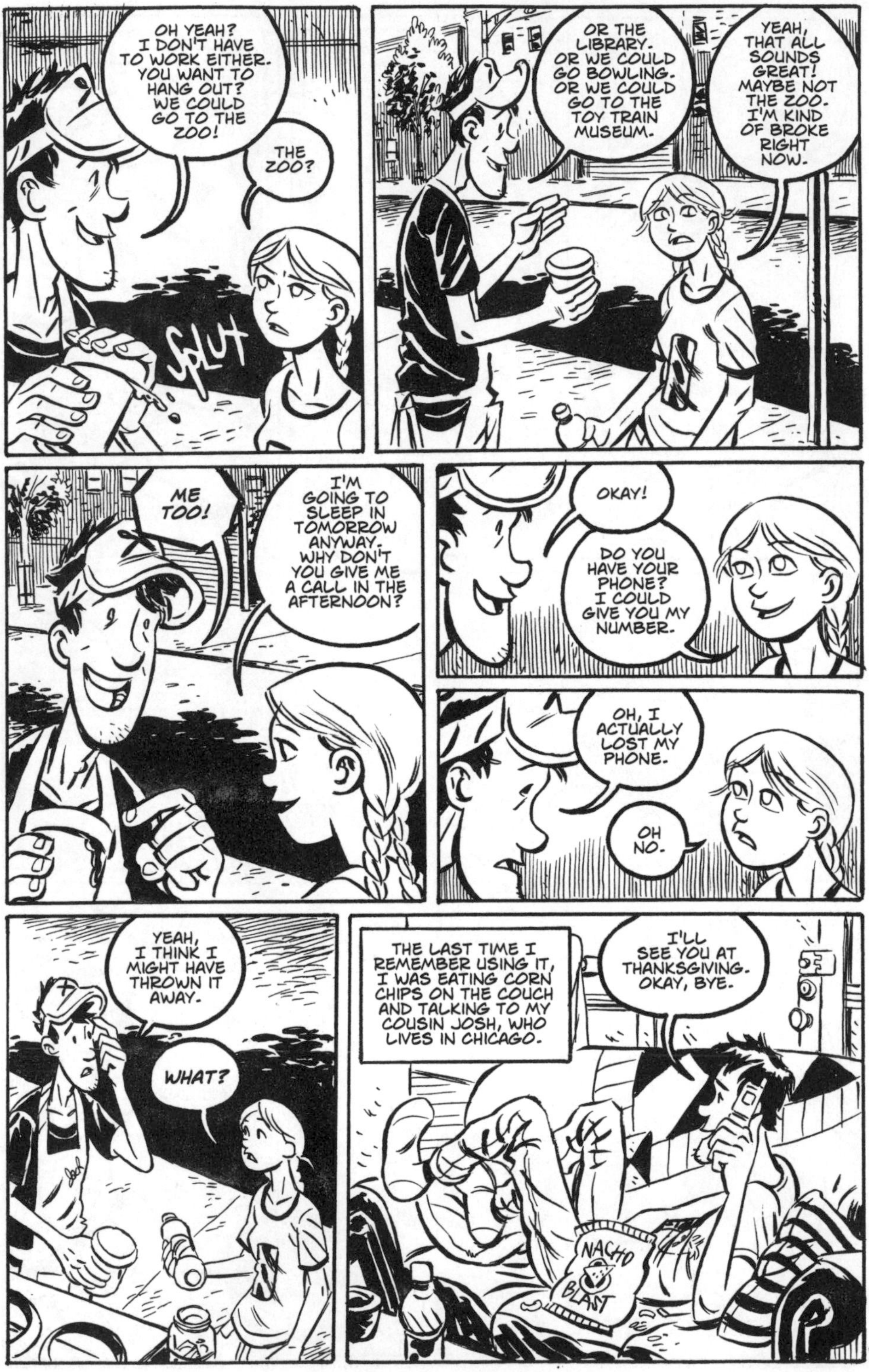

OH YEAH? I DON'T HAVE TO WORK EITHER. YOU WANT TO HANG OUT? WE COULD GO TO THE ZOO!
THE ZOO?
SPLUT
OR THE LIBRARY. OR WE COULD GO BOWLING. OR WE COULD GO TO THE TOY TRAIN MUSEUM.
YEAH, THAT ALL SOUNDS GREAT! MAYBE NOT THE ZOO. I'M KIND OF BROKE RIGHT NOW.
ME TOO!
I'M GOING TO SLEEP IN TOMORROW ANYWAY. WHY DON'T YOU GIVE ME A CALL IN THE AFTERNOON?
OKAY!
DO YOU HAVE YOUR PHONE? I COULD GIVE YOU MY NUMBER.
OH, I ACTUALLY LOST MY PHONE.
OH NO.
YEAH, I THINK I MIGHT HAVE THROWN IT AWAY.
WHAT?
THE LAST TIME I REMEMBER USING IT, I WAS EATING CORN CHIPS ON THE COUCH AND TALKING TO MY COUSIN JOSH, WHO LIVES IN CHICAGO.
I'LL SEE YOU AT THANKSGIVING. OKAY, BYE.
NACHO BLAST

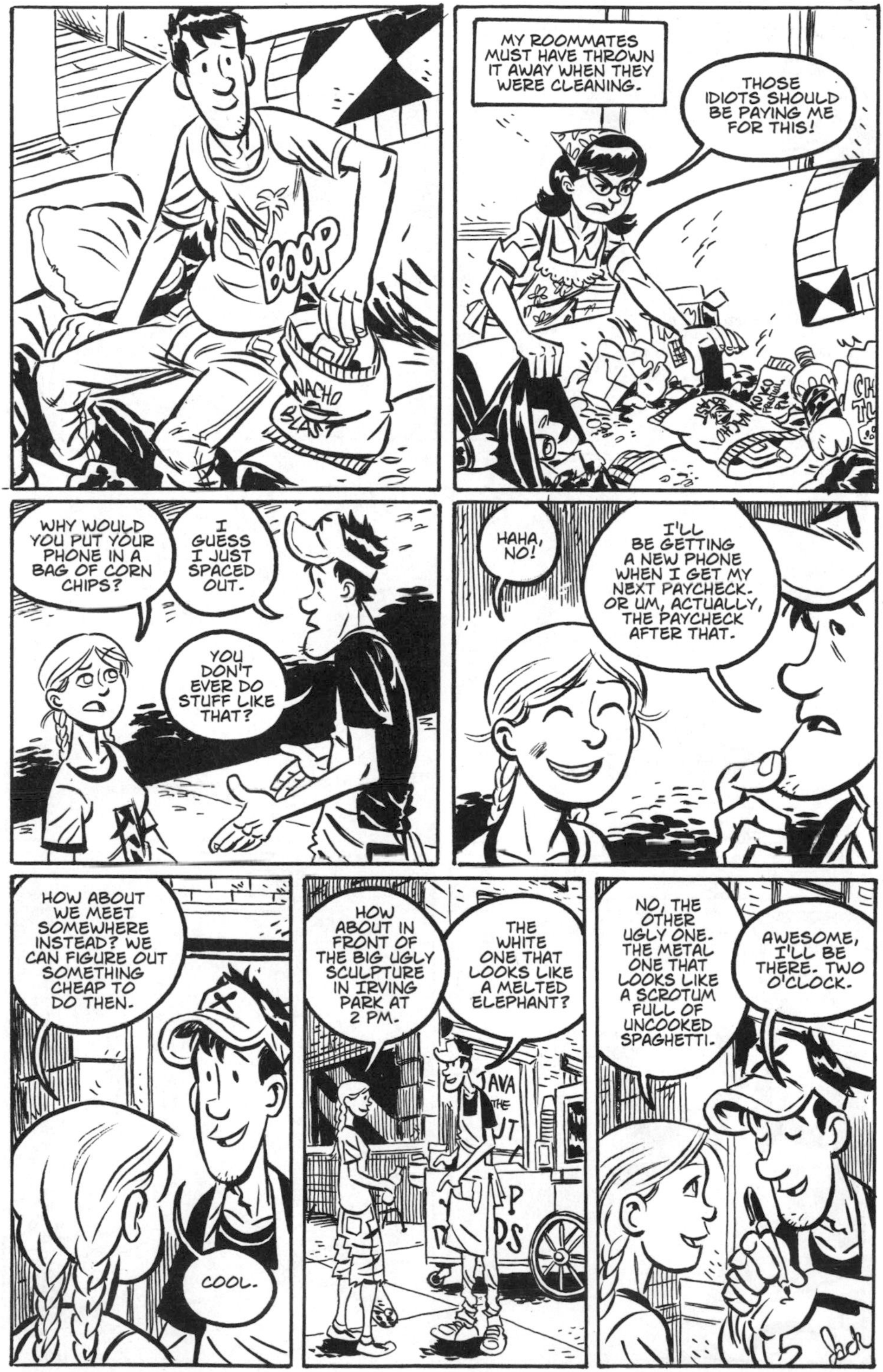
BOOP
NACHO BLAST
MY ROOMMATES MUST HAVE THROWN IT AWAY WHEN THEY WERE CLEANING.
THOSE IDIOTS SHOULD BE PAYING ME FOR THIS!
WHY WOULD YOU PUT YOUR PHONE IN A BAG OF CORN CHIPS?
I GUESS I JUST SPACED OUT.
YOU DON'T EVER DO STUFF LIKE THAT?
HAHA, NO!
I'LL BE GETTING A NEW PHONE WHEN I GET MY NEXT PAYCHECK. OR UM, ACTUALLY, THE PAYCHECK AFTER THAT.
HOW ABOUT WE MEET SOMEWHERE INSTEAD? WE CAN FIGURE OUT SOMETHING CHEAP TO DO THEN.
COOL.
HOW ABOUT IN FRONT OF THE BIG UGLY SCULPTURE IN IRVING PARK AT 2 PM.
THE WHITE ONE THAT LOOKS LIKE A MELTED ELEPHANT?
NO, THE OTHER UGLY ONE. THE METAL ONE THAT LOOKS LIKE A SCROTUM FULL OF UNCOOKED SPAGHETTI.
AWESOME, I'LL BE THERE. TWO O'CLOCK.

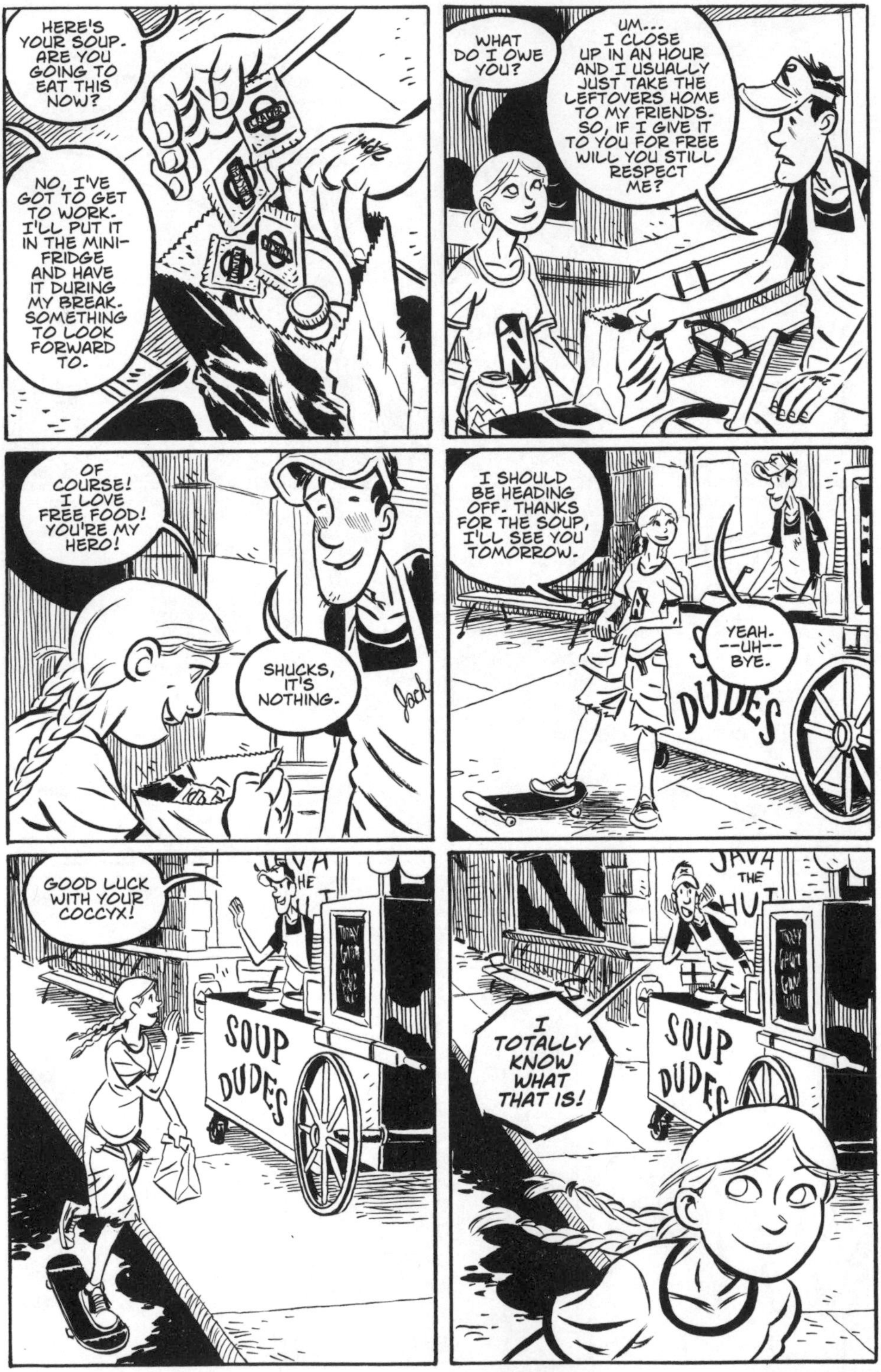
HERE'S YOUR SOUP. ARE YOU GOING TO EAT THIS NOW?
NO, I'VE GOT TO GET TO WORK. I'LL PUT IT IN THE MINI-FRIDGE AND HAVE IT DURING MY BREAK. SOMETHING TO LOOK FORWARD TO.
WHAT DO I OWE YOU?
UM... I CLOSE UP IN AN HOUR AND I USUALLY JUST TAKE THE LEFTOVERS HOME TO MY FRIENDS. SO, IF I GIVE IT TO YOU FOR FREE WILL YOU STILL RESPECT ME?
OF COURSE! I LOVE FREE FOOD! YOU'RE MY HERO!
SHUCKS, IT'S NOTHING.
Jack
I SHOULD BE HEADING OFF. THANKS FOR THE SOUP, I'LL SEE YOU TOMORROW.
YEAH- --UH-- BYE.
DUDES
GOOD LUCK WITH YOUR COCCYX!
SOUP DUDES
I TOTALLY KNOW WHAT THAT IS!
SOUP DUDES

CHAPTER TWO

"The Last People on Earth"

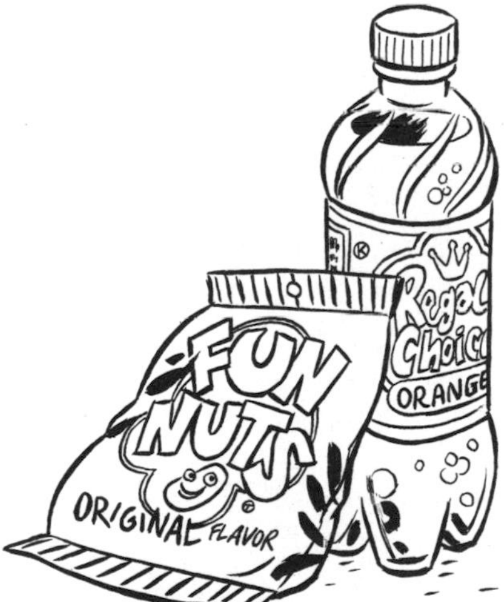

FUN NUTS
ORIGINAL FLAVOR
Regal Choice
ORANGE

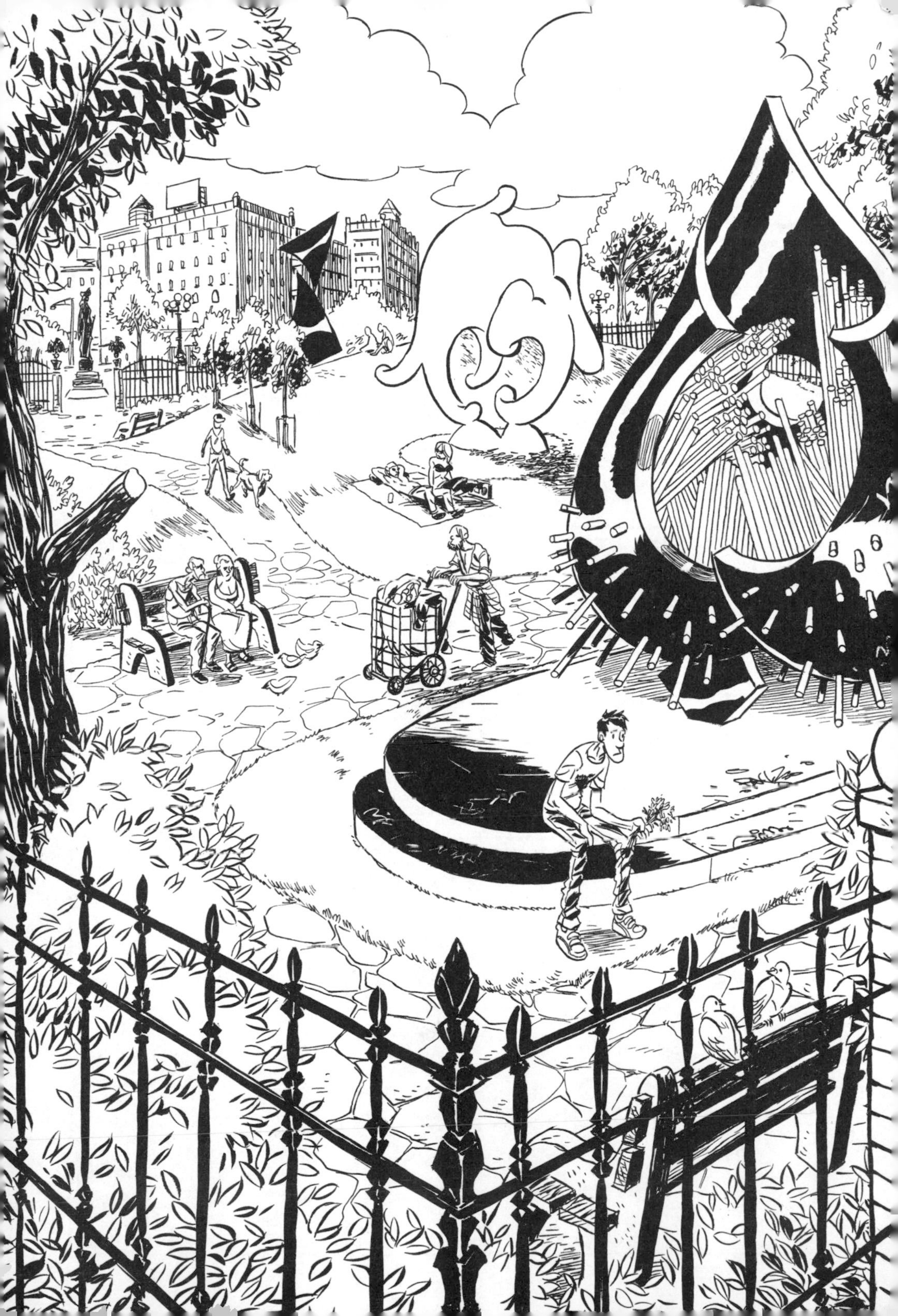

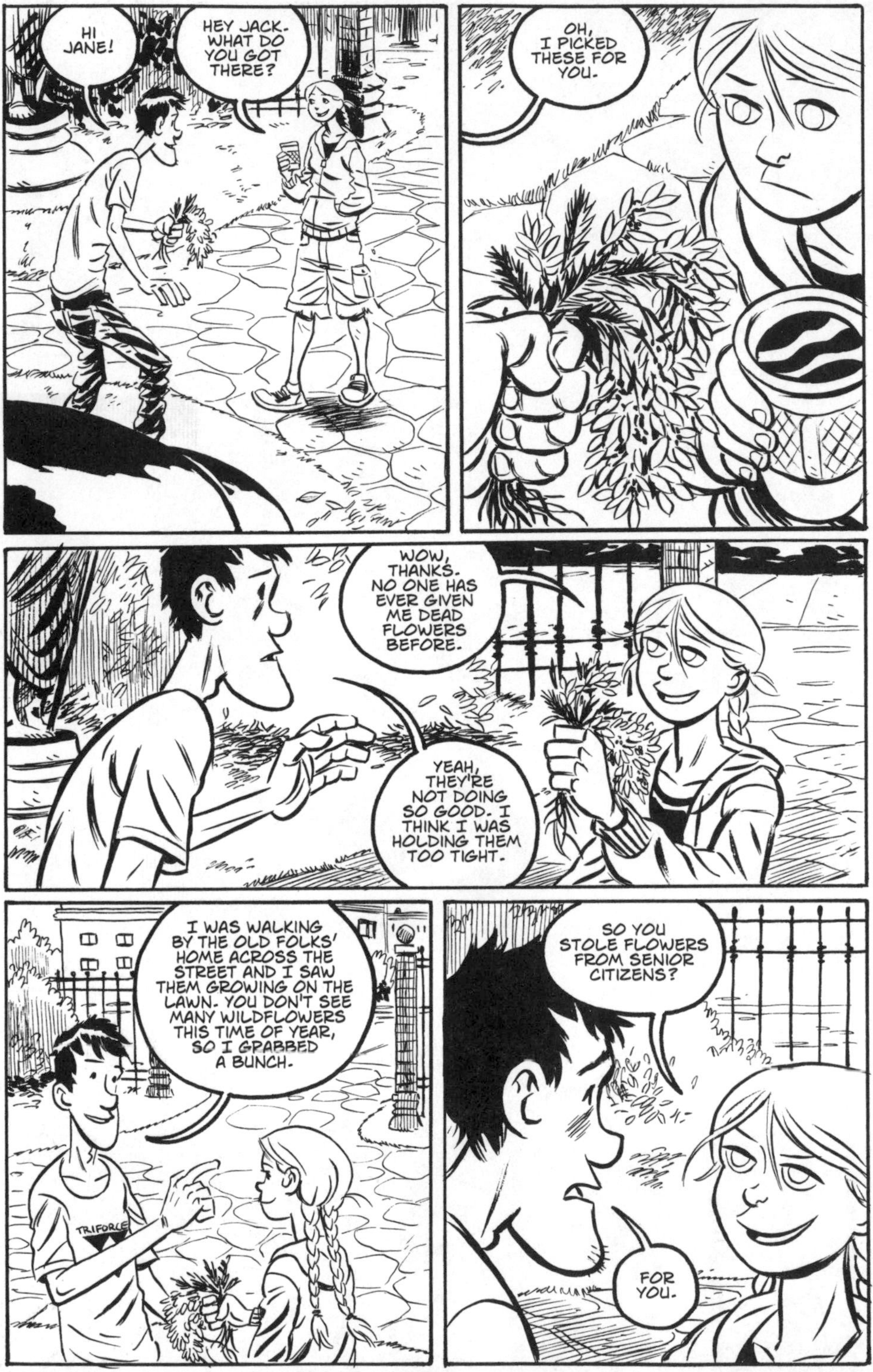
HI JANE!
HEY JACK. WHAT DO YOU GOT THERE?
OH, I PICKED THESE FOR YOU.
WOW, THANKS. NO ONE HAS EVER GIVEN ME DEAD FLOWERS BEFORE.
YEAH, THEY'RE NOT DOING SO GOOD. I THINK I WAS HOLDING THEM TOO TIGHT.
I WAS WALKING BY THE OLD FOLKS' HOME ACROSS THE STREET AND I SAW THEM GROWING ON THE LAWN. YOU DON'T SEE MANY WILDFLOWERS THIS TIME OF YEAR, SO I GRABBED A BUNCH.
TRIFORCE
SO YOU STOLE FLOWERS FROM SENIOR CITIZENS?
FOR YOU.

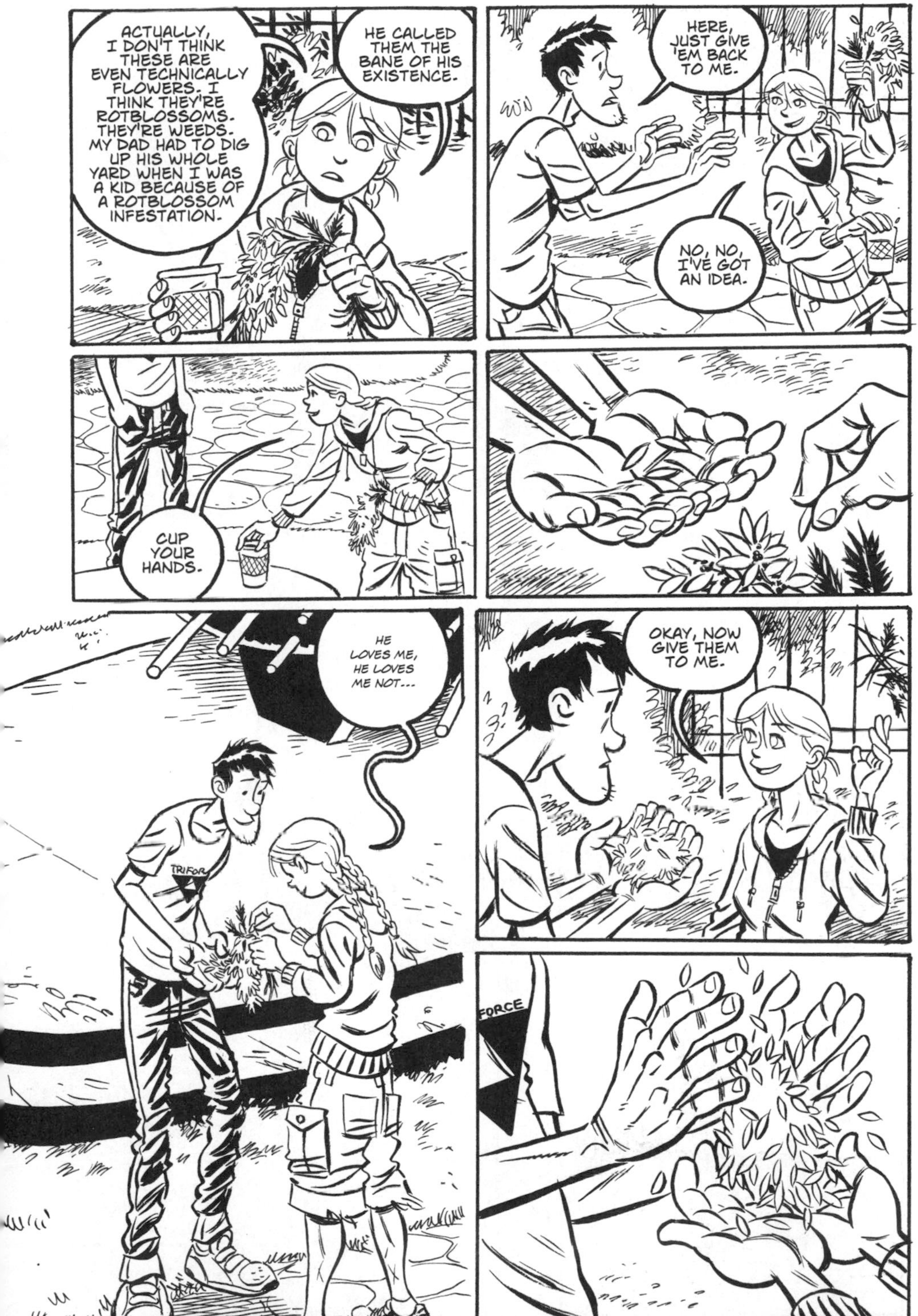
ACTUALLY, I DON'T THINK THESE ARE EVEN TECHNICALLY FLOWERS. I THINK THEY'RE ROTBLOSSOMS. THEY'RE WEEDS. MY DAD HAD TO DIG UP HIS WHOLE YARD WHEN I WAS A KID BECAUSE OF A ROTBLOSSOM INFESTATION.
HE CALLED THEM THE BANE OF HIS EXISTENCE.
HERE, JUST GIVE 'EM BACK TO ME.
NO, NO, I'VE GOT AN IDEA.
CUP YOUR HANDS.
HE LOVES ME, HE LOVES ME NOT...
TRIFOR
OKAY, NOW GIVE THEM TO ME.
FORCE

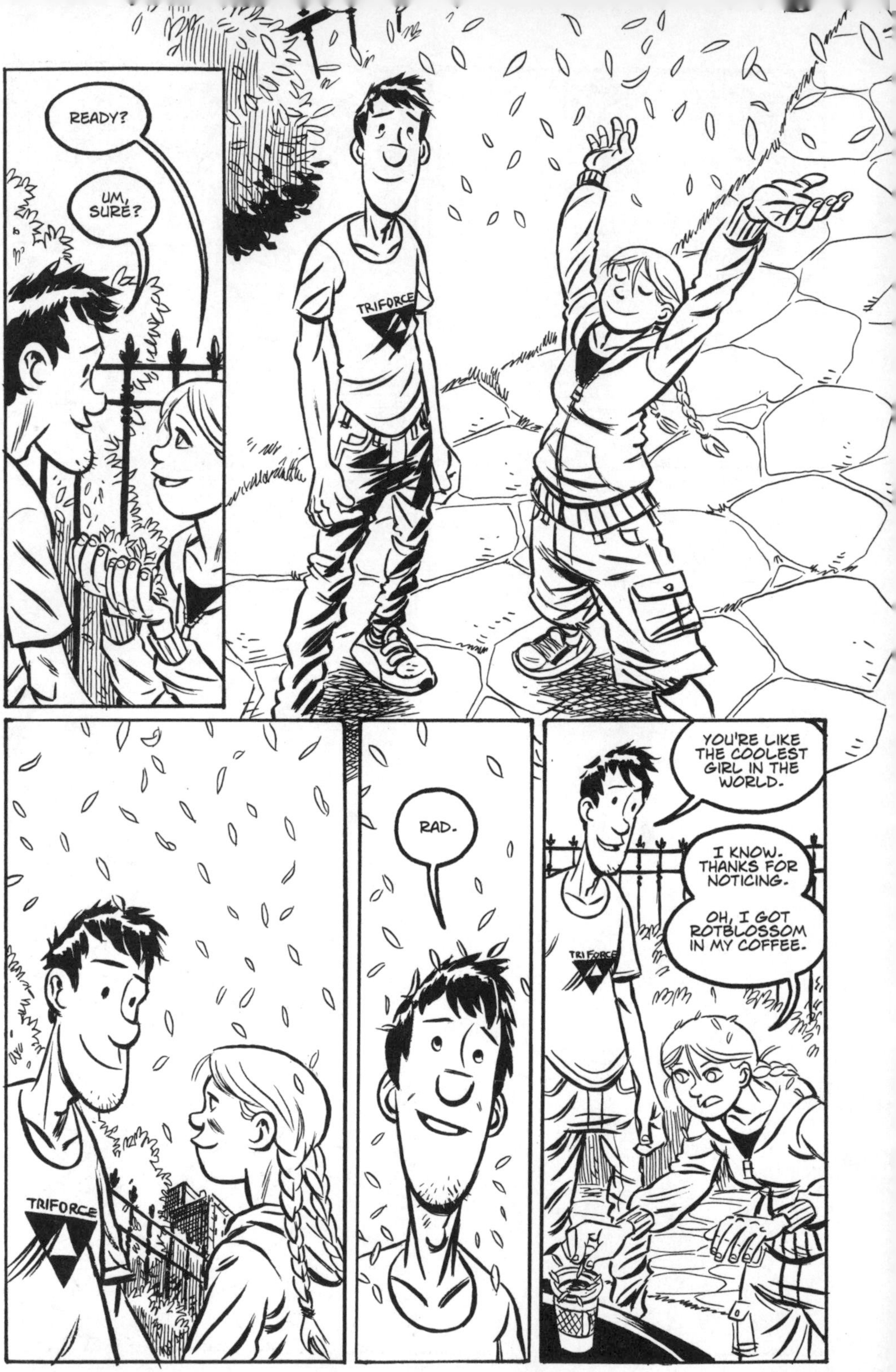
READY?
UM, SURE?
TRIFORCE
TRIFORCE
RAD.
YOU'RE LIKE THE COOLEST GIRL IN THE WORLD.
I KNOW. THANKS FOR NOTICING.
OH, I GOT ROTBLOSSOM IN MY COFFEE.
TRIFORCE

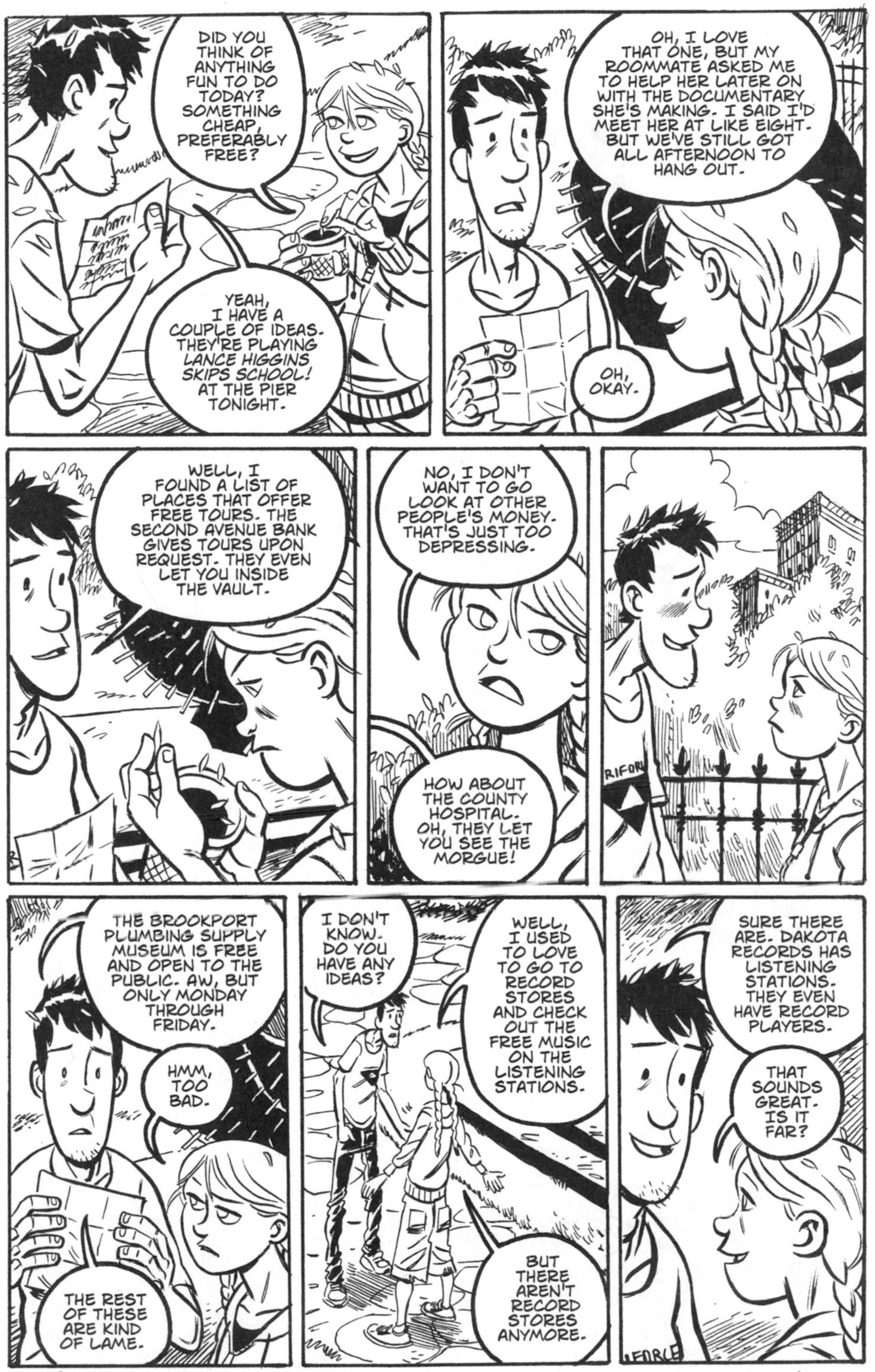
DID YOU THINK OF ANYTHING FUN TO DO TODAY? SOMETHING CHEAP, PREFERABLY FREE?
YEAH, I HAVE A COUPLE OF IDEAS. THEY'RE PLAYING LANCE HIGGINS SKIPS SCHOOL! AT THE PIER TONIGHT.
OH, I LOVE THAT ONE, BUT MY ROOMMATE ASKED ME TO HELP HER LATER ON WITH THE DOCUMENTARY SHE'S MAKING. I SAID I'D MEET HER AT LIKE EIGHT. BUT WE'VE STILL GOT ALL AFTERNOON TO HANG OUT.
OH, OKAY.
WELL, I FOUND A LIST OF PLACES THAT OFFER FREE TOURS. THE SECOND AVENUE BANK GIVES TOURS UPON REQUEST. THEY EVEN LET YOU INSIDE THE VAULT.
NO, I DON'T WANT TO GO LOOK AT OTHER PEOPLE'S MONEY. THAT'S JUST TOO DEPRESSING.
HOW ABOUT THE COUNTY HOSPITAL. OH, THEY LET YOU SEE THE MORGUE!
THE BROOKPORT PLUMBING SUPPLY MUSEUM IS FREE AND OPEN TO THE PUBLIC. AW, BUT ONLY MONDAY THROUGH FRIDAY.
HMM, TOO BAD.
THE REST OF THESE ARE KIND OF LAME.
I DON'T KNOW. DO YOU HAVE ANY IDEAS?
WELL, I USED TO LOVE TO GO TO RECORD STORES AND CHECK OUT THE FREE MUSIC ON THE LISTENING STATIONS.
BUT THERE AREN'T RECORD STORES ANYMORE.
SURE THERE ARE. DAKOTA RECORDS HAS LISTENING STATIONS. THEY EVEN HAVE RECORD PLAYERS.
THAT SOUNDS GREAT. IS IT FAR?

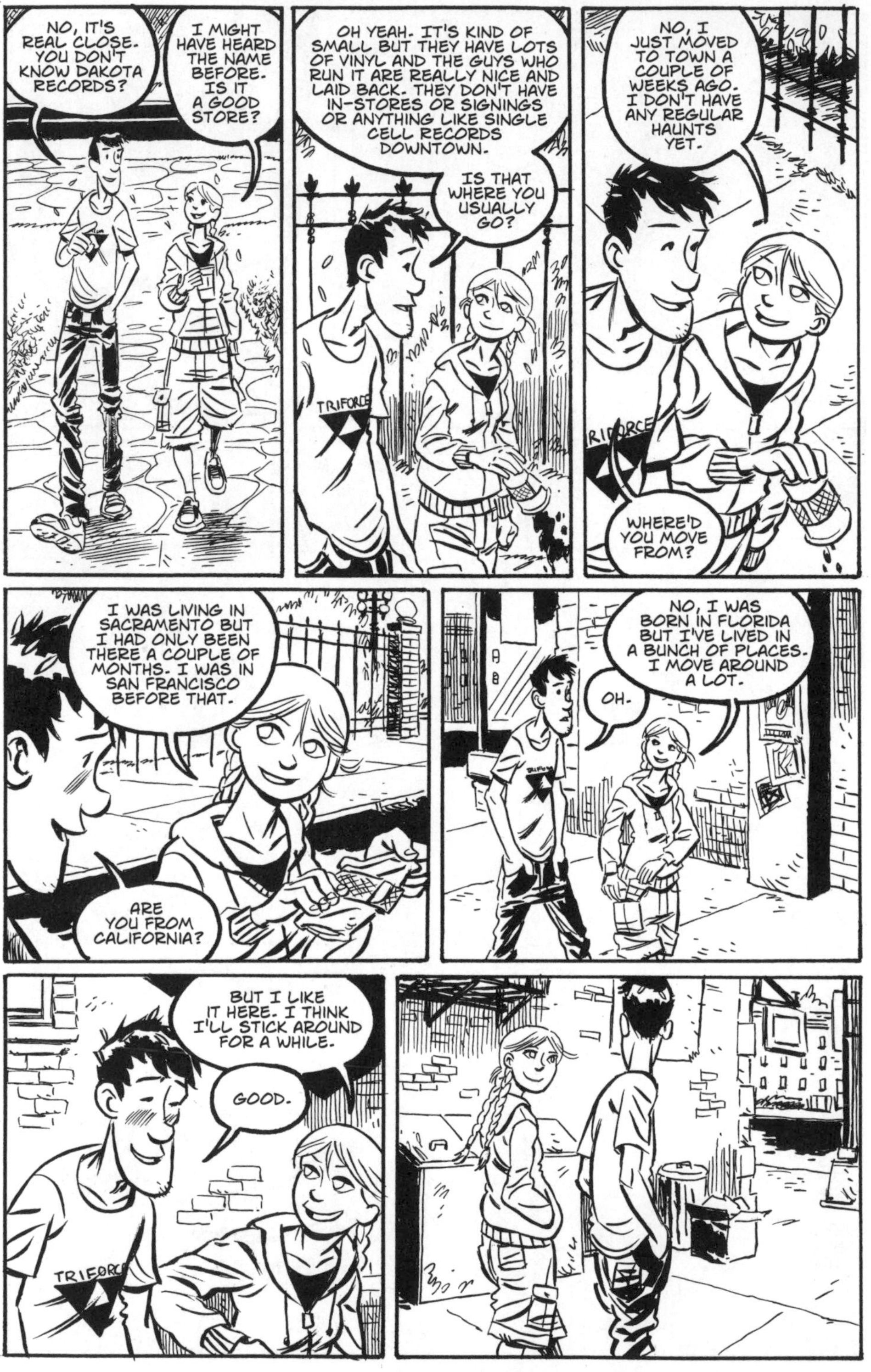

NO, IT'S REAL CLOSE. YOU DON'T KNOW DAKOTA RECORDS?
I MIGHT HAVE HEARD THE NAME BEFORE. IS IT A GOOD STORE?
OH YEAH. IT'S KIND OF SMALL BUT THEY HAVE LOTS OF VINYL AND THE GUYS WHO RUN IT ARE REALLY NICE AND LAID BACK. THEY DON'T HAVE IN-STORES OR SIGNINGS OR ANYTHING LIKE SINGLE CELL RECORDS DOWNTOWN.
IS THAT WHERE YOU USUALLY GO?
TRIFORCE
NO, I JUST MOVED TO TOWN A COUPLE OF WEEKS AGO. I DON'T HAVE ANY REGULAR HAUNTS YET.
RIFORCE
WHERE'D YOU MOVE FROM?
I WAS LIVING IN SACRAMENTO BUT I HAD ONLY BEEN THERE A COUPLE OF MONTHS. I WAS IN SAN FRANCISCO BEFORE THAT.
ARE YOU FROM CALIFORNIA?
NO, I WAS BORN IN FLORIDA BUT I'VE LIVED IN A BUNCH OF PLACES. I MOVE AROUND A LOT.
OH.
BUT I LIKE IT HERE. I THINK I'LL STICK AROUND FOR A WHILE.
GOOD.
TRIFORCE

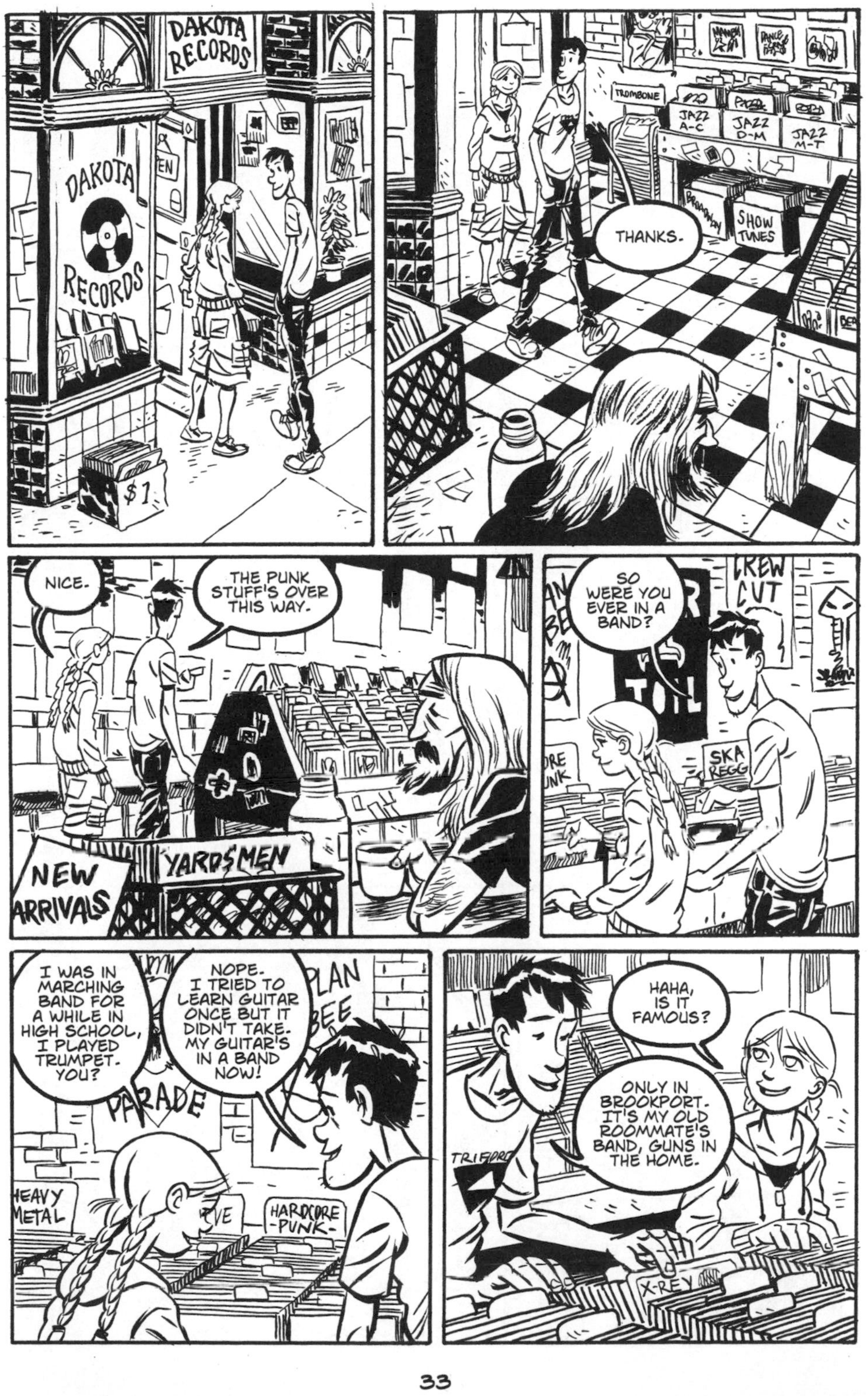
DAKOTA RECORDS
DAKOTA RECORDS
$1
THANKS.
TROMBONE
JAZZ A-C
JAZZ D-M
JAZZ M-T
SHOW TUNES
NICE.
THE PUNK STUFF'S OVER THIS WAY.
NEW ARRIVALS
YARD$MEN
SO WERE YOU EVER IN A BAND?
CREW CUT
SKA REGG
I WAS IN MARCHING BAND FOR A WHILE IN HIGH SCHOOL, I PLAYED TRUMPET. YOU?
NOPE. I TRIED TO LEARN GUITAR ONCE BUT IT DIDN'T TAKE. MY GUITAR'S IN A BAND NOW!
PLAN BEE
PARADE
HEAVY METAL
HARDCORE -PUNK-
HAHA, IS IT FAMOUS?
ONLY IN BROOKPORT. IT'S MY OLD ROOMMATE'S BAND, GUNS IN THE HOME.
X-REY

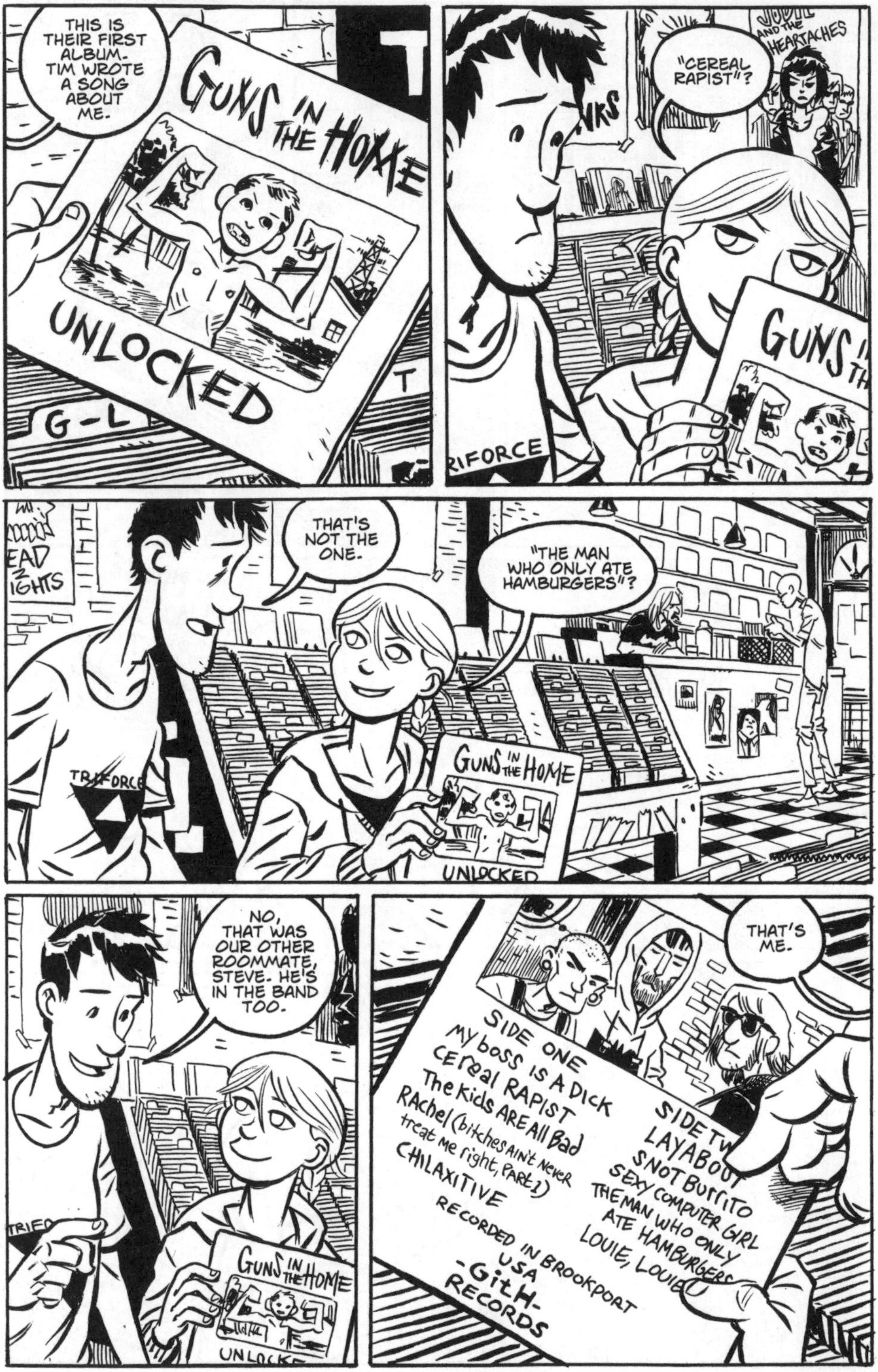
THIS IS THEIR FIRST ALBUM. TIM WROTE A SONG ABOUT ME.
GUNS IN THE HOME
UNLOCKED
G-L
"CEREAL RAPIST"?
JODIE AND THE HEARTACHES
TRIFORCE
THAT'S NOT THE ONE.
"THE MAN WHO ONLY ATE HAMBURGERS"?
GUNS IN THE HOME
UNLOCKED
NO, THAT WAS OUR OTHER ROOMMATE, STEVE. HE'S IN THE BAND TOO.
THAT'S ME.
SIDE ONE
My boss is A Dick
Cereal RAPIST
The Kids ARE All Bad
Rachel (bitches ain't never treat me right, PART 1)
CHILAXITIVE
SIDE TW
LAYABOUT
SNOT BURRITO
SEXY COMPUTER GIRL
THE MAN WHO ONLY ATE HAMBURGERS
LOUIE, LOUIE
RECORDED IN BROOKPORT USA
-Gith- RECORDS

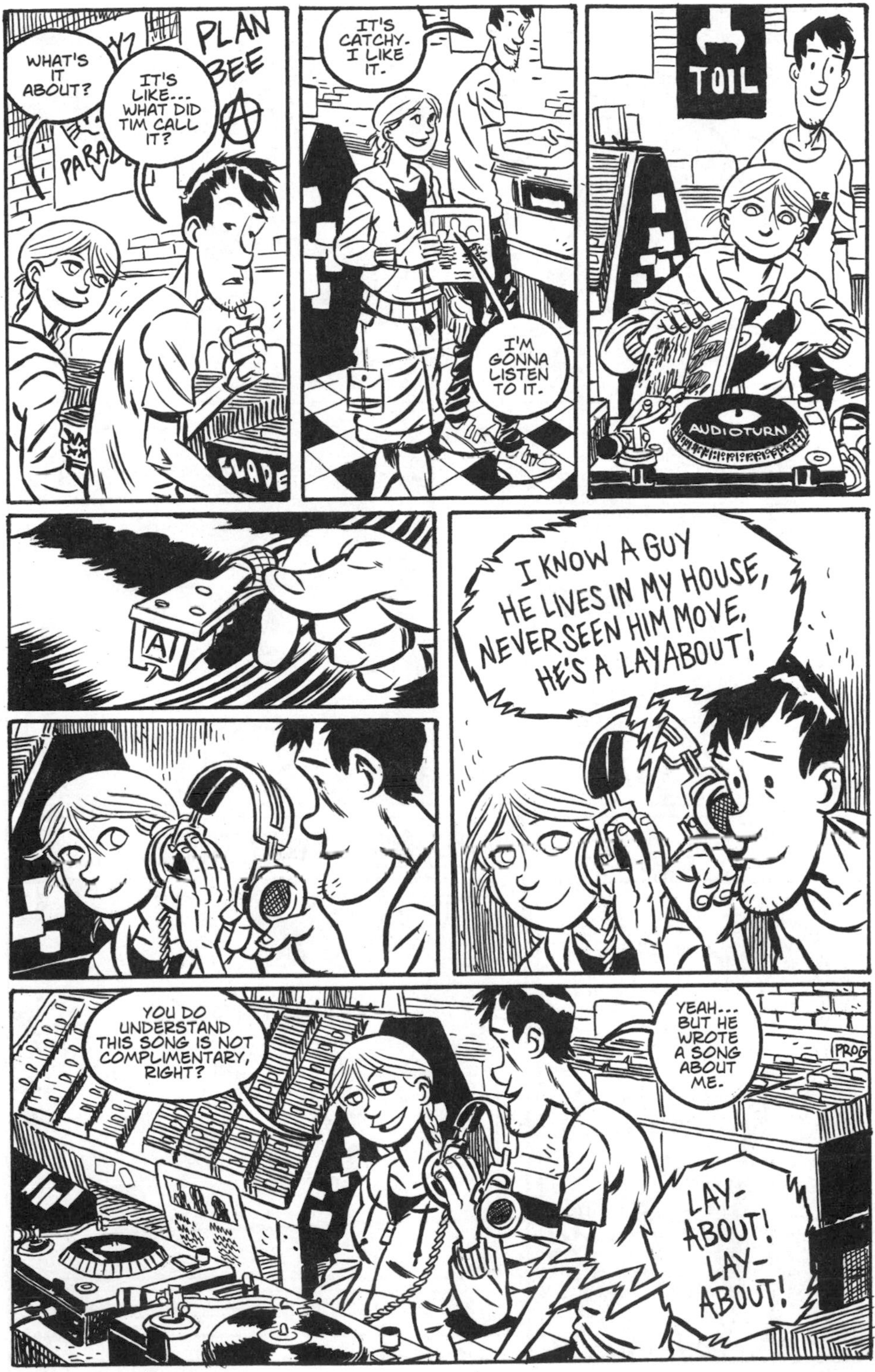
WHAT'S IT ABOUT?
IT'S LIKE... WHAT DID TIM CALL IT?
PLAN BEE
IT'S CATCHY- I LIKE IT.
I'M GONNA LISTEN TO IT.
TOIL
AUDIOTURN
I KNOW A GUY HE LIVES IN MY HOUSE, NEVER SEEN HIM MOVE, HE'S A LAYABOUT!
YOU DO UNDERSTAND THIS SONG IS NOT COMPLIMENTARY, RIGHT?
YEAH... BUT HE WROTE A SONG ABOUT ME.
PROG
LAY-ABOUT! LAY-ABOUT!

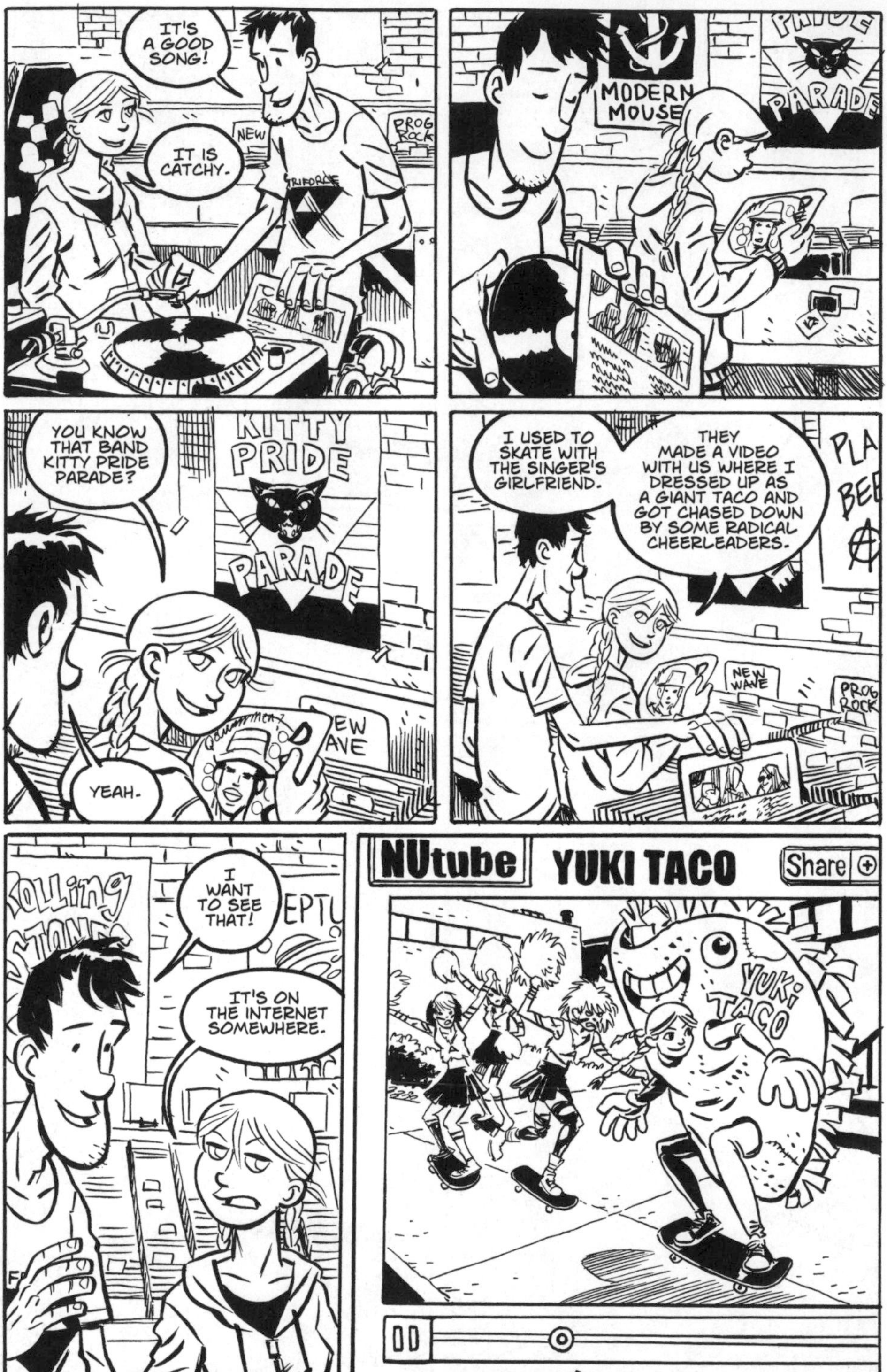
IT'S A GOOD SONG!
IT IS CATCHY.
NEW
PROG ROCK
TRIFORCE
MODERN MOUSE
PRIDE PARADE
YOU KNOW THAT BAND KITTY PRIDE PARADE?
KITTY PRIDE PARADE
YEAH.
I USED TO SKATE WITH THE SINGER'S GIRLFRIEND.
THEY MADE A VIDEO WITH US WHERE I DRESSED UP AS A GIANT TACO AND GOT CHASED DOWN BY SOME RADICAL CHEERLEADERS.
NEW WAVE
PROG ROCK
I WANT TO SEE THAT!
IT'S ON THE INTERNET SOMEWHERE.
NUtube
YUKI TACO
Share
YUKI TACO
comments

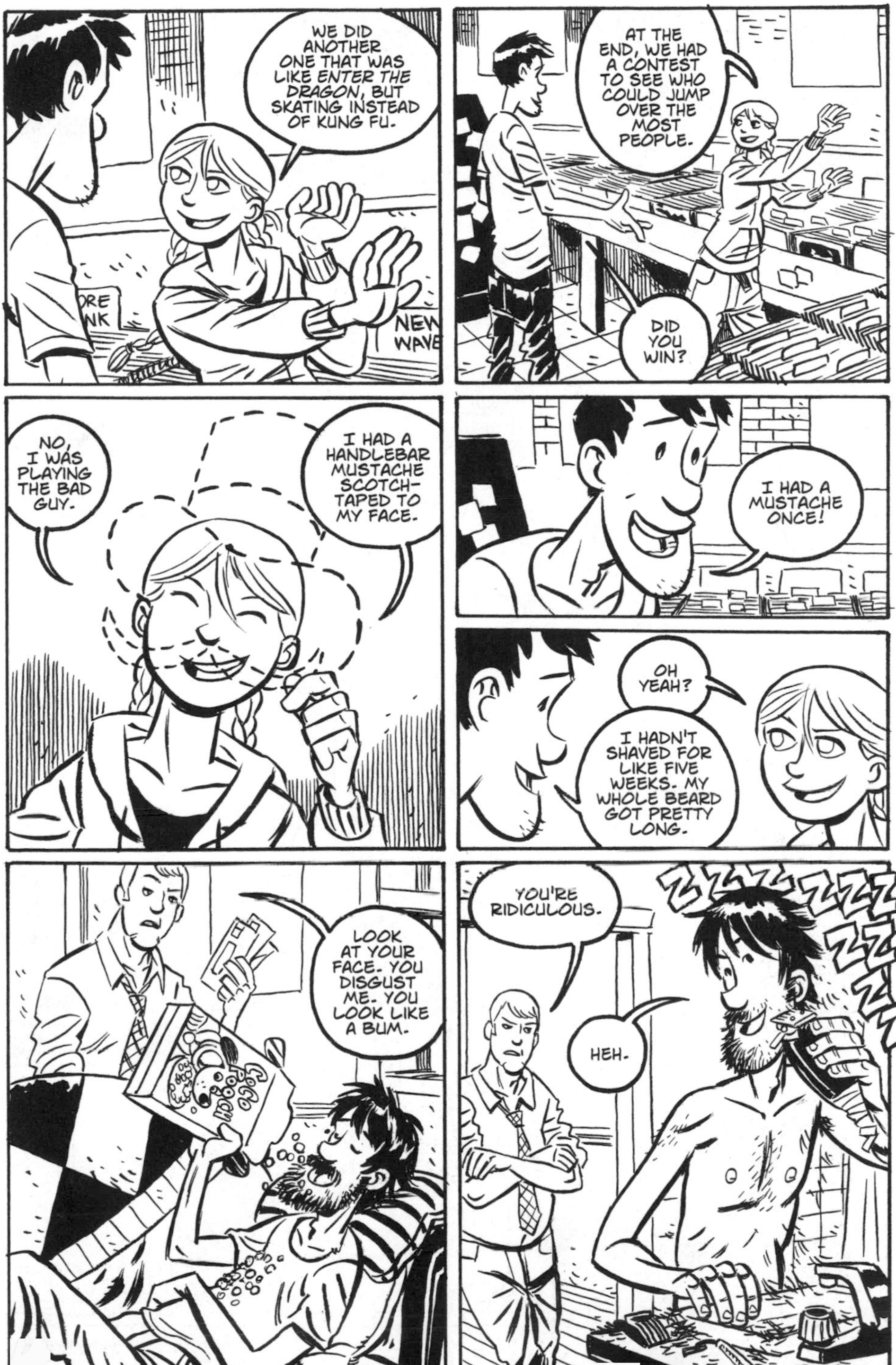
WE DID ANOTHER ONE THAT WAS LIKE ENTER THE DRAGON, BUT SKATING INSTEAD OF KUNG FU.
NEW WAVE
AT THE END, WE HAD A CONTEST TO SEE WHO COULD JUMP OVER THE MOST PEOPLE.
DID YOU WIN?
NO, I WAS PLAYING THE BAD GUY.
I HAD A HANDLEBAR MUSTACHE SCOTCH-TAPED TO MY FACE.
I HAD A MUSTACHE ONCE!
OH YEAH?
I HADN'T SHAVED FOR LIKE FIVE WEEKS. MY WHOLE BEARD GOT PRETTY LONG.
LOOK AT YOUR FACE. YOU DISGUST ME. YOU LOOK LIKE A BUM.
COCO POOCH
YOU'RE RIDICULOUS.
HEH.
ZZZZZZZZZZZ-

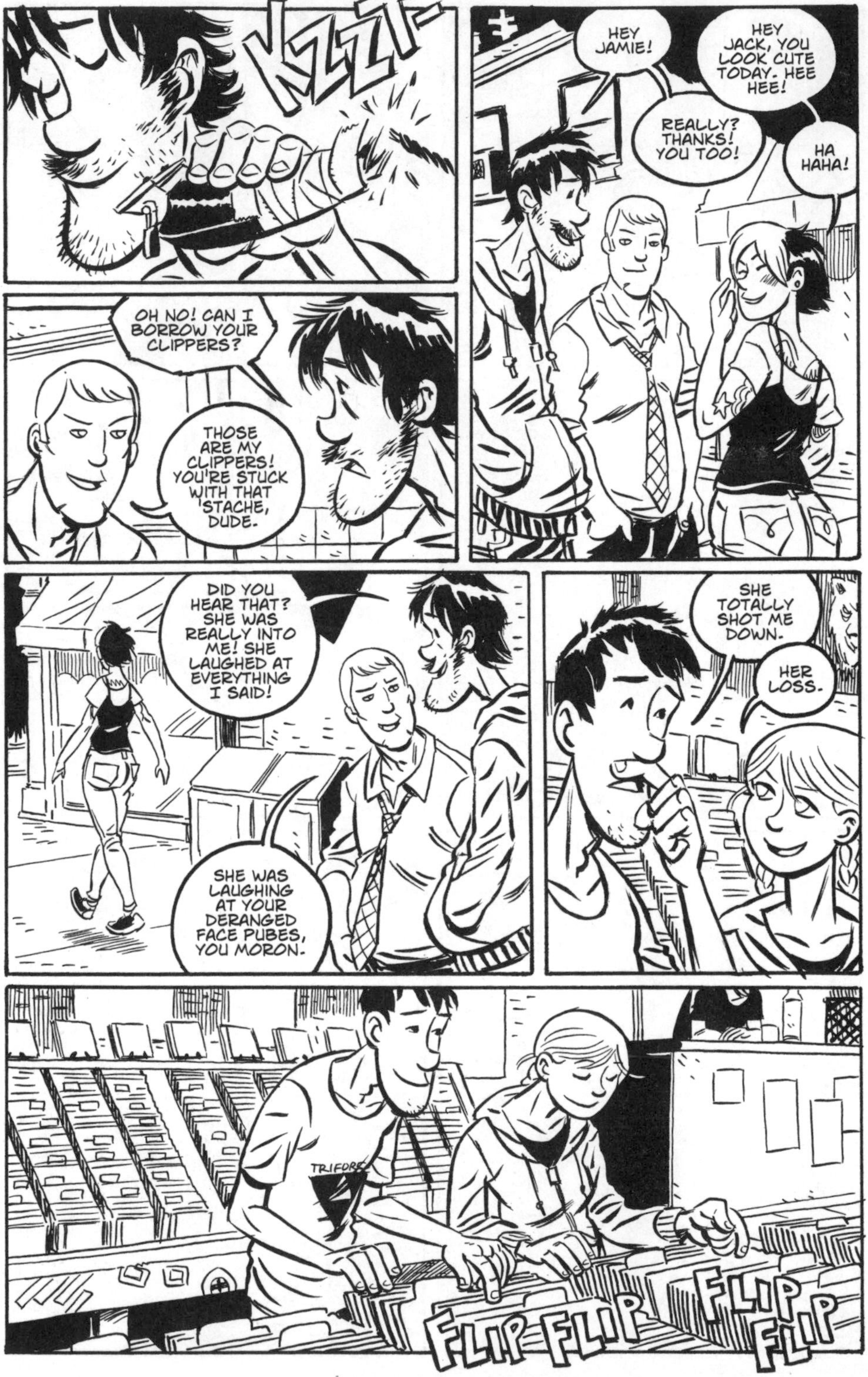
KZZZT-
HEY JAMIE!
HEY JACK, YOU LOOK CUTE TODAY. HEE HEE!
REALLY? THANKS! YOU TOO!
HA HAHA!
OH NO! CAN I BORROW YOUR CLIPPERS?
THOSE ARE MY CLIPPERS! YOU'RE STUCK WITH THAT 'STACHE, DUDE.
DID YOU HEAR THAT? SHE WAS REALLY INTO ME! SHE LAUGHED AT EVERYTHING I SAID!
SHE WAS LAUGHING AT YOUR DERANGED FACE PUBES, YOU MORON.
SHE TOTALLY SHOT ME DOWN.
HER LOSS.
TRIFORCE
FLIP FLIP FLIP FLIP

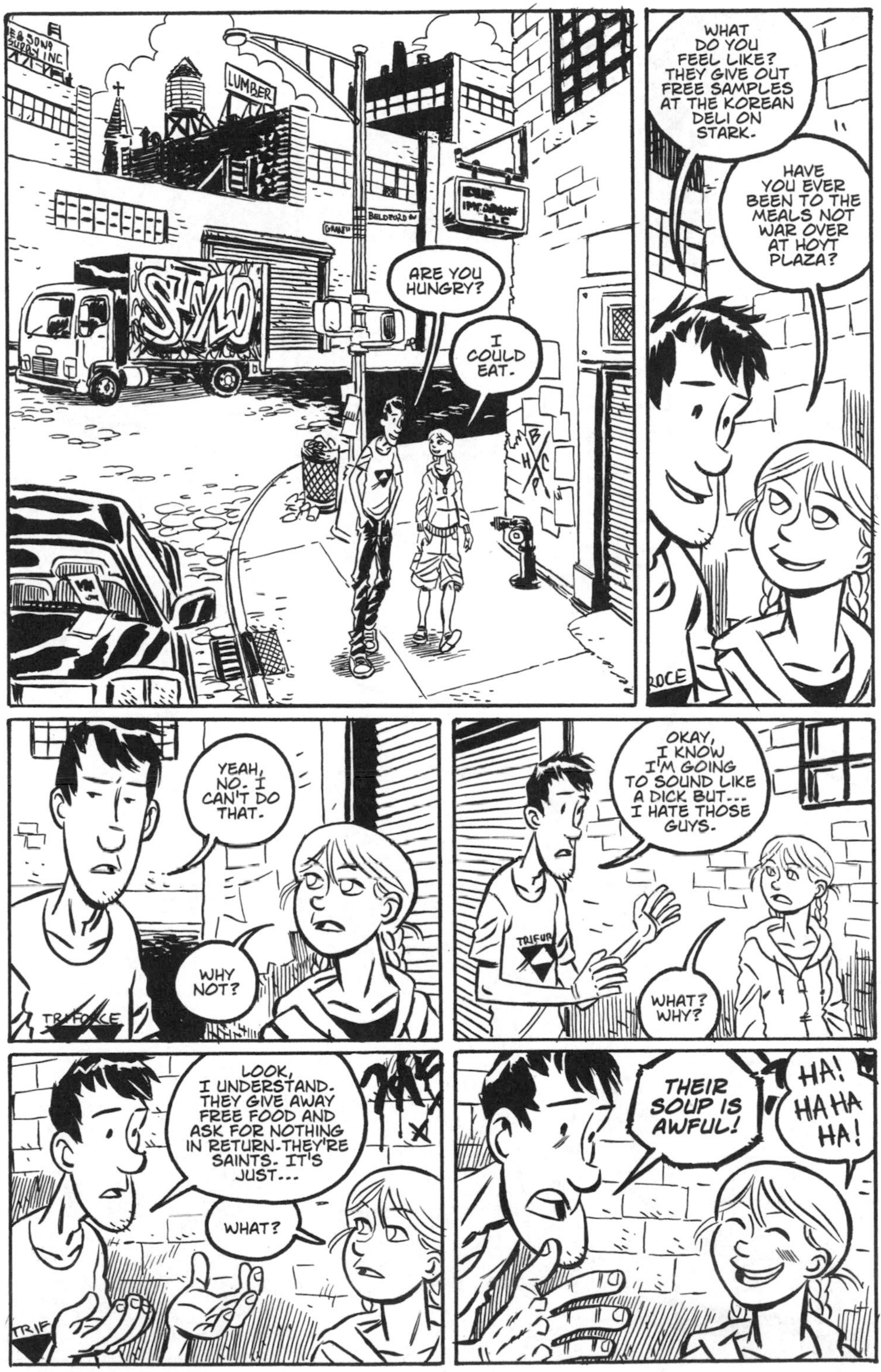
ARE YOU HUNGRY?
I COULD EAT.
WHAT DO YOU FEEL LIKE? THEY GIVE OUT FREE SAMPLES AT THE KOREAN DELI ON STARK.
HAVE YOU EVER BEEN TO THE MEALS NOT WAR OVER AT HOYT PLAZA?
YEAH, NO. I CAN'T DO THAT.
WHY NOT?
OKAY, I KNOW I'M GOING TO SOUND LIKE A DICK BUT... I HATE THOSE GUYS.
WHAT? WHY?
LOOK, I UNDERSTAND. THEY GIVE AWAY FREE FOOD AND ASK FOR NOTHING IN RETURN. THEY'RE SAINTS. IT'S JUST...
WHAT?
THEIR SOUP IS AWFUL!
HA! HA HA HA!

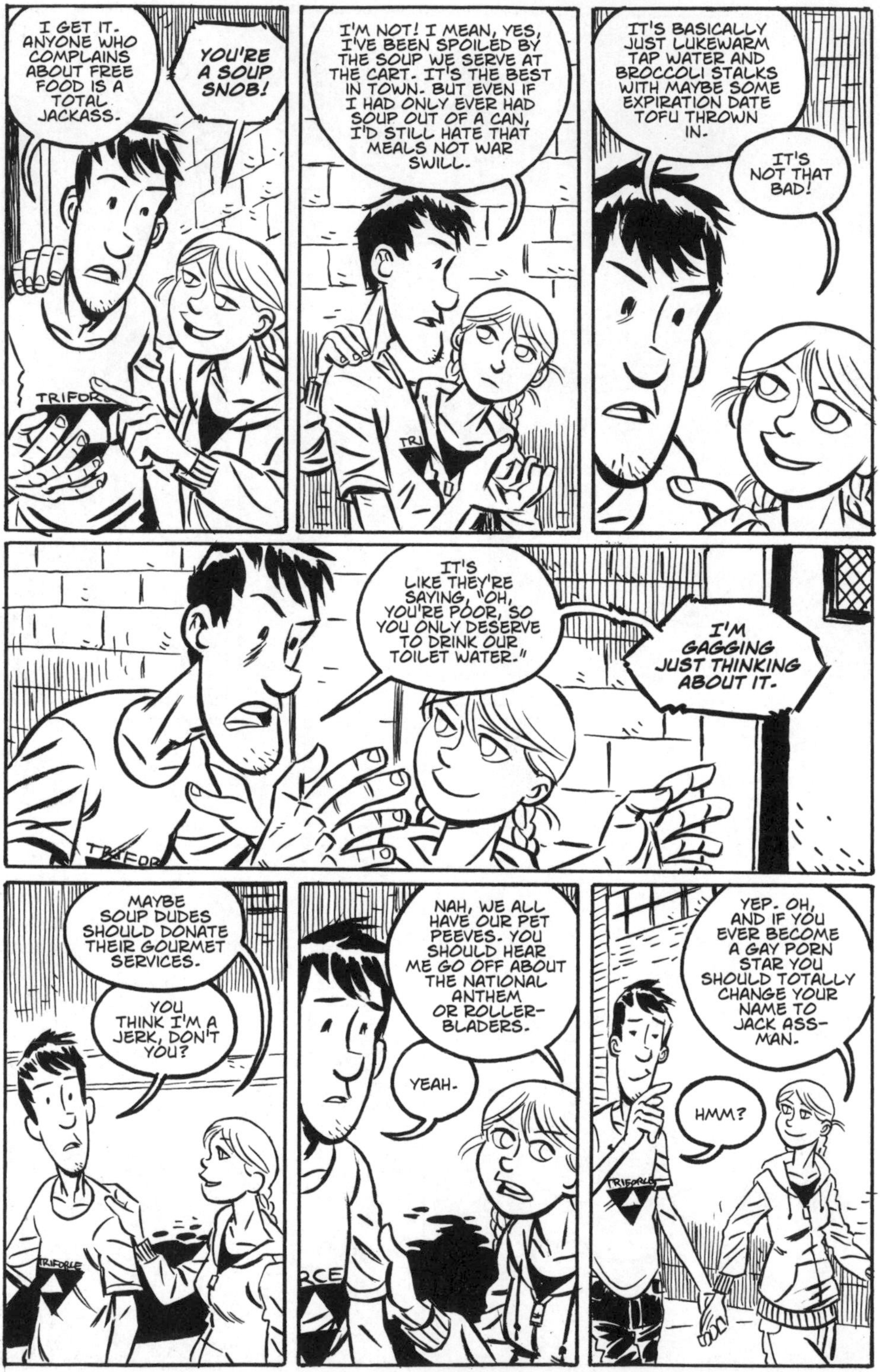
I GET IT. ANYONE WHO COMPLAINS ABOUT FREE FOOD IS A TOTAL JACKASS.
YOU'RE A SOUP SNOB!
TRIFORCE
I'M NOT! I MEAN, YES, I'VE BEEN SPOILED BY THE SOUP WE SERVE AT THE CART. IT'S THE BEST IN TOWN. BUT EVEN IF I HAD ONLY EVER HAD SOUP OUT OF A CAN, I'D STILL HATE THAT MEALS NOT WAR SWILL.
IT'S BASICALLY JUST LUKEWARM TAP WATER AND BROCCOLI STALKS WITH MAYBE SOME EXPIRATION DATE TOFU THROWN IN.
IT'S NOT THAT BAD!
IT'S LIKE THEY'RE SAYING, "OH, YOU'RE POOR, SO YOU ONLY DESERVE TO DRINK OUR TOILET WATER."
I'M GAGGING JUST THINKING ABOUT IT.
MAYBE SOUP DUDES SHOULD DONATE THEIR GOURMET SERVICES.
YOU THINK I'M A JERK, DON'T YOU?
TRIFORCE
NAH, WE ALL HAVE OUR PET PEEVES. YOU SHOULD HEAR ME GO OFF ABOUT THE NATIONAL ANTHEM OR ROLLER-BLADERS.
YEAH.
YEP. OH, AND IF YOU EVER BECOME A GAY PORN STAR YOU SHOULD TOTALLY CHANGE YOUR NAME TO JACK ASS-MAN.
HMM?
TRIFORCE

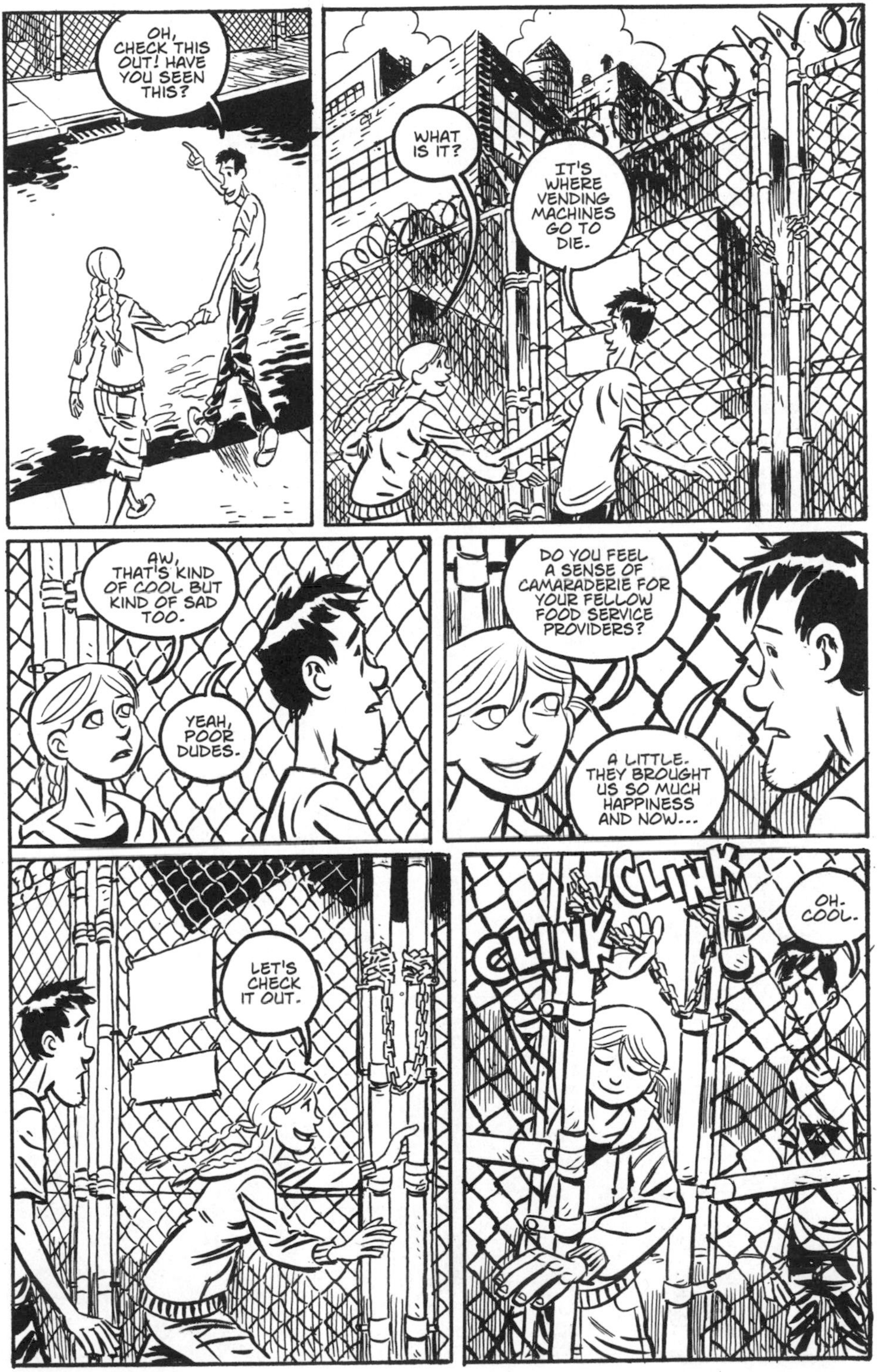
OH, CHECK THIS OUT! HAVE YOU SEEN THIS?
WHAT IS IT?
IT'S WHERE VENDING MACHINES GO TO DIE.
AW, THAT'S KIND OF COOL BUT KIND OF SAD TOO.
YEAH, POOR DUDES.
DO YOU FEEL A SENSE OF CAMARADERIE FOR YOUR FELLOW FOOD SERVICE PROVIDERS?
A LITTLE. THEY BROUGHT US SO MUCH HAPPINESS AND NOW...
LET'S CHECK IT OUT.
CLINK
CLINK
OH. COOL.

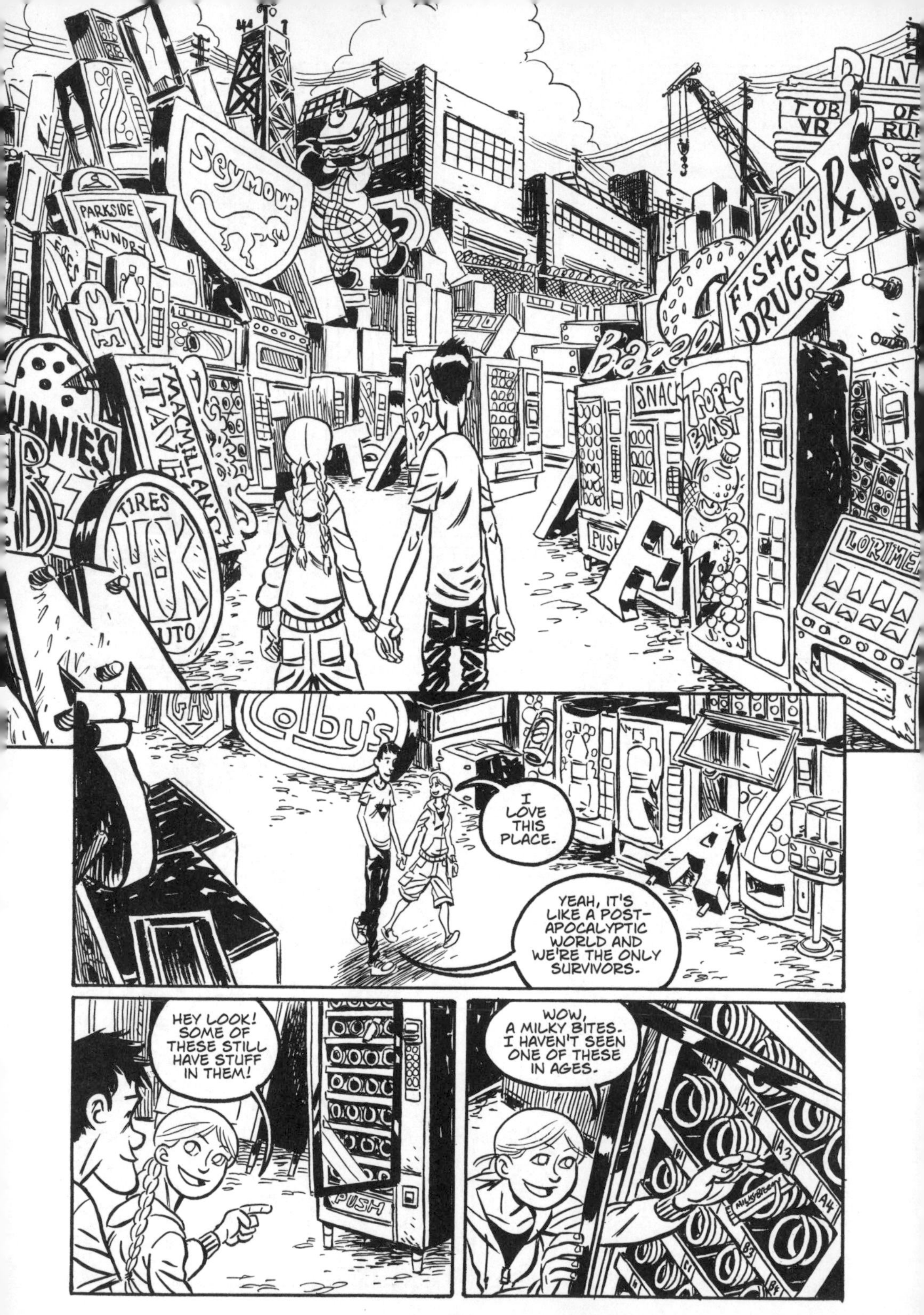
PARKSIDE LAUNDRY
Seymour
FISHER'S DRUGS
SNACK
TROPIC BLAST
TIRES
AUTO
PUSH
LORIMER
GAS
Colby's
I LOVE THIS PLACE.
YEAH, IT'S LIKE A POST-APOCALYPTIC WORLD AND WE'RE THE ONLY SURVIVORS.
HEY LOOK! SOME OF THESE STILL HAVE STUFF IN THEM!
PUSH
WOW, A MILKY BITES. I HAVEN'T SEEN ONE OF THESE IN AGES.

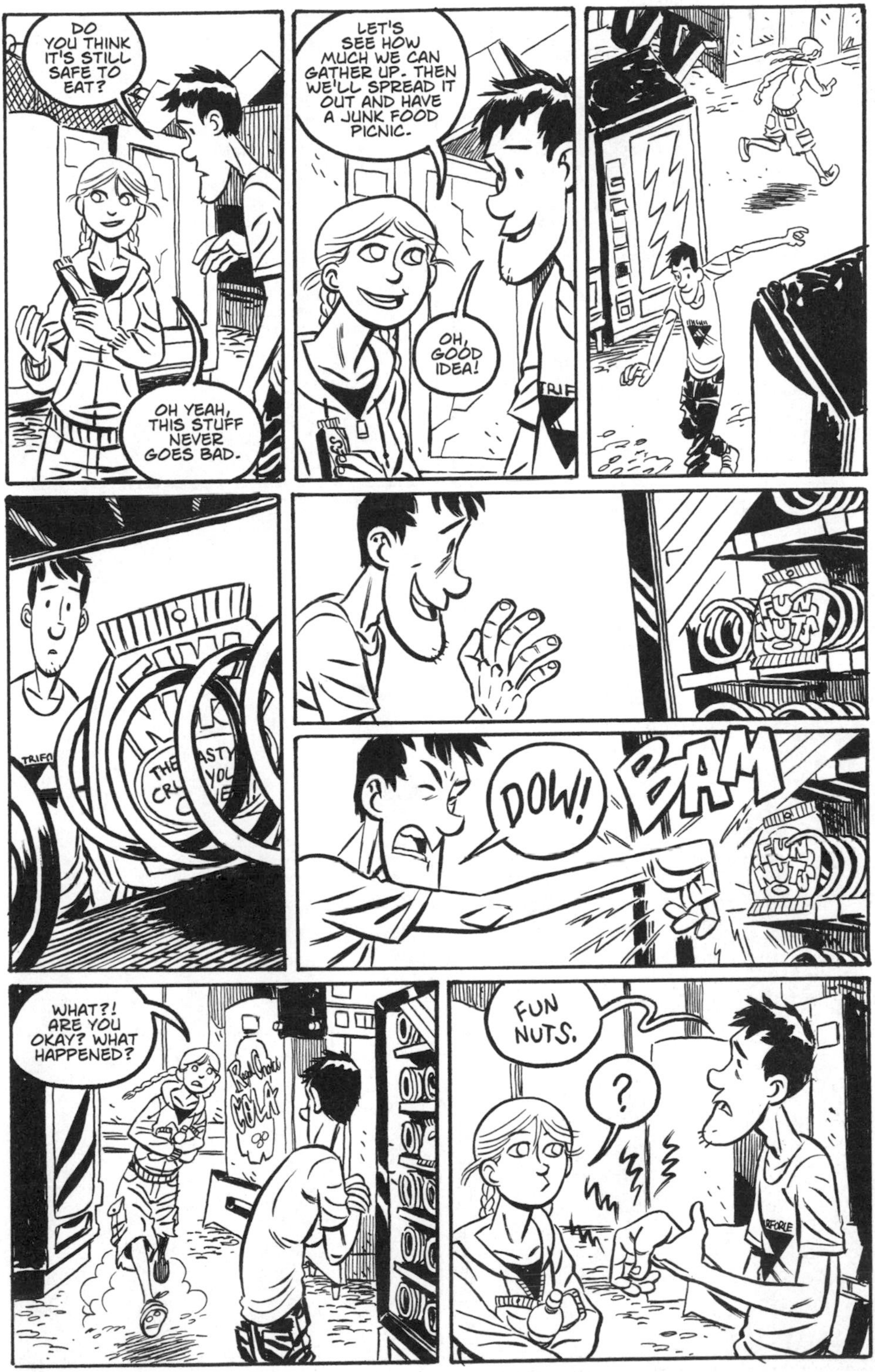
DO YOU THINK IT'S STILL SAFE TO EAT?
OH YEAH, THIS STUFF NEVER GOES BAD.
LET'S SEE HOW MUCH WE CAN GATHER UP. THEN WE'LL SPREAD IT OUT AND HAVE A JUNK FOOD PICNIC.
OH, GOOD IDEA!
FUN NUTS
DOW!
BAM
FUN NUTS
WHAT?! ARE YOU OKAY? WHAT HAPPENED?
FUN NUTS.
?

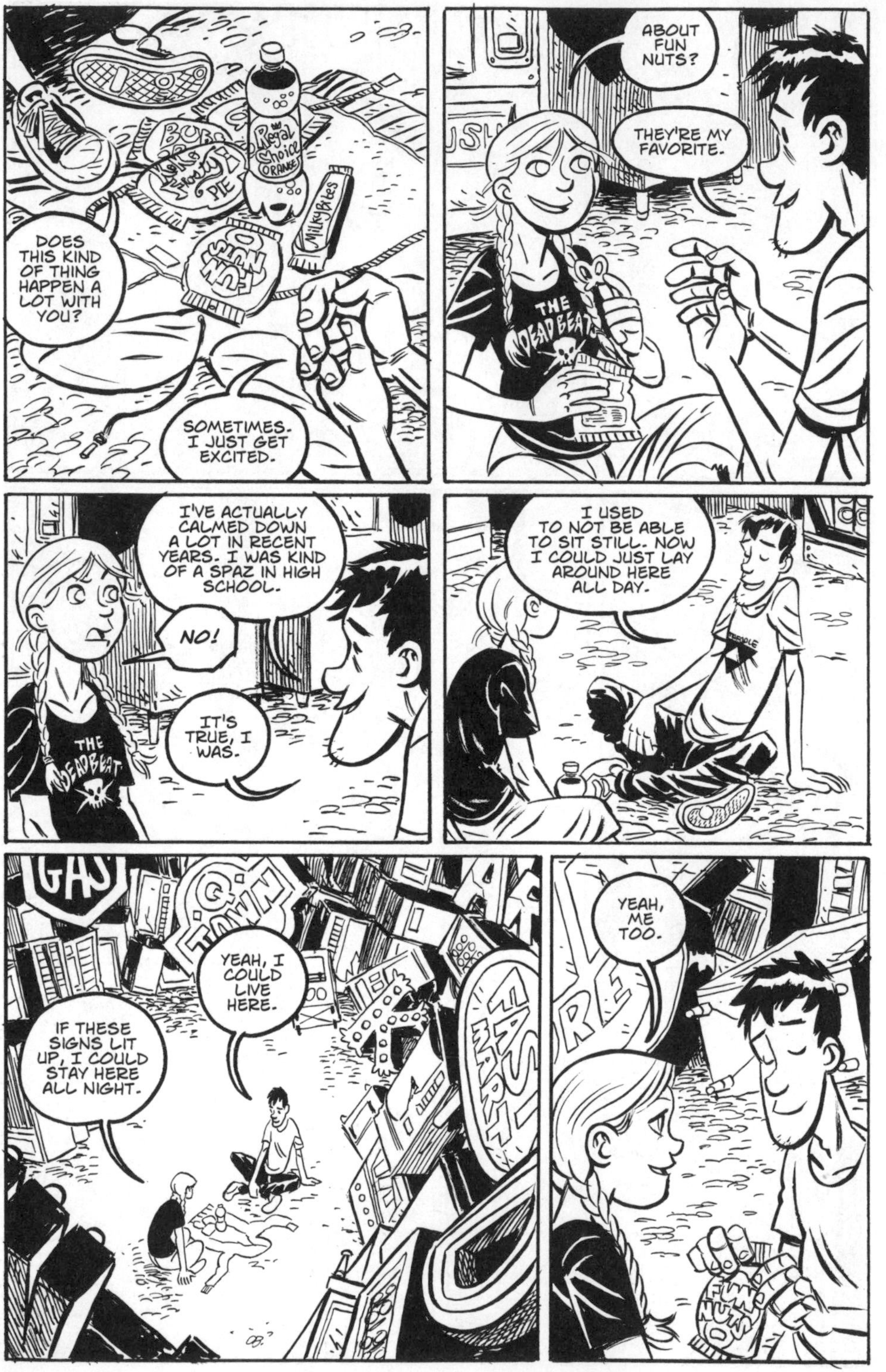

DOES THIS KIND OF THING HAPPEN A LOT WITH YOU?
SOMETIMES. I JUST GET EXCITED.
ABOUT FUN NUTS?
THEY'RE MY FAVORITE.
I'VE ACTUALLY CALMED DOWN A LOT IN RECENT YEARS. I WAS KIND OF A SPAZ IN HIGH SCHOOL.
NO!
IT'S TRUE, I WAS.
I USED TO NOT BE ABLE TO SIT STILL. NOW I COULD JUST LAY AROUND HERE ALL DAY.
IF THESE SIGNS LIT UP, I COULD STAY HERE ALL NIGHT.
YEAH, I COULD LIVE HERE.
YEAH, ME TOO.

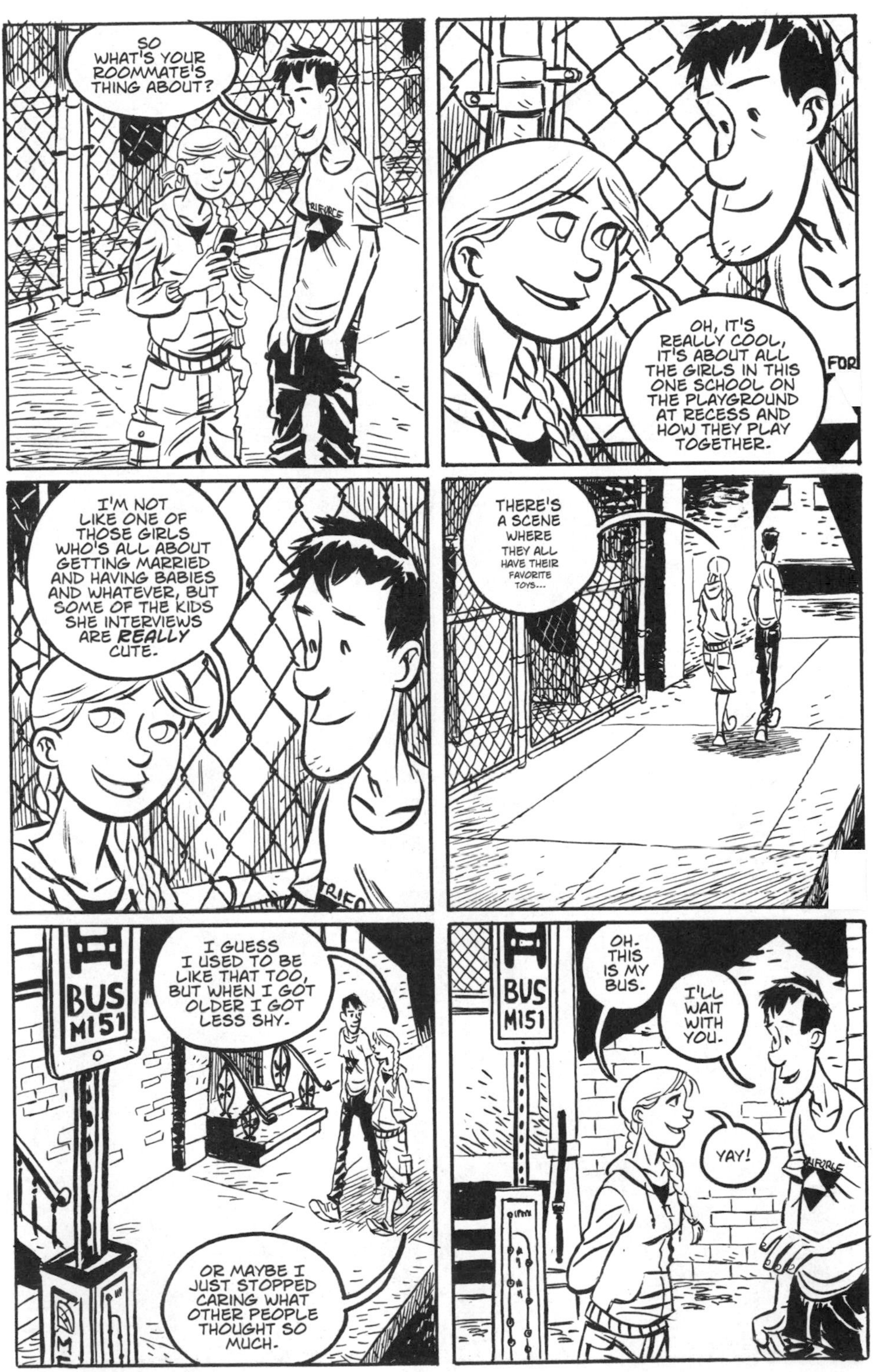
SO WHAT'S YOUR ROOMMATE'S THING ABOUT?
TRIFORCE
OH, IT'S REALLY COOL, IT'S ABOUT ALL THE GIRLS IN THIS ONE SCHOOL ON THE PLAYGROUND AT RECESS AND HOW THEY PLAY TOGETHER.
I'M NOT LIKE ONE OF THOSE GIRLS WHO'S ALL ABOUT GETTING MARRIED AND HAVING BABIES AND WHATEVER, BUT SOME OF THE KIDS SHE INTERVIEWS ARE **REALLY** CUTE.
THERE'S A SCENE WHERE THEY ALL HAVE THEIR FAVORITE TOYS...
BUS M151
I GUESS I USED TO BE LIKE THAT TOO, BUT WHEN I GOT OLDER I GOT LESS SHY.
OR MAYBE I JUST STOPPED CARING WHAT OTHER PEOPLE THOUGHT SO MUCH.
BUS M151
OH. THIS IS MY BUS.
I'LL WAIT WITH YOU.
YAY!
TRIFORCE

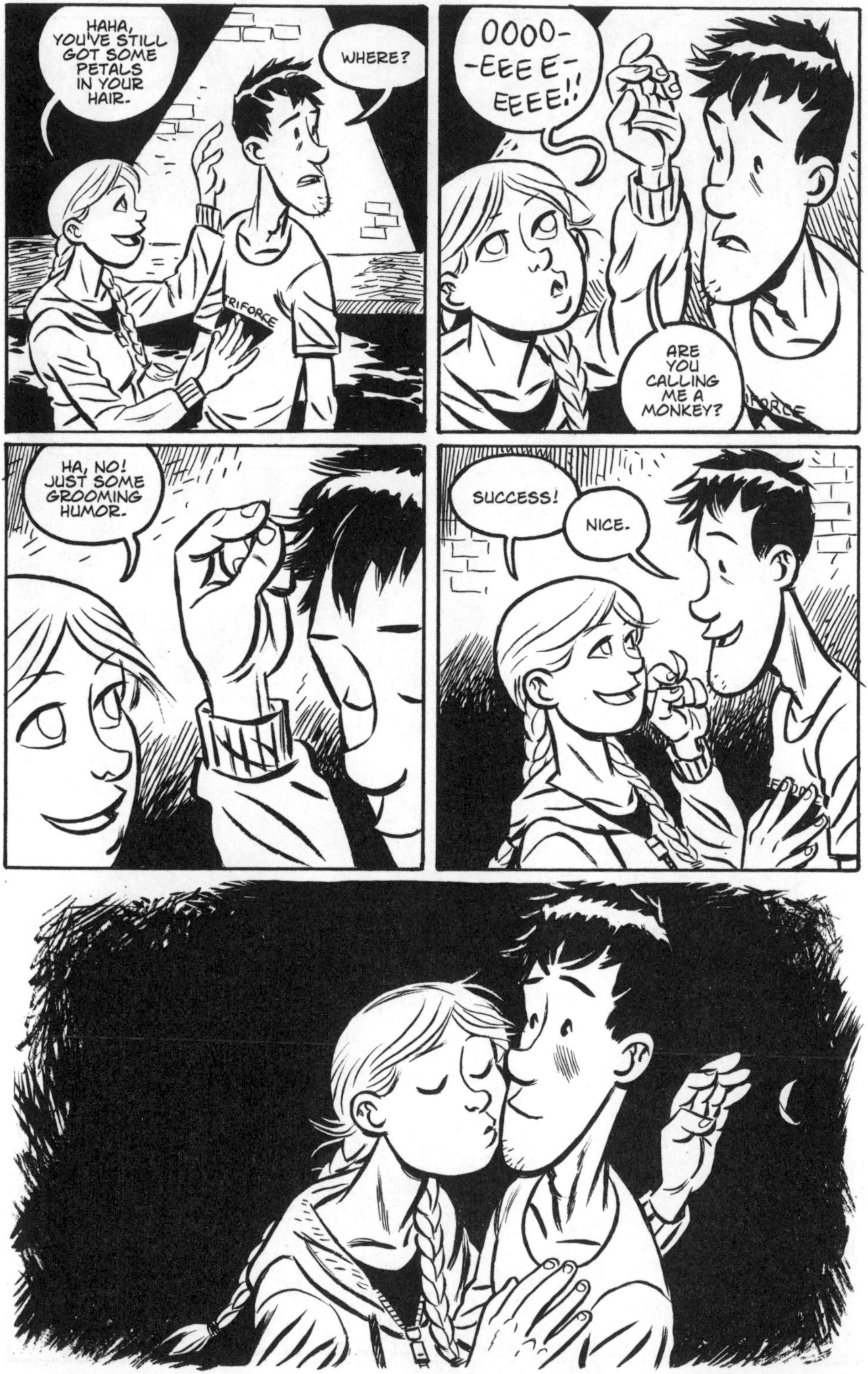
HAHA, YOU'VE STILL GOT SOME PETALS IN YOUR HAIR.
WHERE?
TRIFORCE
OOOO- -EEEE E- EEEE!!
ARE YOU CALLING ME A MONKEY?
HA, NO! JUST SOME GROOMING HUMOR.
SUCCESS!
NICE.

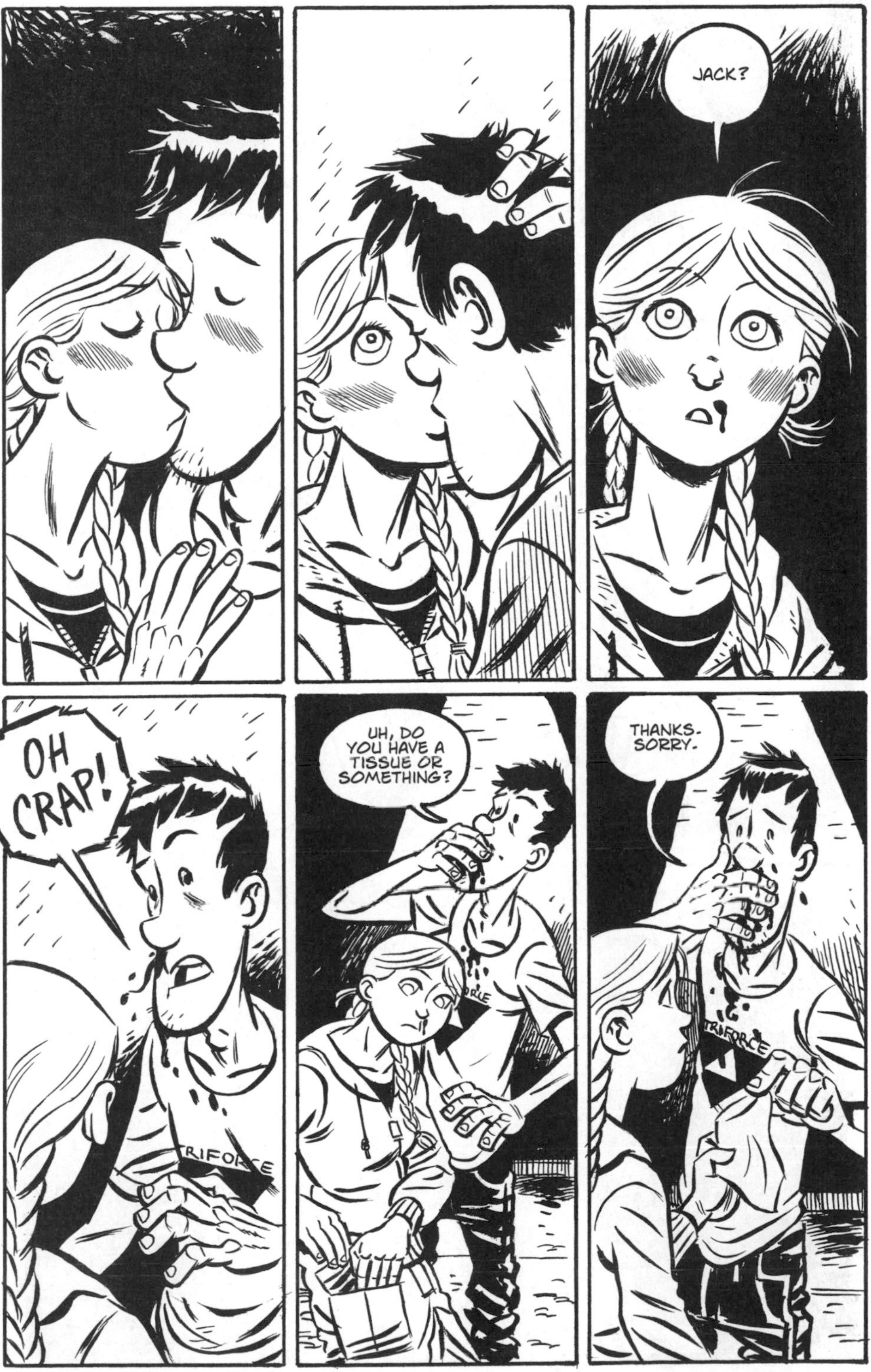
JACK?
OH CRAP!
TRIFORCE
UH, DO YOU HAVE A TISSUE OR SOMETHING?
THANKS. SORRY.
TRIFORCE

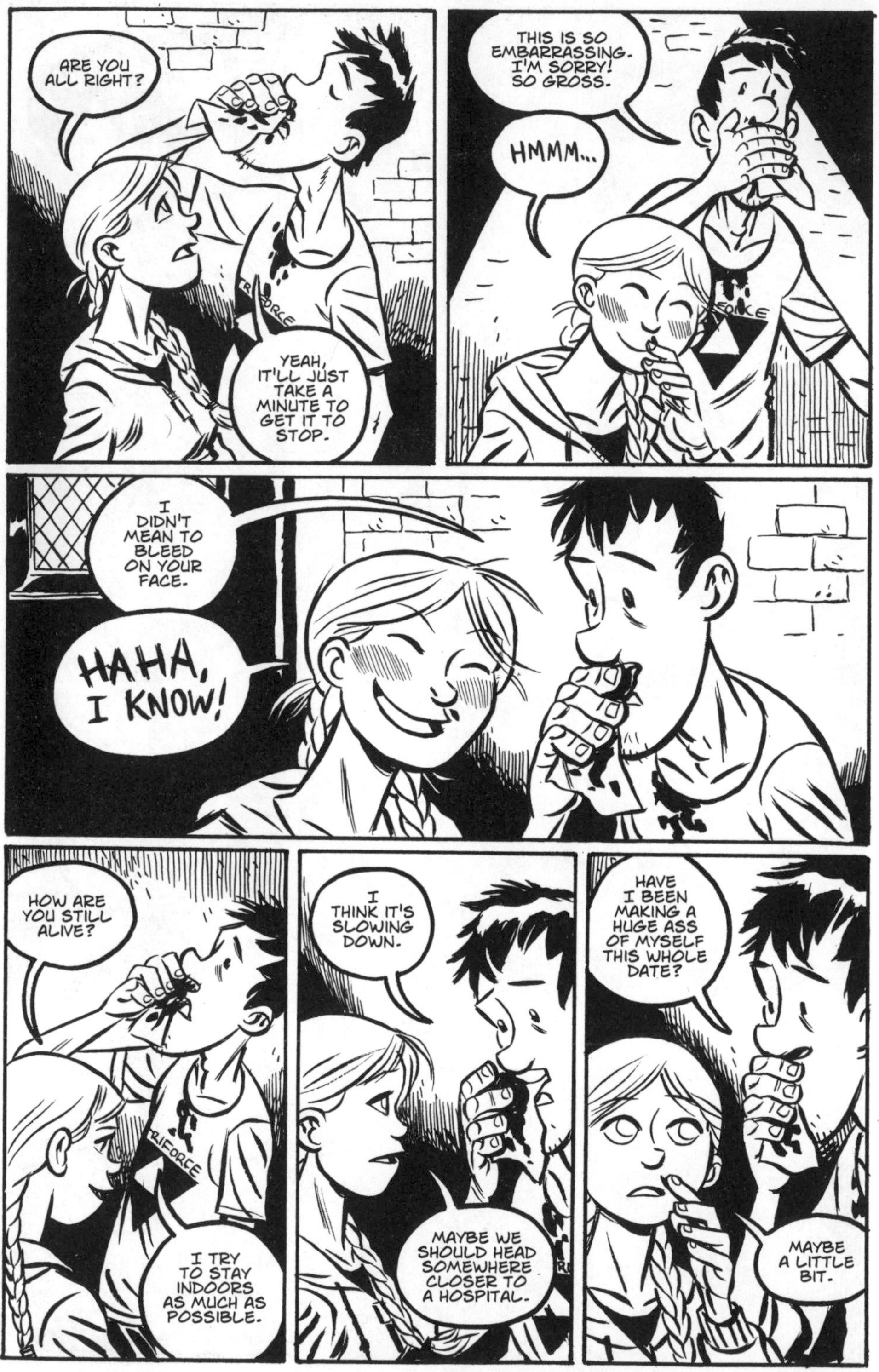
ARE YOU ALL RIGHT?
YEAH, IT'LL JUST TAKE A MINUTE TO GET IT TO STOP.
THIS IS SO EMBARRASSING. I'M SORRY! SO GROSS.
HMMM...
I DIDN'T MEAN TO BLEED ON YOUR FACE.
HAHA, I KNOW!
HOW ARE YOU STILL ALIVE?
I TRY TO STAY INDOORS AS MUCH AS POSSIBLE.
I THINK IT'S SLOWING DOWN.
MAYBE WE SHOULD HEAD SOMEWHERE CLOSER TO A HOSPITAL.
HAVE I BEEN MAKING A HUGE ASS OF MYSELF THIS WHOLE DATE?
MAYBE A LITTLE BIT.

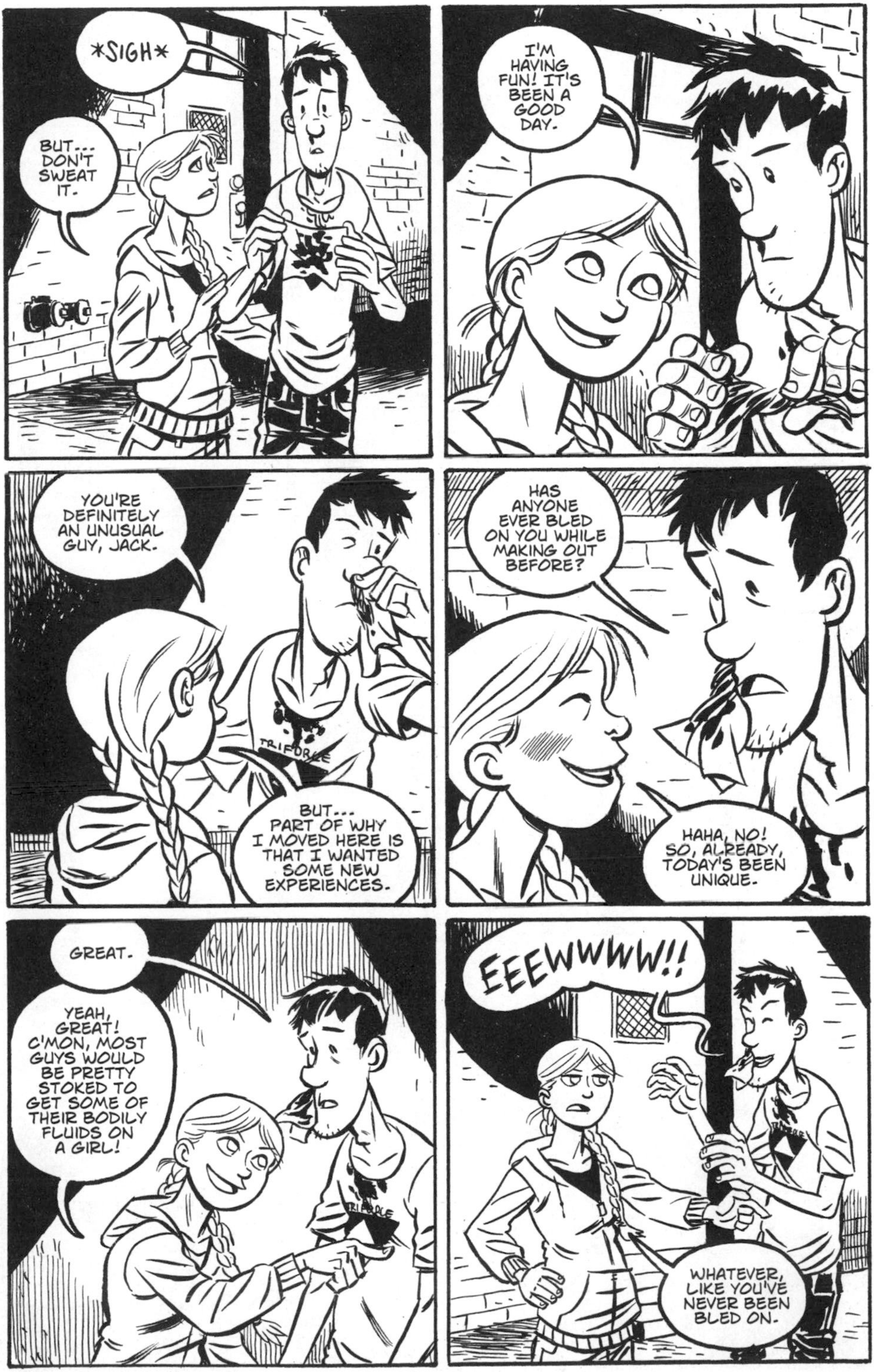
SIGH
BUT... DON'T SWEAT IT.
I'M HAVING FUN! IT'S BEEN A GOOD DAY.
YOU'RE DEFINITELY AN UNUSUAL GUY, JACK.
BUT... PART OF WHY I MOVED HERE IS THAT I WANTED SOME NEW EXPERIENCES.
HAS ANYONE EVER BLED ON YOU WHILE MAKING OUT BEFORE?
HAHA, NO! SO, ALREADY, TODAY'S BEEN UNIQUE.
GREAT.
YEAH, GREAT! C'MON, MOST GUYS WOULD BE PRETTY STOKED TO GET SOME OF THEIR BODILY FLUIDS ON A GIRL!
EEEWWWW!!
WHATEVER, LIKE YOU'VE NEVER BEEN BLED ON.

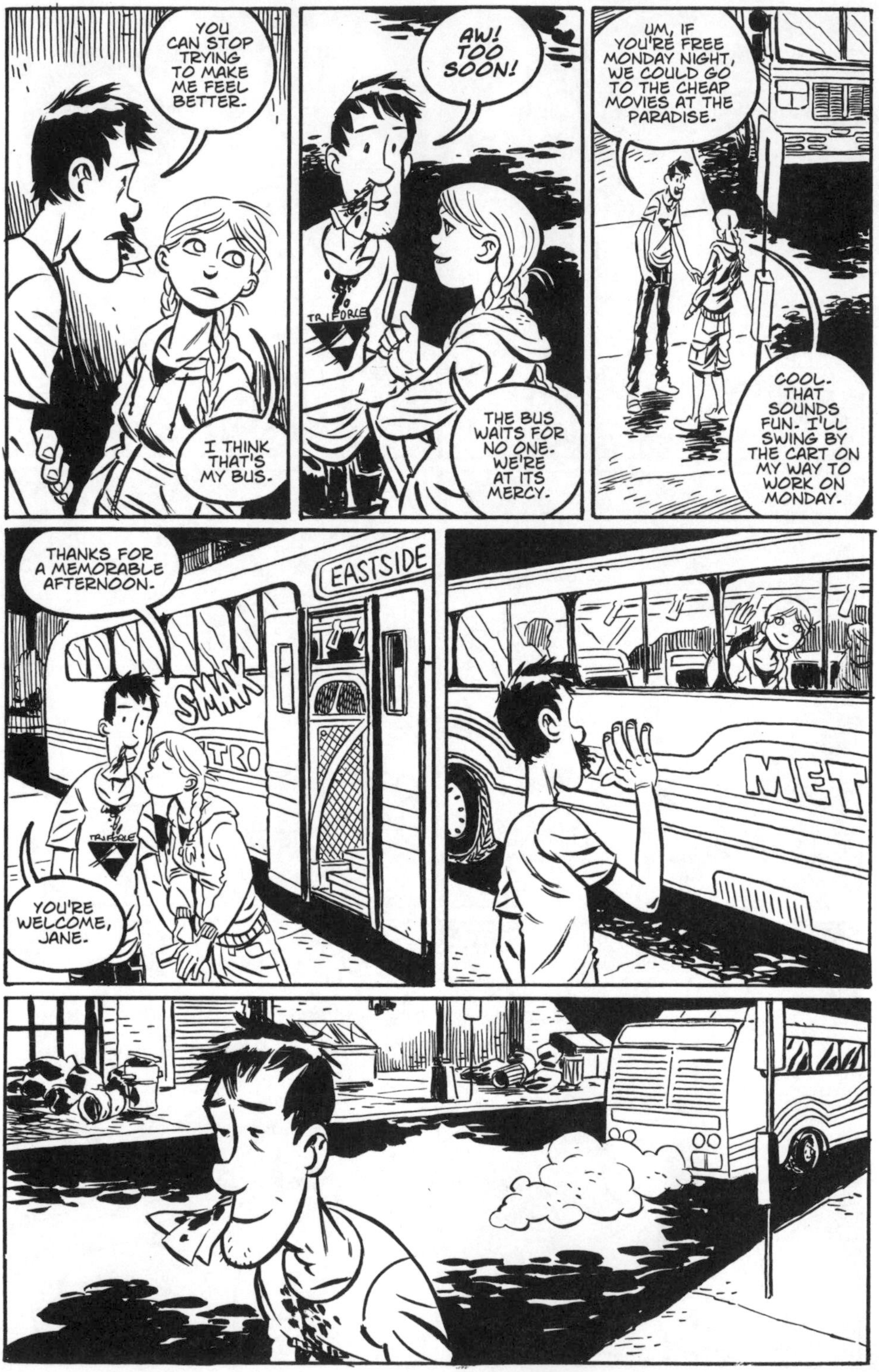
YOU CAN STOP TRYING TO MAKE ME FEEL BETTER.
I THINK THAT'S MY BUS.
AW! TOO SOON!
TRIFORCE
THE BUS WAITS FOR NO ONE. WE'RE AT ITS MERCY.
UM, IF YOU'RE FREE MONDAY NIGHT, WE COULD GO TO THE CHEAP MOVIES AT THE PARADISE.
COOL. THAT SOUNDS FUN. I'LL SWING BY THE CART ON MY WAY TO WORK ON MONDAY.
THANKS FOR A MEMORABLE AFTERNOON.
EASTSIDE
SMAK
TRIFORCE
YOU'RE WELCOME, JANE.
MET

CHAPTER THREE

"The Truth about Heartbreakers"

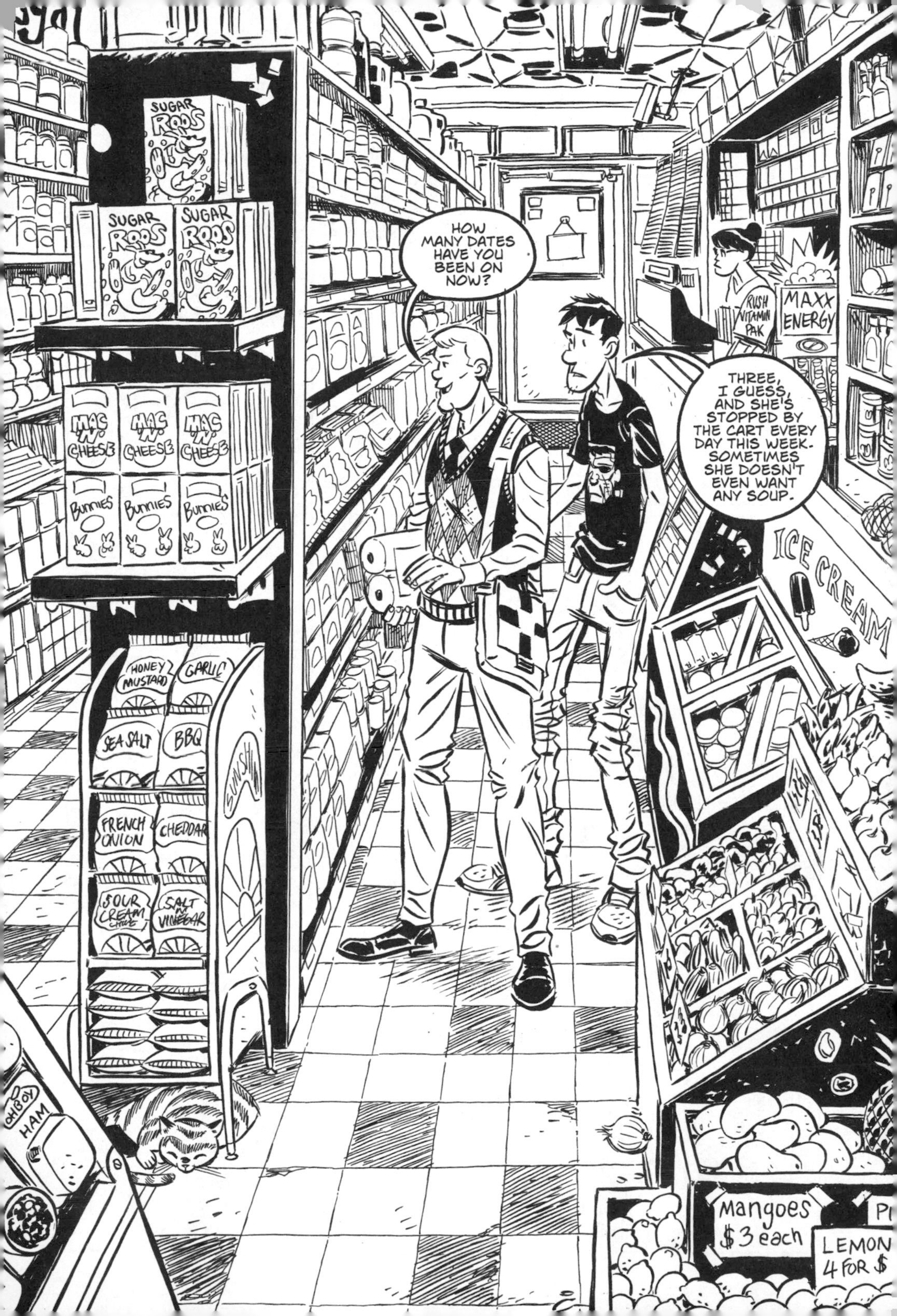
HOW MANY DATES HAVE YOU BEEN ON NOW?
THREE, I GUESS, AND SHE'S STOPPED BY THE CART EVERY DAY THIS WEEK. SOMETIMES SHE DOESN'T EVEN WANT ANY SOUP.
SUGAR ROOS
MAC 'N' CHEESE
Bunnies
HONEY MUSTARD
GARLIC
SEA SALT
BBQ
FRENCH ONION
CHEDDAR
SOUR CREAM
SALT VINEGAR
RUSH VITAMIN PAK
MAXX ENERGY
ICE CREAM
HAM
Mangoes $3 each
LEMON 4 FOR $

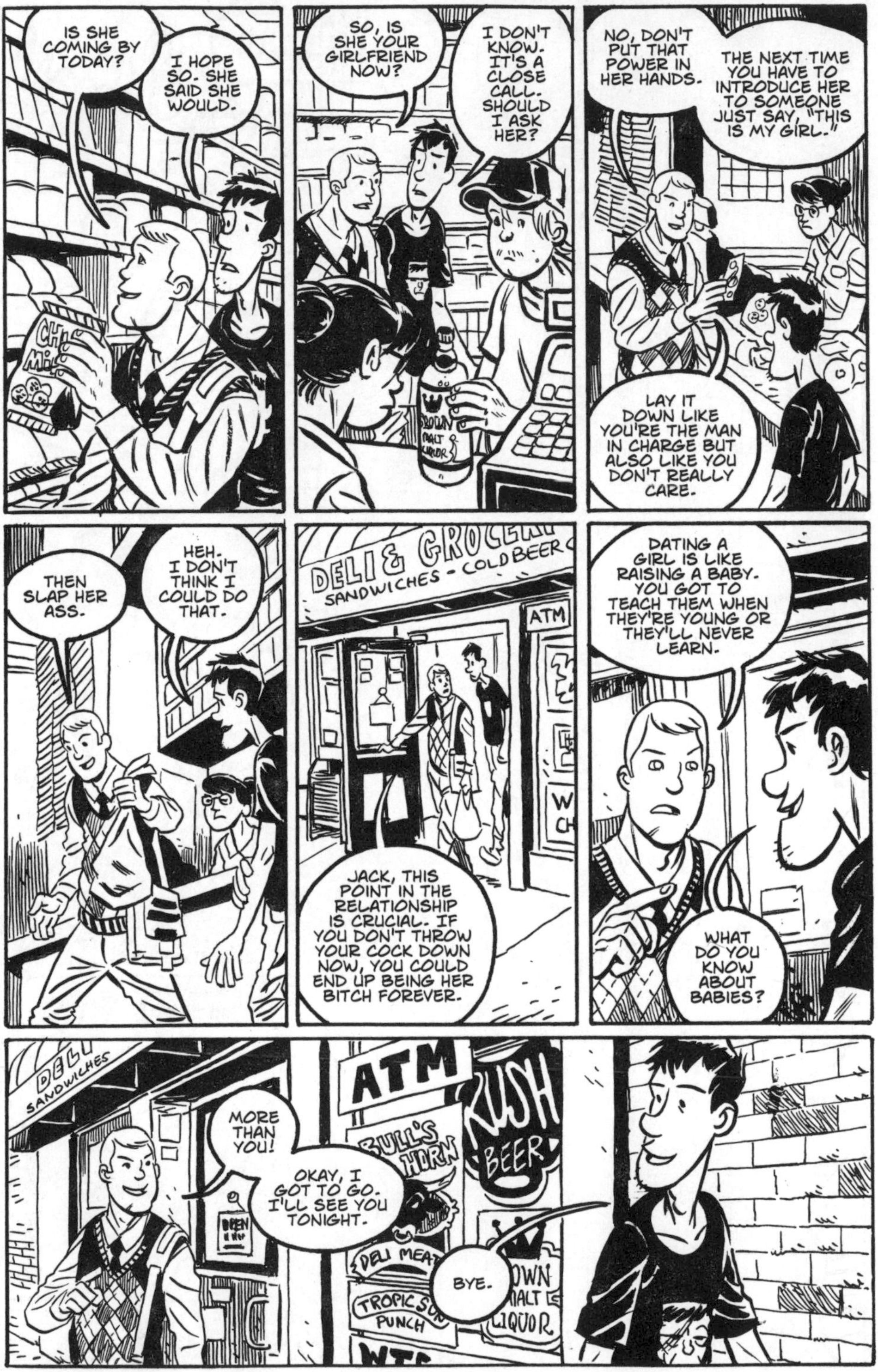

IS SHE COMING BY TODAY?
I HOPE SO. SHE SAID SHE WOULD.
CH MIL
SO, IS SHE YOUR GIRLFRIEND NOW?
I DON'T KNOW. IT'S A CLOSE CALL. SHOULD I ASK HER?
CROWN MALT LIQUOR
NO, DON'T PUT THAT POWER IN HER HANDS.
THE NEXT TIME YOU HAVE TO INTRODUCE HER TO SOMEONE JUST SAY, "THIS IS MY GIRL."
LAY IT DOWN LIKE YOU'RE THE MAN IN CHARGE BUT ALSO LIKE YOU DON'T REALLY CARE.
THEN SLAP HER ASS.
HEH. I DON'T THINK I COULD DO THAT.
DELI & GROCERY
SANDWICHES - COLD BEER
ATM
JACK, THIS POINT IN THE RELATIONSHIP IS CRUCIAL. IF YOU DON'T THROW YOUR COCK DOWN NOW, YOU COULD END UP BEING HER BITCH FOREVER.
DATING A GIRL IS LIKE RAISING A BABY. YOU GOT TO TEACH THEM WHEN THEY'RE YOUNG OR THEY'LL NEVER LEARN.
WHAT DO YOU KNOW ABOUT BABIES?
DELI
SANDWICHES
ATM
RUSH
BEER
BULL'S HORN
MORE THAN YOU!
OKAY, I GOT TO GO. I'LL SEE YOU TONIGHT.
DELI MEAT
TROPIC SUN PUNCH
CROWN MALT LIQUOR
BYE.

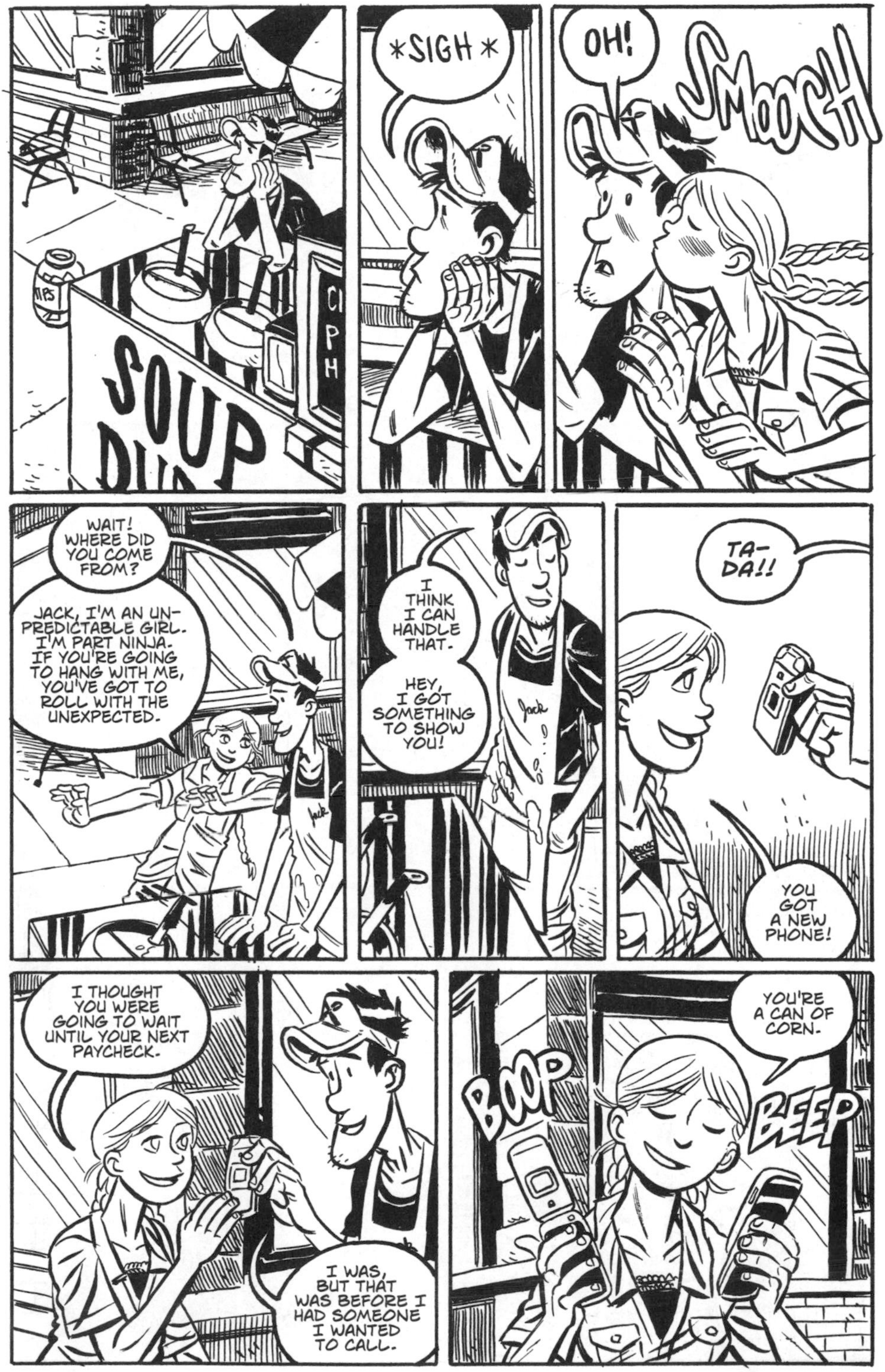
SOUP
CI
P
H
SIGH
OH!
SMOOCH
WAIT! WHERE DID YOU COME FROM?
JACK, I'M AN UN-PREDICTABLE GIRL. I'M PART NINJA. IF YOU'RE GOING TO HANG WITH ME, YOU'VE GOT TO ROLL WITH THE UNEXPECTED.
I THINK I CAN HANDLE THAT.
HEY, I GOT SOMETHING TO SHOW YOU!
TA-DA!!
YOU GOT A NEW PHONE!
I THOUGHT YOU WERE GOING TO WAIT UNTIL YOUR NEXT PAYCHECK.
I WAS, BUT THAT WAS BEFORE I HAD SOMEONE I WANTED TO CALL.
YOU'RE A CAN OF CORN.
BOOP
BEEP

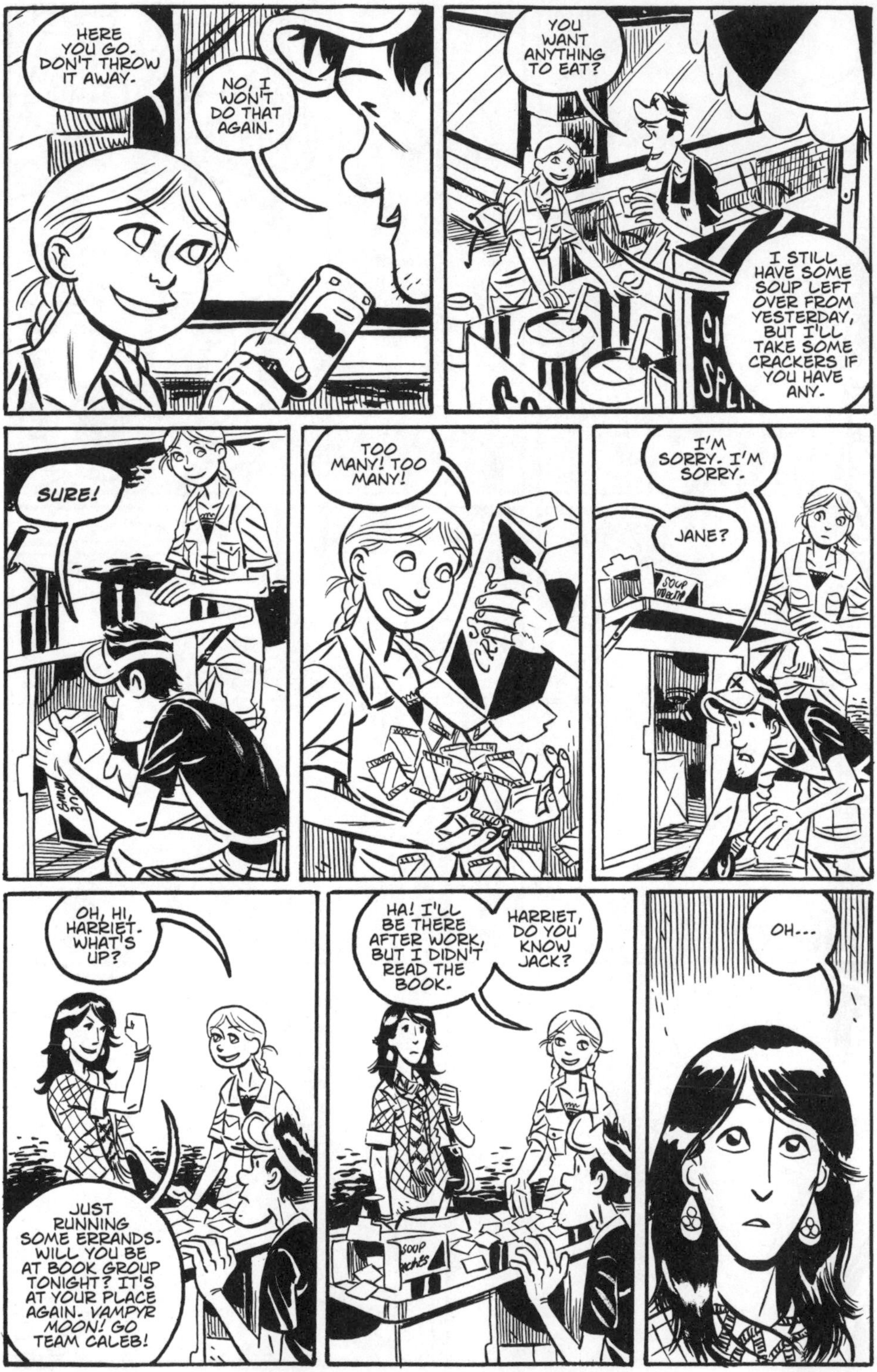
HERE YOU GO. DON'T THROW IT AWAY.
NO, I WON'T DO THAT AGAIN.
YOU WANT ANYTHING TO EAT?
I STILL HAVE SOME SOUP LEFT OVER FROM YESTERDAY, BUT I'LL TAKE SOME CRACKERS IF YOU HAVE ANY.
SURE!
TOO MANY! TOO MANY!
I'M SORRY. I'M SORRY.
JANE?
OH, HI, HARRIET. WHAT'S UP?
JUST RUNNING SOME ERRANDS. WILL YOU BE AT BOOK GROUP TONIGHT? IT'S AT YOUR PLACE AGAIN. *VAMPYR MOON!* GO TEAM CALEB!
HA! I'LL BE THERE AFTER WORK, BUT I DIDN'T READ THE BOOK.
HARRIET, DO YOU KNOW JACK?
OH...

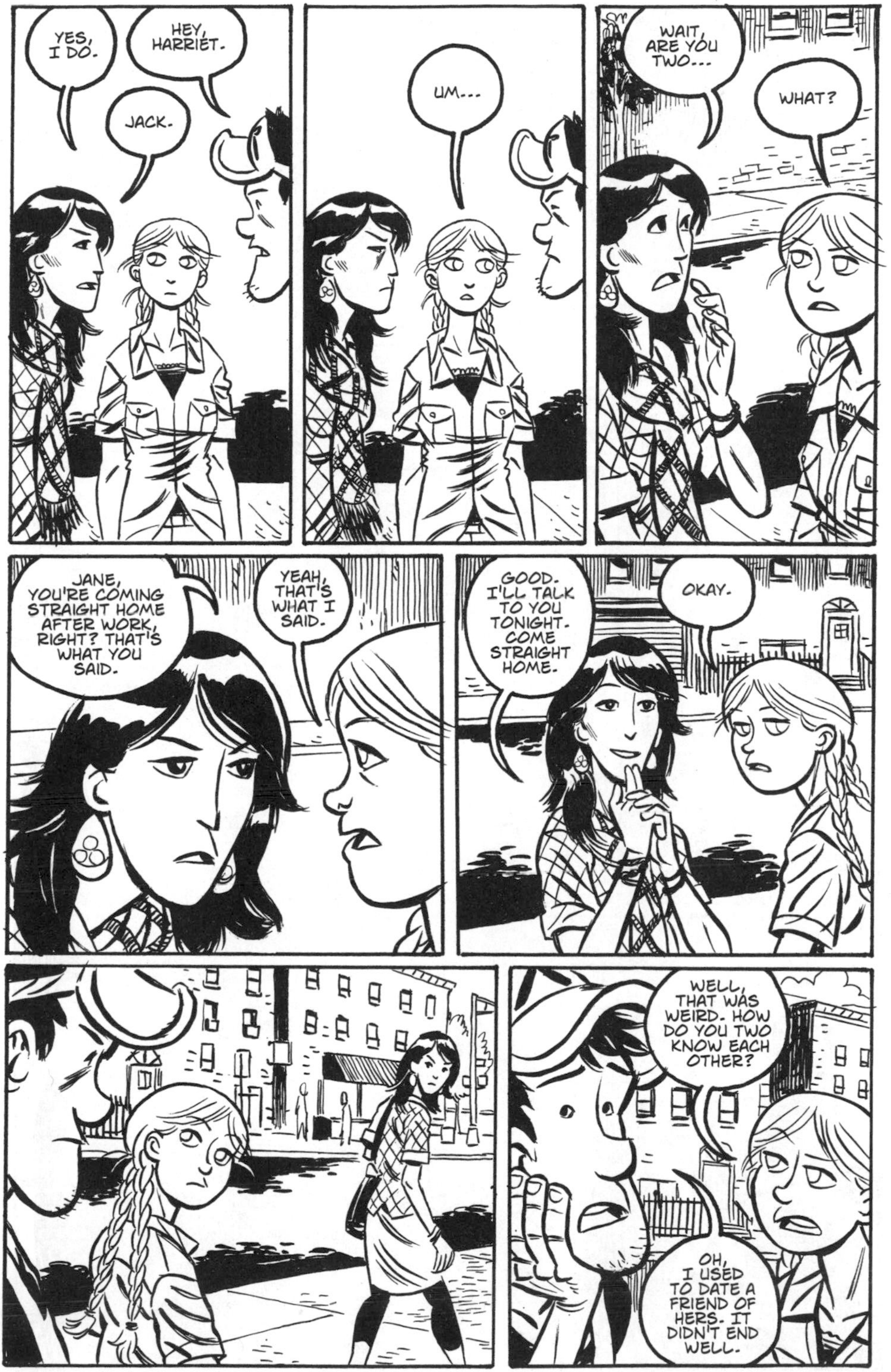
YES, I DO.
HEY, HARRIET.
JACK.
UM...
WAIT, ARE YOU TWO...
WHAT?
JANE, YOU'RE COMING STRAIGHT HOME AFTER WORK, RIGHT? THAT'S WHAT YOU SAID.
YEAH, THAT'S WHAT I SAID.
GOOD. I'LL TALK TO YOU TONIGHT. COME STRAIGHT HOME.
OKAY.
WELL, THAT WAS WEIRD. HOW DO YOU TWO KNOW EACH OTHER?
OH, I USED TO DATE A FRIEND OF HERS. IT DIDN'T END WELL.

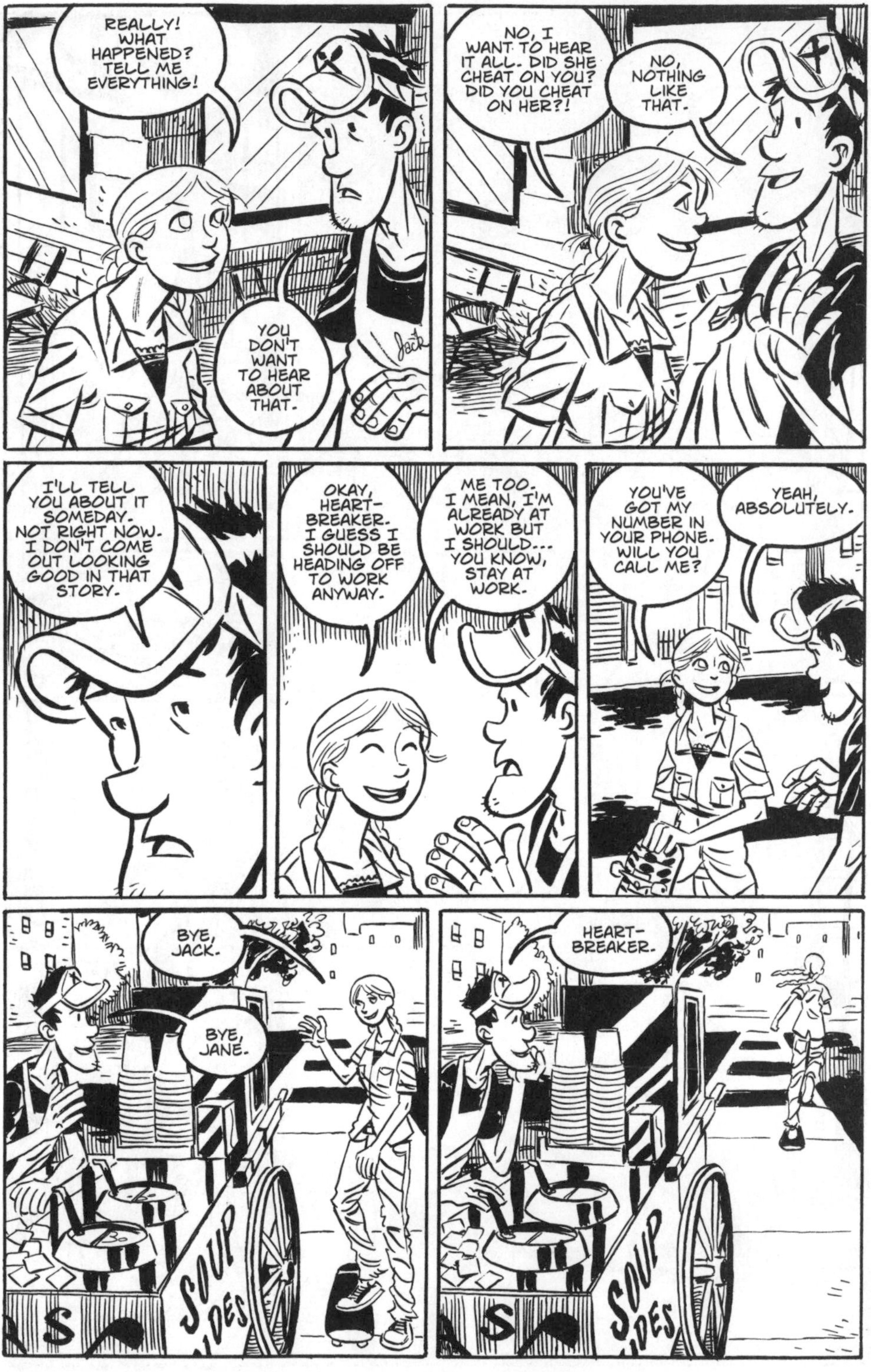

REALLY! WHAT HAPPENED? TELL ME EVERYTHING!
YOU DON'T WANT TO HEAR ABOUT THAT.
Jack
NO, I WANT TO HEAR IT ALL. DID SHE CHEAT ON YOU? DID YOU CHEAT ON HER?!
NO, NOTHING LIKE THAT.
I'LL TELL YOU ABOUT IT SOMEDAY. NOT RIGHT NOW. I DON'T COME OUT LOOKING GOOD IN THAT STORY.
OKAY, HEART-BREAKER. I GUESS I SHOULD BE HEADING OFF TO WORK ANYWAY.
ME TOO. I MEAN, I'M ALREADY AT WORK BUT I SHOULD... YOU KNOW, STAY AT WORK.
YOU'VE GOT MY NUMBER IN YOUR PHONE. WILL YOU CALL ME?
YEAH, ABSOLUTELY.
BYE, JACK.
BYE, JANE.
SOUP
HEART-BREAKER.
SOUP

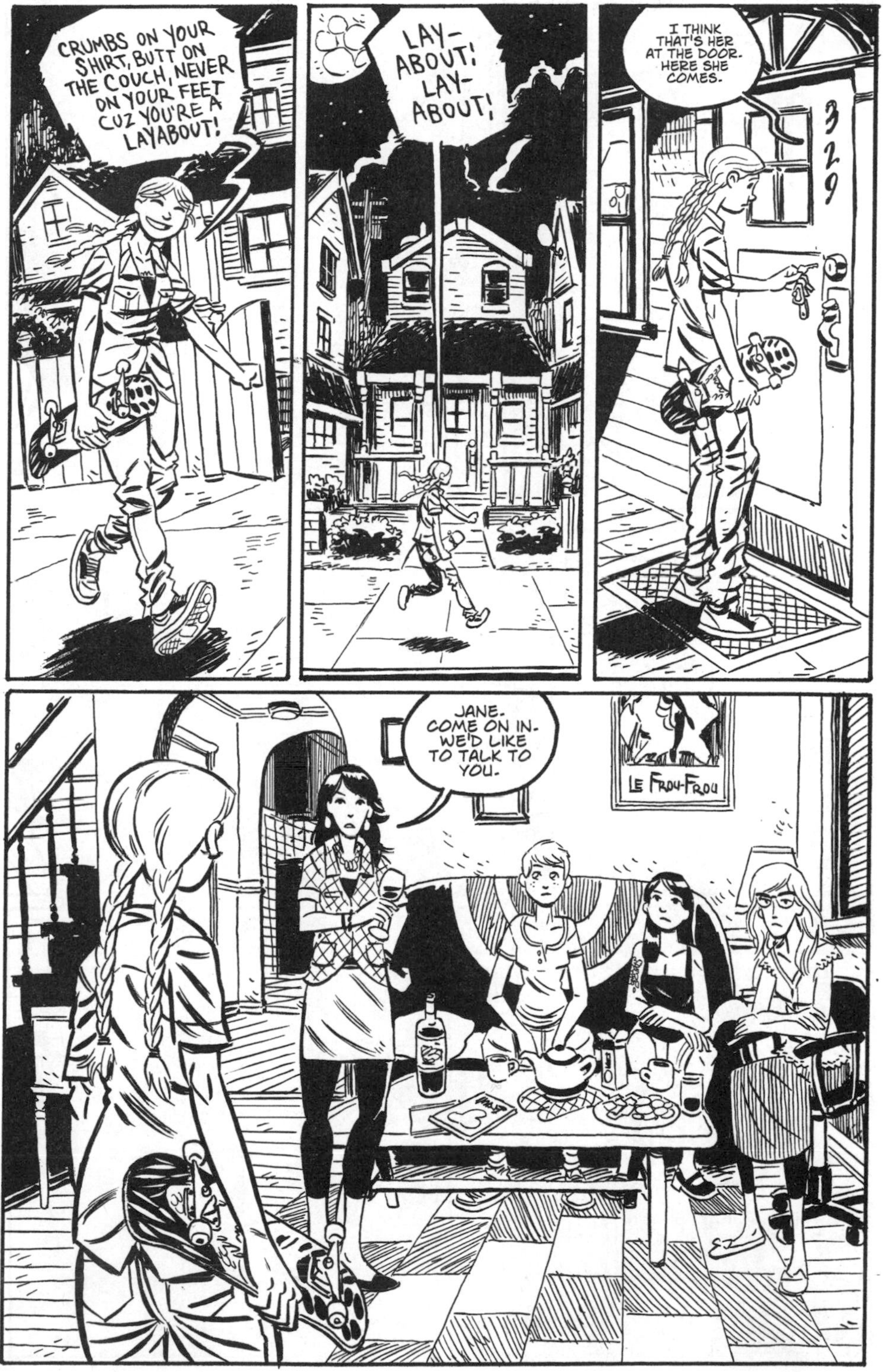
CRUMBS ON YOUR SHIRT, BUTT ON THE COUCH, NEVER ON YOUR FEET CUZ YOU'RE A LAYABOUT!
LAY-ABOUT! LAY-ABOUT!
I THINK THAT'S HER AT THE DOOR. HERE SHE COMES.
329
JANE. COME ON IN. WE'D LIKE TO TALK TO YOU.
LE FROU-FROU

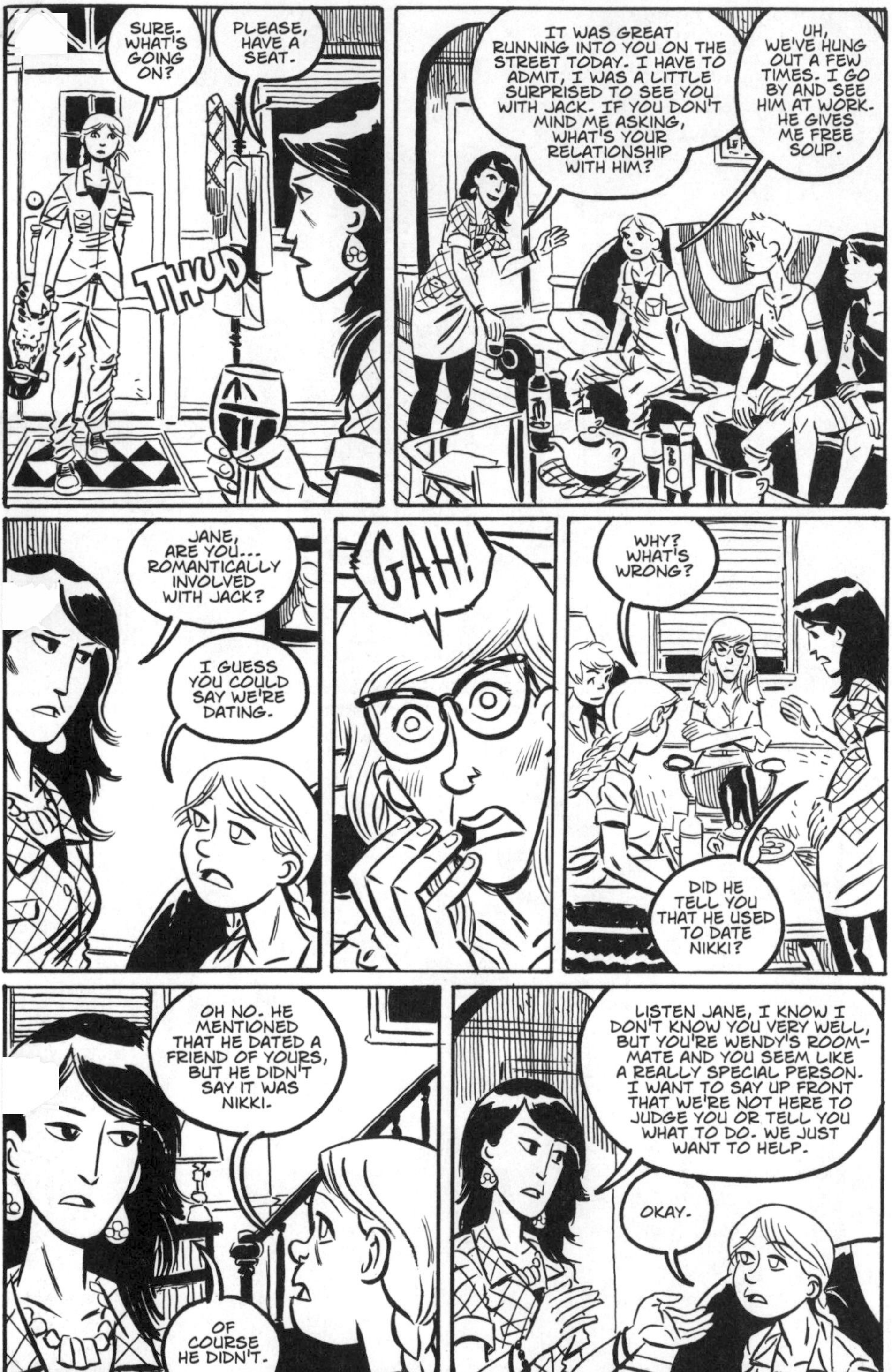
SURE. WHAT'S GOING ON?
PLEASE, HAVE A SEAT.
THUD
IT WAS GREAT RUNNING INTO YOU ON THE STREET TODAY. I HAVE TO ADMIT, I WAS A LITTLE SURPRISED TO SEE YOU WITH JACK. IF YOU DON'T MIND ME ASKING, WHAT'S YOUR RELATIONSHIP WITH HIM?
UH, WE'VE HUNG OUT A FEW TIMES. I GO BY AND SEE HIM AT WORK. HE GIVES ME FREE SOUP.
JANE, ARE YOU... ROMANTICALLY INVOLVED WITH JACK?
I GUESS YOU COULD SAY WE'RE DATING.
GAH!
WHY? WHAT'S WRONG?
DID HE TELL YOU THAT HE USED TO DATE NIKKI?
OH NO. HE MENTIONED THAT HE DATED A FRIEND OF YOURS, BUT HE DIDN'T SAY IT WAS NIKKI.
OF COURSE HE DIDN'T.
LISTEN JANE, I KNOW I DON'T KNOW YOU VERY WELL, BUT YOU'RE WENDY'S ROOM-MATE AND YOU SEEM LIKE A REALLY SPECIAL PERSON. I WANT TO SAY UP FRONT THAT WE'RE NOT HERE TO JUDGE YOU OR TELL YOU WHAT TO DO. WE JUST WANT TO HELP.
OKAY.

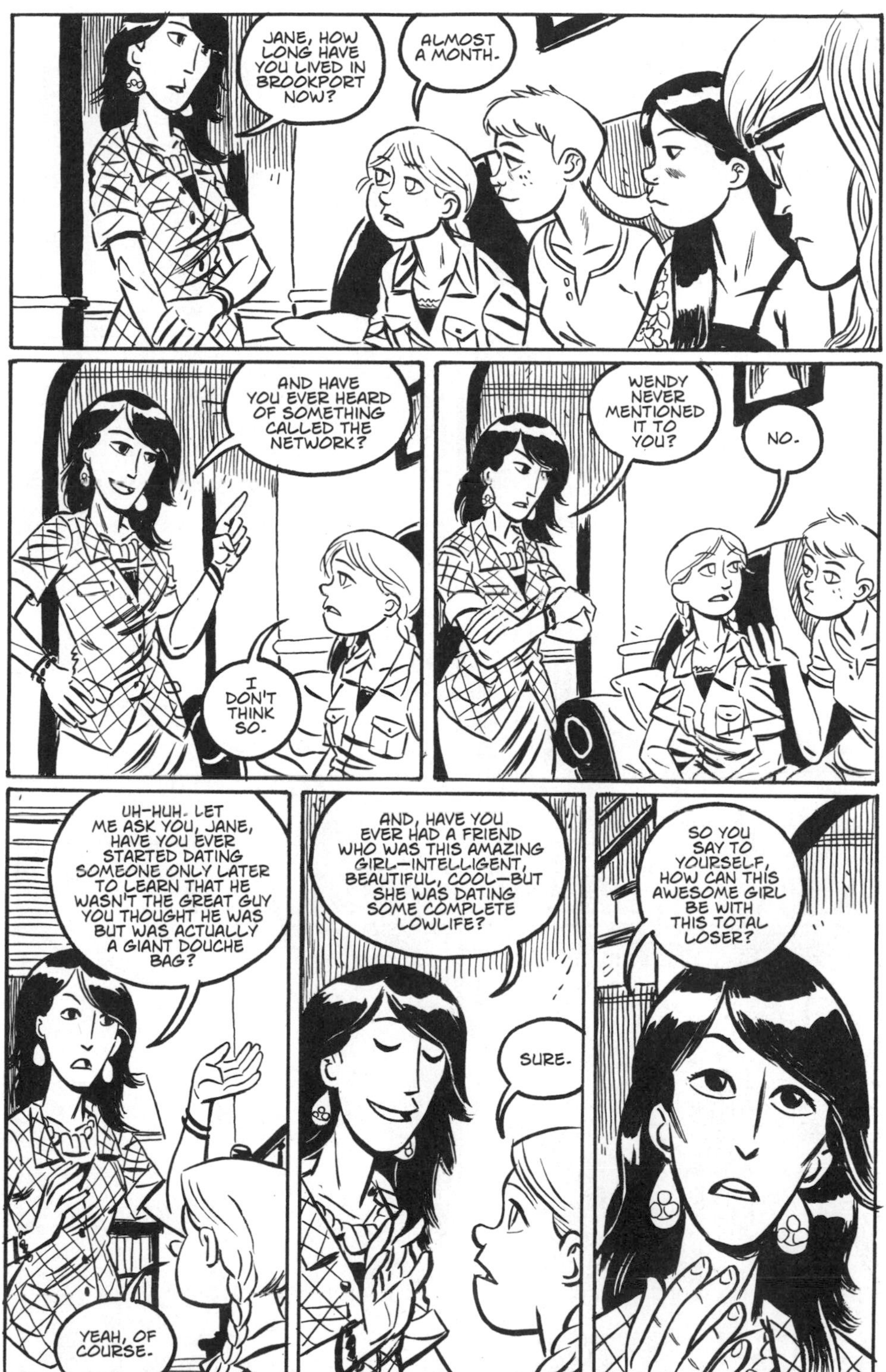
JANE, HOW LONG HAVE YOU LIVED IN BROOKPORT NOW?
ALMOST A MONTH.
AND HAVE YOU EVER HEARD OF SOMETHING CALLED THE NETWORK?
I DON'T THINK SO.
WENDY NEVER MENTIONED IT TO YOU?
NO.
UH-HUH. LET ME ASK YOU, JANE, HAVE YOU EVER STARTED DATING SOMEONE ONLY LATER TO LEARN THAT HE WASN'T THE GREAT GUY YOU THOUGHT HE WAS BUT WAS ACTUALLY A GIANT DOUCHE BAG?
YEAH, OF COURSE.
AND, HAVE YOU EVER HAD A FRIEND WHO WAS THIS AMAZING GIRL—INTELLIGENT, BEAUTIFUL, COOL—BUT SHE WAS DATING SOME COMPLETE LOWLIFE?
SURE.
SO YOU SAY TO YOURSELF, HOW CAN THIS AWESOME GIRL BE WITH THIS TOTAL LOSER?

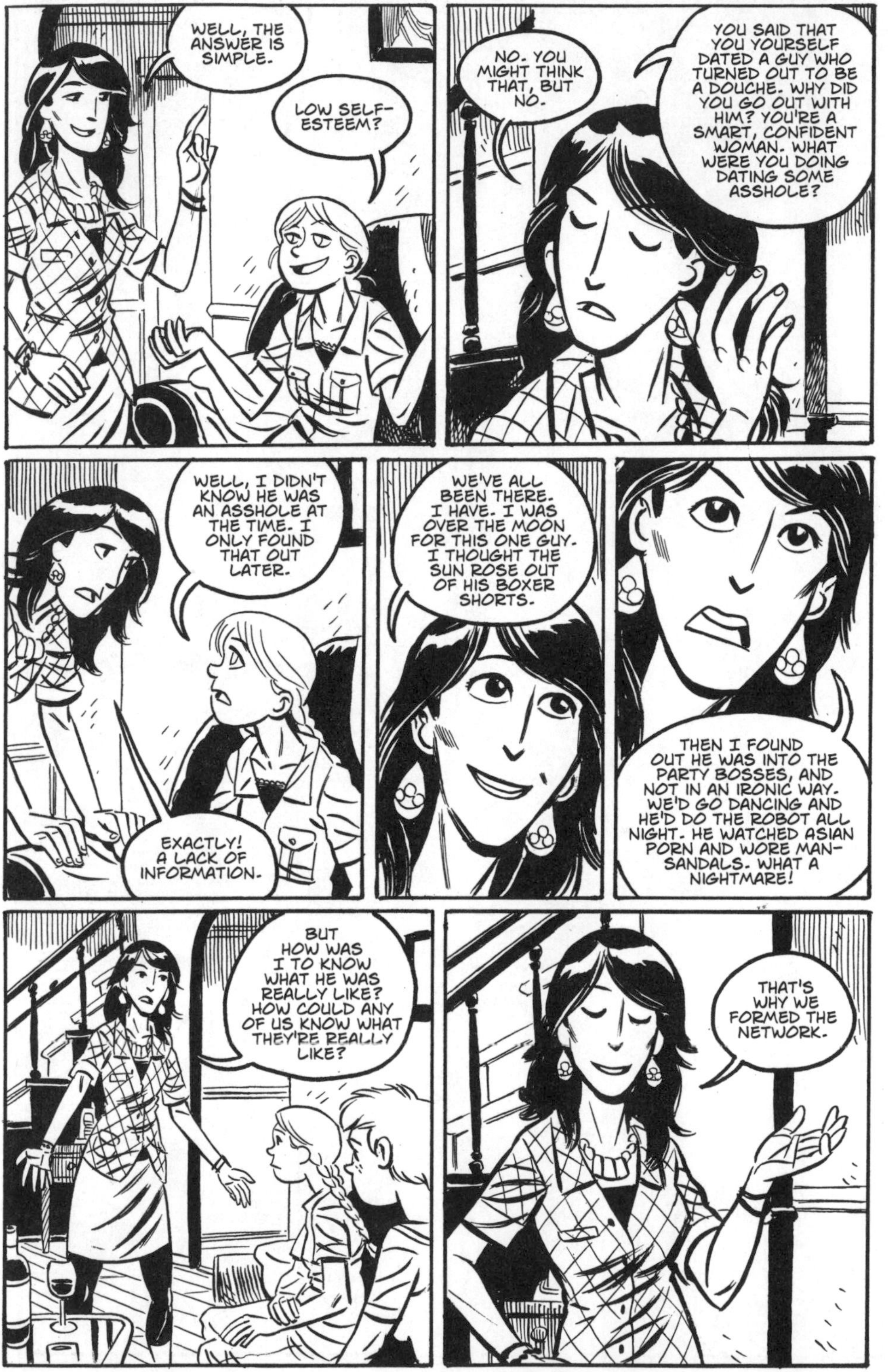
WELL, THE ANSWER IS SIMPLE.
LOW SELF-ESTEEM?
NO. YOU MIGHT THINK THAT, BUT NO.
YOU SAID THAT YOU YOURSELF DATED A GUY WHO TURNED OUT TO BE A DOUCHE. WHY DID YOU GO OUT WITH HIM? YOU'RE A SMART, CONFIDENT WOMAN. WHAT WERE YOU DOING DATING SOME ASSHOLE?
WELL, I DIDN'T KNOW HE WAS AN ASSHOLE AT THE TIME. I ONLY FOUND THAT OUT LATER.
EXACTLY! A LACK OF INFORMATION.
WE'VE ALL BEEN THERE. I HAVE. I WAS OVER THE MOON FOR THIS ONE GUY. I THOUGHT THE SUN ROSE OUT OF HIS BOXER SHORTS.
THEN I FOUND OUT HE WAS INTO THE PARTY BOSSES, AND NOT IN AN IRONIC WAY. WE'D GO DANCING AND HE'D DO THE ROBOT ALL NIGHT. HE WATCHED ASIAN PORN AND WORE MAN-SANDALS. WHAT A NIGHTMARE!
BUT HOW WAS I TO KNOW WHAT HE WAS REALLY LIKE? HOW COULD ANY OF US KNOW WHAT THEY'RE REALLY LIKE?
THAT'S WHY WE FORMED THE NETWORK.

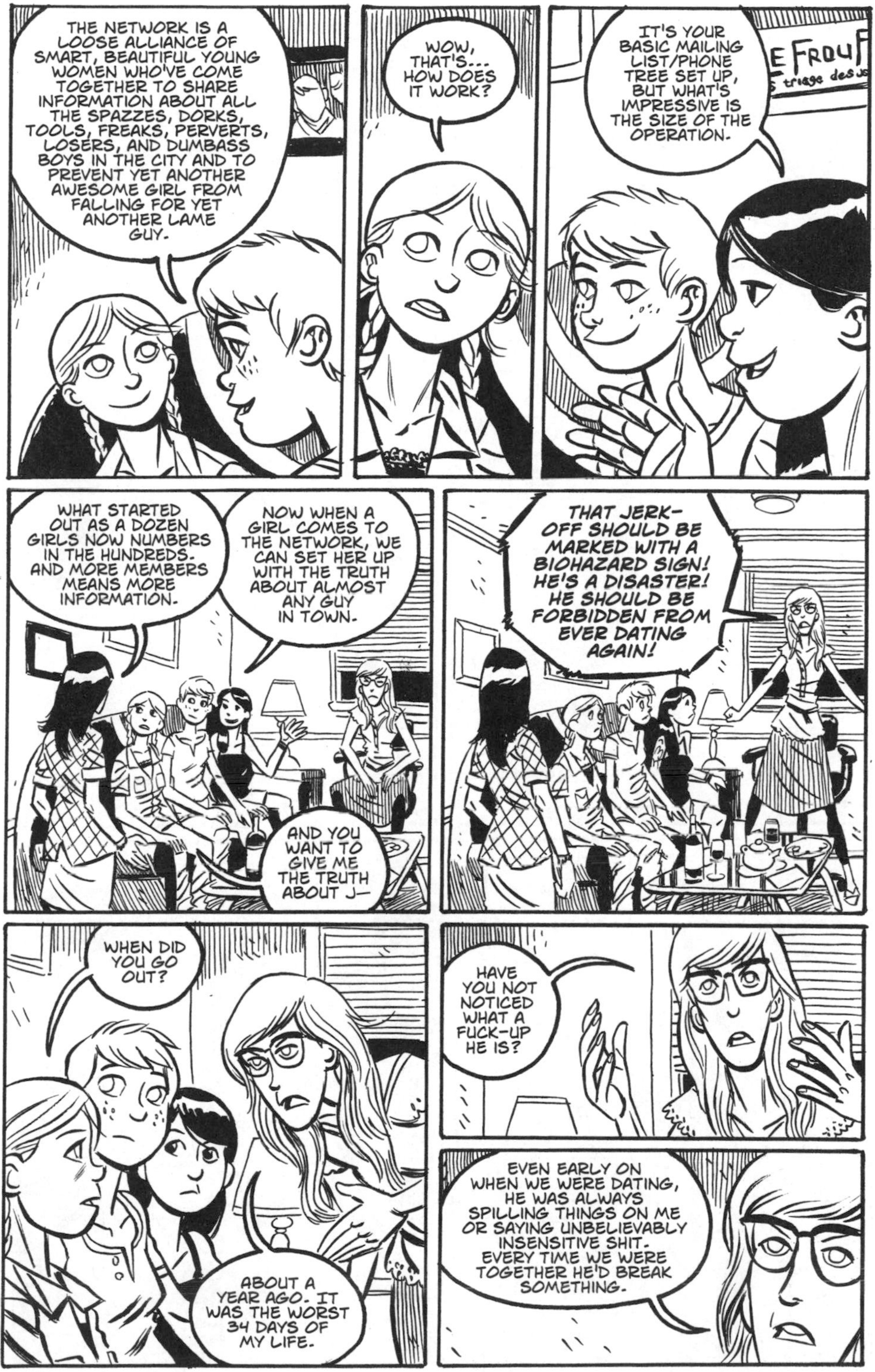
THE NETWORK IS A LOOSE ALLIANCE OF SMART, BEAUTIFUL YOUNG WOMEN WHO'VE COME TOGETHER TO SHARE INFORMATION ABOUT ALL THE SPAZZES, DORKS, TOOLS, FREAKS, PERVERTS, LOSERS, AND DUMBASS BOYS IN THE CITY AND TO PREVENT YET ANOTHER AWESOME GIRL FROM FALLING FOR YET ANOTHER LAME GUY.
WOW, THAT'S... HOW DOES IT WORK?
IT'S YOUR BASIC MAILING LIST/PHONE TREE SET UP, BUT WHAT'S IMPRESSIVE IS THE SIZE OF THE OPERATION.
WHAT STARTED OUT AS A DOZEN GIRLS NOW NUMBERS IN THE HUNDREDS. AND MORE MEMBERS MEANS MORE INFORMATION.
NOW WHEN A GIRL COMES TO THE NETWORK, WE CAN SET HER UP WITH THE TRUTH ABOUT ALMOST ANY GUY IN TOWN.
AND YOU WANT TO GIVE ME THE TRUTH ABOUT J—
THAT JERK-OFF SHOULD BE MARKED WITH A BIOHAZARD SIGN! HE'S A DISASTER! HE SHOULD BE FORBIDDEN FROM EVER DATING AGAIN!
WHEN DID YOU GO OUT?
ABOUT A YEAR AGO. IT WAS THE WORST 34 DAYS OF MY LIFE.
HAVE YOU NOT NOTICED WHAT A FUCK-UP HE IS?
EVEN EARLY ON WHEN WE WERE DATING, HE WAS ALWAYS SPILLING THINGS ON ME OR SAYING UNBELIEVABLY INSENSITIVE SHIT. EVERY TIME WE WERE TOGETHER HE'D BREAK SOMETHING.

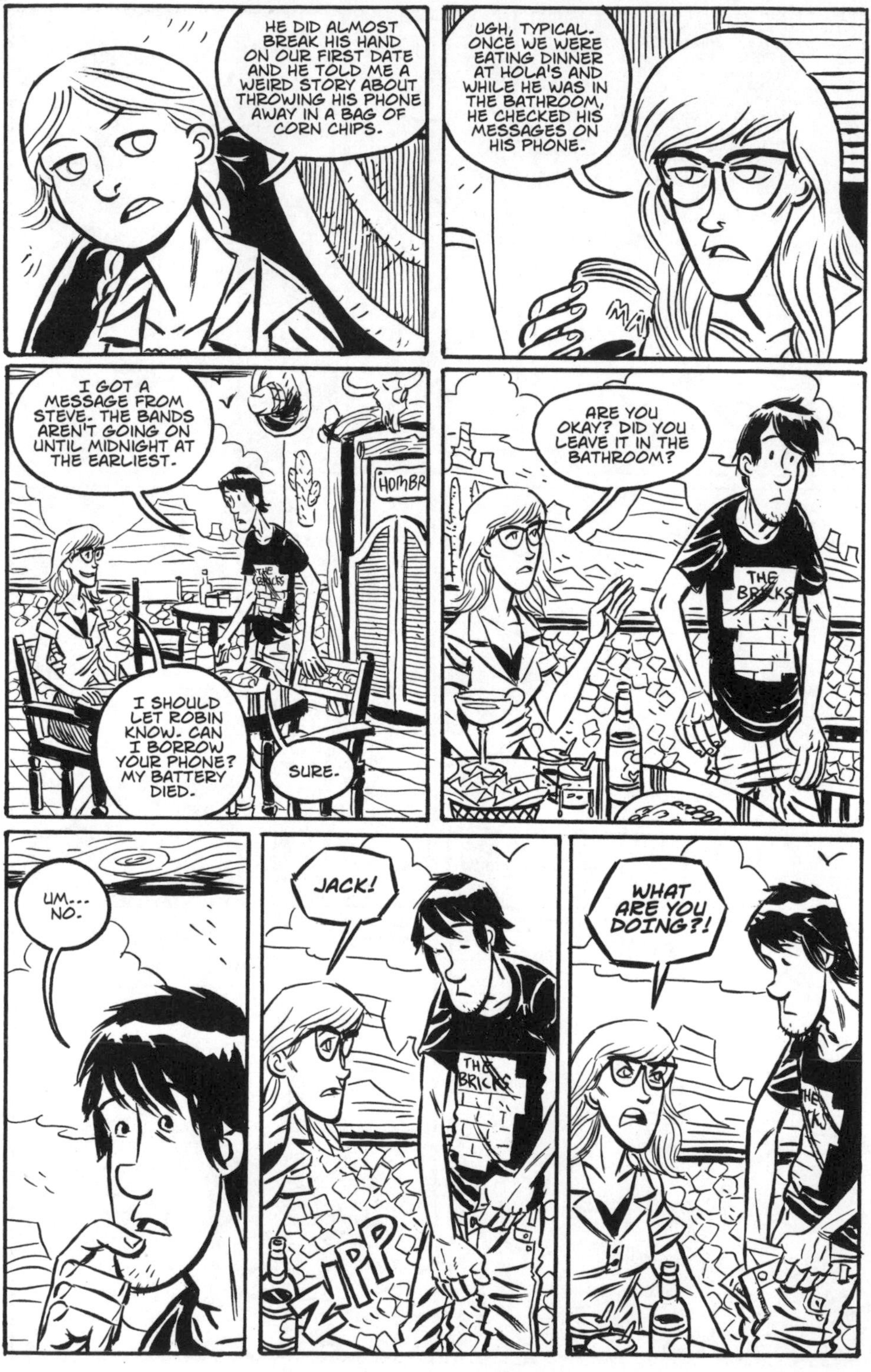
HE DID ALMOST BREAK HIS HAND ON OUR FIRST DATE AND HE TOLD ME A WEIRD STORY ABOUT THROWING HIS PHONE AWAY IN A BAG OF CORN CHIPS.
UGH, TYPICAL. ONCE WE WERE EATING DINNER AT HOLA'S AND WHILE HE WAS IN THE BATHROOM, HE CHECKED HIS MESSAGES ON HIS PHONE.
I GOT A MESSAGE FROM STEVE. THE BANDS AREN'T GOING ON UNTIL MIDNIGHT AT THE EARLIEST.
HOMBR
THE BRICKS
I SHOULD LET ROBIN KNOW. CAN I BORROW YOUR PHONE? MY BATTERY DIED.
SURE.
ARE YOU OKAY? DID YOU LEAVE IT IN THE BATHROOM?
THE BRICKS
UM... NO.
JACK!
THE BRICKS
ZIPP
WHAT ARE YOU DOING?!

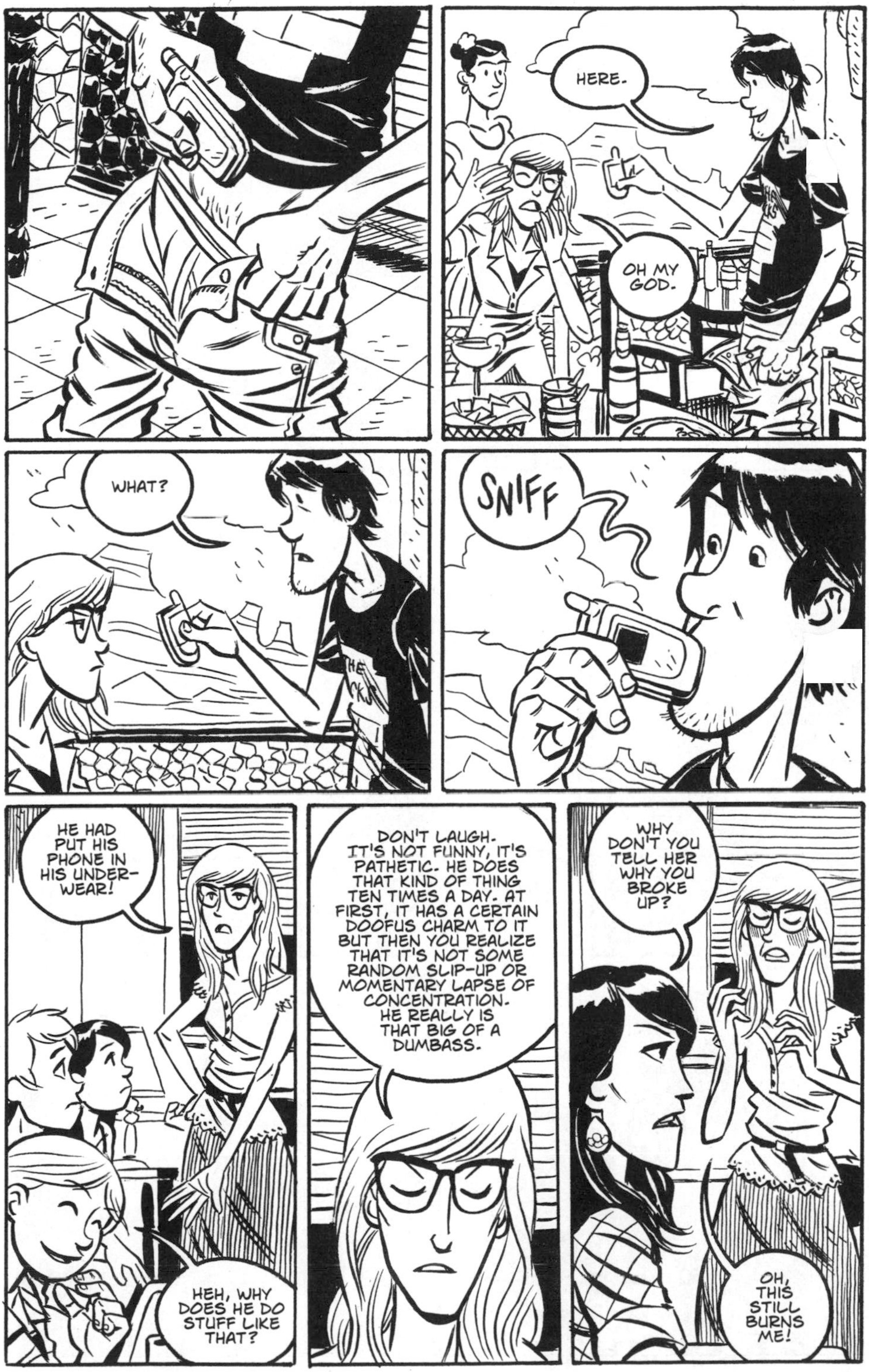
HERE.
OH MY GOD.
WHAT?
SNIFF
HE HAD PUT HIS PHONE IN HIS UNDER-WEAR!
HEH, WHY DOES HE DO STUFF LIKE THAT?
DON'T LAUGH. IT'S NOT FUNNY, IT'S PATHETIC. HE DOES THAT KIND OF THING TEN TIMES A DAY. AT FIRST, IT HAS A CERTAIN DOOFUS CHARM TO IT BUT THEN YOU REALIZE THAT IT'S NOT SOME RANDOM SLIP-UP OR MOMENTARY LAPSE OF CONCENTRATION. HE REALLY IS THAT BIG OF A DUMBASS.
WHY DON'T YOU TELL HER WHY YOU BROKE UP?
OH, THIS STILL BURNS ME!

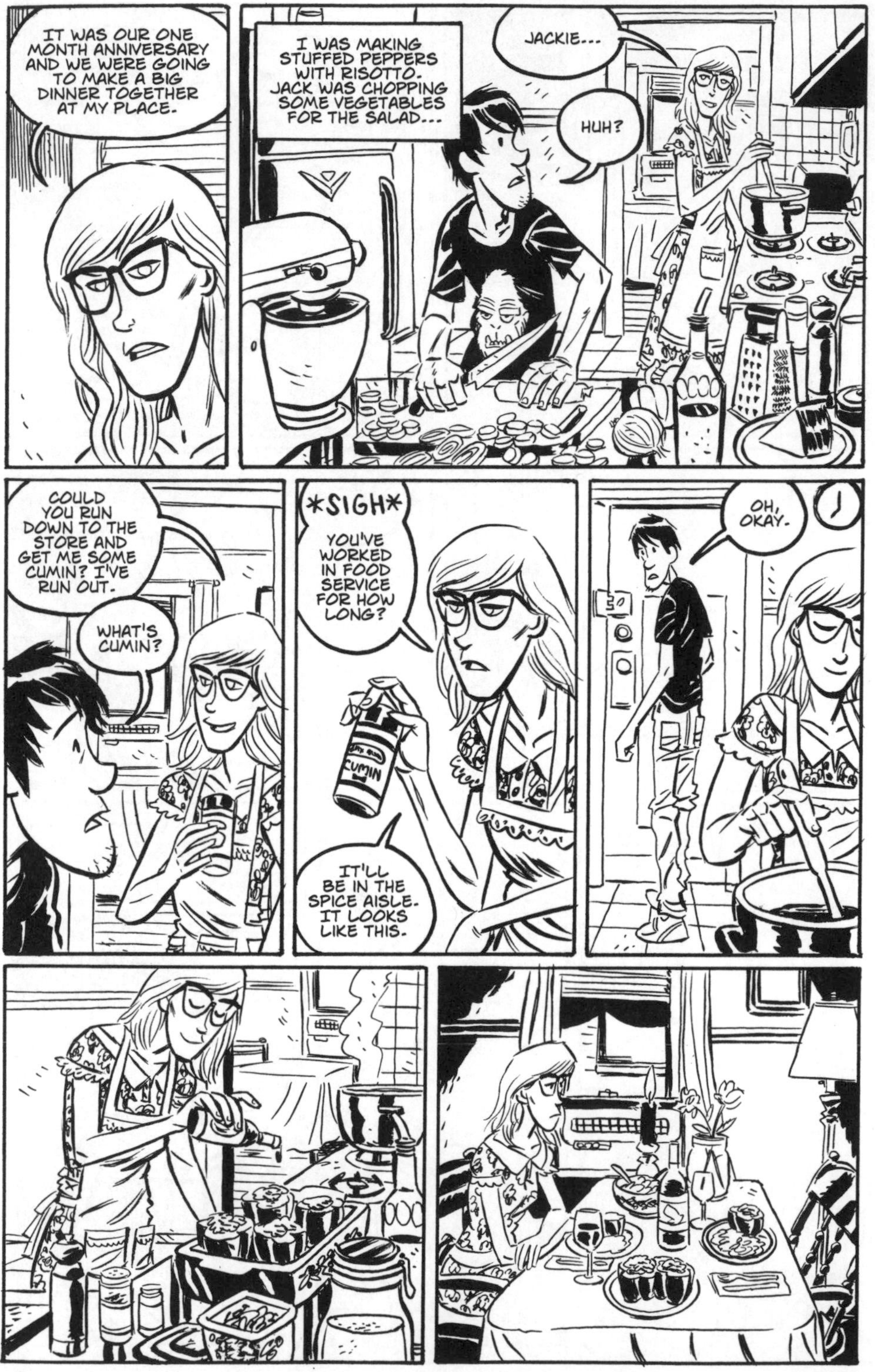
IT WAS OUR ONE MONTH ANNIVERSARY AND WE WERE GOING TO MAKE A BIG DINNER TOGETHER AT MY PLACE.
I WAS MAKING STUFFED PEPPERS WITH RISOTTO. JACK WAS CHOPPING SOME VEGETABLES FOR THE SALAD...
JACKIE...
HUH?
COULD YOU RUN DOWN TO THE STORE AND GET ME SOME CUMIN? I'VE RUN OUT.
WHAT'S CUMIN?
SIGH
YOU'VE WORKED IN FOOD SERVICE FOR HOW LONG?
CUMIN
IT'LL BE IN THE SPICE AISLE. IT LOOKS LIKE THIS.
OH, OKAY.

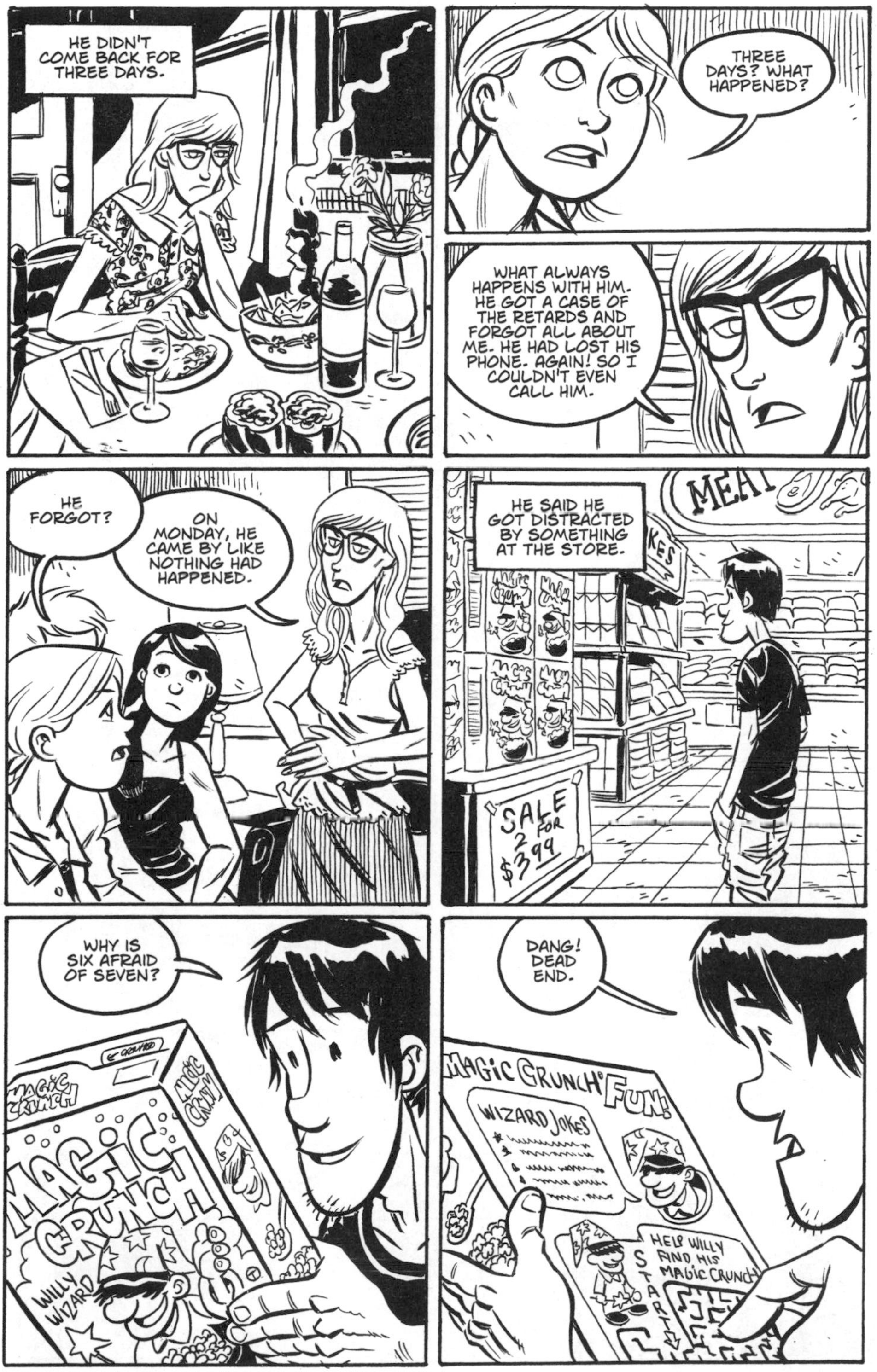

HE DIDN'T COME BACK FOR THREE DAYS.
THREE DAYS? WHAT HAPPENED?
WHAT ALWAYS HAPPENS WITH HIM. HE GOT A CASE OF THE RETARDS AND FORGOT ALL ABOUT ME. HE HAD LOST HIS PHONE. AGAIN! SO I COULDN'T EVEN CALL HIM.
HE FORGOT?
ON MONDAY, HE CAME BY LIKE NOTHING HAD HAPPENED.
HE SAID HE GOT DISTRACTED BY SOMETHING AT THE STORE.
MEAT
SALE 2 FOR $3.99
WHY IS SIX AFRAID OF SEVEN?
MAGIC CRUNCH
WILLY WIZARD
DANG! DEAD END.
MAGIC CRUNCH® FUN!
WIZARD JOKES
HELP WILLY FIND HIS MAGIC CRUNCH
START

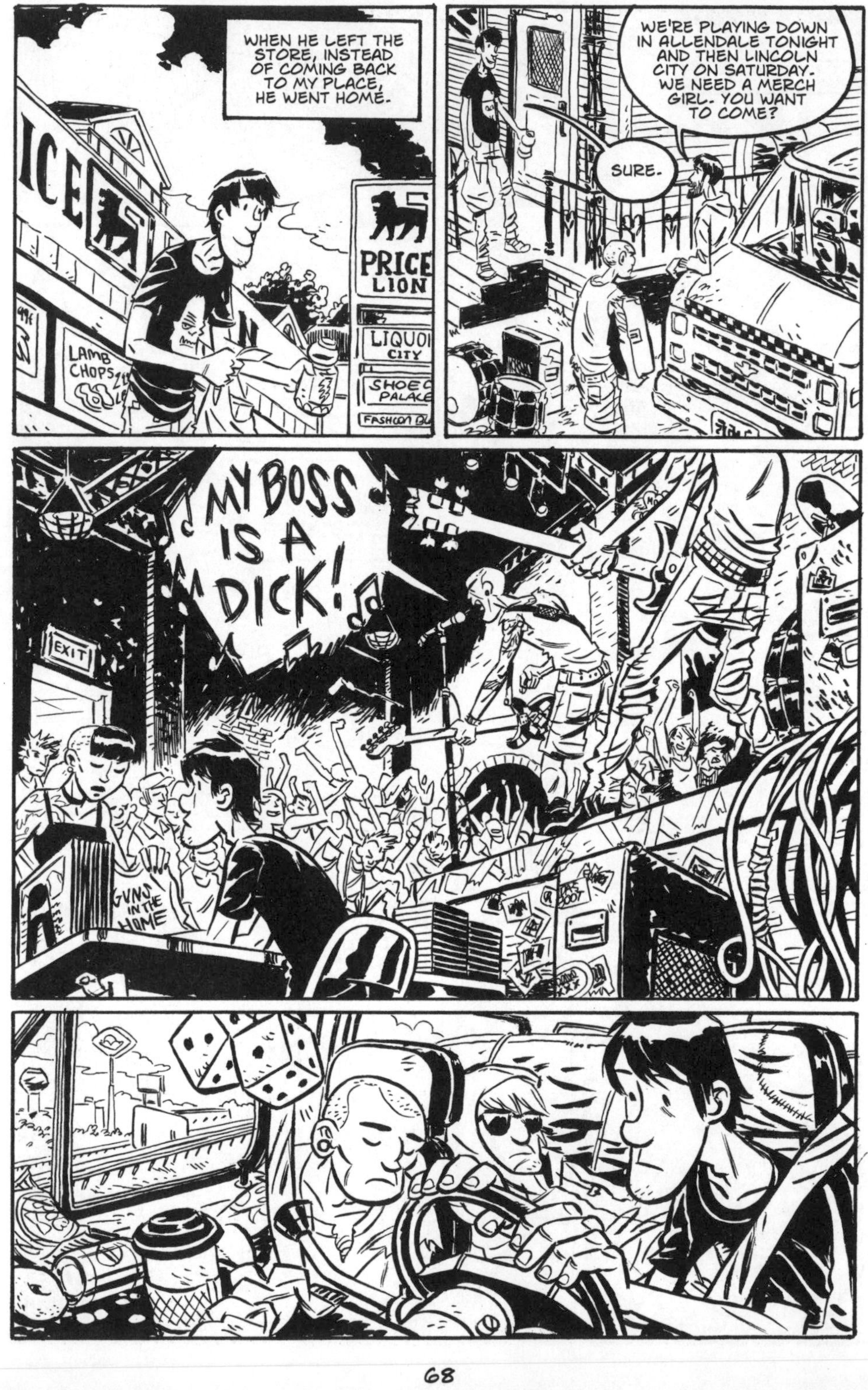
WHEN HE LEFT THE STORE, INSTEAD OF COMING BACK TO MY PLACE, HE WENT HOME.
PRICE LION
LAMB CHOPS
WE'RE PLAYING DOWN IN ALLENDALE TONIGHT AND THEN LINCOLN CITY ON SATURDAY. WE NEED A MERCH GIRL. YOU WANT TO COME?
SURE.
MY BOSS IS A DICK!
EXIT
GUNS IN THE HOME

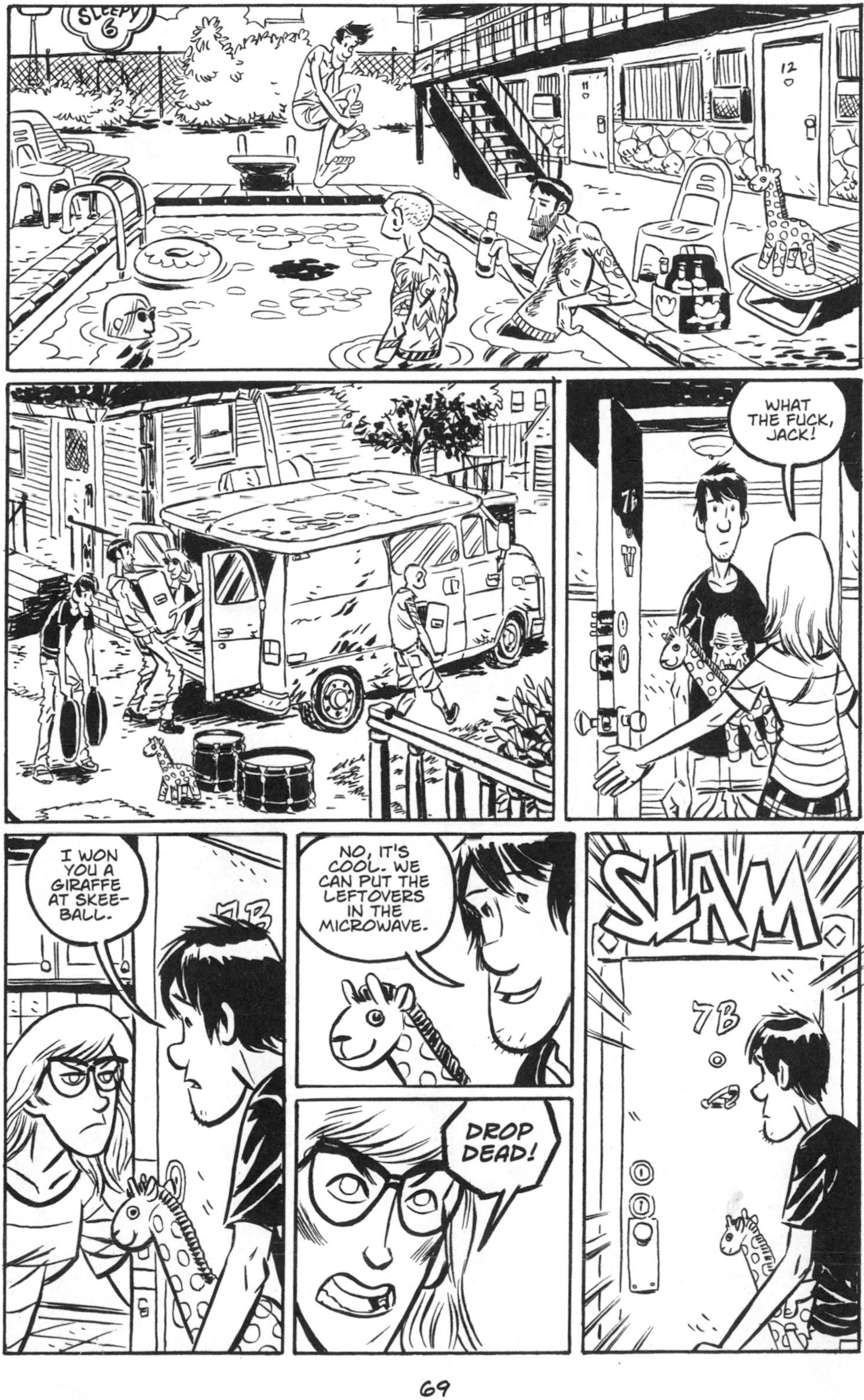
SLEEPY 6
11
12
WHAT THE FUCK, JACK!
I WON YOU A GIRAFFE AT SKEE-BALL.
NO, IT'S COOL. WE CAN PUT THE LEFTOVERS IN THE MICROWAVE.
DROP DEAD!
SLAM
7B

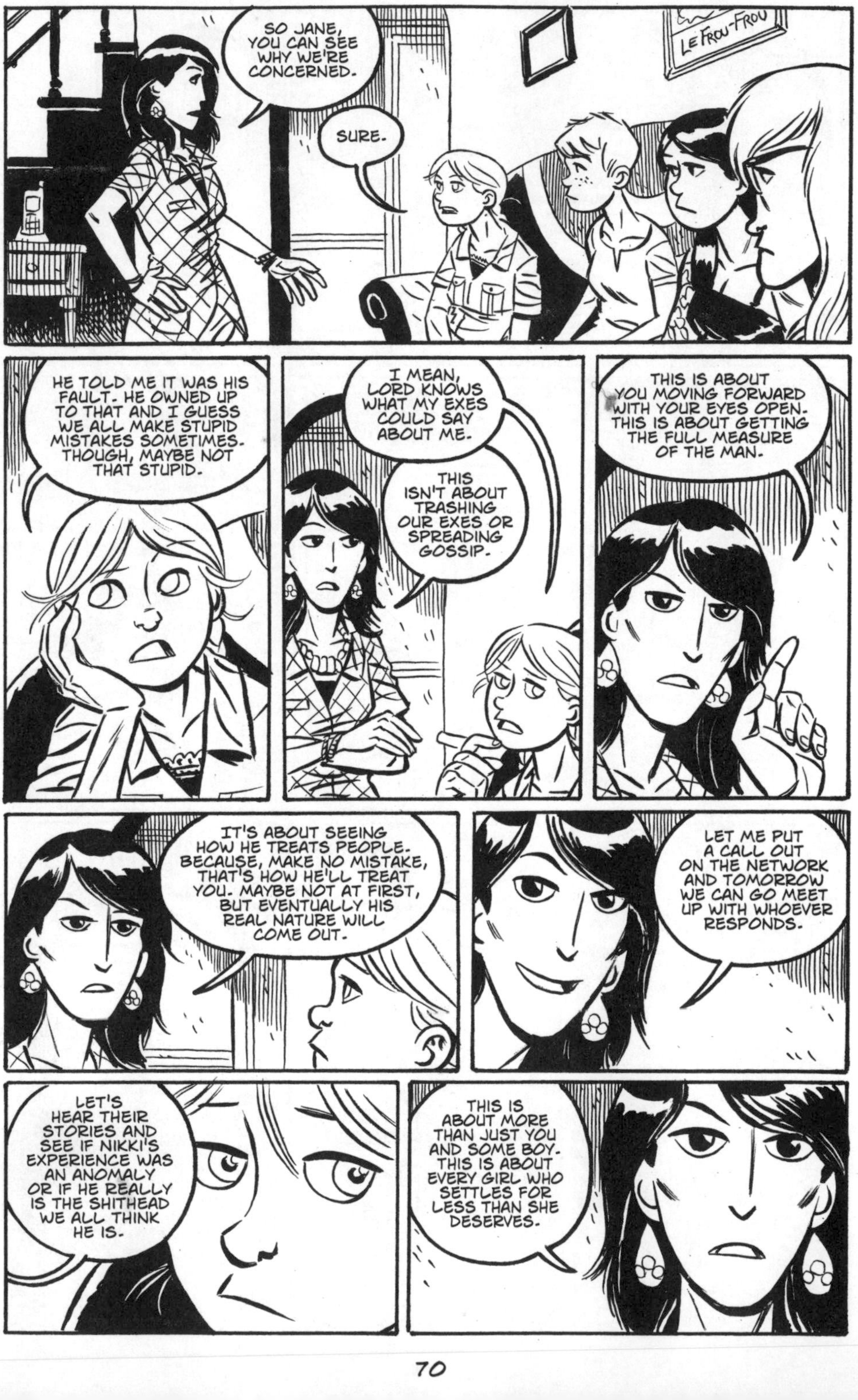
LE FROU-FROU
SO JANE, YOU CAN SEE WHY WE'RE CONCERNED.
SURE.
HE TOLD ME IT WAS HIS FAULT. HE OWNED UP TO THAT AND I GUESS WE ALL MAKE STUPID MISTAKES SOMETIMES. THOUGH, MAYBE NOT THAT STUPID.
I MEAN, LORD KNOWS WHAT MY EXES COULD SAY ABOUT ME.
THIS ISN'T ABOUT TRASHING OUR EXES OR SPREADING GOSSIP.
THIS IS ABOUT YOU MOVING FORWARD WITH YOUR EYES OPEN. THIS IS ABOUT GETTING THE FULL MEASURE OF THE MAN.
IT'S ABOUT SEEING HOW HE TREATS PEOPLE. BECAUSE, MAKE NO MISTAKE, THAT'S HOW HE'LL TREAT YOU. MAYBE NOT AT FIRST, BUT EVENTUALLY HIS REAL NATURE WILL COME OUT.
LET ME PUT A CALL OUT ON THE NETWORK AND TOMORROW WE CAN GO MEET UP WITH WHOEVER RESPONDS.
LET'S HEAR THEIR STORIES AND SEE IF NIKKI'S EXPERIENCE WAS AN ANOMALY OR IF HE REALLY IS THE SHITHEAD WE ALL THINK HE IS.
THIS IS ABOUT MORE THAN JUST YOU AND SOME BOY. THIS IS ABOUT EVERY GIRL WHO SETTLES FOR LESS THAN SHE DESERVES.

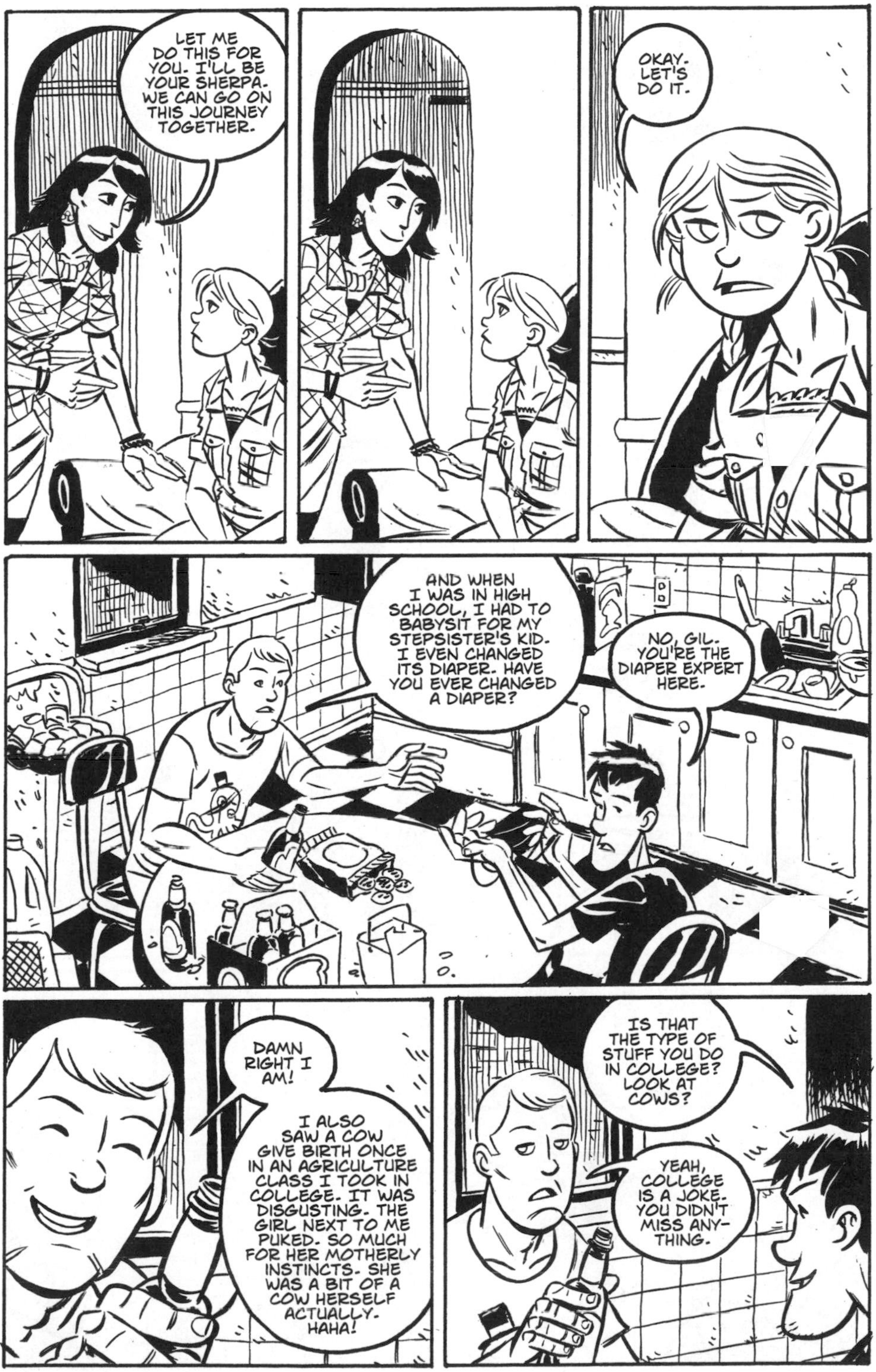
LET ME DO THIS FOR YOU. I'LL BE YOUR SHERPA. WE CAN GO ON THIS JOURNEY TOGETHER.
OKAY. LET'S DO IT.
AND WHEN I WAS IN HIGH SCHOOL, I HAD TO BABYSIT FOR MY STEPSISTER'S KID. I EVEN CHANGED ITS DIAPER. HAVE YOU EVER CHANGED A DIAPER?
NO, GIL. YOU'RE THE DIAPER EXPERT HERE.
DAMN RIGHT I AM!
I ALSO SAW A COW GIVE BIRTH ONCE IN AN AGRICULTURE CLASS I TOOK IN COLLEGE. IT WAS DISGUSTING. THE GIRL NEXT TO ME PUKED. SO MUCH FOR HER MOTHERLY INSTINCTS. SHE WAS A BIT OF A COW HERSELF ACTUALLY. HAHA!
IS THAT THE TYPE OF STUFF YOU DO IN COLLEGE? LOOK AT COWS?
YEAH, COLLEGE IS A JOKE. YOU DIDN'T MISS ANY-THING.

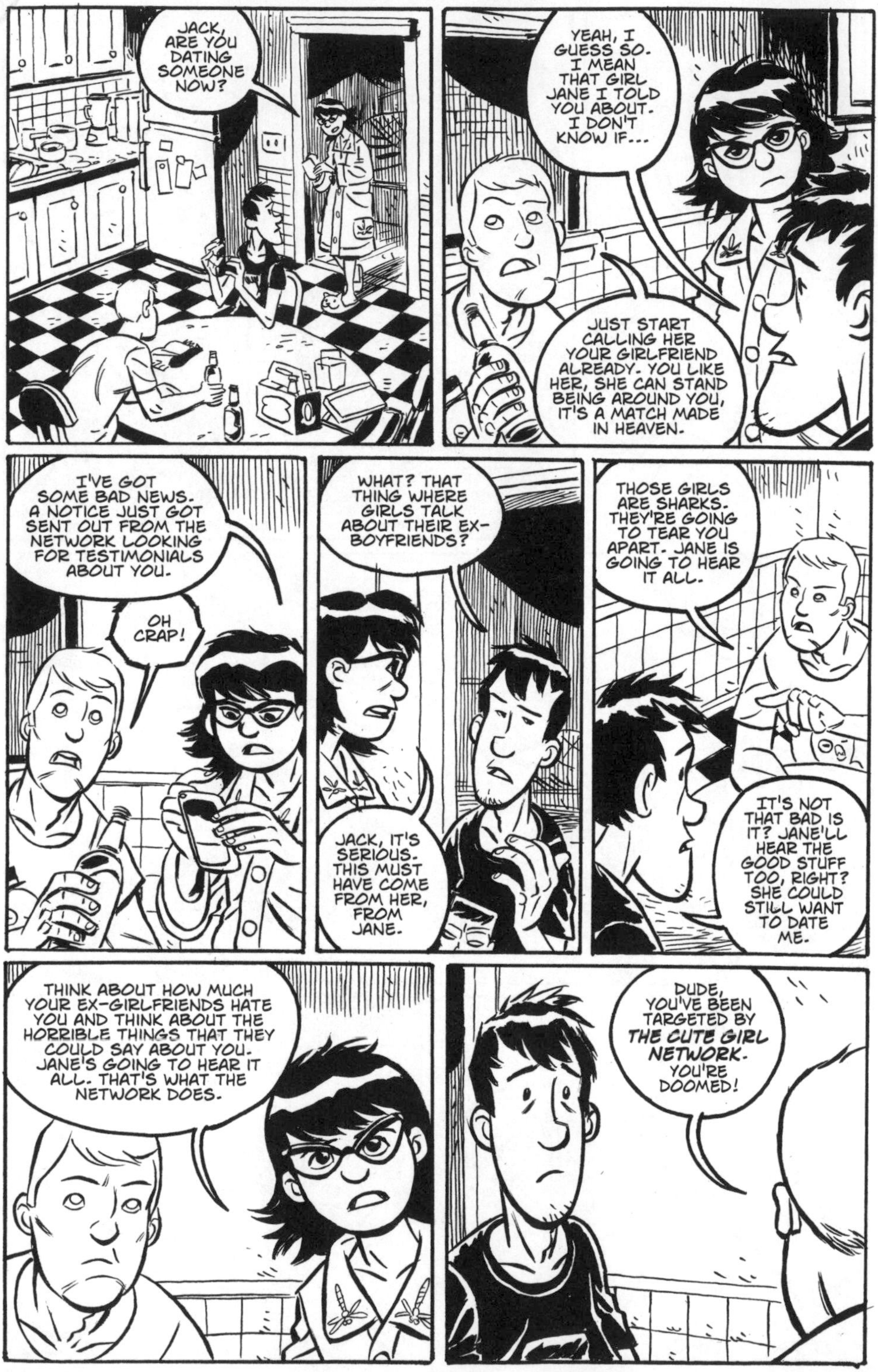

JACK, ARE YOU DATING SOMEONE NOW?
YEAH, I GUESS SO. I MEAN THAT GIRL JANE I TOLD YOU ABOUT. I DON'T KNOW IF...
JUST START CALLING HER YOUR GIRLFRIEND ALREADY. YOU LIKE HER, SHE CAN STAND BEING AROUND YOU, IT'S A MATCH MADE IN HEAVEN.
I'VE GOT SOME BAD NEWS. A NOTICE JUST GOT SENT OUT FROM THE NETWORK LOOKING FOR TESTIMONIALS ABOUT YOU.
OH CRAP!
WHAT? THAT THING WHERE GIRLS TALK ABOUT THEIR EX-BOYFRIENDS?
JACK, IT'S SERIOUS. THIS MUST HAVE COME FROM HER, FROM JANE.
THOSE GIRLS ARE SHARKS. THEY'RE GOING TO TEAR YOU APART. JANE IS GOING TO HEAR IT ALL.
IT'S NOT THAT BAD IS IT? JANE'LL HEAR THE GOOD STUFF TOO, RIGHT? SHE COULD STILL WANT TO DATE ME.
THINK ABOUT HOW MUCH YOUR EX-GIRLFRIENDS HATE YOU AND THINK ABOUT THE HORRIBLE THINGS THAT THEY COULD SAY ABOUT YOU. JANE'S GOING TO HEAR IT ALL. THAT'S WHAT THE NETWORK DOES.
DUDE, YOU'VE BEEN TARGETED BY **THE CUTE GIRL NETWORK**. YOU'RE DOOMED!

CHAPTER FOUR

"Whither the Mathlete"

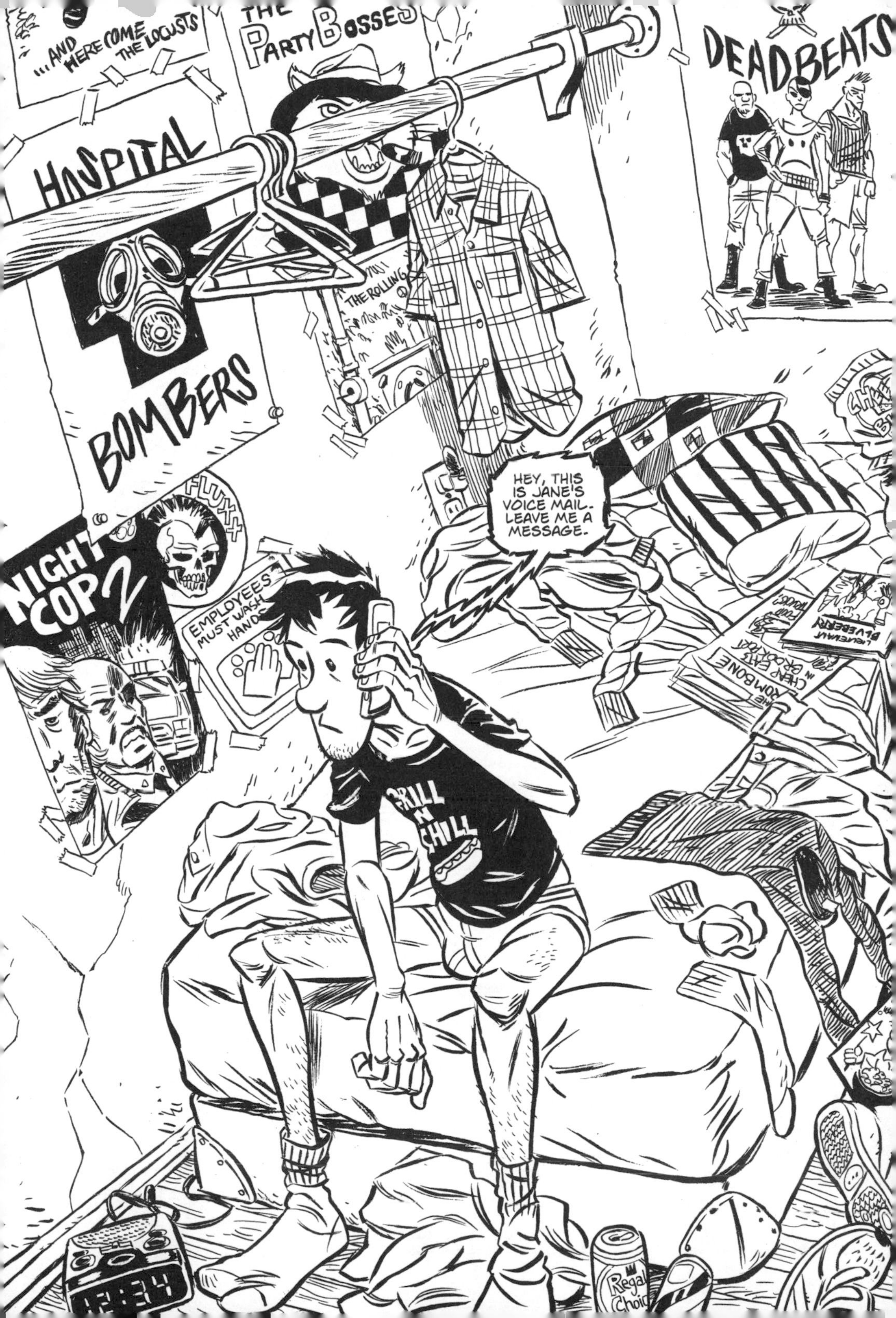
...AND HERE COME THE LOCUSTS
THE PARTY BOSSES
DEADBEATS
HOSPITAL BOMBERS
THE ROLLING
NIGHT COP 2
FLUXX
EMPLOYEES MUST WASH HANDS
HEY, THIS IS JANE'S VOICE MAIL. LEAVE ME A MESSAGE.
GRILL N CHILL
THE TROMBONE CHEF EATS IN BROOKLYN
LIEUTENANT BLUEBERRY
Regal Choice

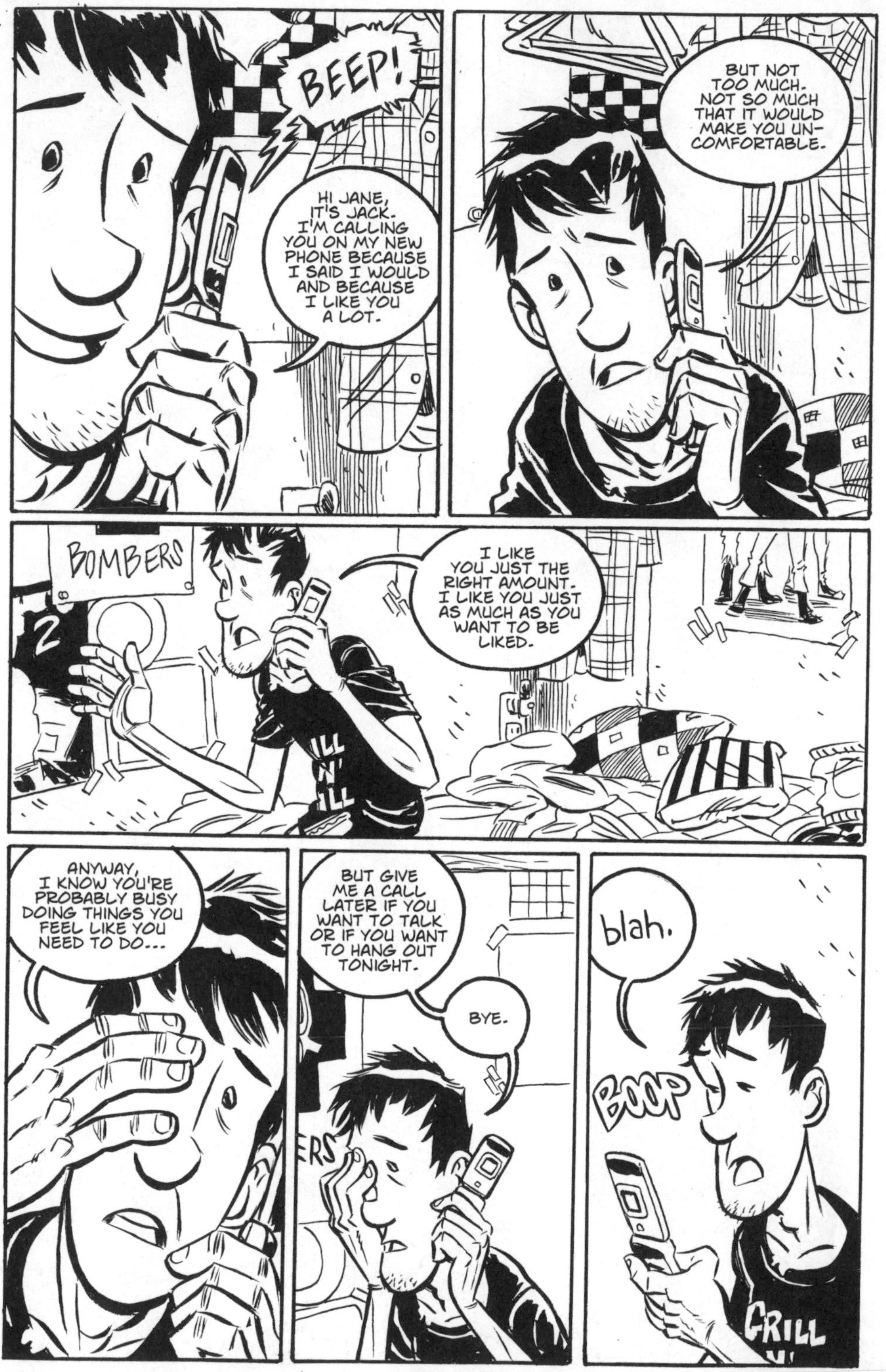

BEEP!
HI JANE, IT'S JACK. I'M CALLING YOU ON MY NEW PHONE BECAUSE I SAID I WOULD AND BECAUSE I LIKE YOU A LOT.
BUT NOT TOO MUCH. NOT SO MUCH THAT IT WOULD MAKE YOU UN-COMFORTABLE.
BOMBERS
I LIKE YOU JUST THE RIGHT AMOUNT. I LIKE YOU JUST AS MUCH AS YOU WANT TO BE LIKED.
ANYWAY, I KNOW YOU'RE PROBABLY BUSY DOING THINGS YOU FEEL LIKE YOU NEED TO DO...
BUT GIVE ME A CALL LATER IF YOU WANT TO TALK OR IF YOU WANT TO HANG OUT TONIGHT.
BYE.
blah.
BOOP
GRILL

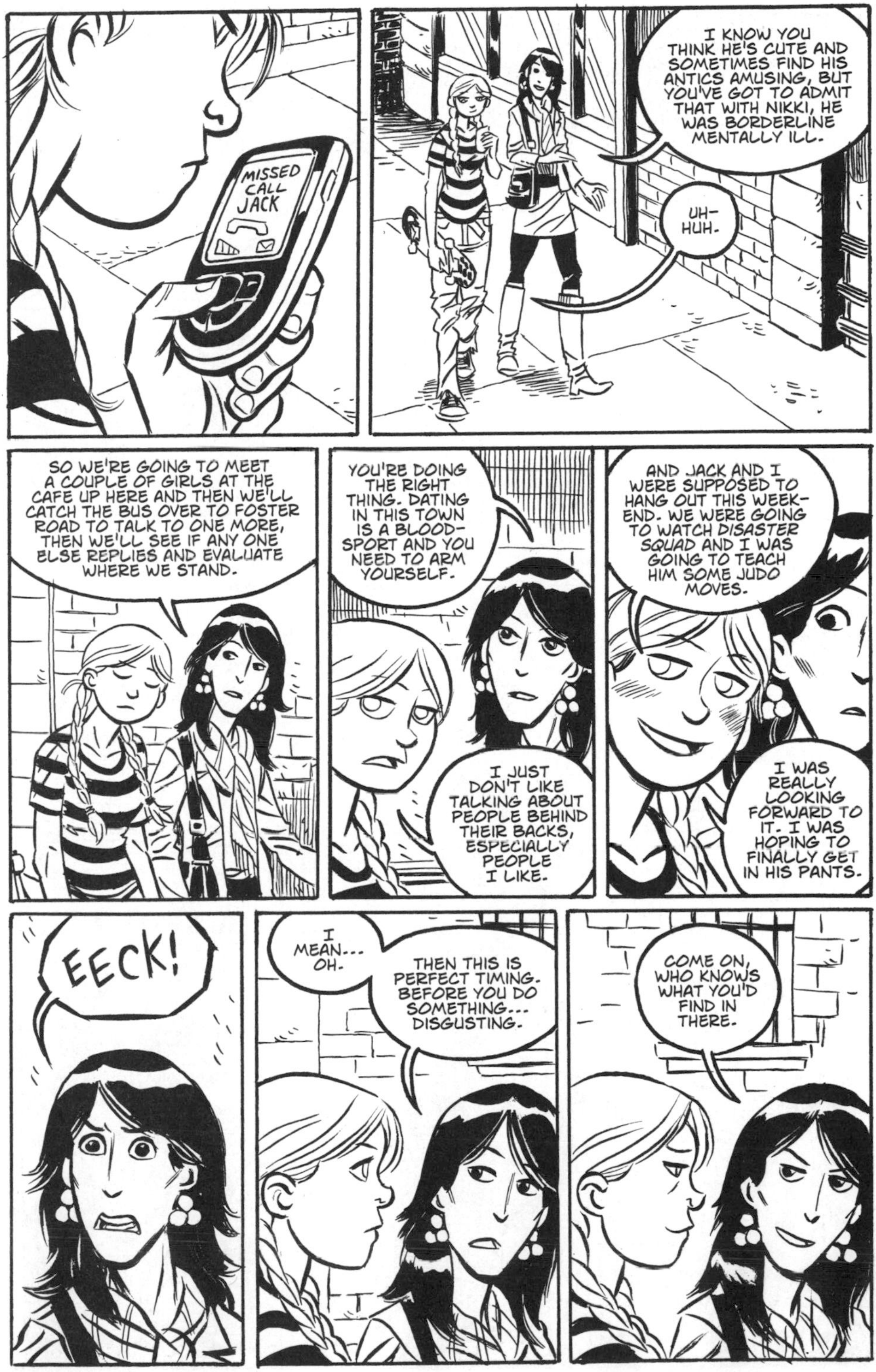
MISSED CALL JACK
I KNOW YOU THINK HE'S CUTE AND SOMETIMES FIND HIS ANTICS AMUSING, BUT YOU'VE GOT TO ADMIT THAT WITH NIKKI, HE WAS BORDERLINE MENTALLY ILL.
UH-HUH.
SO WE'RE GOING TO MEET A COUPLE OF GIRLS AT THE CAFE UP HERE AND THEN WE'LL CATCH THE BUS OVER TO FOSTER ROAD TO TALK TO ONE MORE, THEN WE'LL SEE IF ANY ONE ELSE REPLIES AND EVALUATE WHERE WE STAND.
YOU'RE DOING THE RIGHT THING. DATING IN THIS TOWN IS A BLOOD-SPORT AND YOU NEED TO ARM YOURSELF.
I JUST DON'T LIKE TALKING ABOUT PEOPLE BEHIND THEIR BACKS, ESPECIALLY PEOPLE I LIKE.
AND JACK AND I WERE SUPPOSED TO HANG OUT THIS WEEK-END. WE WERE GOING TO WATCH DISASTER SQUAD AND I WAS GOING TO TEACH HIM SOME JUDO MOVES.
I WAS REALLY LOOKING FORWARD TO IT. I WAS HOPING TO FINALLY GET IN HIS PANTS.
EECK!
I MEAN... OH.
THEN THIS IS PERFECT TIMING. BEFORE YOU DO SOMETHING... DISGUSTING.
COME ON, WHO KNOWS WHAT YOU'D FIND IN THERE.

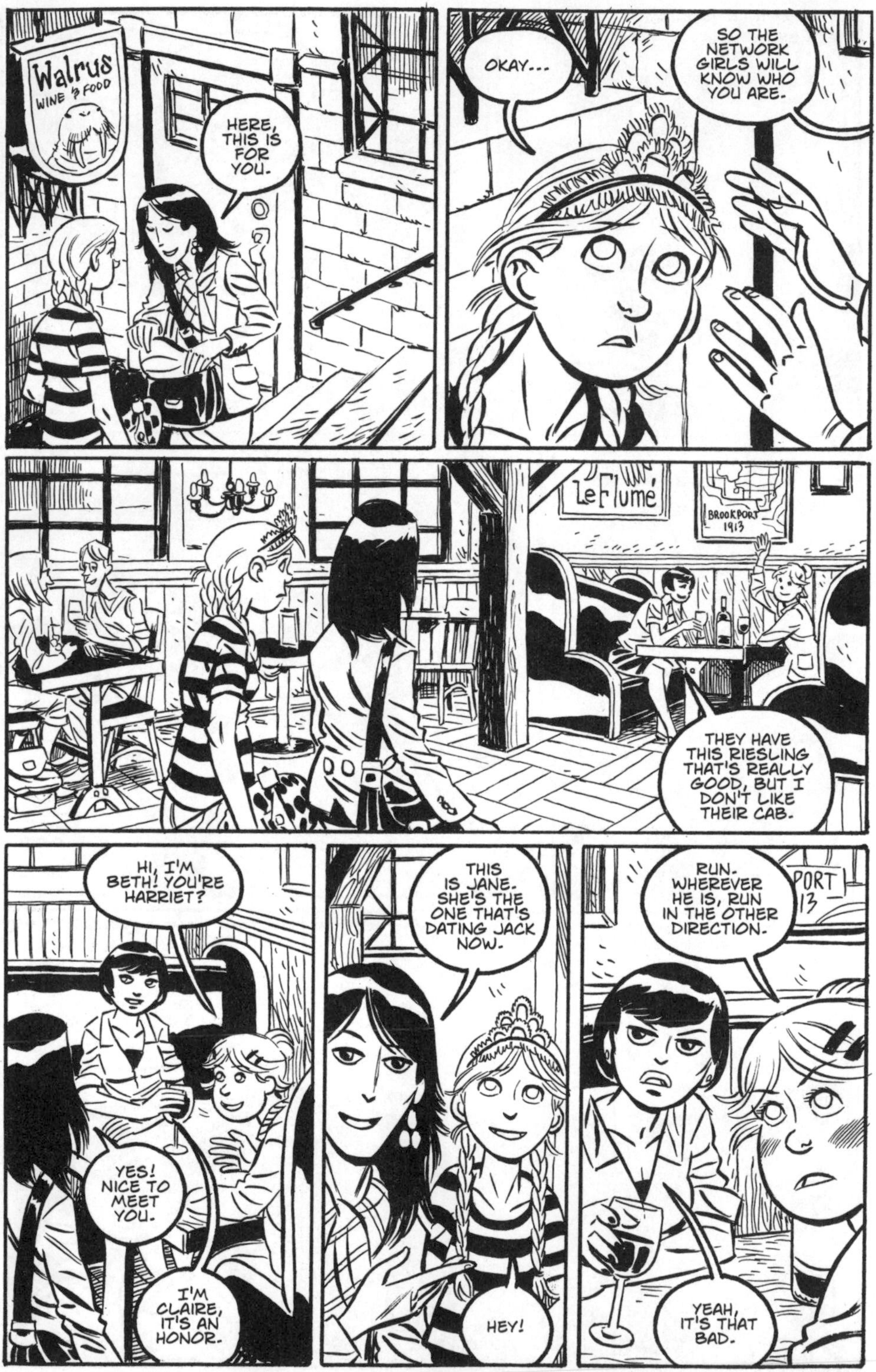
Walrus
WINE & FOOD
HERE, THIS IS FOR YOU.
OKAY...
SO THE NETWORK GIRLS WILL KNOW WHO YOU ARE.
Le Flumé
BROOKPORT 1913
THEY HAVE THIS RIESLING THAT'S REALLY GOOD, BUT I DON'T LIKE THEIR CAB.
HI, I'M BETH! YOU'RE HARRIET?
YES! NICE TO MEET YOU.
I'M CLAIRE, IT'S AN HONOR.
THIS IS JANE. SHE'S THE ONE THAT'S DATING JACK NOW.
HEY!
RUN. WHEREVER HE IS, RUN IN THE OTHER DIRECTION.
PORT 13
YEAH, IT'S THAT BAD.

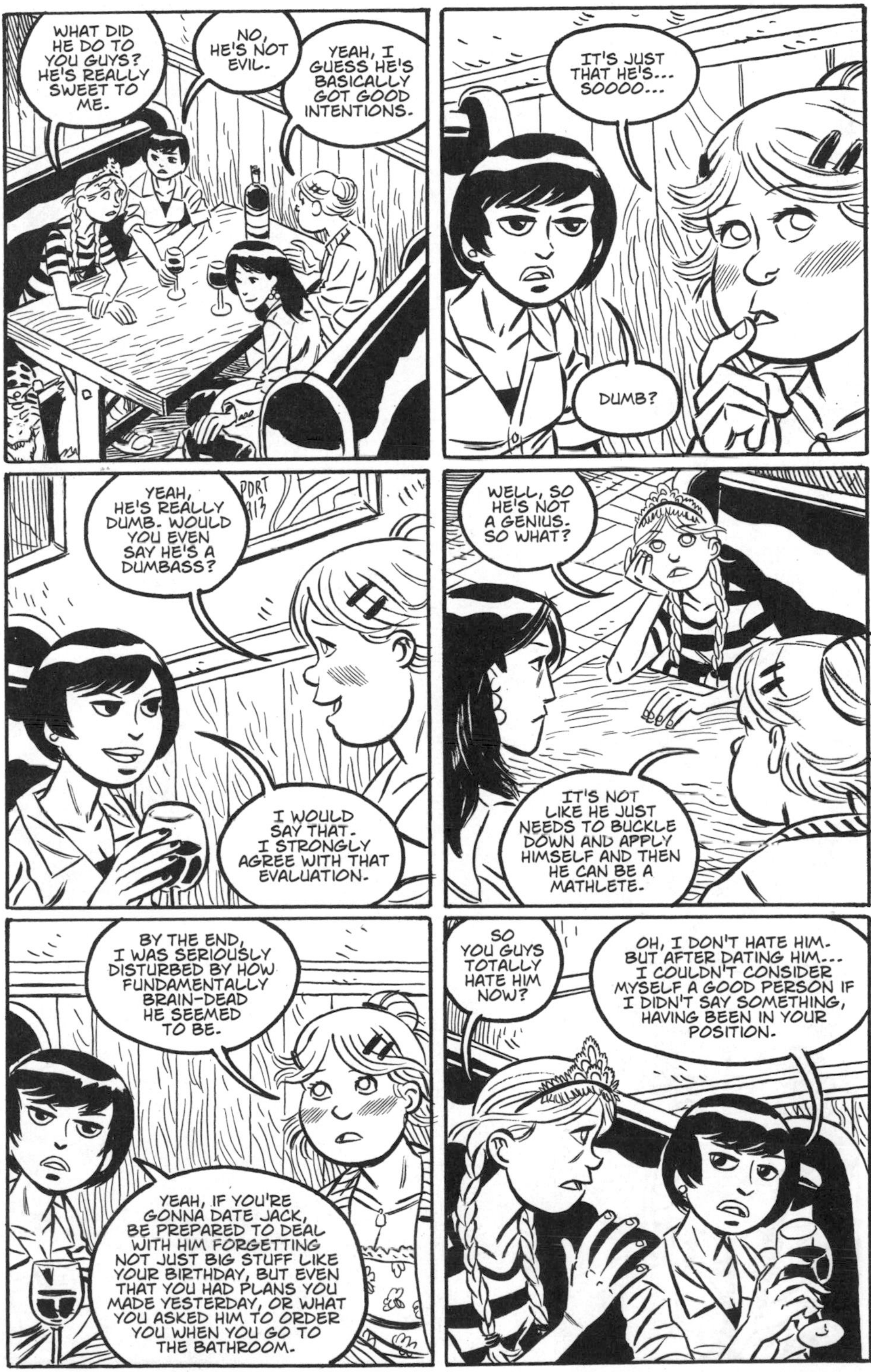
WHAT DID HE DO TO YOU GUYS? HE'S REALLY SWEET TO ME.
NO, HE'S NOT EVIL.
YEAH, I GUESS HE'S BASICALLY GOT GOOD INTENTIONS.
IT'S JUST THAT HE'S... SOOOO...
DUMB?
YEAH, HE'S REALLY DUMB. WOULD YOU EVEN SAY HE'S A DUMBASS?
I WOULD SAY THAT. I STRONGLY AGREE WITH THAT EVALUATION.
WELL, SO HE'S NOT A GENIUS. SO WHAT?
IT'S NOT LIKE HE JUST NEEDS TO BUCKLE DOWN AND APPLY HIMSELF AND THEN HE CAN BE A MATHLETE.
BY THE END, I WAS SERIOUSLY DISTURBED BY HOW FUNDAMENTALLY BRAIN-DEAD HE SEEMED TO BE.
YEAH, IF YOU'RE GONNA DATE JACK, BE PREPARED TO DEAL WITH HIM FORGETTING NOT JUST BIG STUFF LIKE YOUR BIRTHDAY, BUT EVEN THAT YOU HAD PLANS YOU MADE YESTERDAY, OR WHAT YOU ASKED HIM TO ORDER YOU WHEN YOU GO TO THE BATHROOM.
SO YOU GUYS TOTALLY HATE HIM NOW?
OH, I DON'T HATE HIM. BUT AFTER DATING HIM... I COULDN'T CONSIDER MYSELF A GOOD PERSON IF I DIDN'T SAY SOMETHING, HAVING BEEN IN YOUR POSITION.

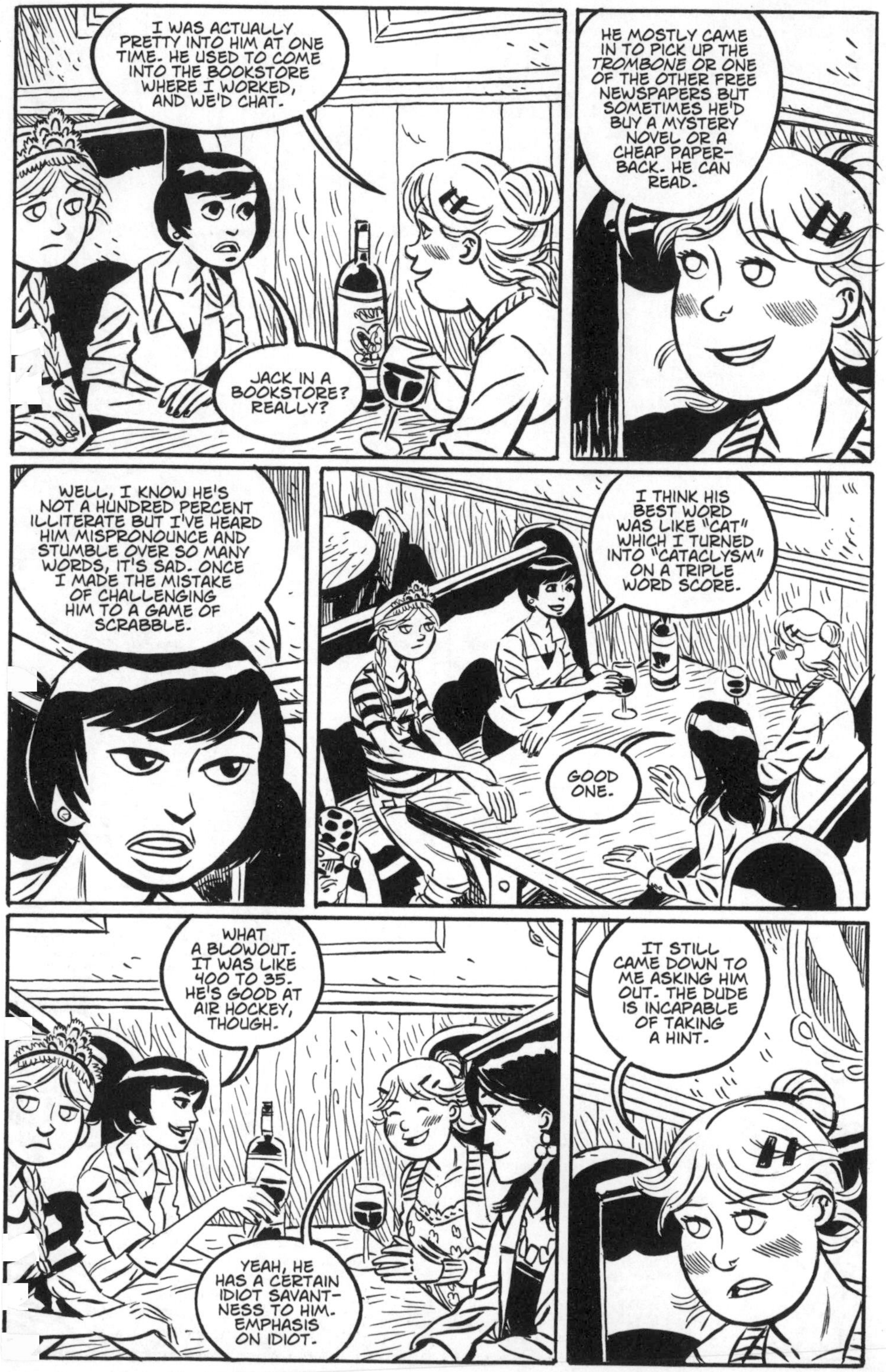
I WAS ACTUALLY PRETTY INTO HIM AT ONE TIME. HE USED TO COME INTO THE BOOKSTORE WHERE I WORKED, AND WE'D CHAT.
JACK IN A BOOKSTORE? REALLY?
HE MOSTLY CAME IN TO PICK UP THE *TROMBONE* OR ONE OF THE OTHER FREE NEWSPAPERS BUT SOMETIMES HE'D BUY A MYSTERY NOVEL OR A CHEAP PAPER-BACK. HE CAN READ.
WELL, I KNOW HE'S NOT A HUNDRED PERCENT ILLITERATE BUT I'VE HEARD HIM MISPRONOUNCE AND STUMBLE OVER SO MANY WORDS, IT'S SAD. ONCE I MADE THE MISTAKE OF CHALLENGING HIM TO A GAME OF SCRABBLE.
I THINK HIS BEST WORD WAS LIKE "CAT" WHICH I TURNED INTO "CATACLYSM" ON A TRIPLE WORD SCORE.
GOOD ONE.
WHAT A BLOWOUT. IT WAS LIKE 400 TO 35. HE'S GOOD AT AIR HOCKEY, THOUGH.
YEAH, HE HAS A CERTAIN IDIOT SAVANT-NESS TO HIM. EMPHASIS ON IDIOT.
IT STILL CAME DOWN TO ME ASKING HIM OUT. THE DUDE IS INCAPABLE OF TAKING A HINT.

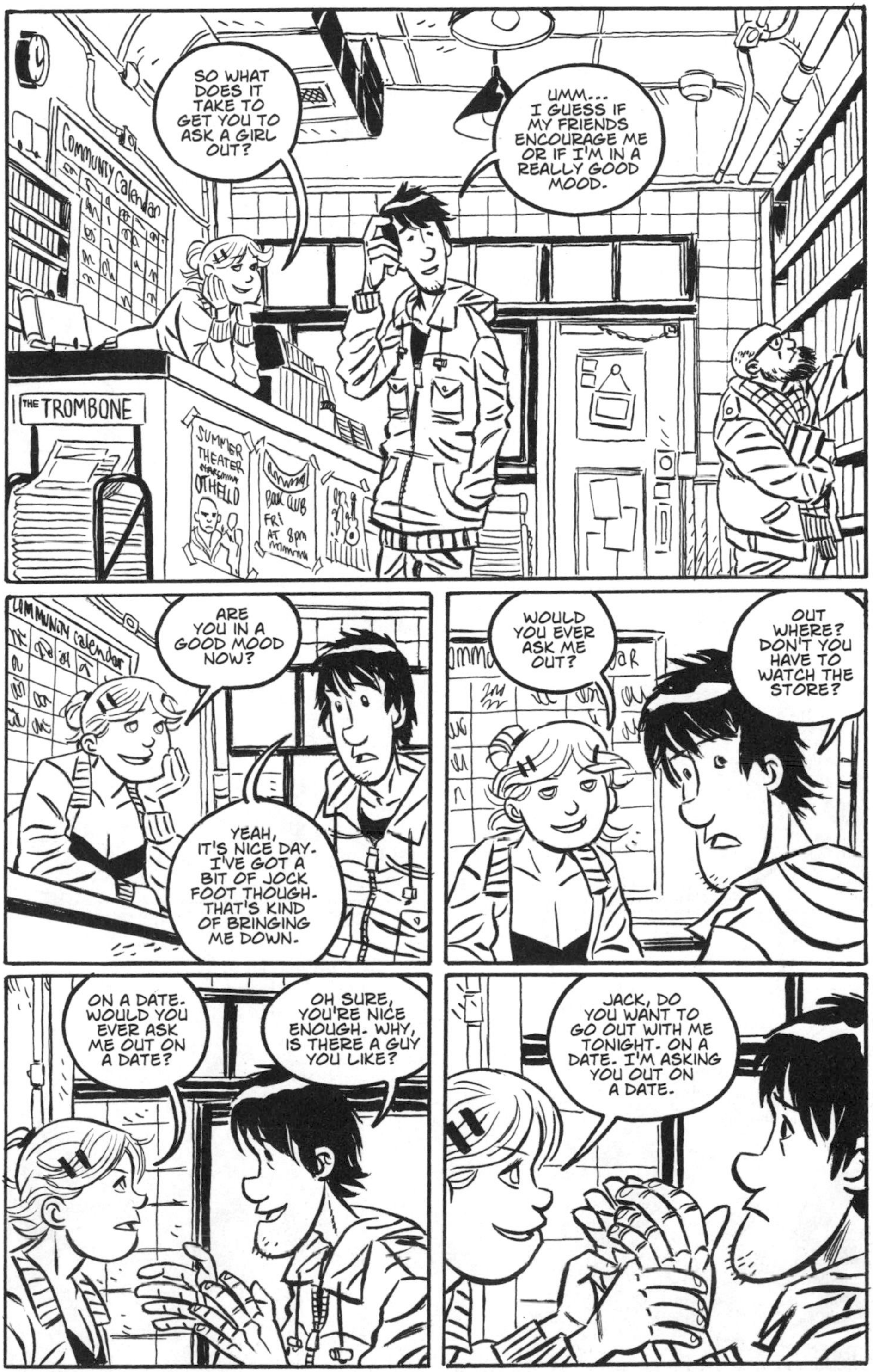
COMMUNITY CALENDAR
THE TROMBONE
SUMMER THEATER OTHELLO
BOOK CLUB FRI AT 8PM
SO WHAT DOES IT TAKE TO GET YOU TO ASK A GIRL OUT?
UMM... I GUESS IF MY FRIENDS ENCOURAGE ME OR IF I'M IN A REALLY GOOD MOOD.
ARE YOU IN A GOOD MOOD NOW?
YEAH, IT'S NICE DAY. I'VE GOT A BIT OF JOCK FOOT THOUGH. THAT'S KIND OF BRINGING ME DOWN.
WOULD YOU EVER ASK ME OUT?
OUT WHERE? DON'T YOU HAVE TO WATCH THE STORE?
ON A DATE. WOULD YOU EVER ASK ME OUT ON A DATE?
OH SURE, YOU'RE NICE ENOUGH. WHY, IS THERE A GUY YOU LIKE?
JACK, DO YOU WANT TO GO OUT WITH ME TONIGHT. ON A DATE. I'M ASKING YOU OUT ON A DATE.

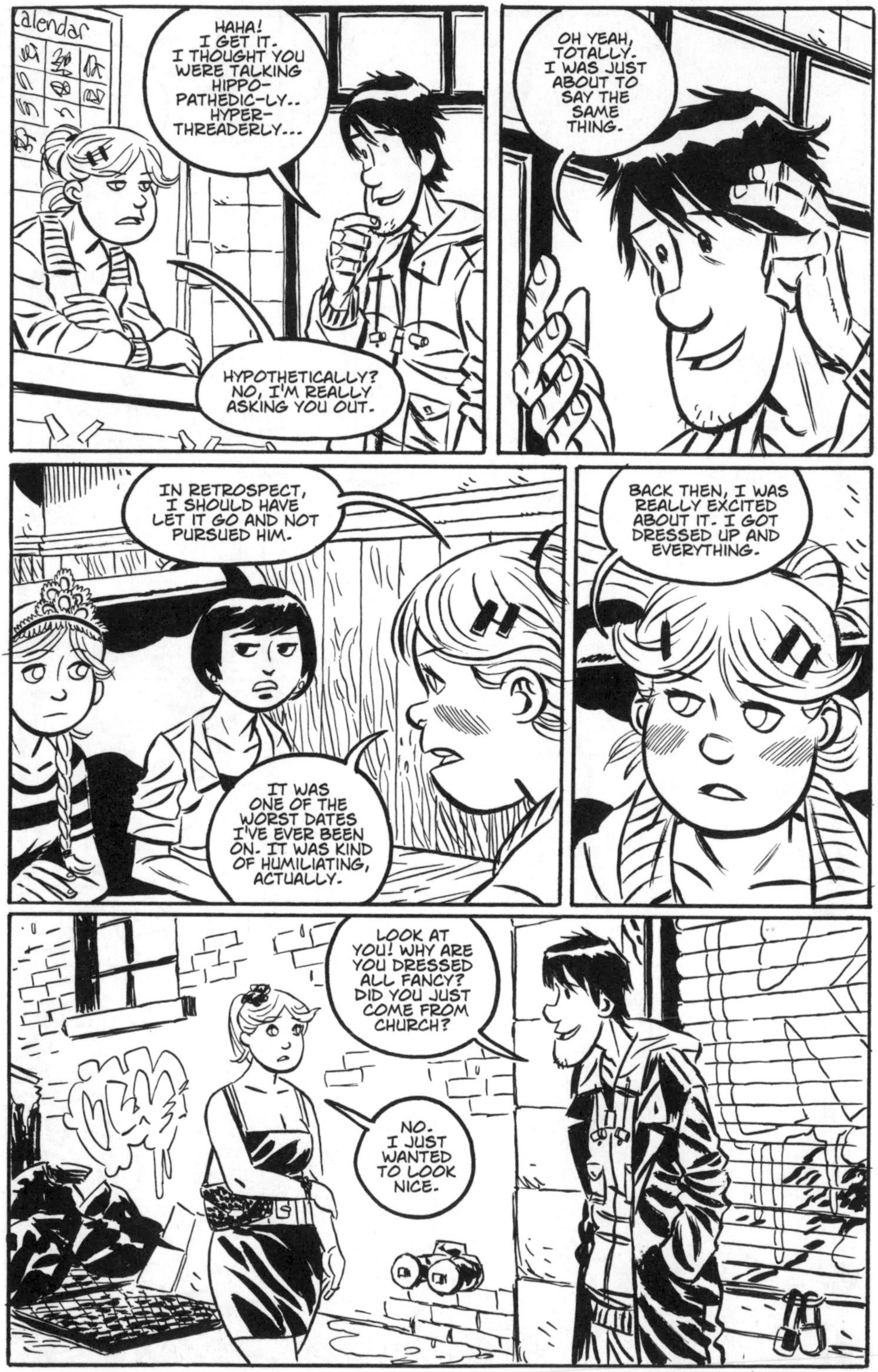
Calendar
HAHA! I GET IT. I THOUGHT YOU WERE TALKING HIPPO-PATHEDIC-LY.. HYPER-THREADERLY...
HYPOTHETICALLY? NO, I'M REALLY ASKING YOU OUT.
OH YEAH, TOTALLY. I WAS JUST ABOUT TO SAY THE SAME THING.
IN RETROSPECT, I SHOULD HAVE LET IT GO AND NOT PURSUED HIM.
IT WAS ONE OF THE WORST DATES I'VE EVER BEEN ON. IT WAS KIND OF HUMILIATING, ACTUALLY.
BACK THEN, I WAS REALLY EXCITED ABOUT IT. I GOT DRESSED UP AND EVERYTHING.
LOOK AT YOU! WHY ARE YOU DRESSED ALL FANCY? DID YOU JUST COME FROM CHURCH?
NO. I JUST WANTED TO LOOK NICE.

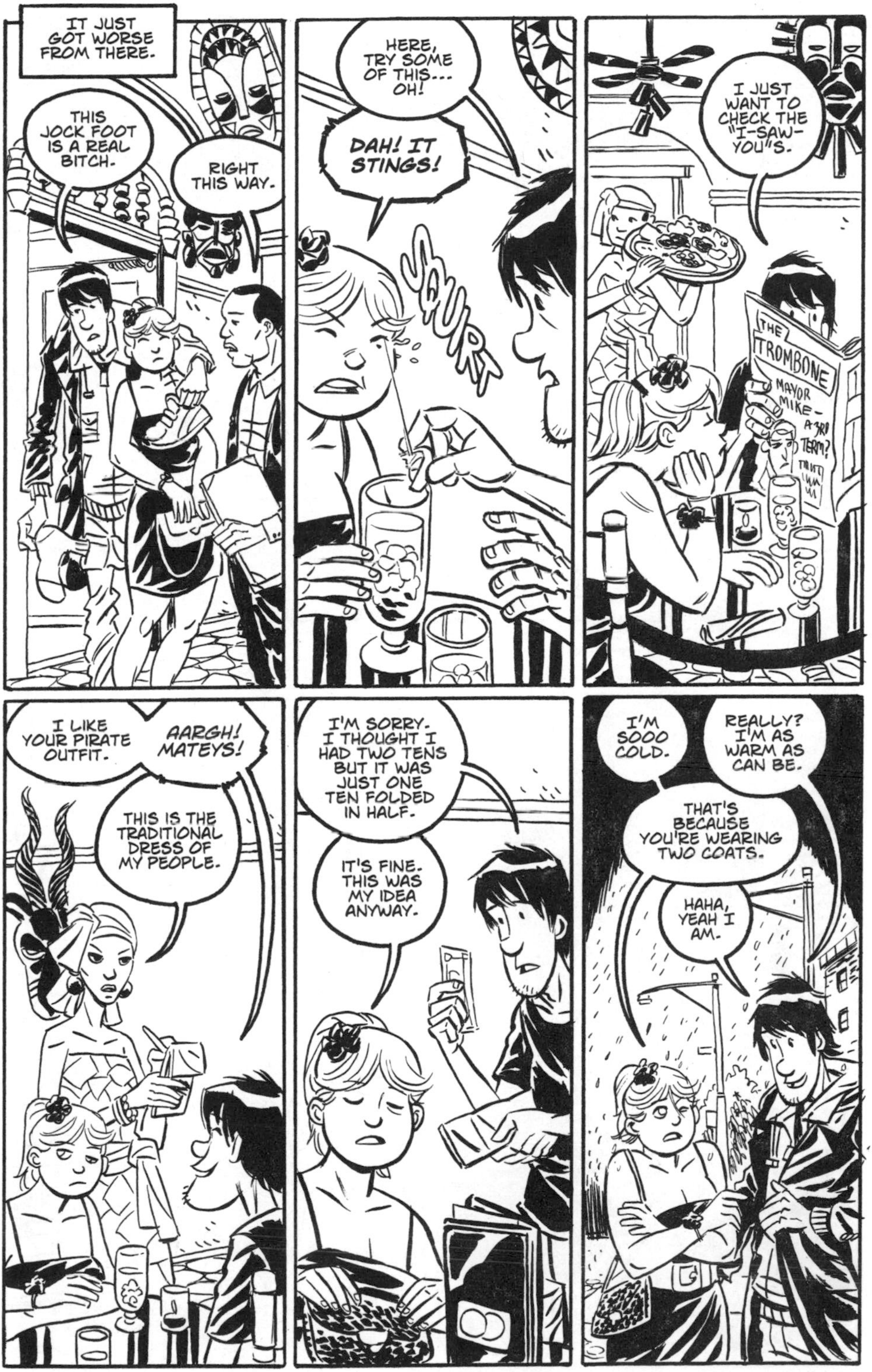

IT JUST GOT WORSE FROM THERE.
THIS JOCK FOOT IS A REAL BITCH.
RIGHT THIS WAY.
HERE, TRY SOME OF THIS... OH!
DAH! IT STINGS!
SQUIRT
I JUST WANT TO CHECK THE "I-SAW-YOU"S.
THE TROMBONE
MAYOR MIKE-
TERM?
I LIKE YOUR PIRATE OUTFIT.
AARGH! MATEYS!
THIS IS THE TRADITIONAL DRESS OF MY PEOPLE.
I'M SORRY. I THOUGHT I HAD TWO TENS BUT IT WAS JUST ONE TEN FOLDED IN HALF.
IT'S FINE. THIS WAS MY IDEA ANYWAY.
I'M SOOO COLD.
REALLY? I'M AS WARM AS CAN BE.
THAT'S BECAUSE YOU'RE WEARING TWO COATS.
HAHA, YEAH I AM.

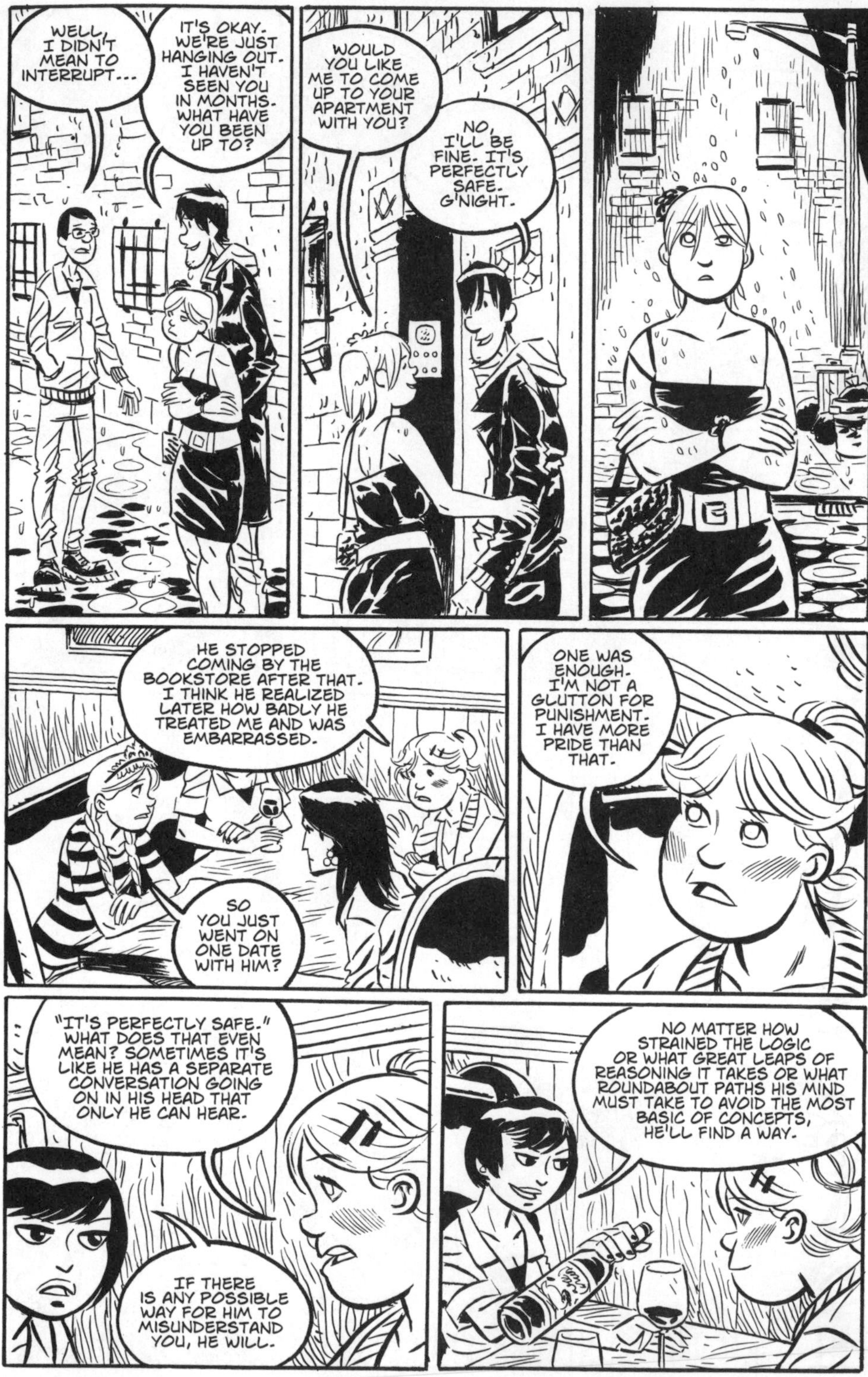
WELL, I DIDN'T MEAN TO INTERRUPT...
IT'S OKAY. WE'RE JUST HANGING OUT. I HAVEN'T SEEN YOU IN MONTHS. WHAT HAVE YOU BEEN UP TO?
WOULD YOU LIKE ME TO COME UP TO YOUR APARTMENT WITH YOU?
NO, I'LL BE FINE. IT'S PERFECTLY SAFE. G'NIGHT.
HE STOPPED COMING BY THE BOOKSTORE AFTER THAT. I THINK HE REALIZED LATER HOW BADLY HE TREATED ME AND WAS EMBARRASSED.
SO YOU JUST WENT ON ONE DATE WITH HIM?
ONE WAS ENOUGH. I'M NOT A GLUTTON FOR PUNISHMENT. I HAVE MORE PRIDE THAN THAT.
"IT'S PERFECTLY SAFE." WHAT DOES THAT EVEN MEAN? SOMETIMES IT'S LIKE HE HAS A SEPARATE CONVERSATION GOING ON IN HIS HEAD THAT ONLY HE CAN HEAR.
IF THERE IS ANY POSSIBLE WAY FOR HIM TO MISUNDERSTAND YOU, HE WILL.
NO MATTER HOW STRAINED THE LOGIC OR WHAT GREAT LEAPS OF REASONING IT TAKES OR WHAT ROUNDABOUT PATHS HIS MIND MUST TAKE TO AVOID THE MOST BASIC OF CONCEPTS, HE'LL FIND A WAY.

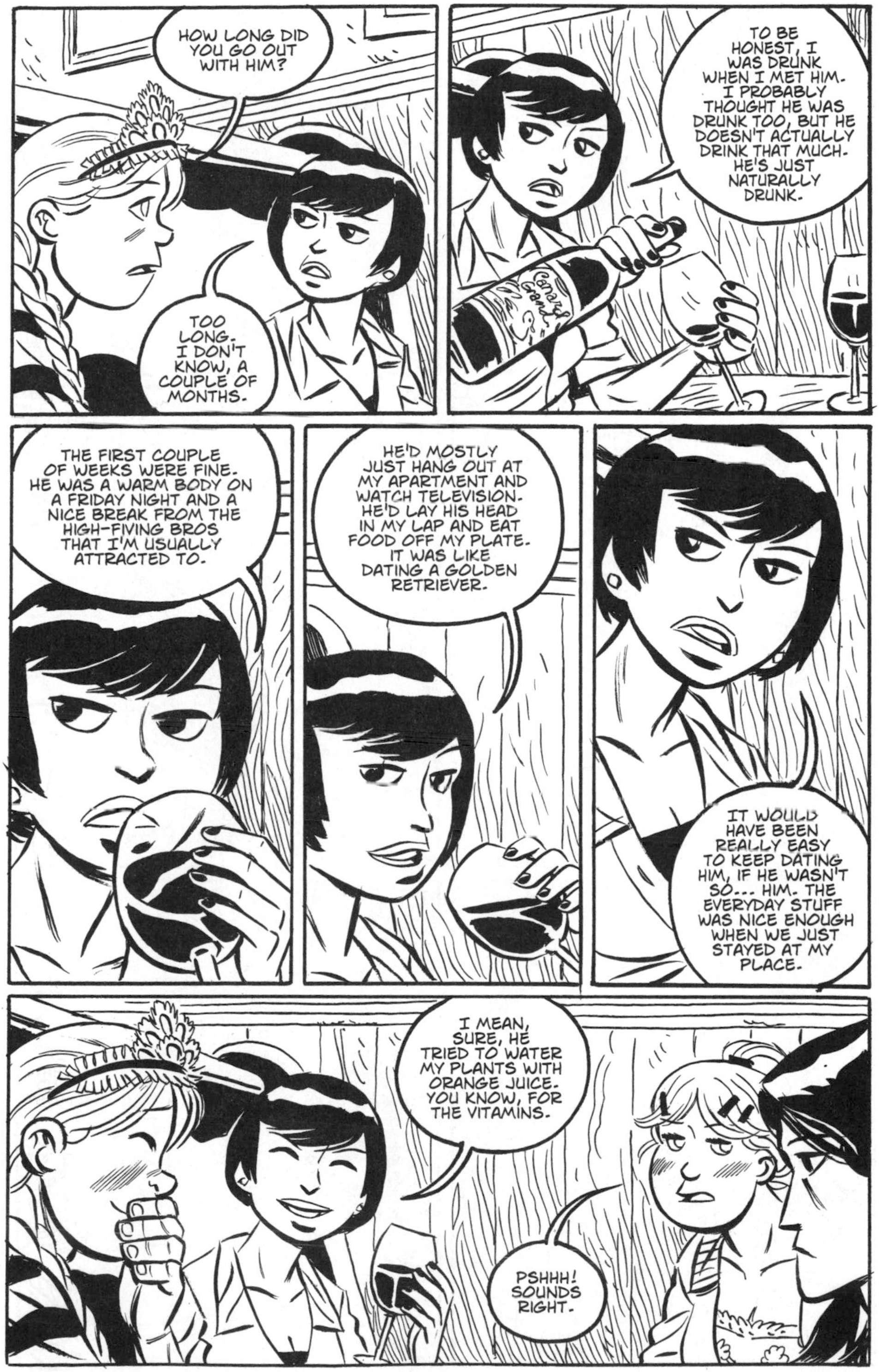
HOW LONG DID YOU GO OUT WITH HIM?
TOO LONG. I DON'T KNOW, A COUPLE OF MONTHS.
TO BE HONEST, I WAS DRUNK WHEN I MET HIM. I PROBABLY THOUGHT HE WAS DRUNK TOO, BUT HE DOESN'T ACTUALLY DRINK THAT MUCH. HE'S JUST NATURALLY DRUNK.
THE FIRST COUPLE OF WEEKS WERE FINE. HE WAS A WARM BODY ON A FRIDAY NIGHT AND A NICE BREAK FROM THE HIGH-FIVING BROS THAT I'M USUALLY ATTRACTED TO.
HE'D MOSTLY JUST HANG OUT AT MY APARTMENT AND WATCH TELEVISION. HE'D LAY HIS HEAD IN MY LAP AND EAT FOOD OFF MY PLATE. IT WAS LIKE DATING A GOLDEN RETRIEVER.
IT WOULD HAVE BEEN REALLY EASY TO KEEP DATING HIM, IF HE WASN'T SO... HIM. THE EVERYDAY STUFF WAS NICE ENOUGH WHEN WE JUST STAYED AT MY PLACE.
I MEAN, SURE, HE TRIED TO WATER MY PLANTS WITH ORANGE JUICE. YOU KNOW, FOR THE VITAMINS.
PSHHH! SOUNDS RIGHT.

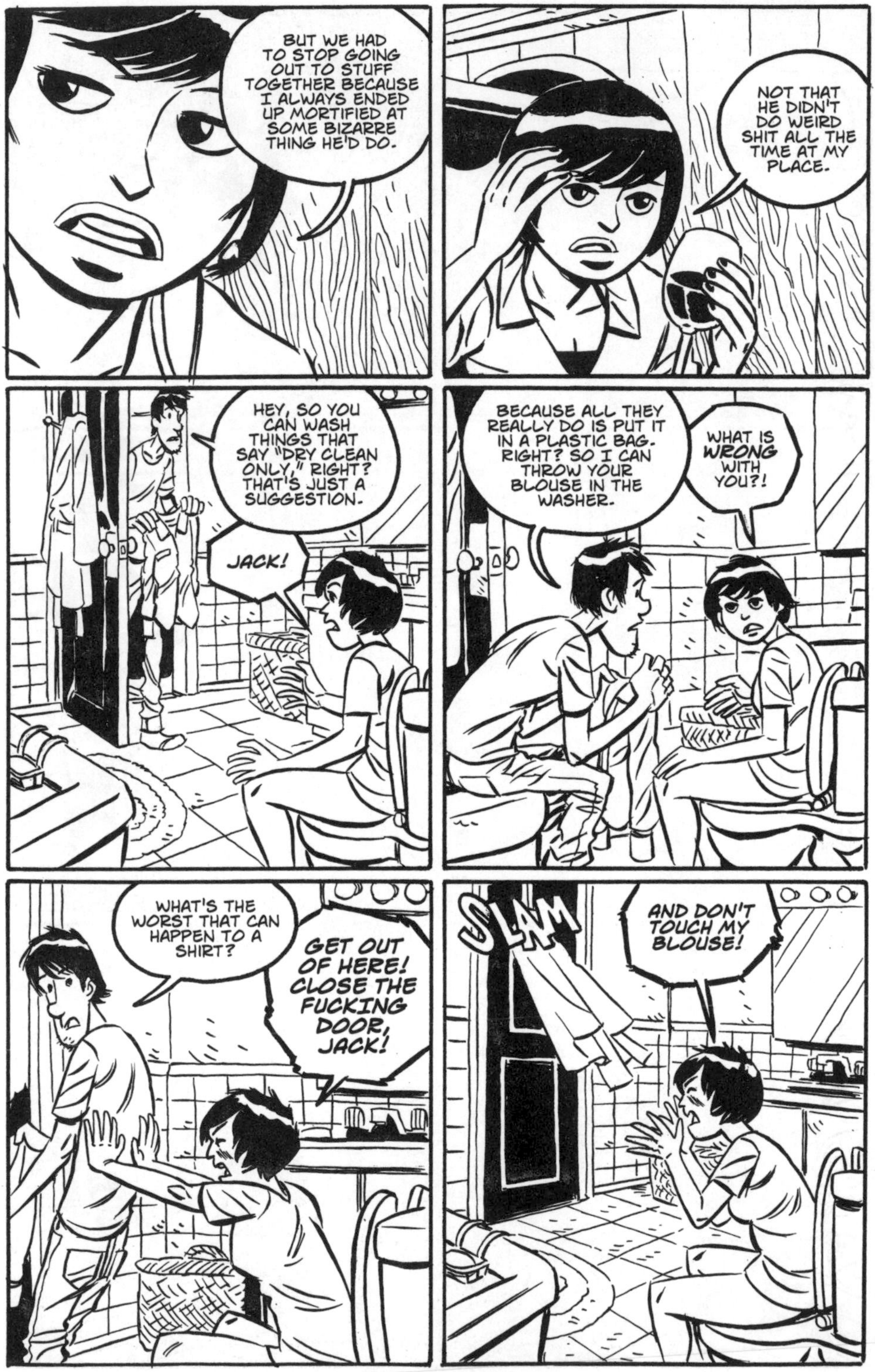
BUT WE HAD TO STOP GOING OUT TO STUFF TOGETHER BECAUSE I ALWAYS ENDED UP MORTIFIED AT SOME BIZARRE THING HE'D DO.
NOT THAT HE DIDN'T DO WEIRD SHIT ALL THE TIME AT MY PLACE.
HEY, SO YOU CAN WASH THINGS THAT SAY "DRY CLEAN ONLY," RIGHT? THAT'S JUST A SUGGESTION.
JACK!
BECAUSE ALL THEY REALLY DO IS PUT IT IN A PLASTIC BAG. RIGHT? SO I CAN THROW YOUR BLOUSE IN THE WASHER.
WHAT IS WRONG WITH YOU?!
WHAT'S THE WORST THAT CAN HAPPEN TO A SHIRT?
GET OUT OF HERE! CLOSE THE FUCKING DOOR, JACK!
SLAM
AND DON'T TOUCH MY BLOUSE!

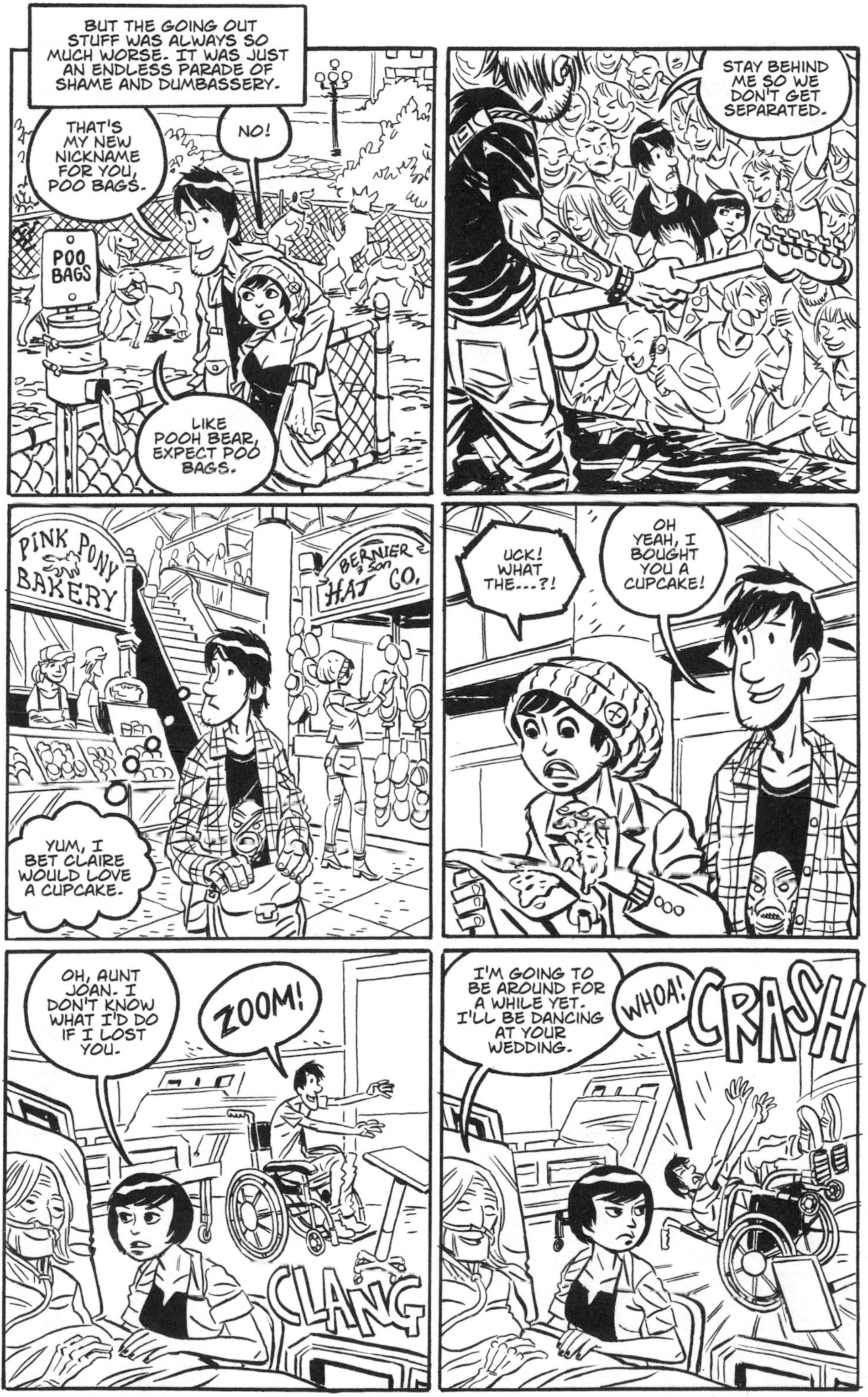
BUT THE GOING OUT STUFF WAS ALWAYS SO MUCH WORSE. IT WAS JUST AN ENDLESS PARADE OF SHAME AND DUMBASSERY.
THAT'S MY NEW NICKNAME FOR YOU, POO BAGS.
NO!
POO BAGS
LIKE POOH BEAR, EXPECT POO BAGS.
STAY BEHIND ME SO WE DON'T GET SEPARATED.
PINK PONY BAKERY
BERNIER & SON HAT CO.
YUM, I BET CLAIRE WOULD LOVE A CUPCAKE.
UCK! WHAT THE...?!
OH YEAH, I BOUGHT YOU A CUPCAKE!
OH, AUNT JOAN. I DON'T KNOW WHAT I'D DO IF I LOST YOU.
ZOOM!
CLANG
I'M GOING TO BE AROUND FOR A WHILE YET. I'LL BE DANCING AT YOUR WEDDING.
WHOA!
CRASH

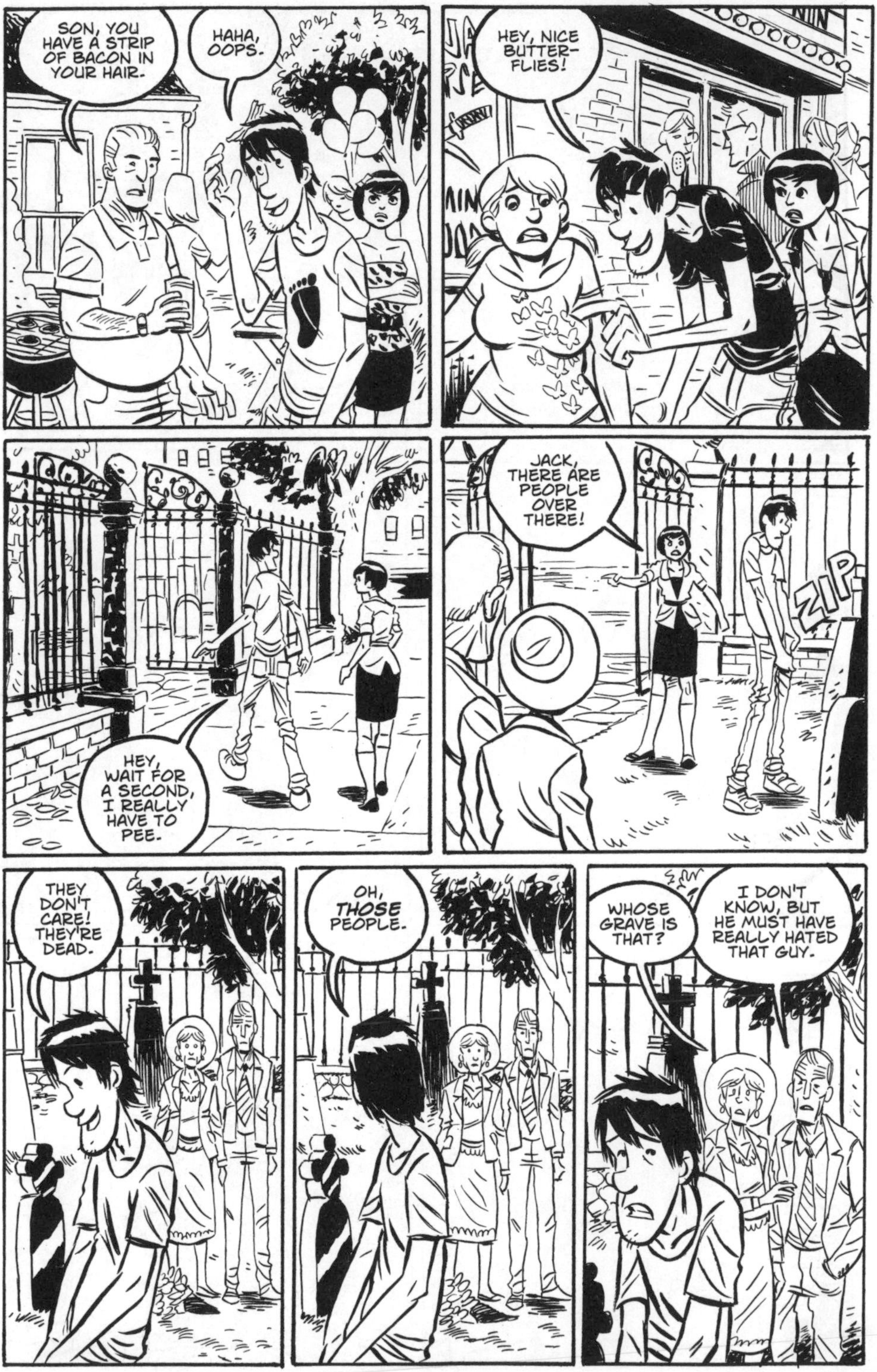
SON, YOU HAVE A STRIP OF BACON IN YOUR HAIR.
HAHA, OOPS.
HEY, NICE BUTTER-FLIES!
HEY, WAIT FOR A SECOND, I REALLY HAVE TO PEE.
JACK, THERE ARE PEOPLE OVER THERE!
ZIP
THEY DON'T CARE! THEY'RE DEAD.
OH, *THOSE* PEOPLE.
WHOSE GRAVE IS THAT?
I DON'T KNOW, BUT HE MUST HAVE REALLY HATED THAT GUY.

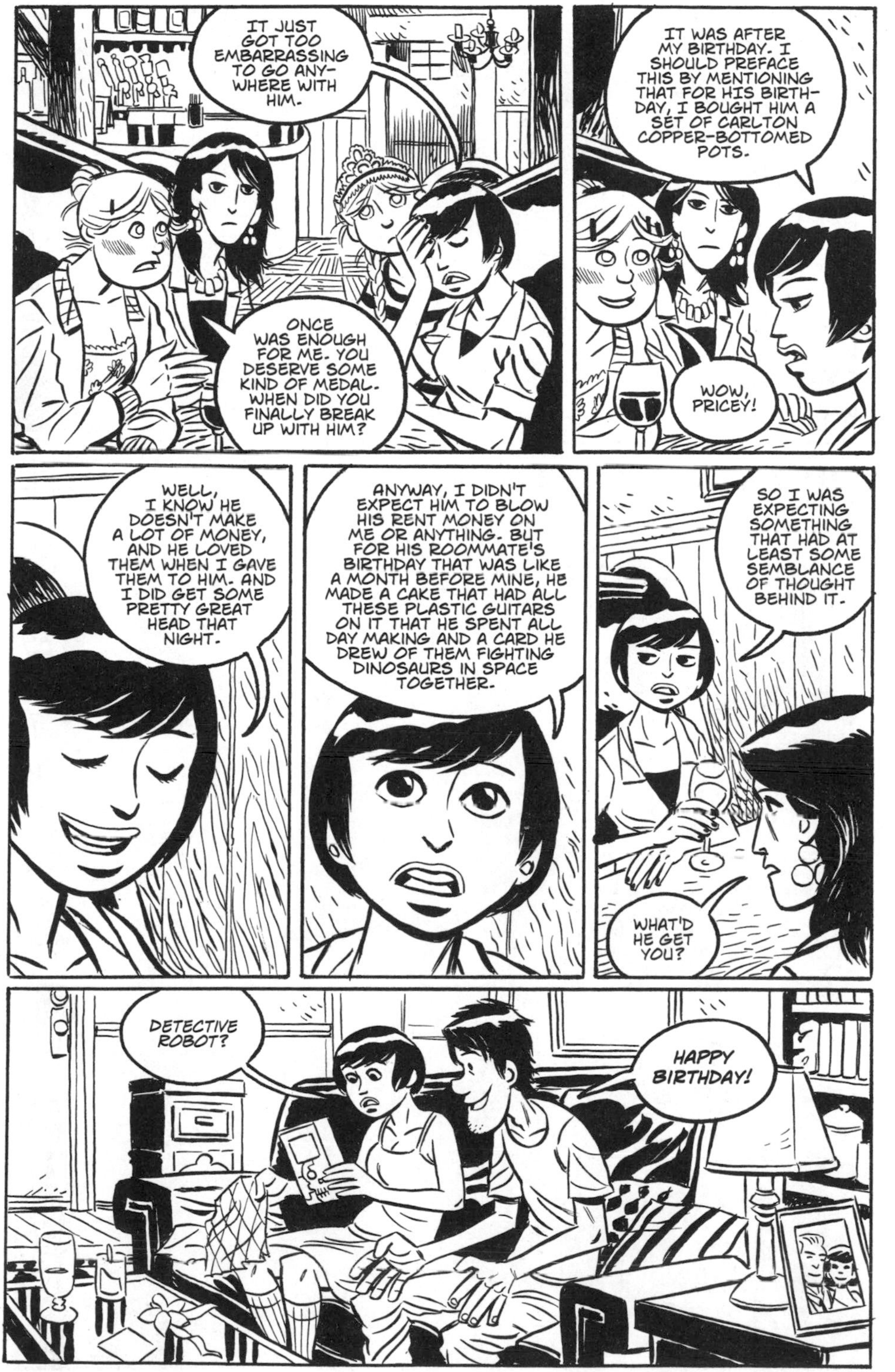
IT JUST GOT TOO EMBARRASSING TO GO ANY-WHERE WITH HIM.
ONCE WAS ENOUGH FOR ME. YOU DESERVE SOME KIND OF MEDAL. WHEN DID YOU FINALLY BREAK UP WITH HIM?
IT WAS AFTER MY BIRTHDAY. I SHOULD PREFACE THIS BY MENTIONING THAT FOR HIS BIRTH-DAY, I BOUGHT HIM A SET OF CARLTON COPPER-BOTTOMED POTS.
WOW, PRICEY!
WELL, I KNOW HE DOESN'T MAKE A LOT OF MONEY, AND HE LOVED THEM WHEN I GAVE THEM TO HIM. AND I DID GET SOME PRETTY GREAT HEAD THAT NIGHT.
ANYWAY, I DIDN'T EXPECT HIM TO BLOW HIS RENT MONEY ON ME OR ANYTHING. BUT FOR HIS ROOMMATE'S BIRTHDAY THAT WAS LIKE A MONTH BEFORE MINE, HE MADE A CAKE THAT HAD ALL THESE PLASTIC GUITARS ON IT THAT HE SPENT ALL DAY MAKING AND A CARD HE DREW OF THEM FIGHTING DINOSAURS IN SPACE TOGETHER.
SO I WAS EXPECTING SOMETHING THAT HAD AT LEAST SOME SEMBLANCE OF THOUGHT BEHIND IT.
WHAT'D HE GET YOU?
DETECTIVE ROBOT?
HAPPY BIRTHDAY!

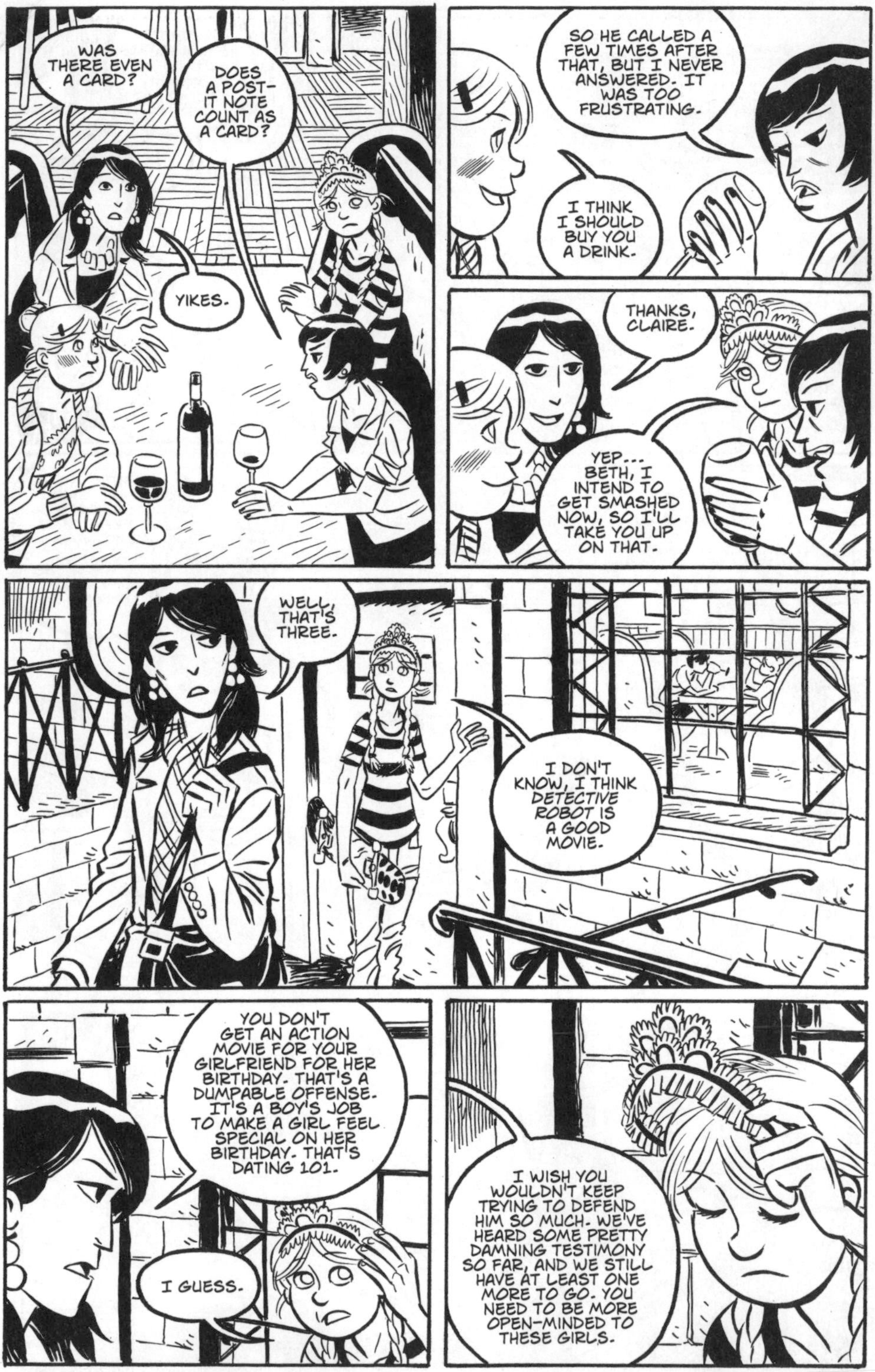
WAS THERE EVEN A CARD?
DOES A POST-IT NOTE COUNT AS A CARD?
YIKES.
SO HE CALLED A FEW TIMES AFTER THAT, BUT I NEVER ANSWERED. IT WAS TOO FRUSTRATING.
I THINK I SHOULD BUY YOU A DRINK.
THANKS, CLAIRE.
YEP... BETH, I INTEND TO GET SMASHED NOW, SO I'LL TAKE YOU UP ON THAT.
WELL, THAT'S THREE.
I DON'T KNOW, I THINK *DETECTIVE ROBOT* IS A GOOD MOVIE.
YOU DON'T GET AN ACTION MOVIE FOR YOUR GIRLFRIEND FOR HER BIRTHDAY. THAT'S A DUMPABLE OFFENSE. IT'S A BOY'S JOB TO MAKE A GIRL FEEL SPECIAL ON HER BIRTHDAY. THAT'S DATING 101.
I GUESS.
I WISH YOU WOULDN'T KEEP TRYING TO DEFEND HIM SO MUCH. WE'VE HEARD SOME PRETTY DAMNING TESTIMONY SO FAR, AND WE STILL HAVE AT LEAST ONE MORE TO GO. YOU NEED TO BE MORE OPEN-MINDED TO THESE GIRLS.

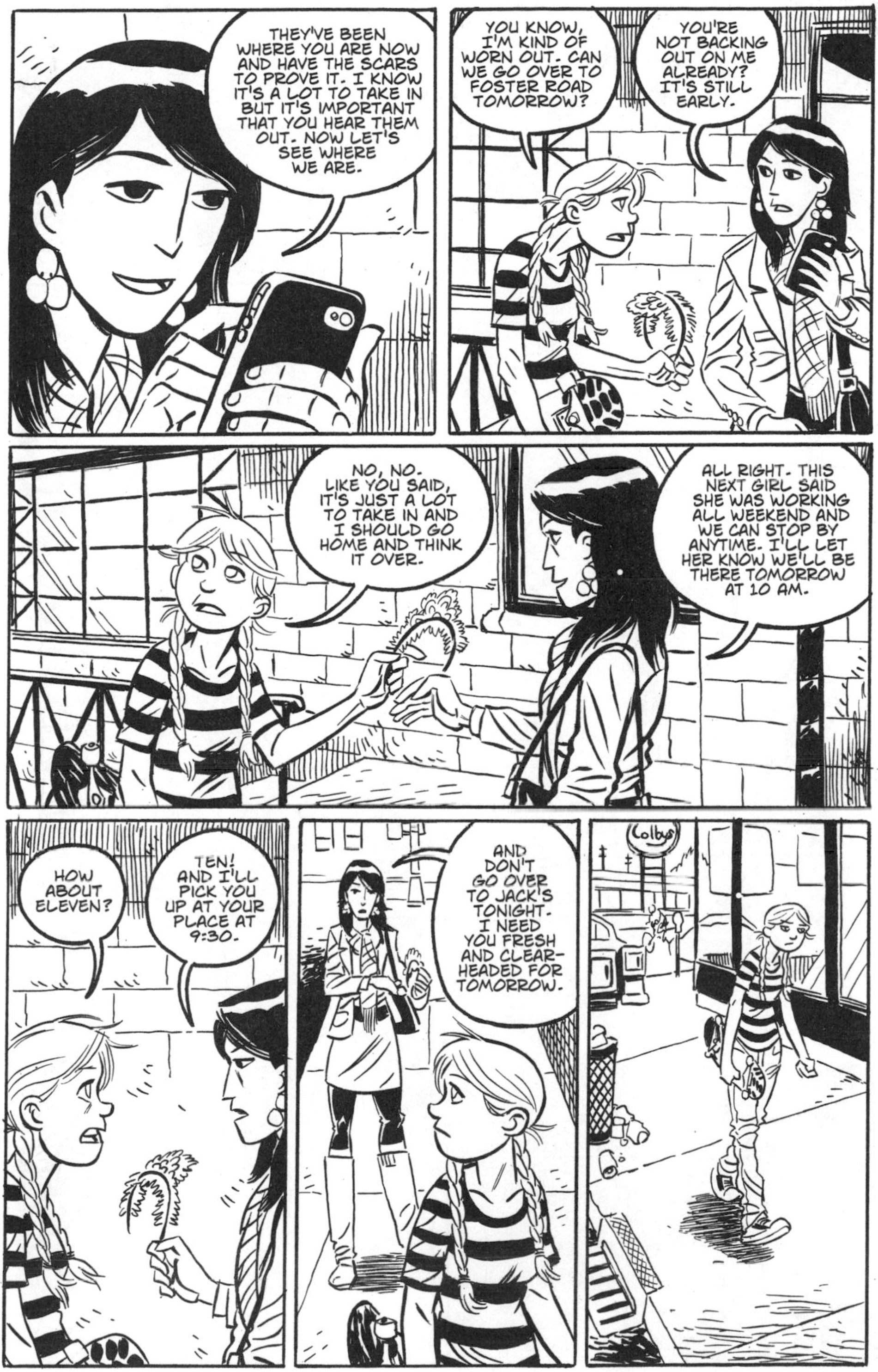
THEY'VE BEEN WHERE YOU ARE NOW AND HAVE THE SCARS TO PROVE IT. I KNOW IT'S A LOT TO TAKE IN BUT IT'S IMPORTANT THAT YOU HEAR THEM OUT. NOW LET'S SEE WHERE WE ARE.
YOU KNOW, I'M KIND OF WORN OUT. CAN WE GO OVER TO FOSTER ROAD TOMORROW?
YOU'RE NOT BACKING OUT ON ME ALREADY? IT'S STILL EARLY.
NO, NO. LIKE YOU SAID, IT'S JUST A LOT TO TAKE IN AND I SHOULD GO HOME AND THINK IT OVER.
ALL RIGHT. THIS NEXT GIRL SAID SHE WAS WORKING ALL WEEKEND AND WE CAN STOP BY ANYTIME. I'LL LET HER KNOW WE'LL BE THERE TOMORROW AT 10 AM.
HOW ABOUT ELEVEN?
TEN! AND I'LL PICK YOU UP AT YOUR PLACE AT 9:30.
AND DON'T GO OVER TO JACK'S TONIGHT. I NEED YOU FRESH AND CLEAR-HEADED FOR TOMORROW.
Colbys

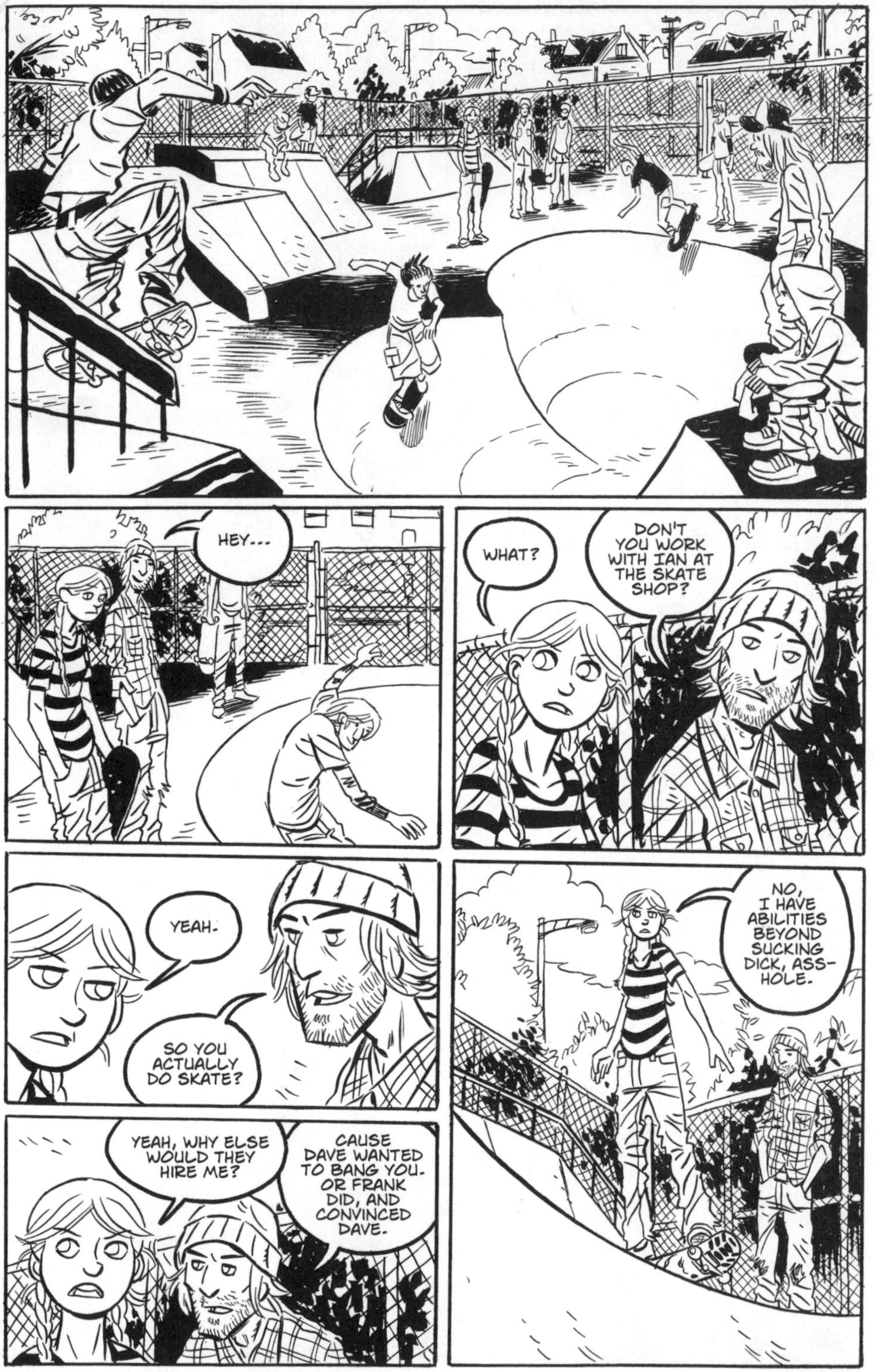
HEY...
WHAT?
DON'T YOU WORK WITH IAN AT THE SKATE SHOP?
YEAH.
SO YOU ACTUALLY DO SKATE?
YEAH, WHY ELSE WOULD THEY HIRE ME?
CAUSE DAVE WANTED TO BANG YOU. OR FRANK DID, AND CONVINCED DAVE.
NO, I HAVE ABILITIES BEYOND SUCKING DICK, ASS-HOLE.

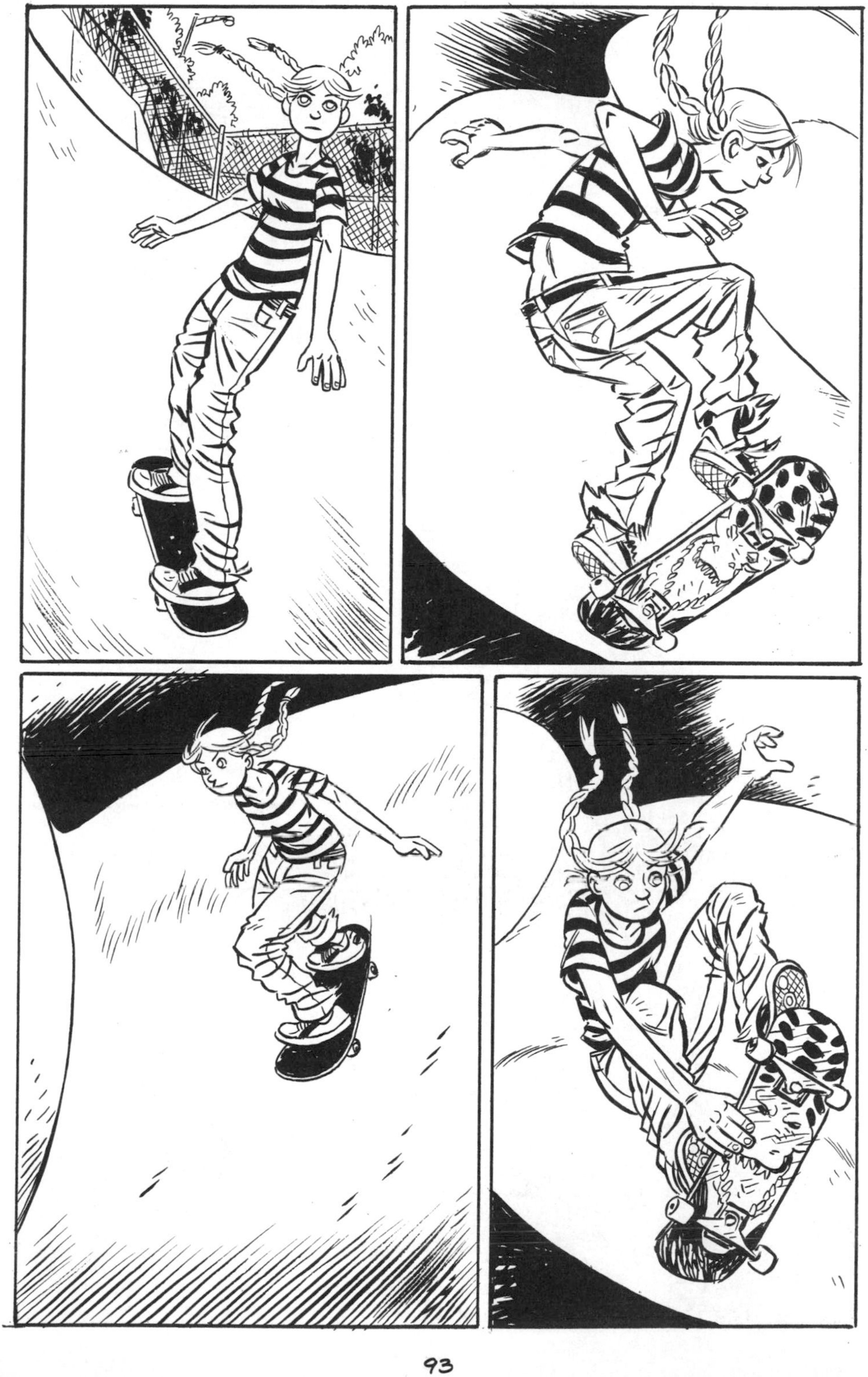

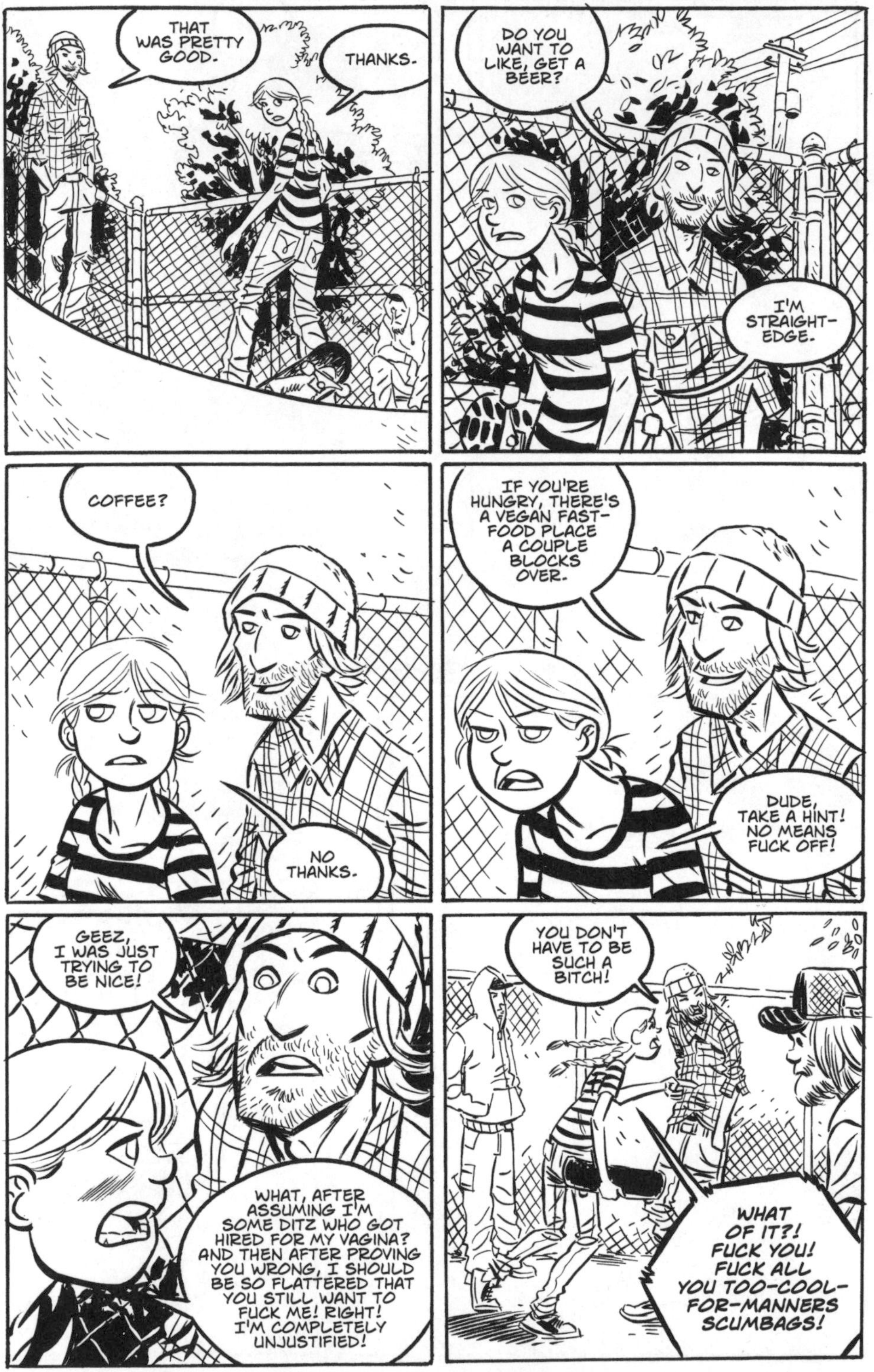
THAT WAS PRETTY GOOD.
THANKS.
DO YOU WANT TO LIKE, GET A BEER?
I'M STRAIGHT-EDGE.
COFFEE?
NO THANKS.
IF YOU'RE HUNGRY, THERE'S A VEGAN FAST-FOOD PLACE A COUPLE BLOCKS OVER.
DUDE, TAKE A HINT! NO MEANS FUCK OFF!
GEEZ, I WAS JUST TRYING TO BE NICE!
WHAT, AFTER ASSUMING I'M SOME DITZ WHO GOT HIRED FOR MY VAGINA? AND THEN AFTER PROVING YOU WRONG, I SHOULD BE SO FLATTERED THAT YOU STILL WANT TO FUCK ME! RIGHT! I'M COMPLETELY UNJUSTIFIED!
YOU DON'T HAVE TO BE SUCH A BITCH!
WHAT OF IT?! FUCK YOU! FUCK ALL YOU TOO-COOL-FOR-MANNERS SCUMBAGS!

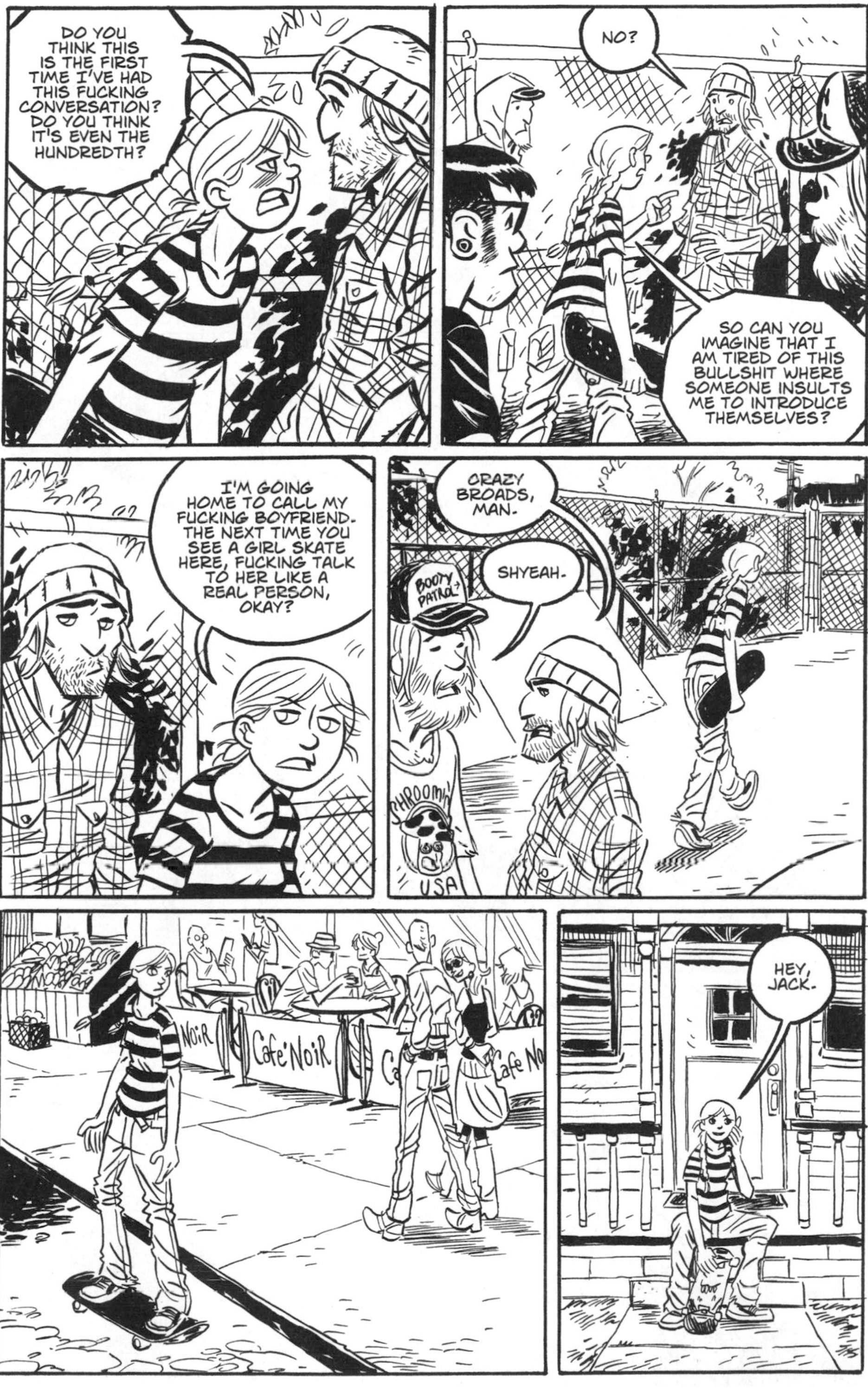
DO YOU THINK THIS IS THE FIRST TIME I'VE HAD THIS FUCKING CONVERSATION? DO YOU THINK IT'S EVEN THE HUNDREDTH?
NO?
SO CAN YOU IMAGINE THAT I AM TIRED OF THIS BULLSHIT WHERE SOMEONE INSULTS ME TO INTRODUCE THEMSELVES?
I'M GOING HOME TO CALL MY FUCKING BOYFRIEND. THE NEXT TIME YOU SEE A GIRL SKATE HERE, FUCKING TALK TO HER LIKE A REAL PERSON, OKAY?
CRAZY BROADS, MAN.
SHYEAH.
BOOTY PATROL
SHROOMIN
USA
Café Noir
Café Noir
HEY, JACK.

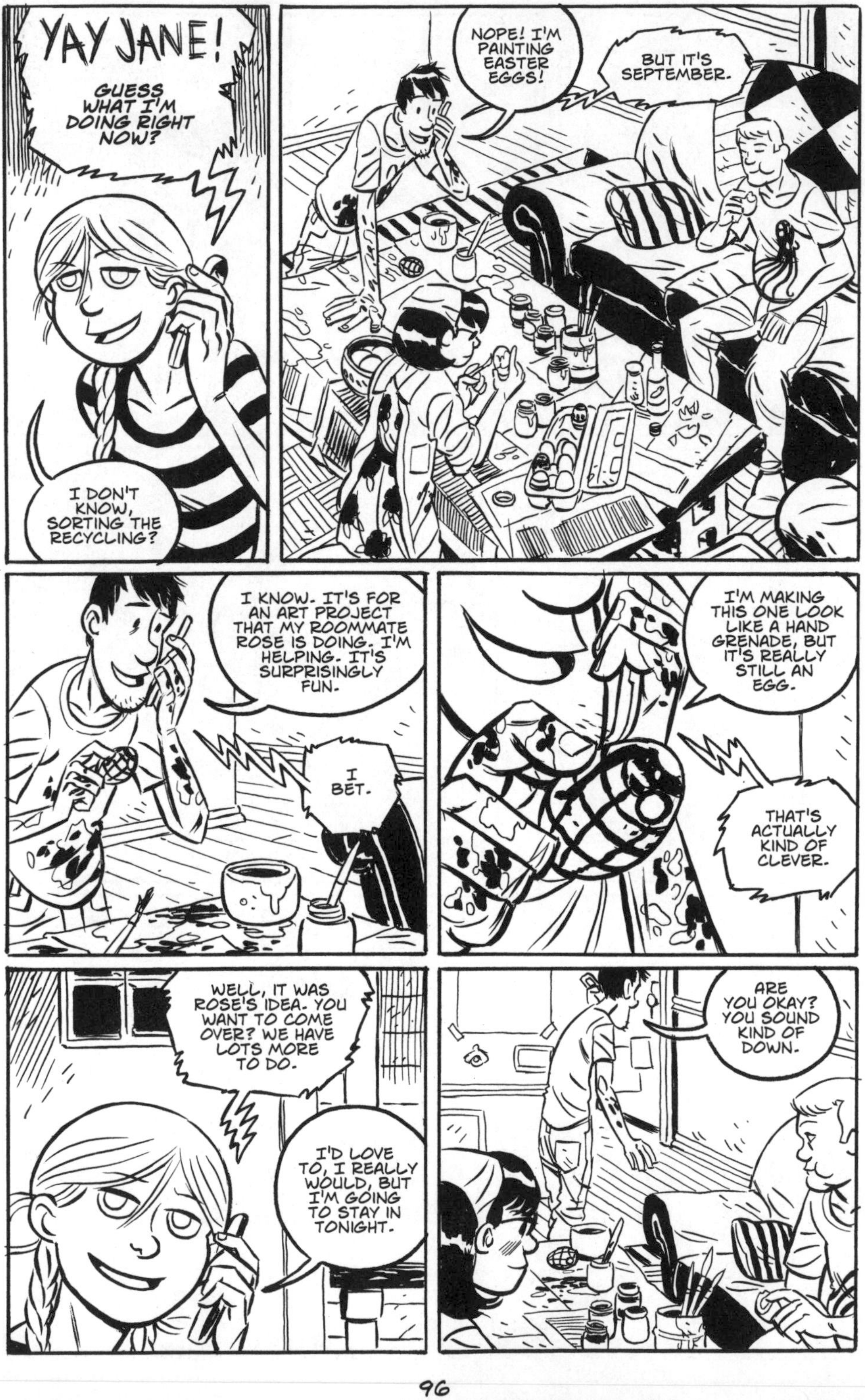
YAY JANE!
GUESS WHAT I'M DOING RIGHT NOW?
I DON'T KNOW, SORTING THE RECYCLING?
NOPE! I'M PAINTING EASTER EGGS!
BUT IT'S SEPTEMBER.
I KNOW. IT'S FOR AN ART PROJECT THAT MY ROOMMATE ROSE IS DOING. I'M HELPING. IT'S SURPRISINGLY FUN.
I BET.
I'M MAKING THIS ONE LOOK LIKE A HAND GRENADE, BUT IT'S REALLY STILL AN EGG.
THAT'S ACTUALLY KIND OF CLEVER.
WELL, IT WAS ROSE'S IDEA. YOU WANT TO COME OVER? WE HAVE LOTS MORE TO DO.
I'D LOVE TO, I REALLY WOULD, BUT I'M GOING TO STAY IN TONIGHT.
ARE YOU OKAY? YOU SOUND KIND OF DOWN.

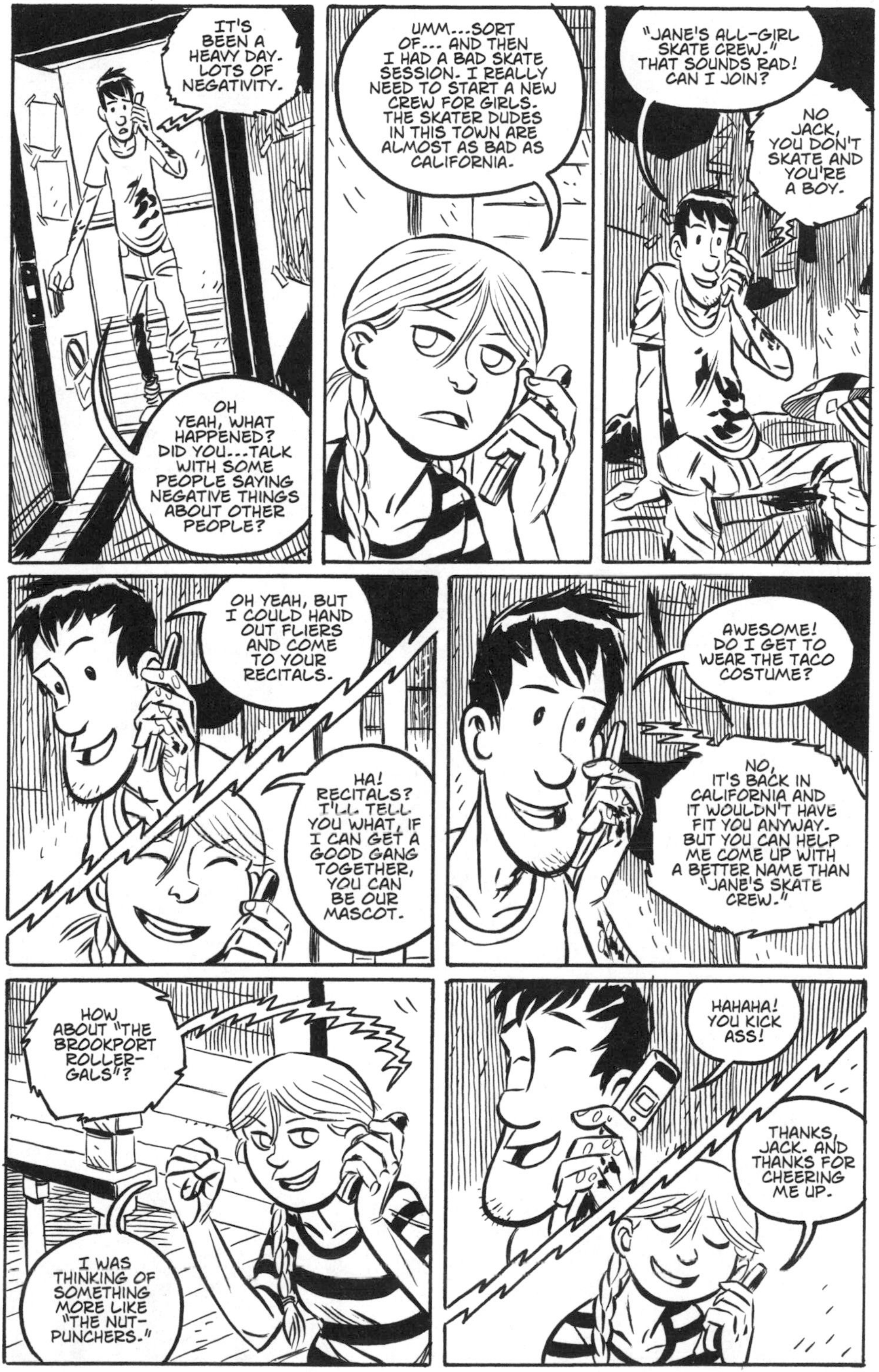
IT'S BEEN A HEAVY DAY. LOTS OF NEGATIVITY.
OH YEAH, WHAT HAPPENED? DID YOU...TALK WITH SOME PEOPLE SAYING NEGATIVE THINGS ABOUT OTHER PEOPLE?
UMM...SORT OF... AND THEN I HAD A BAD SKATE SESSION. I REALLY NEED TO START A NEW CREW FOR GIRLS. THE SKATER DUDES IN THIS TOWN ARE ALMOST AS BAD AS CALIFORNIA.
"JANE'S ALL-GIRL SKATE CREW." THAT SOUNDS RAD! CAN I JOIN?
NO JACK, YOU DON'T SKATE AND YOU'RE A BOY.
OH YEAH, BUT I COULD HAND OUT FLIERS AND COME TO YOUR RECITALS.
HA! RECITALS? I'LL TELL YOU WHAT, IF I CAN GET A GOOD GANG TOGETHER, YOU CAN BE OUR MASCOT.
AWESOME! DO I GET TO WEAR THE TACO COSTUME?
NO, IT'S BACK IN CALIFORNIA AND IT WOULDN'T HAVE FIT YOU ANYWAY. BUT YOU CAN HELP ME COME UP WITH A BETTER NAME THAN "JANE'S SKATE CREW."
HOW ABOUT "THE BROOKPORT ROLLER-GALS"?
I WAS THINKING OF SOMETHING MORE LIKE "THE NUT-PUNCHERS."
HAHAHA! YOU KICK ASS!
THANKS, JACK. AND THANKS FOR CHEERING ME UP.

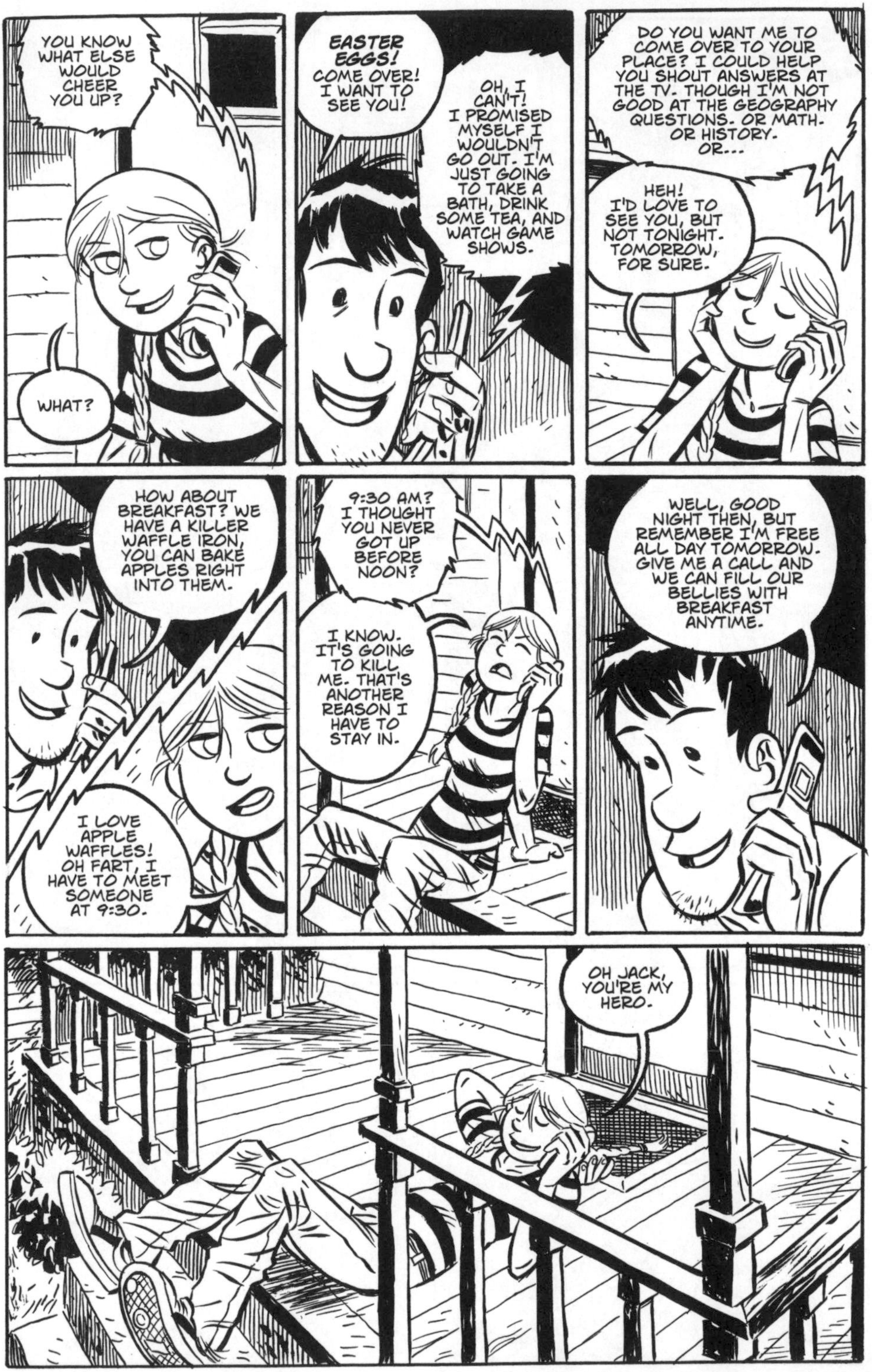
YOU KNOW WHAT ELSE WOULD CHEER YOU UP?
WHAT?
EASTER EGGS! COME OVER! I WANT TO SEE YOU!
OH, I CAN'T! I PROMISED MYSELF I WOULDN'T GO OUT. I'M JUST GOING TO TAKE A BATH, DRINK SOME TEA, AND WATCH GAME SHOWS.
DO YOU WANT ME TO COME OVER TO YOUR PLACE? I COULD HELP YOU SHOUT ANSWERS AT THE TV. THOUGH I'M NOT GOOD AT THE GEOGRAPHY QUESTIONS. OR MATH. OR HISTORY. OR...
HEH! I'D LOVE TO SEE YOU, BUT NOT TONIGHT. TOMORROW, FOR SURE.
HOW ABOUT BREAKFAST? WE HAVE A KILLER WAFFLE IRON, YOU CAN BAKE APPLES RIGHT INTO THEM.
I LOVE APPLE WAFFLES! OH FART, I HAVE TO MEET SOMEONE AT 9:30.
9:30 AM? I THOUGHT YOU NEVER GOT UP BEFORE NOON?
I KNOW. IT'S GOING TO KILL ME. THAT'S ANOTHER REASON I HAVE TO STAY IN.
WELL, GOOD NIGHT THEN, BUT REMEMBER I'M FREE ALL DAY TOMORROW. GIVE ME A CALL AND WE CAN FILL OUR BELLIES WITH BREAKFAST ANYTIME.
OH JACK, YOU'RE MY HERO.

CHAPTER FIVE

"Last Stand at the Bagelarium"

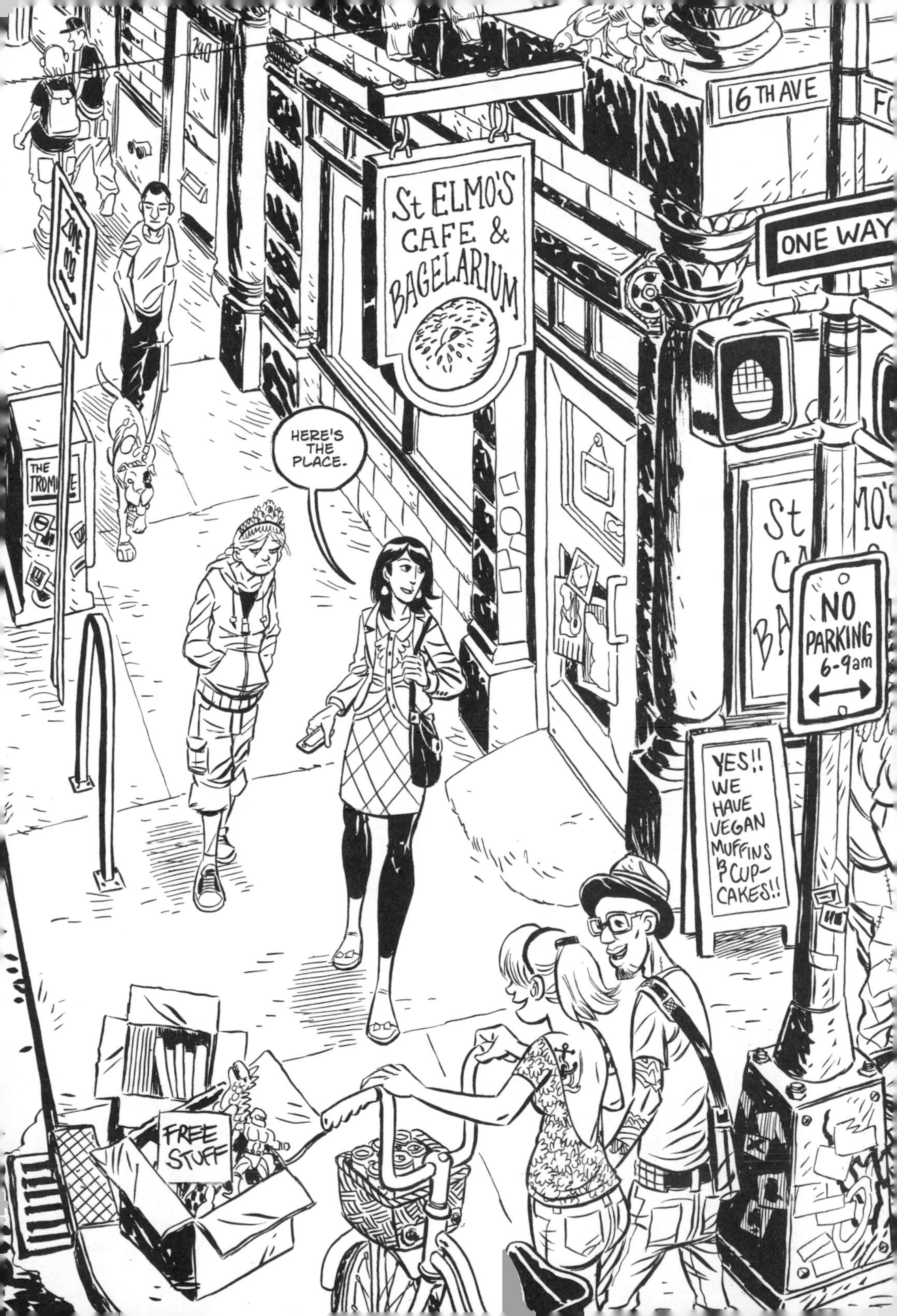
16TH AVE
ST ELMO'S CAFE & BAGELARIUM
ONE WAY
HERE'S THE PLACE.
NO PARKING 6-9am
YES!! WE HAVE VEGAN MUFFINS & CUP-CAKES!!
FREE STUFF

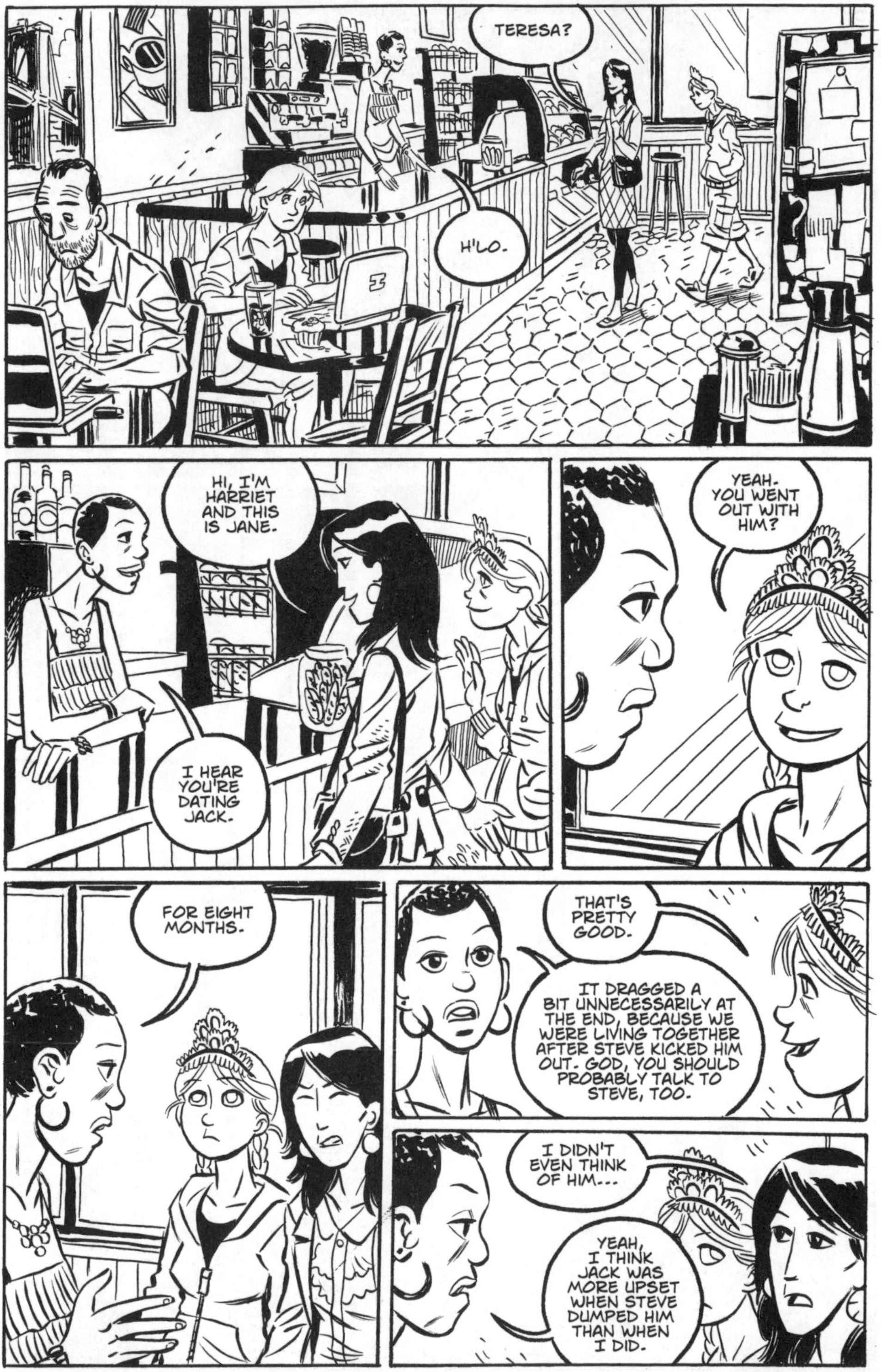

TERESA?
H'LO.
HI, I'M HARRIET AND THIS IS JANE.
I HEAR YOU'RE DATING JACK.
YEAH. YOU WENT OUT WITH HIM?
FOR EIGHT MONTHS.
THAT'S PRETTY GOOD.
IT DRAGGED A BIT UNNECESSARILY AT THE END, BECAUSE WE WERE LIVING TOGETHER AFTER STEVE KICKED HIM OUT. GOD, YOU SHOULD PROBABLY TALK TO STEVE, TOO.
I DIDN'T EVEN THINK OF HIM...
YEAH, I THINK JACK WAS MORE UPSET WHEN STEVE DUMPED HIM THAN WHEN I DID.

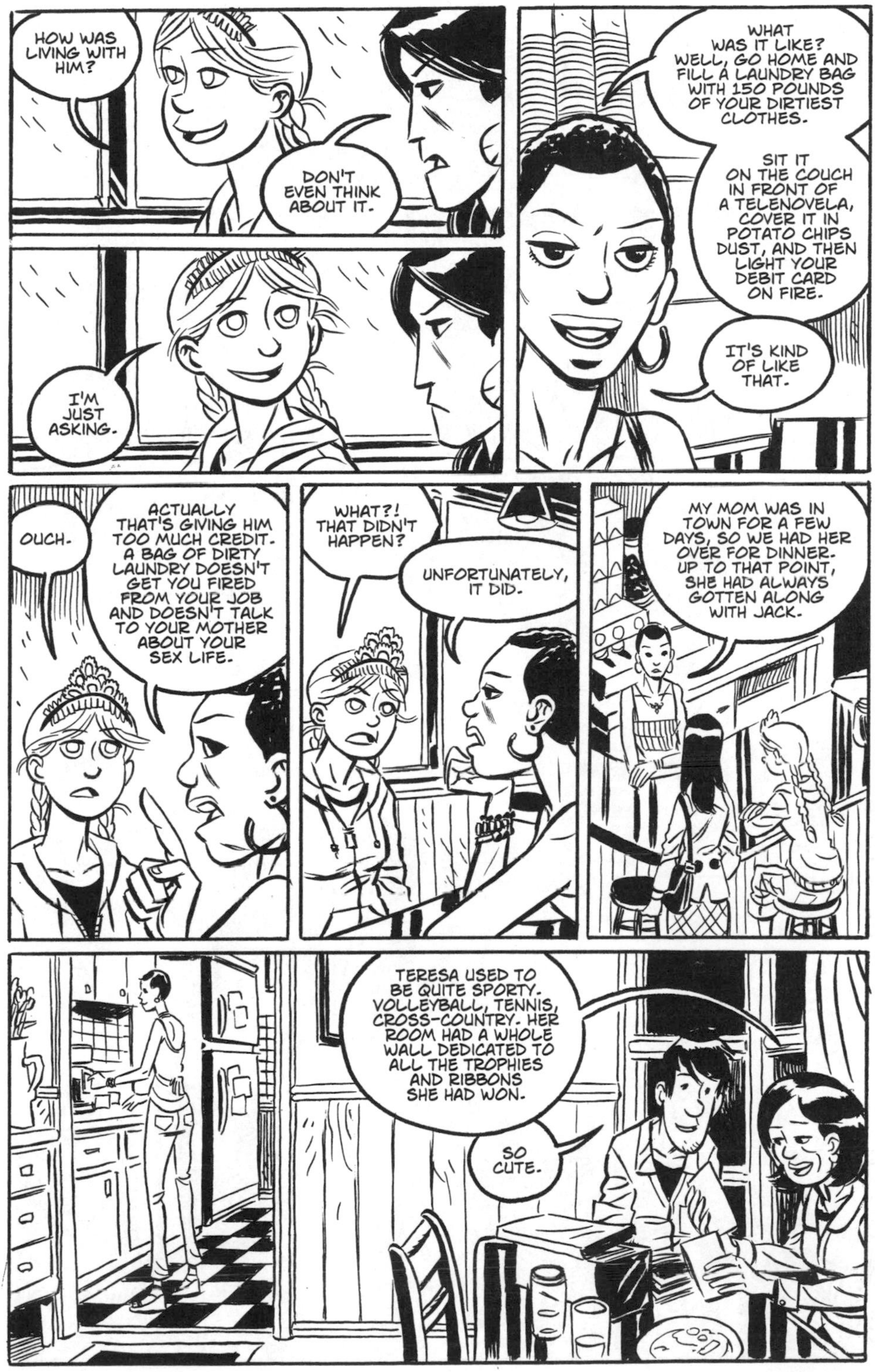
HOW WAS LIVING WITH HIM?
DON'T EVEN THINK ABOUT IT.
I'M JUST ASKING.
WHAT WAS IT LIKE? WELL, GO HOME AND FILL A LAUNDRY BAG WITH 150 POUNDS OF YOUR DIRTIEST CLOTHES.
SIT IT ON THE COUCH IN FRONT OF A TELENOVELA, COVER IT IN POTATO CHIPS DUST, AND THEN LIGHT YOUR DEBIT CARD ON FIRE.
IT'S KIND OF LIKE THAT.
OUCH.
ACTUALLY THAT'S GIVING HIM TOO MUCH CREDIT. A BAG OF DIRTY LAUNDRY DOESN'T GET YOU FIRED FROM YOUR JOB AND DOESN'T TALK TO YOUR MOTHER ABOUT YOUR SEX LIFE.
WHAT?! THAT DIDN'T HAPPEN?
UNFORTUNATELY, IT DID.
MY MOM WAS IN TOWN FOR A FEW DAYS, SO WE HAD HER OVER FOR DINNER. UP TO THAT POINT, SHE HAD ALWAYS GOTTEN ALONG WITH JACK.
TERESA USED TO BE QUITE SPORTY. VOLLEYBALL, TENNIS, CROSS-COUNTRY. HER ROOM HAD A WHOLE WALL DEDICATED TO ALL THE TROPHIES AND RIBBONS SHE HAD WON.
SO CUTE.

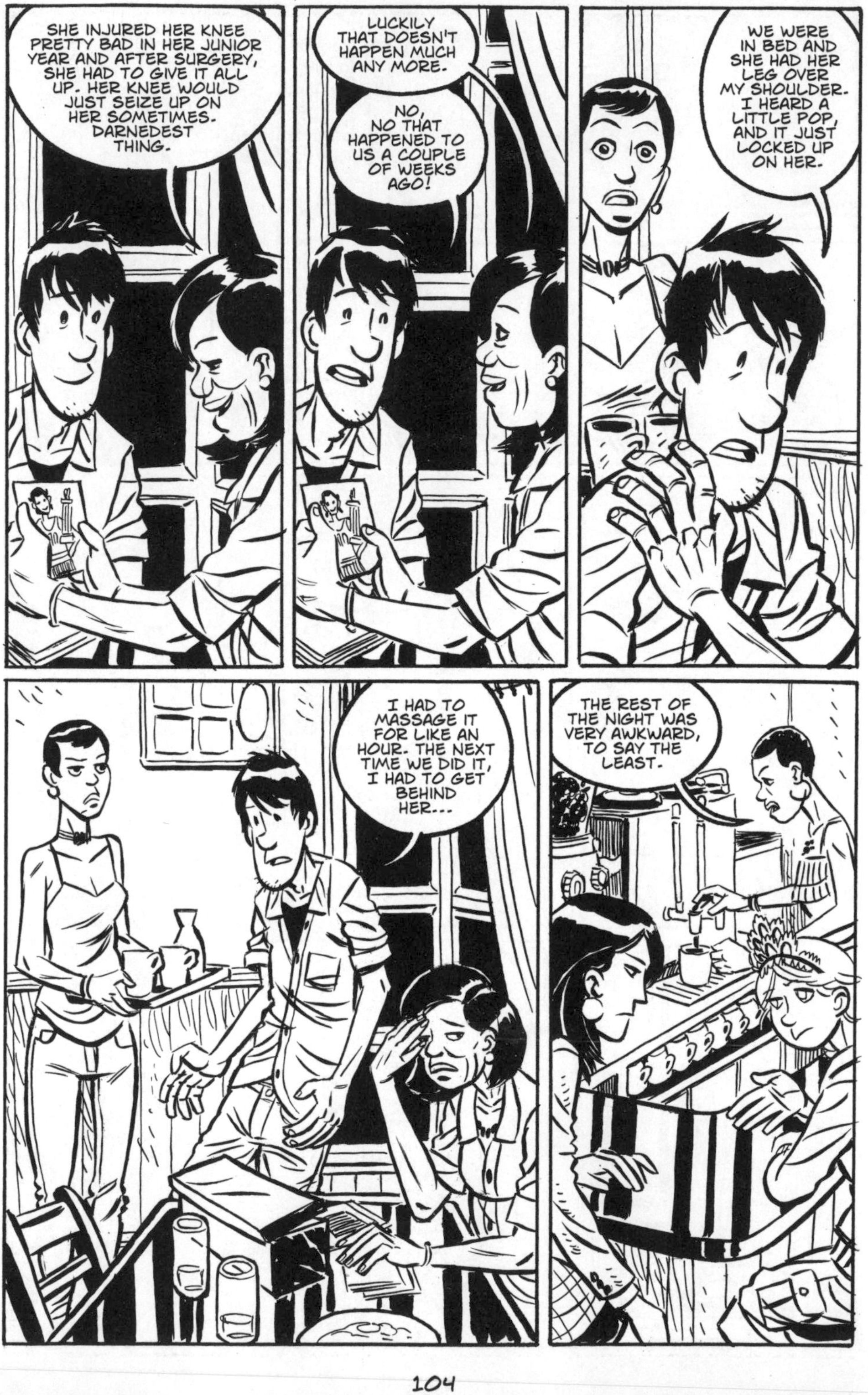
SHE INJURED HER KNEE PRETTY BAD IN HER JUNIOR YEAR AND AFTER SURGERY, SHE HAD TO GIVE IT ALL UP. HER KNEE WOULD JUST SEIZE UP ON HER SOMETIMES. DARNEDEST THING.
LUCKILY THAT DOESN'T HAPPEN MUCH ANY MORE.
NO, NO THAT HAPPENED TO US A COUPLE OF WEEKS AGO!
WE WERE IN BED AND SHE HAD HER LEG OVER MY SHOULDER. I HEARD A LITTLE POP, AND IT JUST LOCKED UP ON HER.
I HAD TO MASSAGE IT FOR LIKE AN HOUR. THE NEXT TIME WE DID IT, I HAD TO GET BEHIND HER...
THE REST OF THE NIGHT WAS VERY AWKWARD, TO SAY THE LEAST.

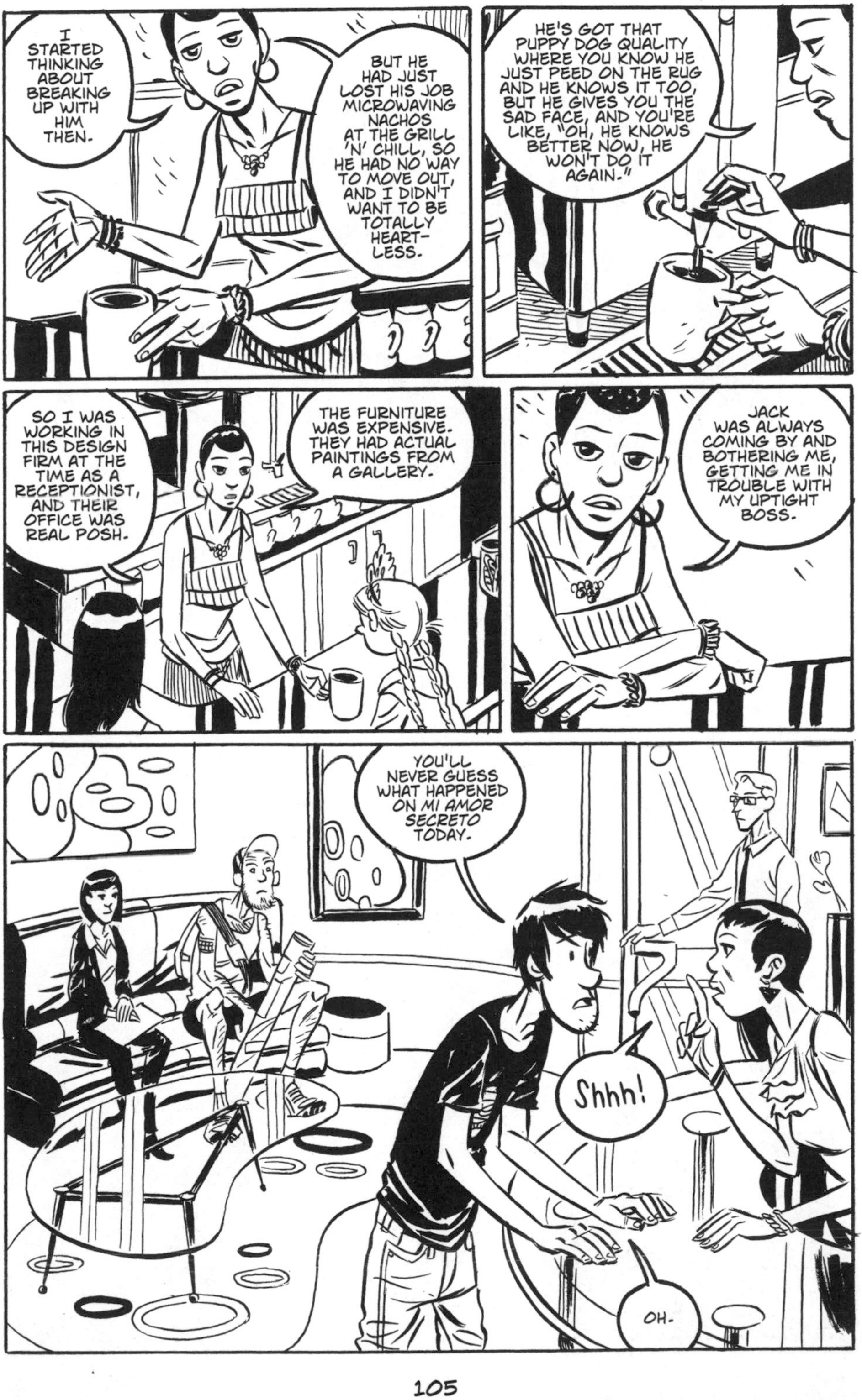
I STARTED THINKING ABOUT BREAKING UP WITH HIM THEN.
BUT HE HAD JUST LOST HIS JOB MICROWAVING NACHOS AT THE GRILL 'N' CHILL, SO HE HAD NO WAY TO MOVE OUT, AND I DIDN'T WANT TO BE TOTALLY HEART-LESS.
HE'S GOT THAT PUPPY DOG QUALITY WHERE YOU KNOW HE JUST PEED ON THE RUG AND HE KNOWS IT TOO, BUT HE GIVES YOU THE SAD FACE, AND YOU'RE LIKE, "OH, HE KNOWS BETTER NOW, HE WON'T DO IT AGAIN."
SO I WAS WORKING IN THIS DESIGN FIRM AT THE TIME AS A RECEPTIONIST, AND THEIR OFFICE WAS REAL POSH.
THE FURNITURE WAS EXPENSIVE. THEY HAD ACTUAL PAINTINGS FROM A GALLERY.
JACK WAS ALWAYS COMING BY AND BOTHERING ME, GETTING ME IN TROUBLE WITH MY UPTIGHT BOSS.
YOU'LL NEVER GUESS WHAT HAPPENED ON MI AMOR SECRETO TODAY.
Shhh!
OH.

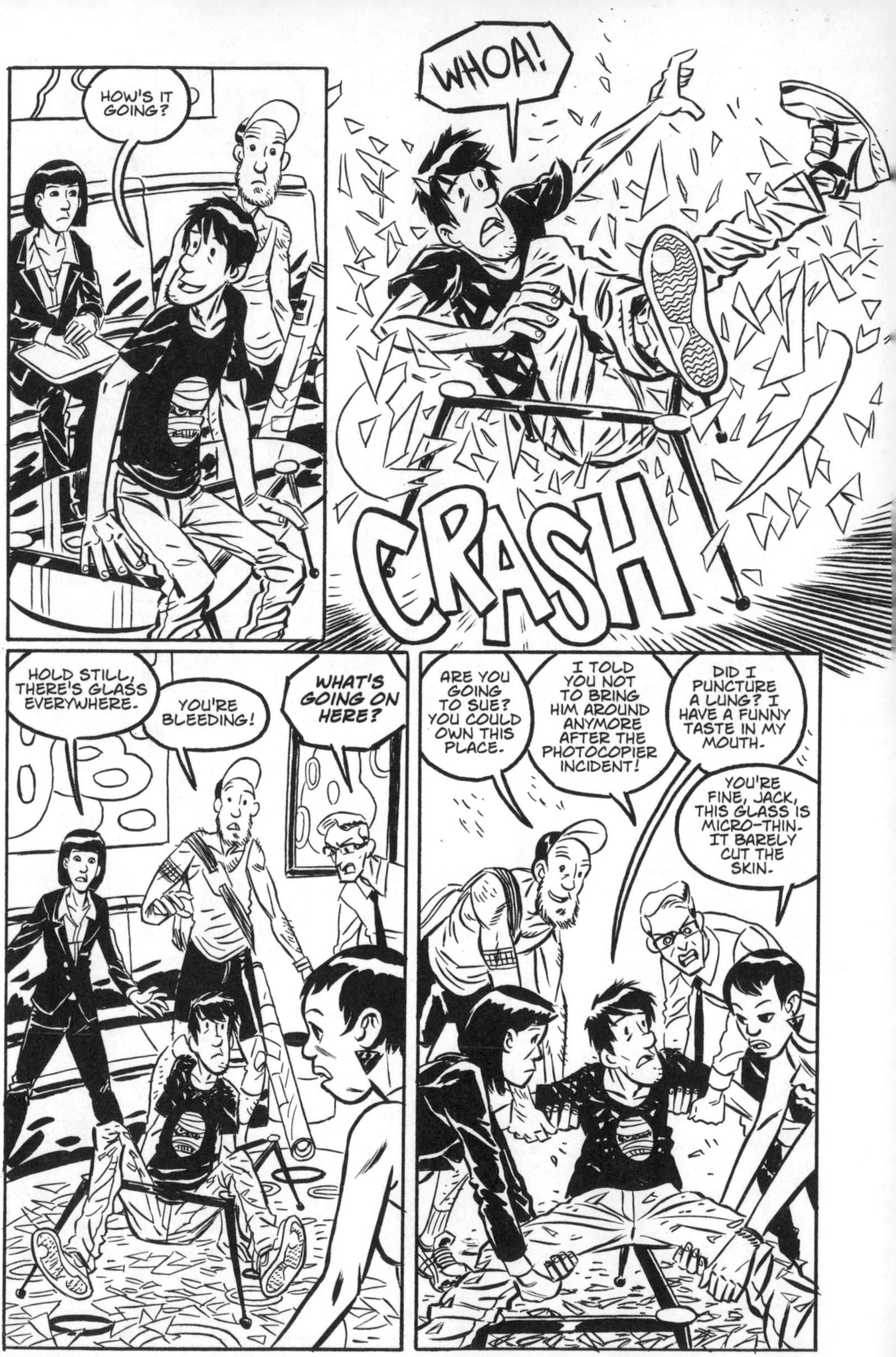
HOW'S IT GOING?
WHOA!
CRASH
HOLD STILL, THERE'S GLASS EVERYWHERE.
YOU'RE BLEEDING!
WHAT'S GOING ON HERE?
ARE YOU GOING TO SUE? YOU COULD OWN THIS PLACE.
I TOLD YOU NOT TO BRING HIM AROUND ANYMORE AFTER THE PHOTOCOPIER INCIDENT!
DID I PUNCTURE A LUNG? I HAVE A FUNNY TASTE IN MY MOUTH.
YOU'RE FINE, JACK, THIS GLASS IS MICRO-THIN. IT BARELY CUT THE SKIN.

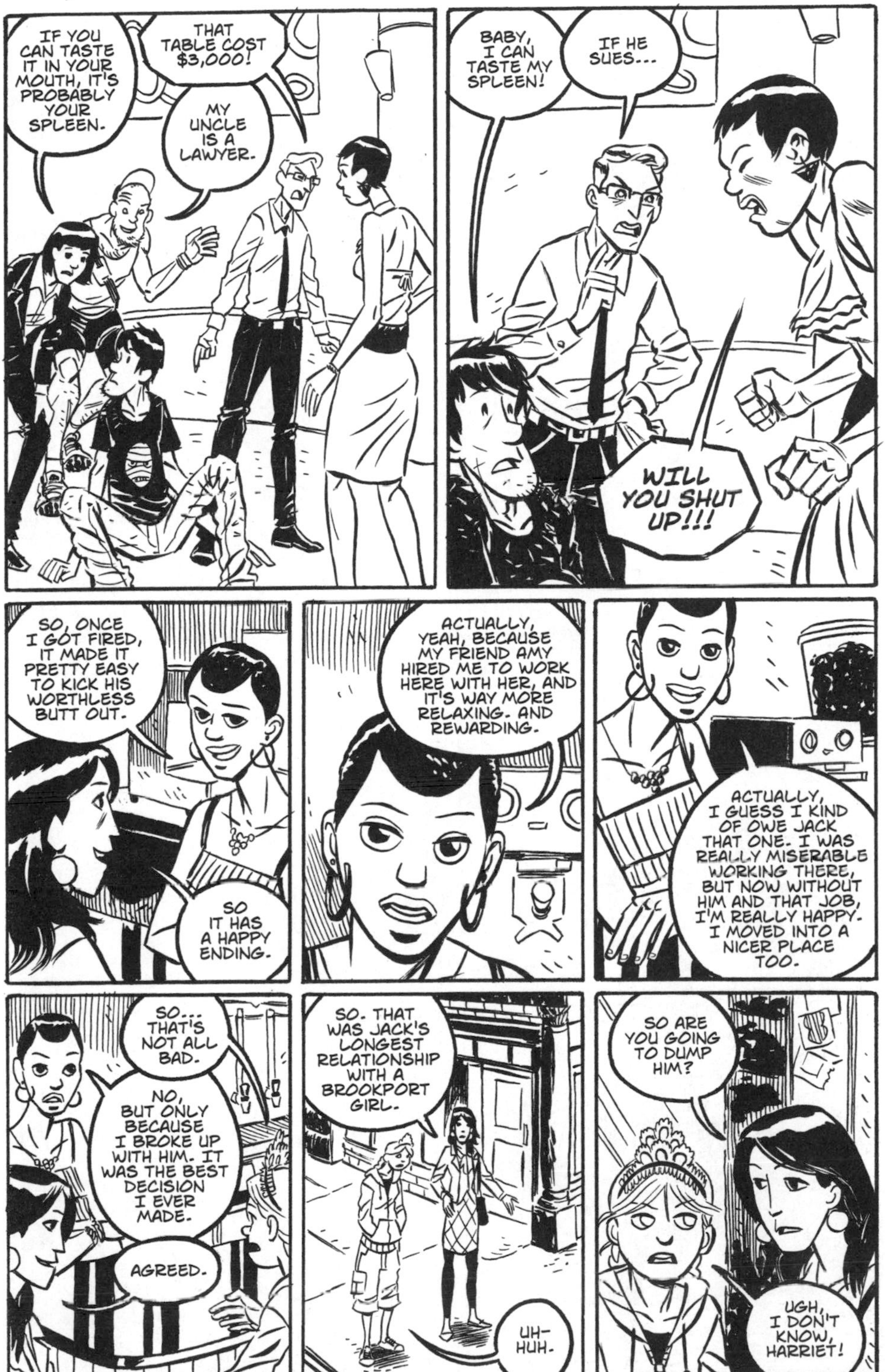
IF YOU CAN TASTE IT IN YOUR MOUTH, IT'S PROBABLY YOUR SPLEEN.
THAT TABLE COST $3,000!
MY UNCLE IS A LAWYER.
BABY, I CAN TASTE MY SPLEEN!
IF HE SUES...
WILL YOU SHUT UP!!!
SO, ONCE I GOT FIRED, IT MADE IT PRETTY EASY TO KICK HIS WORTHLESS BUTT OUT.
SO IT HAS A HAPPY ENDING.
ACTUALLY, YEAH, BECAUSE MY FRIEND AMY HIRED ME TO WORK HERE WITH HER, AND IT'S WAY MORE RELAXING. AND REWARDING.
ACTUALLY, I GUESS I KIND OF OWE JACK THAT ONE. I WAS REALLY MISERABLE WORKING THERE, BUT NOW WITHOUT HIM AND THAT JOB, I'M REALLY HAPPY. I MOVED INTO A NICER PLACE TOO.
SO... THAT'S NOT ALL BAD.
NO, BUT ONLY BECAUSE I BROKE UP WITH HIM. IT WAS THE BEST DECISION I EVER MADE.
AGREED.
SO. THAT WAS JACK'S LONGEST RELATIONSHIP WITH A BROOKPORT GIRL.
UH-HUH.
SO ARE YOU GOING TO DUMP HIM?
UGH, I DON'T KNOW, HARRIET!

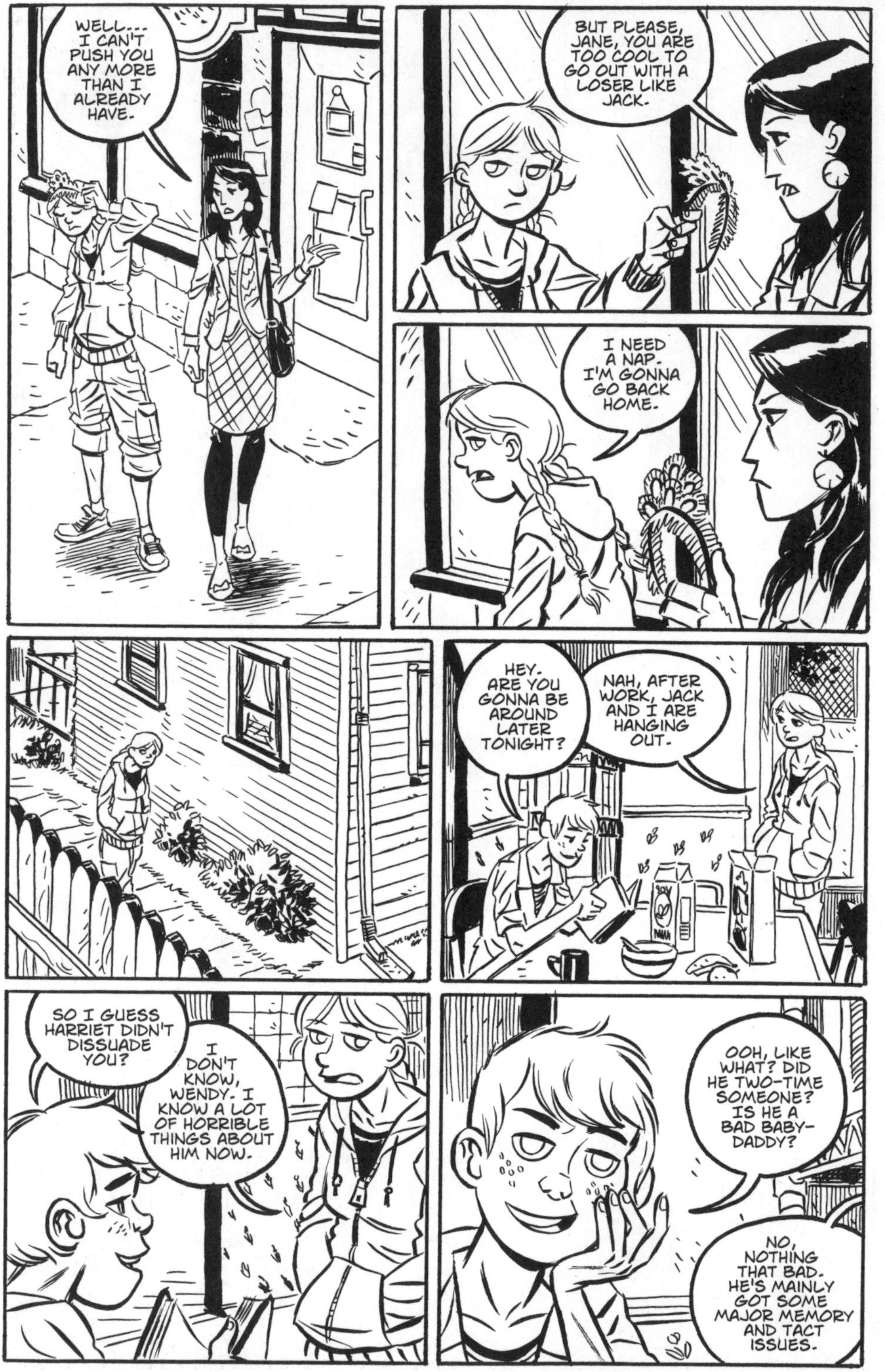
WELL... I CAN'T PUSH YOU ANY MORE THAN I ALREADY HAVE.
BUT PLEASE, JANE, YOU ARE TOO COOL TO GO OUT WITH A LOSER LIKE JACK.
I NEED A NAP. I'M GONNA GO BACK HOME.
HEY. ARE YOU GONNA BE AROUND LATER TONIGHT?
NAH, AFTER WORK, JACK AND I ARE HANGING OUT.
SO I GUESS HARRIET DIDN'T DISSUADE YOU?
I DON'T KNOW, WENDY. I KNOW A LOT OF HORRIBLE THINGS ABOUT HIM NOW.
OOH, LIKE WHAT? DID HE TWO-TIME SOMEONE? IS HE A BAD BABY-DADDY?
NO, NOTHING THAT BAD. HE'S MAINLY GOT SOME MAJOR MEMORY AND TACT ISSUES.

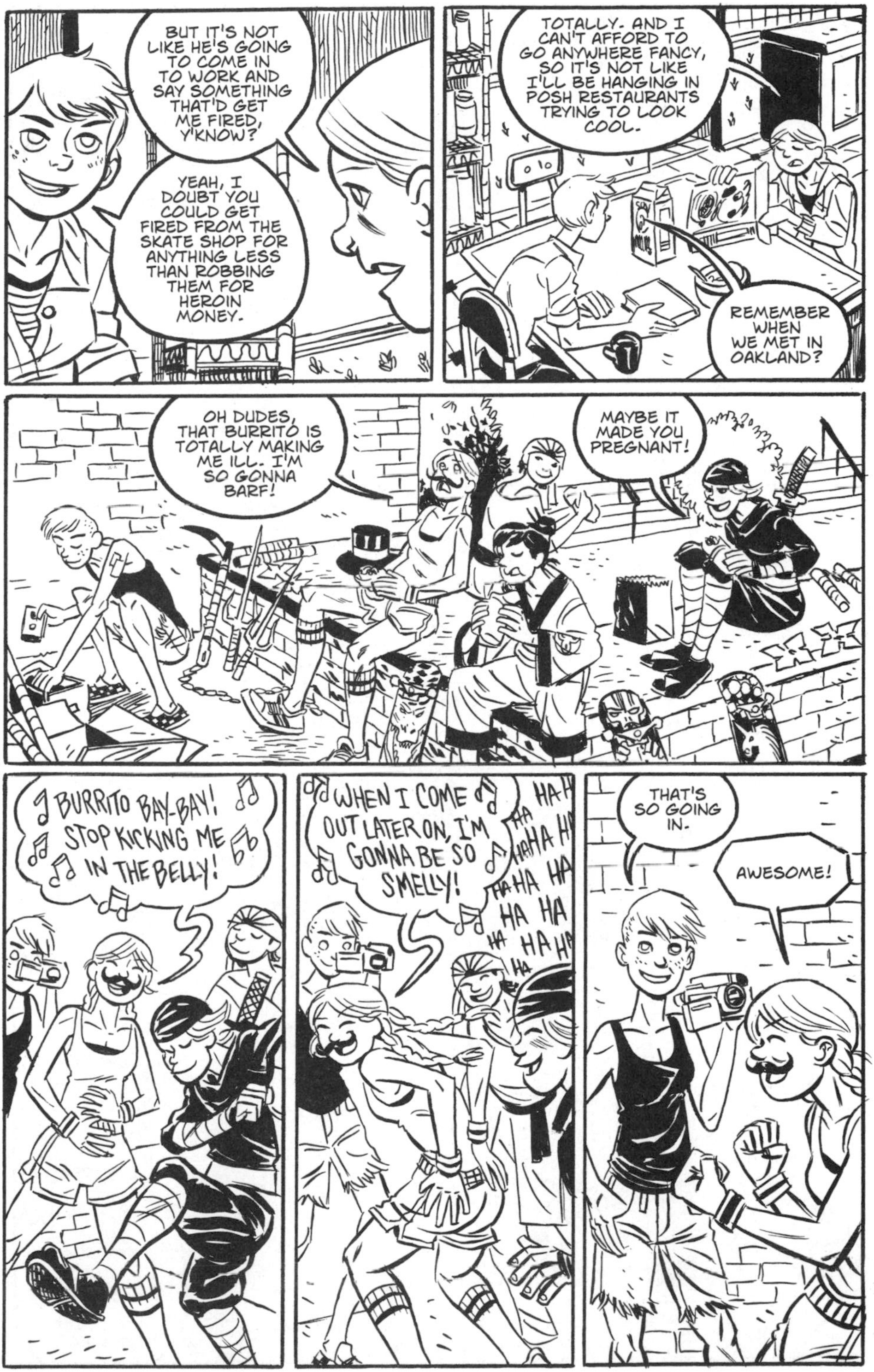
BUT IT'S NOT LIKE HE'S GOING TO COME IN TO WORK AND SAY SOMETHING THAT'D GET ME FIRED, Y'KNOW?
YEAH, I DOUBT YOU COULD GET FIRED FROM THE SKATE SHOP FOR ANYTHING LESS THAN ROBBING THEM FOR HEROIN MONEY.
TOTALLY. AND I CAN'T AFFORD TO GO ANYWHERE FANCY, SO IT'S NOT LIKE I'LL BE HANGING IN POSH RESTAURANTS TRYING TO LOOK COOL.
REMEMBER WHEN WE MET IN OAKLAND?
OH DUDES, THAT BURRITO IS TOTALLY MAKING ME ILL. I'M SO GONNA BARF!
MAYBE IT MADE YOU PREGNANT!
BURRITO BAY-BAY! STOP KICKING ME IN THE BELLY!
WHEN I COME OUT LATER ON, I'M GONNA BE SO SMELLY!
HA HA HA HA HA HA HA HA HA HA HA HA HA HA HA HA
THAT'S SO GOING IN.
AWESOME!

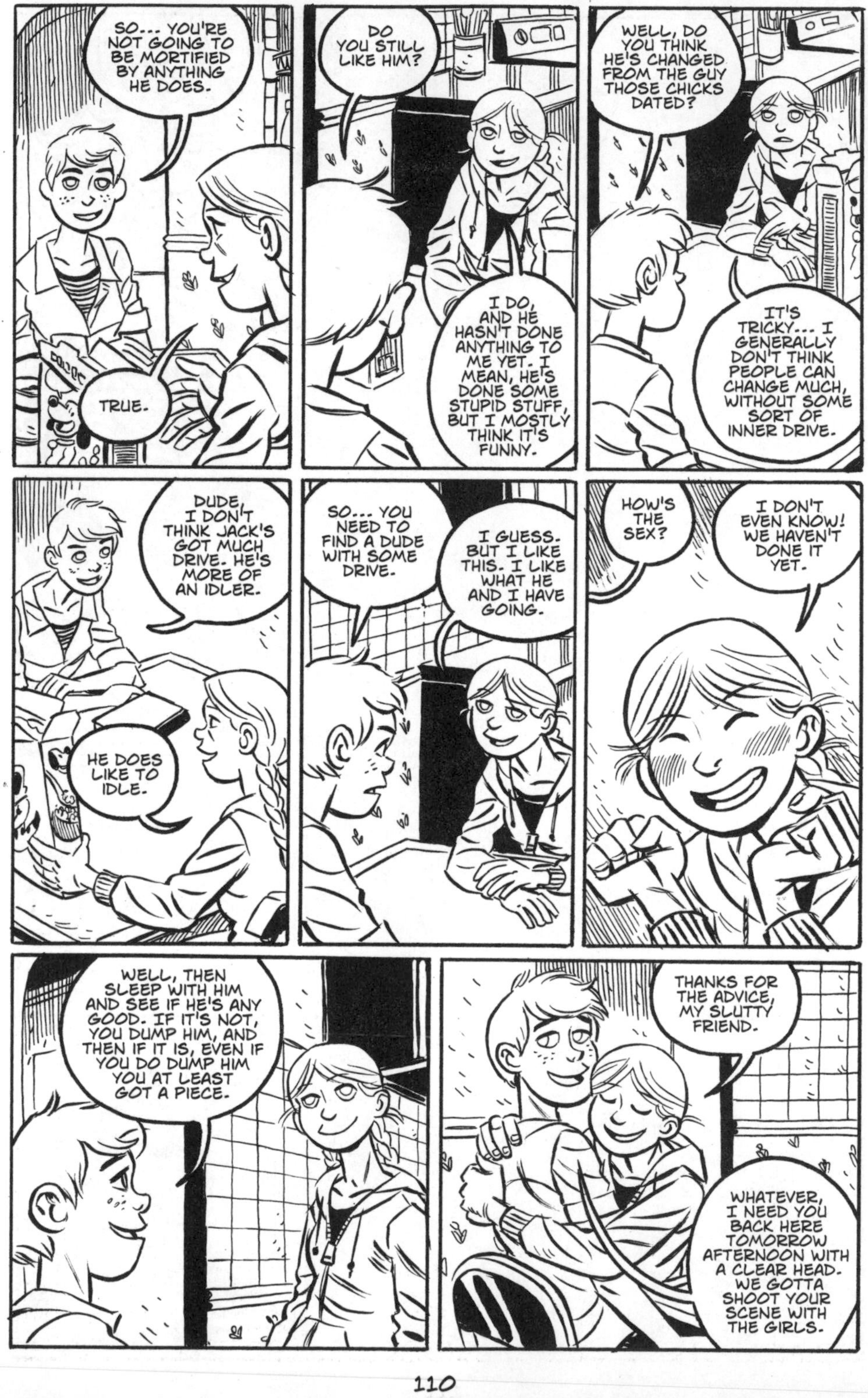

SO... YOU'RE NOT GOING TO BE MORTIFIED BY ANYTHING HE DOES.
TRUE.
DO YOU STILL LIKE HIM?
I DO, AND HE HASN'T DONE ANYTHING TO ME YET. I MEAN, HE'S DONE SOME STUPID STUFF, BUT I MOSTLY THINK IT'S FUNNY.
WELL, DO YOU THINK HE'S CHANGED FROM THE GUY THOSE CHICKS DATED?
IT'S TRICKY... I GENERALLY DON'T THINK PEOPLE CAN CHANGE MUCH, WITHOUT SOME SORT OF INNER DRIVE.
DUDE, I DON'T THINK JACK'S GOT MUCH DRIVE. HE'S MORE OF AN IDLER.
HE DOES LIKE TO IDLE.
SO... YOU NEED TO FIND A DUDE WITH SOME DRIVE.
I GUESS. BUT I LIKE THIS. I LIKE WHAT HE AND I HAVE GOING.
HOW'S THE SEX?
I DON'T EVEN KNOW! WE HAVEN'T DONE IT YET.
WELL, THEN SLEEP WITH HIM AND SEE IF HE'S ANY GOOD. IF IT'S NOT, YOU DUMP HIM, AND THEN IF IT IS, EVEN IF YOU DO DUMP HIM YOU AT LEAST GOT A PIECE.
THANKS FOR THE ADVICE, MY SLUTTY FRIEND.
WHATEVER, I NEED YOU BACK HERE TOMORROW AFTERNOON WITH A CLEAR HEAD. WE GOTTA SHOOT YOUR SCENE WITH THE GIRLS.

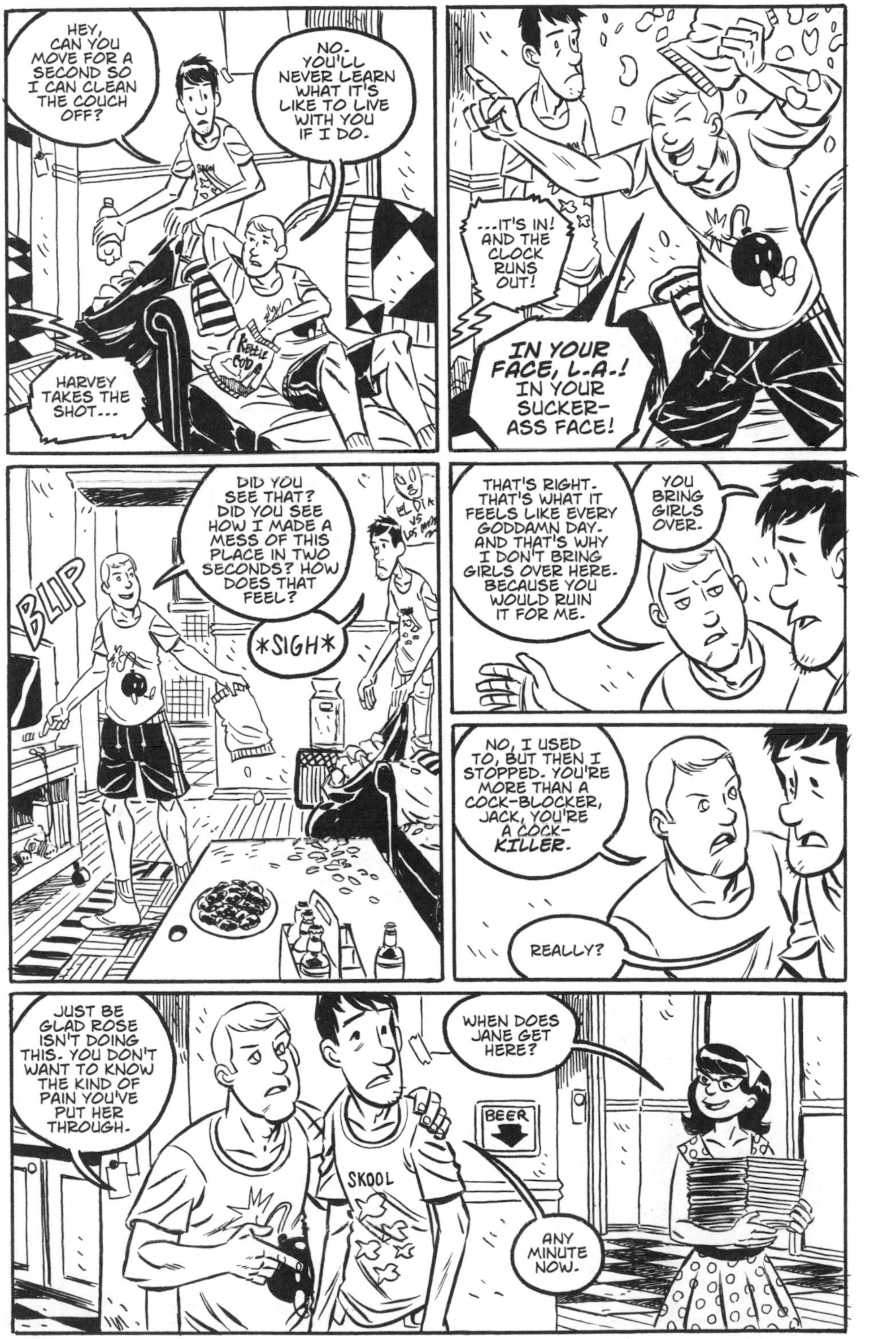
HEY, CAN YOU MOVE FOR A SECOND SO I CAN CLEAN THE COUCH OFF?
NO. YOU'LL NEVER LEARN WHAT IT'S LIKE TO LIVE WITH YOU IF I DO.
HARVEY TAKES THE SHOT...
...IT'S IN! AND THE CLOCK RUNS OUT!
IN YOUR FACE, L.A.! IN YOUR SUCKER-ASS FACE!
BLIP
DID YOU SEE THAT? DID YOU SEE HOW I MADE A MESS OF THIS PLACE IN TWO SECONDS? HOW DOES THAT FEEL?
SIGH
THAT'S RIGHT. THAT'S WHAT IT FEELS LIKE EVERY GODDAMN DAY. AND THAT'S WHY I DON'T BRING GIRLS OVER HERE. BECAUSE YOU WOULD RUIN IT FOR ME.
YOU BRING GIRLS OVER.
NO, I USED TO, BUT THEN I STOPPED. YOU'RE MORE THAN A COCK-BLOCKER, JACK, YOU'RE A COCK-KILLER.
REALLY?
JUST BE GLAD ROSE ISN'T DOING THIS. YOU DON'T WANT TO KNOW THE KIND OF PAIN YOU'VE PUT HER THROUGH.
WHEN DOES JANE GET HERE?
BEER
SKOOL
ANY MINUTE NOW.

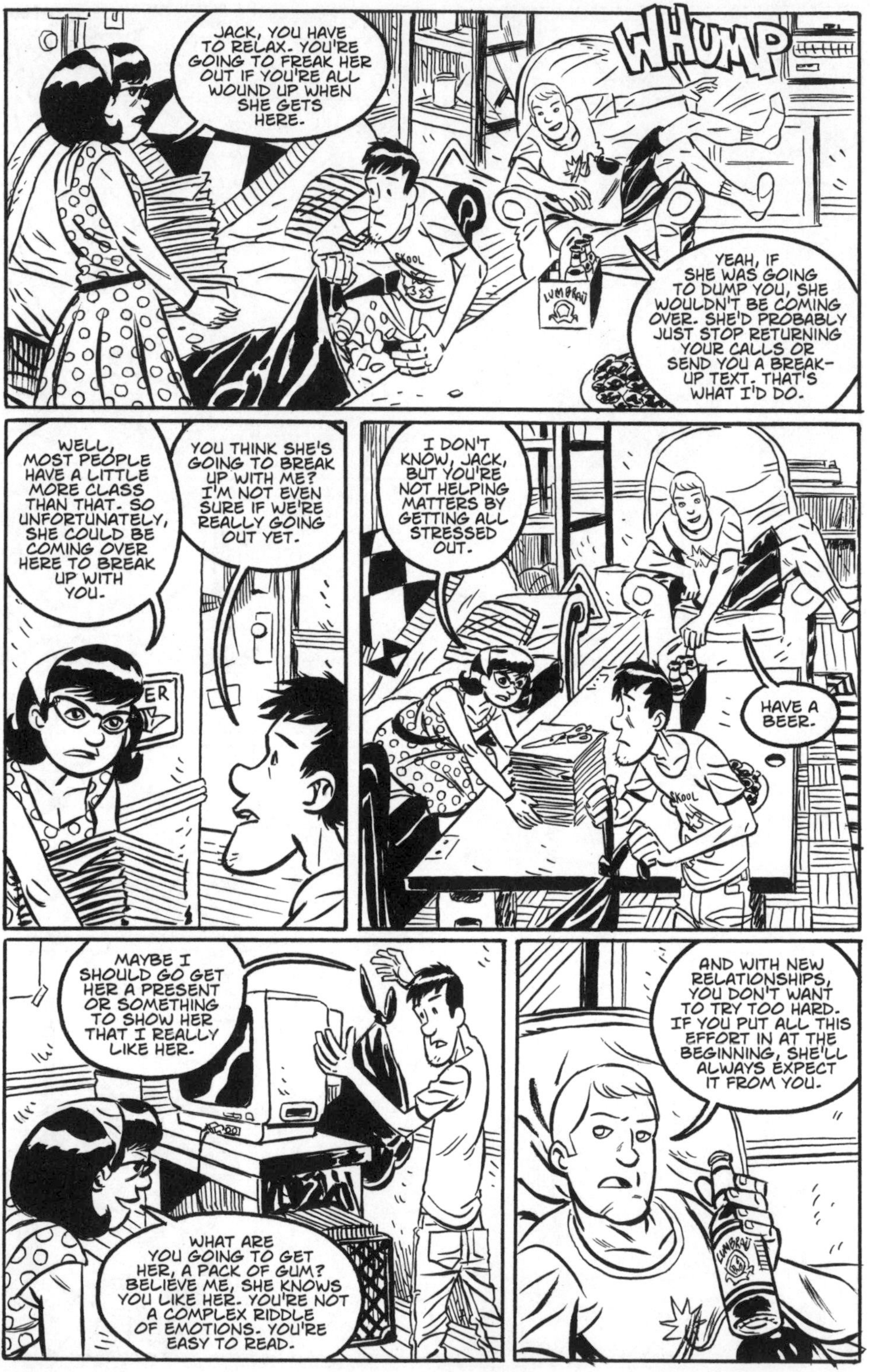
WHUMP
JACK, YOU HAVE TO RELAX. YOU'RE GOING TO FREAK HER OUT IF YOU'RE ALL WOUND UP WHEN SHE GETS HERE.
YEAH, IF SHE WAS GOING TO DUMP YOU, SHE WOULDN'T BE COMING OVER. SHE'D PROBABLY JUST STOP RETURNING YOUR CALLS OR SEND YOU A BREAK-UP TEXT. THAT'S WHAT I'D DO.
WELL, MOST PEOPLE HAVE A LITTLE MORE CLASS THAN THAT. SO UNFORTUNATELY, SHE COULD BE COMING OVER HERE TO BREAK UP WITH YOU.
YOU THINK SHE'S GOING TO BREAK UP WITH ME? I'M NOT EVEN SURE IF WE'RE REALLY GOING OUT YET.
I DON'T KNOW, JACK, BUT YOU'RE NOT HELPING MATTERS BY GETTING ALL STRESSED OUT.
HAVE A BEER.
MAYBE I SHOULD GO GET HER A PRESENT OR SOMETHING TO SHOW HER THAT I REALLY LIKE HER.
WHAT ARE YOU GOING TO GET HER, A PACK OF GUM? BELIEVE ME, SHE KNOWS YOU LIKE HER. YOU'RE NOT A COMPLEX RIDDLE OF EMOTIONS. YOU'RE EASY TO READ.
AND WITH NEW RELATIONSHIPS, YOU DON'T WANT TO TRY TOO HARD. IF YOU PUT ALL THIS EFFORT IN AT THE BEGINNING, SHE'LL ALWAYS EXPECT IT FROM YOU.

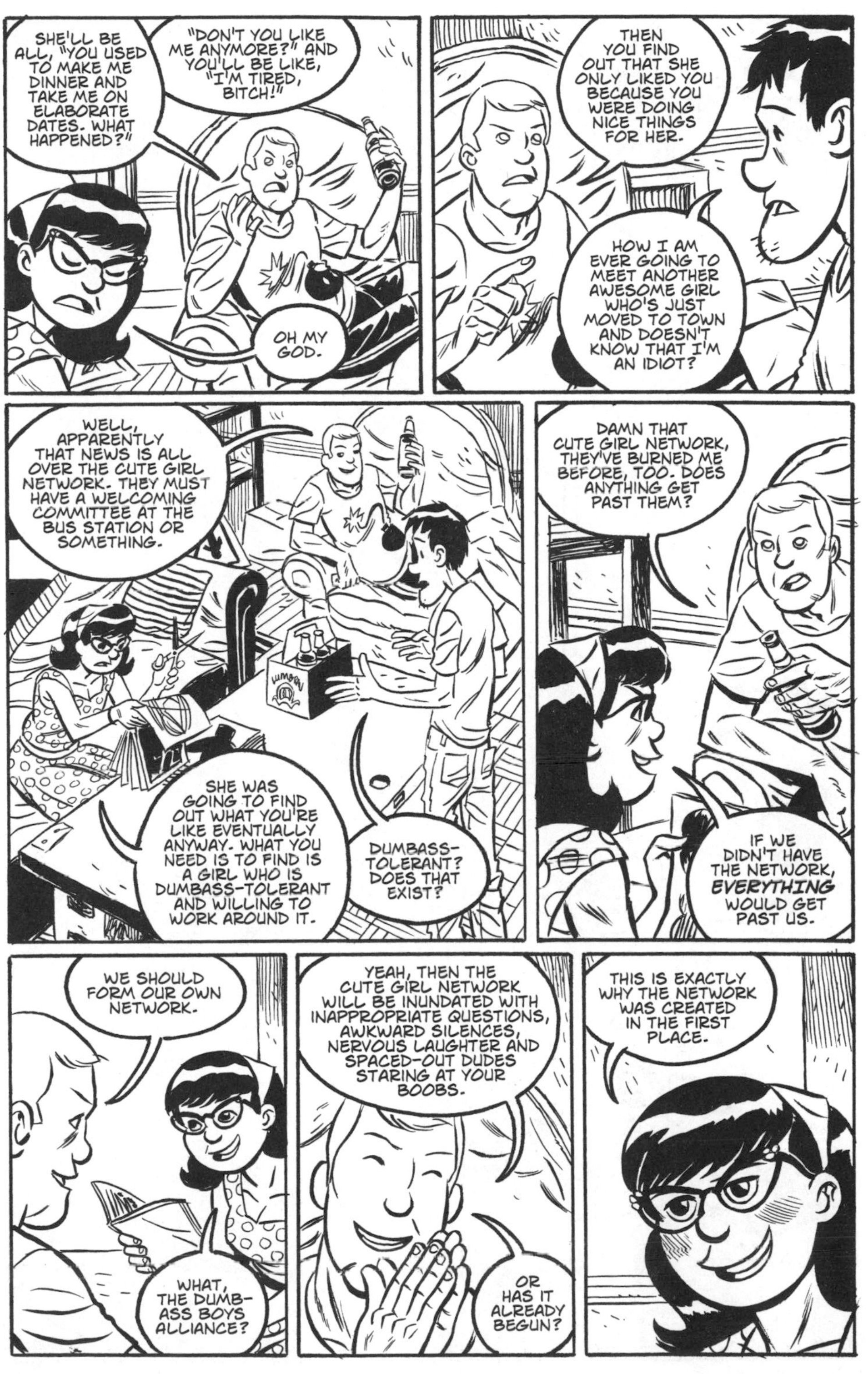
SHE'LL BE ALL, "YOU USED TO MAKE ME DINNER AND TAKE ME ON ELABORATE DATES. WHAT HAPPENED?"
"DON'T YOU LIKE ME ANYMORE?" AND YOU'LL BE LIKE, "I'M TIRED, BITCH!"
OH MY GOD.
THEN YOU FIND OUT THAT SHE ONLY LIKED YOU BECAUSE YOU WERE DOING NICE THINGS FOR HER.
HOW I AM EVER GOING TO MEET ANOTHER AWESOME GIRL WHO'S JUST MOVED TO TOWN AND DOESN'T KNOW THAT I'M AN IDIOT?
WELL, APPARENTLY THAT NEWS IS ALL OVER THE CUTE GIRL NETWORK. THEY MUST HAVE A WELCOMING COMMITTEE AT THE BUS STATION OR SOMETHING.
SHE WAS GOING TO FIND OUT WHAT YOU'RE LIKE EVENTUALLY ANYWAY. WHAT YOU NEED IS TO FIND IS A GIRL WHO IS DUMBASS-TOLERANT AND WILLING TO WORK AROUND IT.
DUMBASS-TOLERANT? DOES THAT EXIST?
DAMN THAT CUTE GIRL NETWORK, THEY'VE BURNED ME BEFORE, TOO. DOES ANYTHING GET PAST THEM?
IF WE DIDN'T HAVE THE NETWORK, EVERYTHING WOULD GET PAST US.
WE SHOULD FORM OUR OWN NETWORK.
WHAT, THE DUMBASS BOYS ALLIANCE?
YEAH, THEN THE CUTE GIRL NETWORK WILL BE INUNDATED WITH INAPPROPRIATE QUESTIONS, AWKWARD SILENCES, NERVOUS LAUGHTER AND SPACED-OUT DUDES STARING AT YOUR BOOBS.
OR HAS IT ALREADY BEGUN?
THIS IS EXACTLY WHY THE NETWORK WAS CREATED IN THE FIRST PLACE.

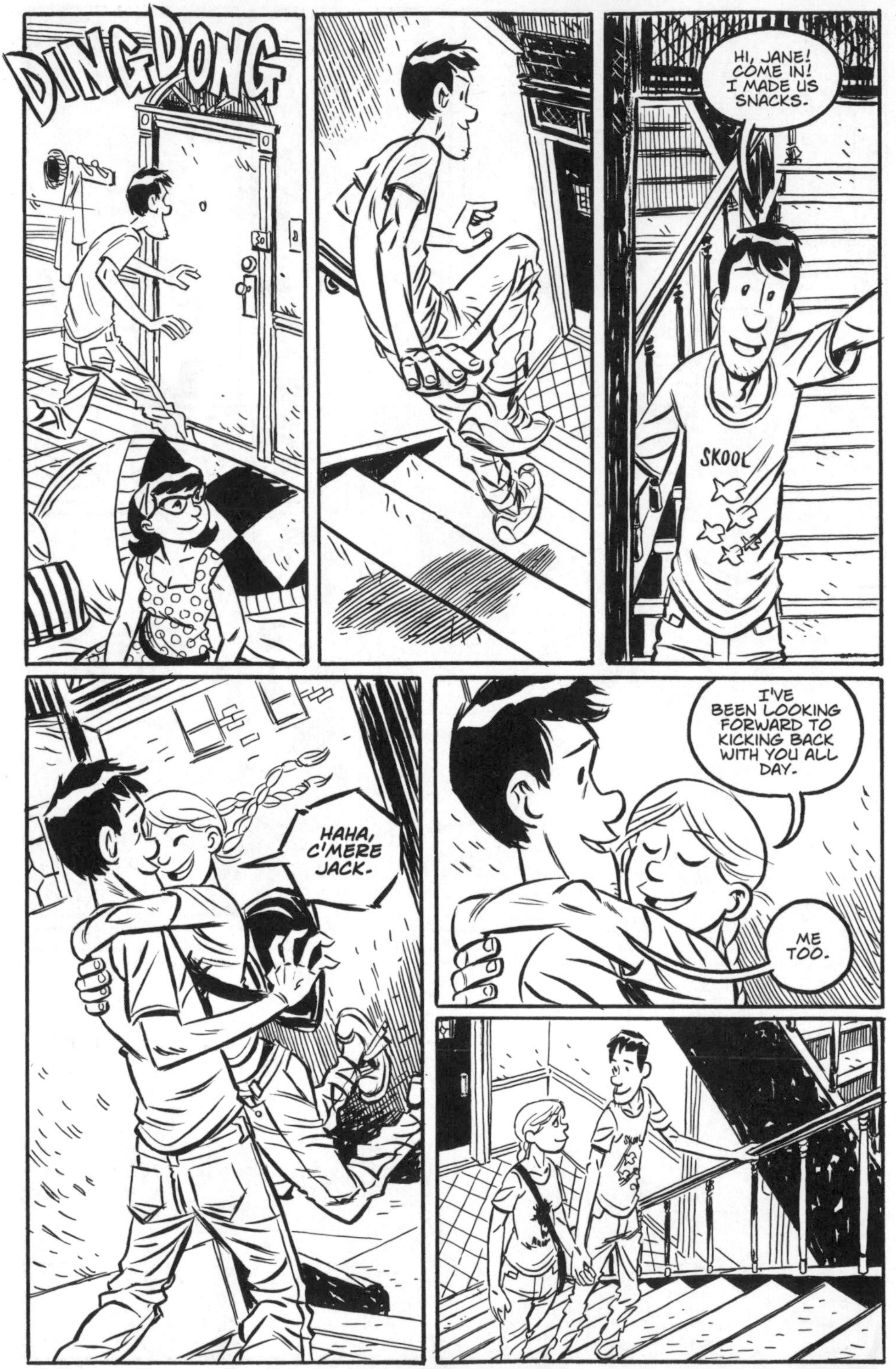
DING DONG
HI, JANE! COME IN! I MADE US SNACKS.
SKOOL
HAHA, C'MERE JACK.
I'VE BEEN LOOKING FORWARD TO KICKING BACK WITH YOU ALL DAY.
ME TOO.

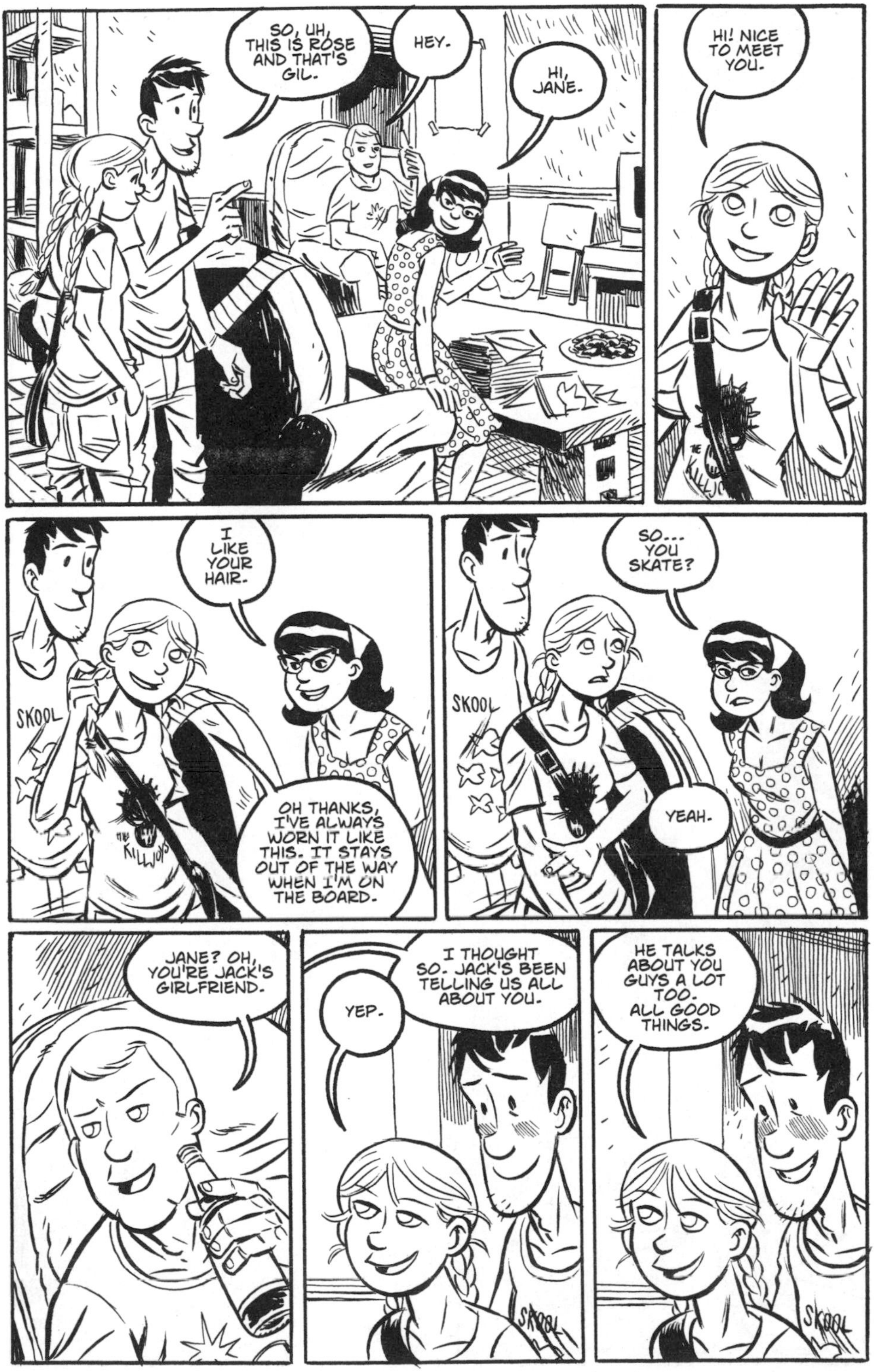
SO, UH, THIS IS ROSE AND THAT'S GIL.
HEY.
HI, JANE.
HI! NICE TO MEET YOU.
I LIKE YOUR HAIR.
OH THANKS, I'VE ALWAYS WORN IT LIKE THIS. IT STAYS OUT OF THE WAY WHEN I'M ON THE BOARD.
SKOOL
THE KILLJOYS
SO... YOU SKATE?
YEAH.
JANE? OH, YOU'RE JACK'S GIRLFRIEND.
YEP.
I THOUGHT SO. JACK'S BEEN TELLING US ALL ABOUT YOU.
HE TALKS ABOUT YOU GUYS A LOT TOO. ALL GOOD THINGS.

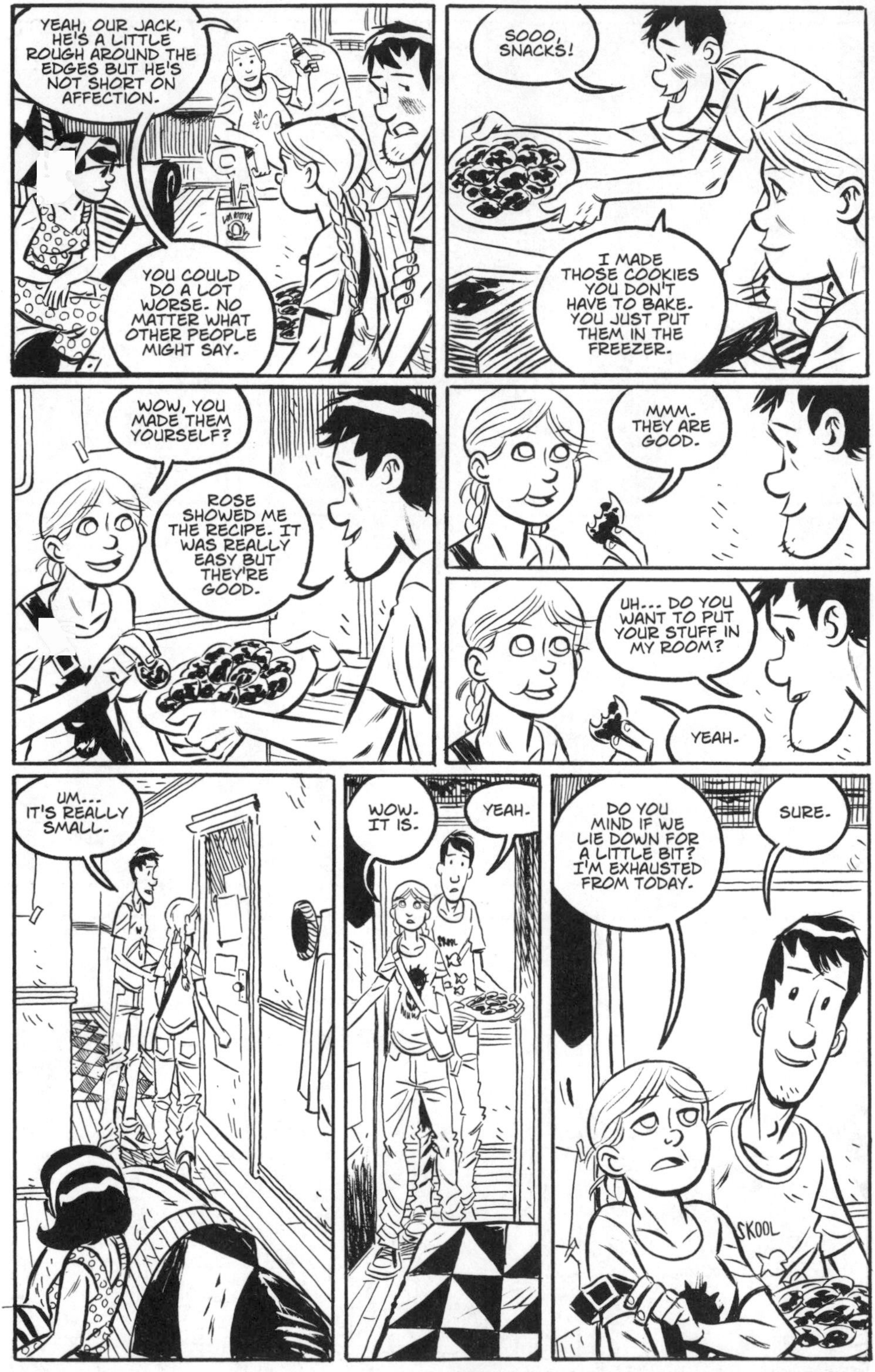
YEAH, OUR JACK, HE'S A LITTLE ROUGH AROUND THE EDGES BUT HE'S NOT SHORT ON AFFECTION.
YOU COULD DO A LOT WORSE. NO MATTER WHAT OTHER PEOPLE MIGHT SAY.
SOOO, SNACKS!
I MADE THOSE COOKIES YOU DON'T HAVE TO BAKE. YOU JUST PUT THEM IN THE FREEZER.
WOW, YOU MADE THEM YOURSELF?
ROSE SHOWED ME THE RECIPE. IT WAS REALLY EASY BUT THEY'RE GOOD.
MMM. THEY ARE GOOD.
UH... DO YOU WANT TO PUT YOUR STUFF IN MY ROOM?
YEAH.
UM... IT'S REALLY SMALL.
WOW. IT IS.
YEAH.
DO YOU MIND IF WE LIE DOWN FOR A LITTLE BIT? I'M EXHAUSTED FROM TODAY.
SURE.
SKOOL

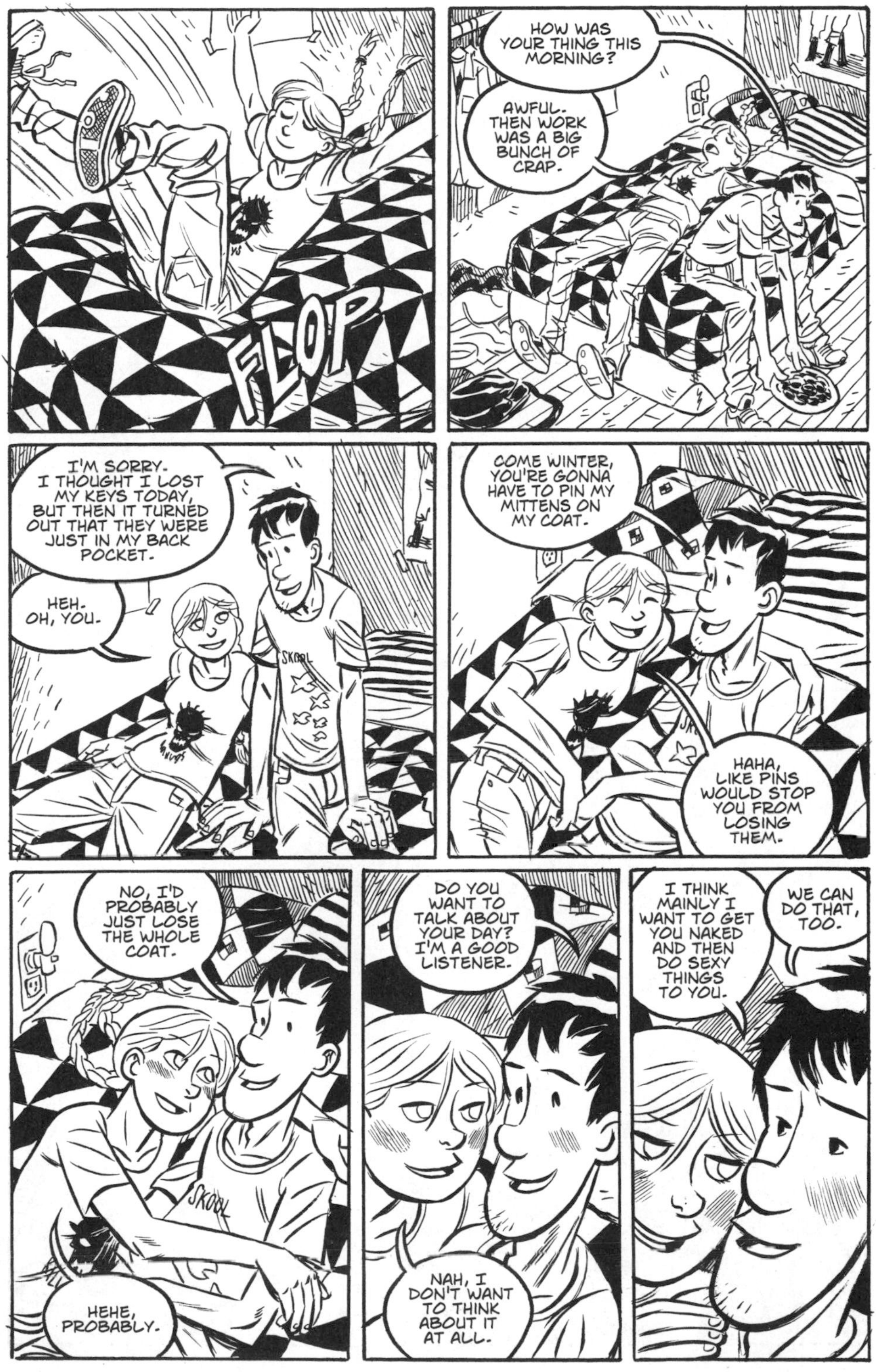
FLOP
HOW WAS YOUR THING THIS MORNING?
AWFUL. THEN WORK WAS A BIG BUNCH OF CRAP.
I'M SORRY. I THOUGHT I LOST MY KEYS TODAY, BUT THEN IT TURNED OUT THAT THEY WERE JUST IN MY BACK POCKET.
HEH. OH, YOU.
SKOOL
COME WINTER, YOU'RE GONNA HAVE TO PIN MY MITTENS ON MY COAT.
HAHA, LIKE PINS WOULD STOP YOU FROM LOSING THEM.
NO, I'D PROBABLY JUST LOSE THE WHOLE COAT.
SKOOL
HEHE, PROBABLY.
DO YOU WANT TO TALK ABOUT YOUR DAY? I'M A GOOD LISTENER.
NAH, I DON'T WANT TO THINK ABOUT IT AT ALL.
I THINK MAINLY I WANT TO GET YOU NAKED AND THEN DO SEXY THINGS TO YOU.
WE CAN DO THAT, TOO.

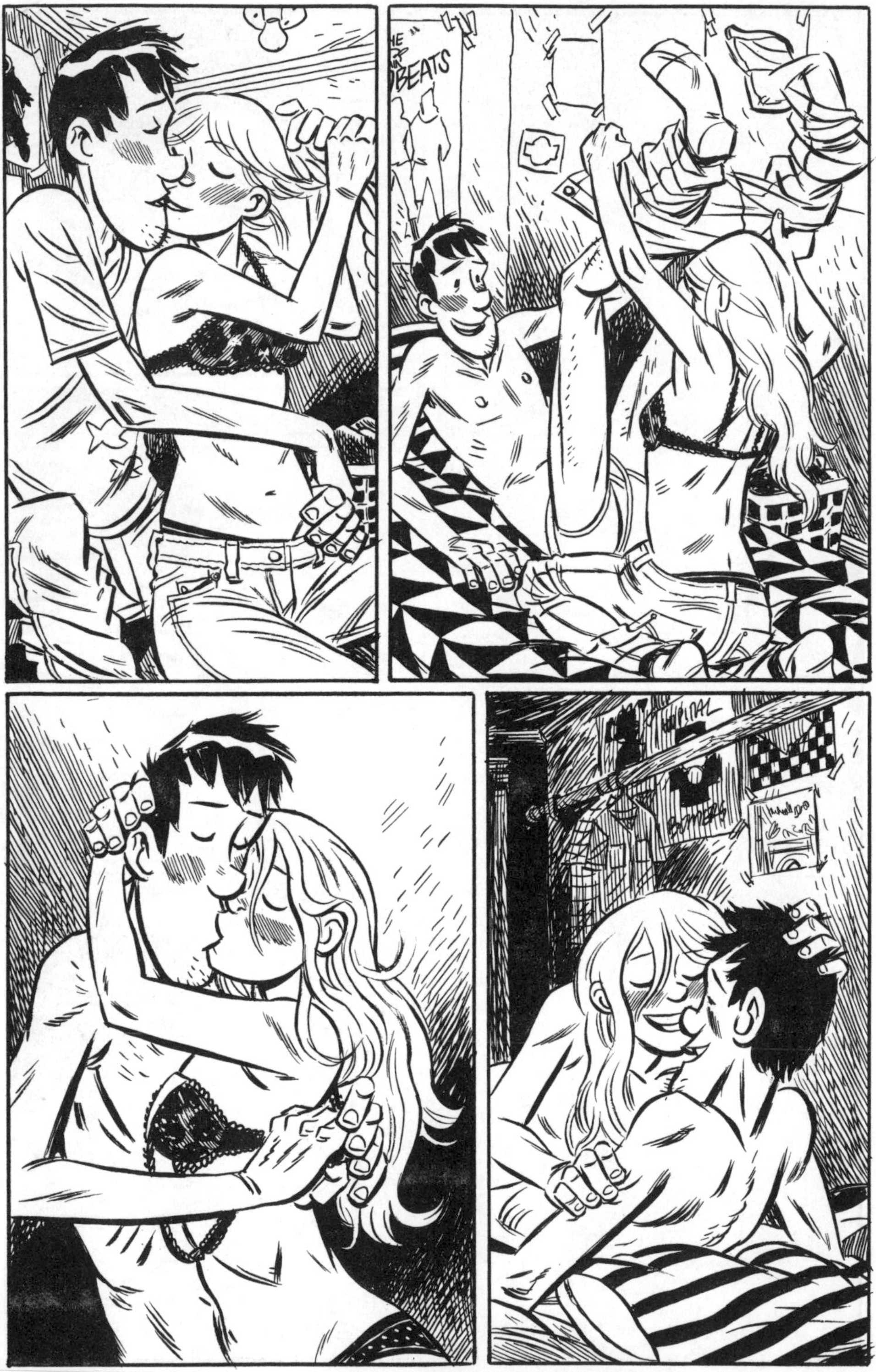

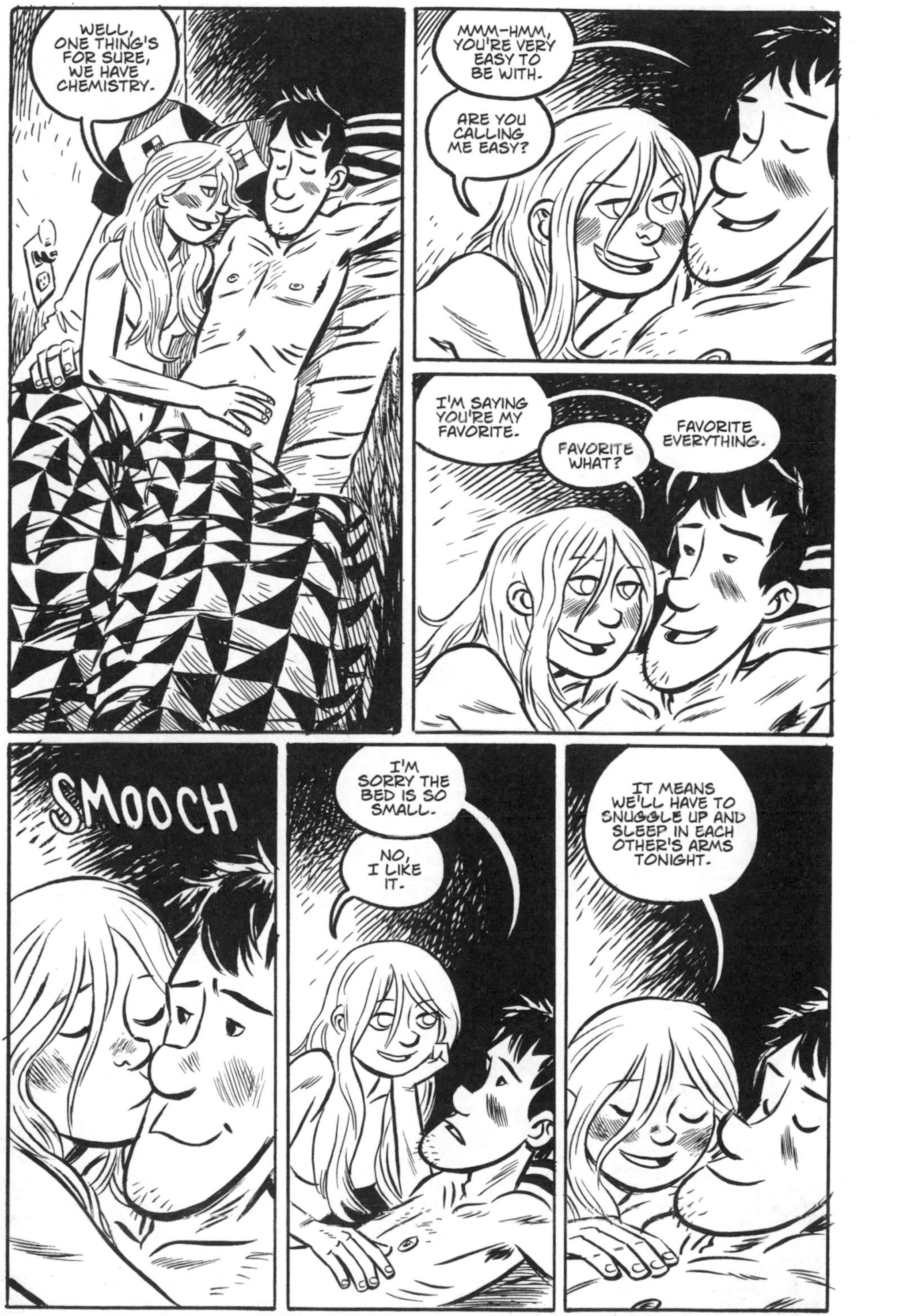
WELL, ONE THING'S FOR SURE, WE HAVE CHEMISTRY.
MMM-HMM, YOU'RE VERY EASY TO BE WITH.
ARE YOU CALLING ME EASY?
I'M SAYING YOU'RE MY FAVORITE.
FAVORITE WHAT?
FAVORITE EVERYTHING.
SMOOCH
I'M SORRY THE BED IS SO SMALL.
NO, I LIKE IT.
IT MEANS WE'LL HAVE TO SNUGGLE UP AND SLEEP IN EACH OTHER'S ARMS TONIGHT.

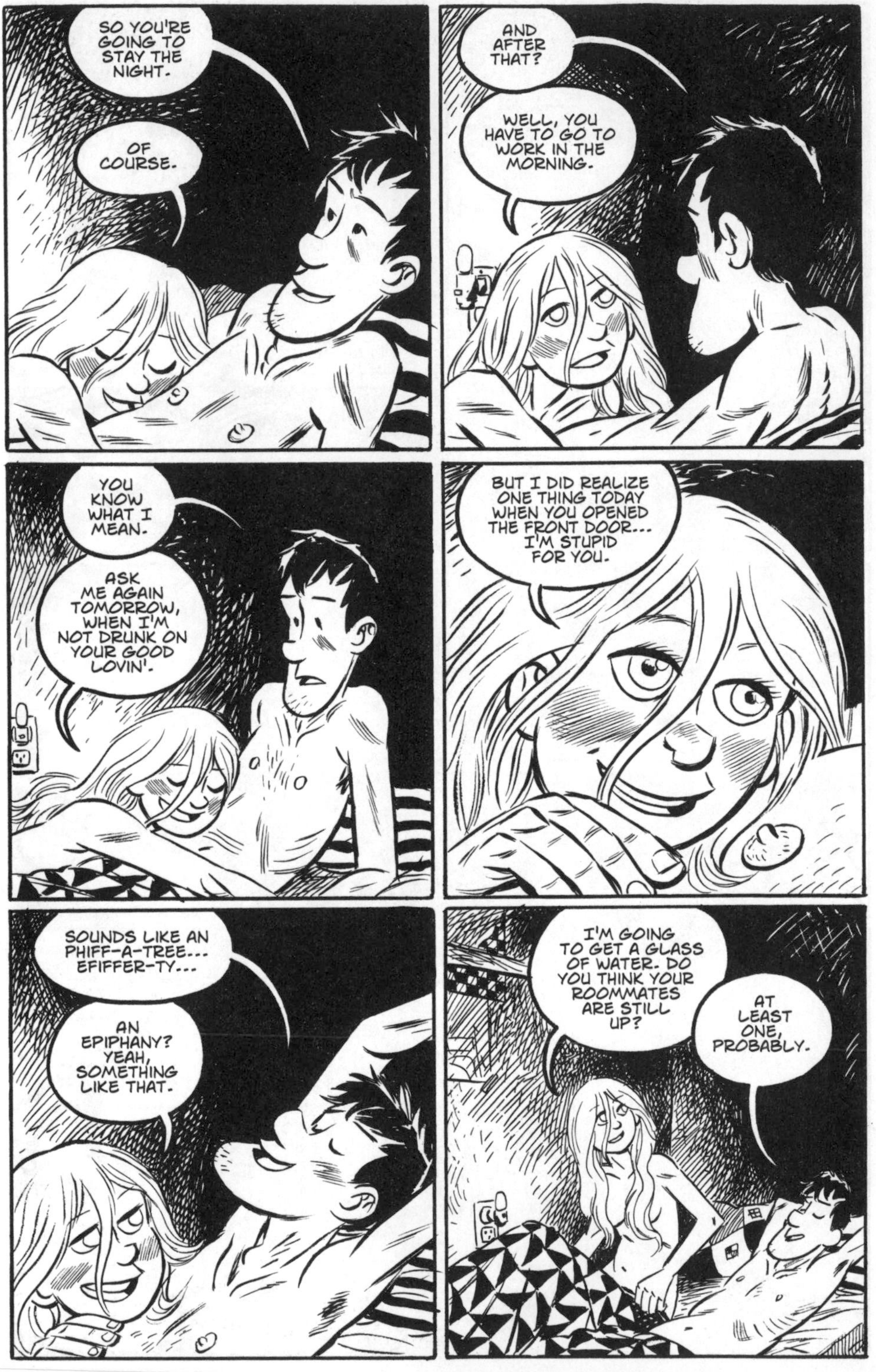
SO YOU'RE GOING TO STAY THE NIGHT.
OF COURSE.
AND AFTER THAT?
WELL, YOU HAVE TO GO TO WORK IN THE MORNING.
YOU KNOW WHAT I MEAN.
ASK ME AGAIN TOMORROW, WHEN I'M NOT DRUNK ON YOUR GOOD LOVIN'.
BUT I DID REALIZE ONE THING TODAY WHEN YOU OPENED THE FRONT DOOR... I'M STUPID FOR YOU.
SOUNDS LIKE AN PHIFF-A-TREE... EFIFFER-TY...
AN EPIPHANY? YEAH, SOMETHING LIKE THAT.
I'M GOING TO GET A GLASS OF WATER. DO YOU THINK YOUR ROOMMATES ARE STILL UP?
AT LEAST ONE, PROBABLY.

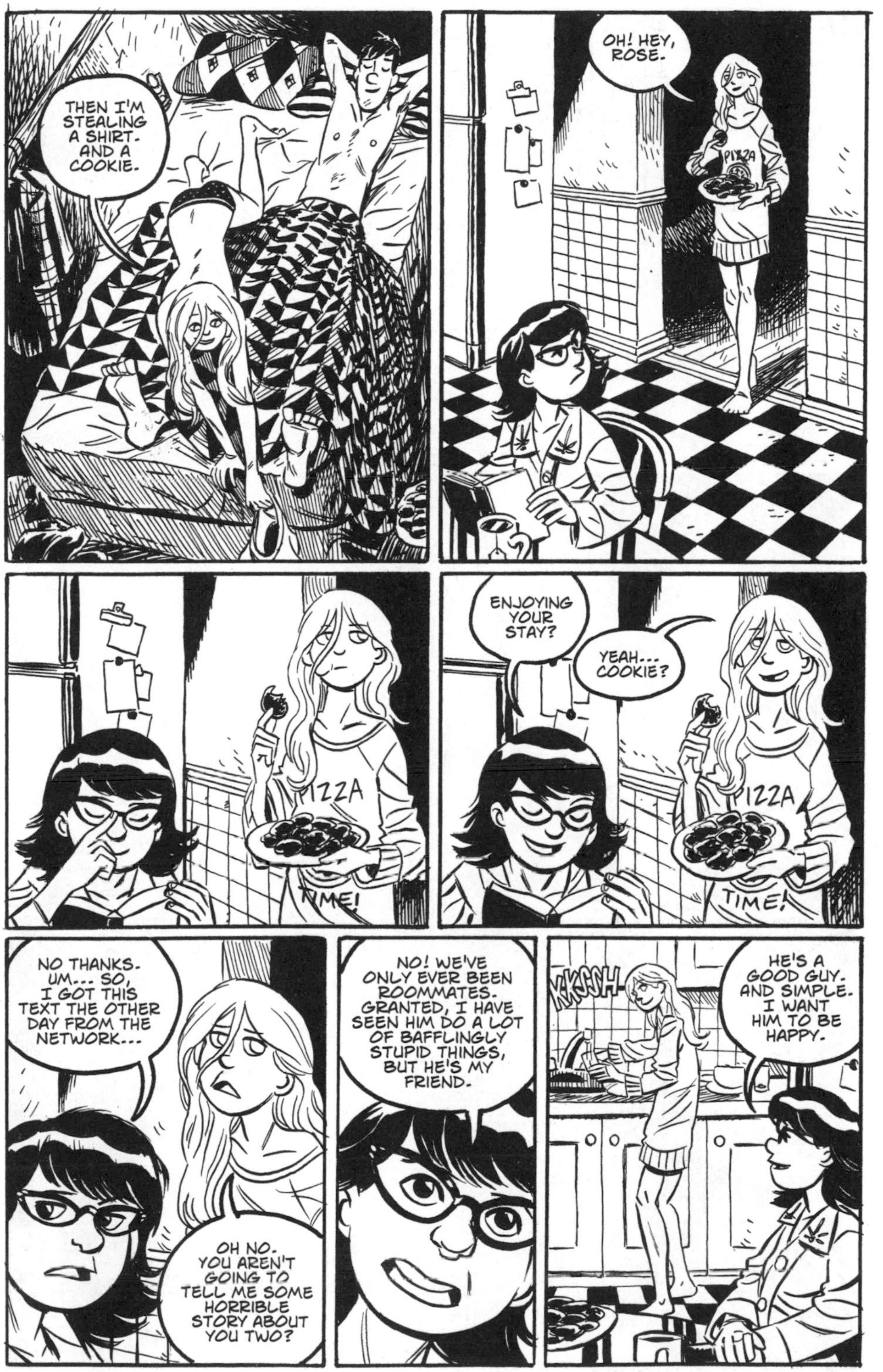
THEN I'M STEALING A SHIRT. AND A COOKIE.
OH! HEY, ROSE.
PIZZA
PIZZA TIME!
ENJOYING YOUR STAY?
YEAH... COOKIE?
PIZZA TIME!
NO THANKS. UM... SO, I GOT THIS TEXT THE OTHER DAY FROM THE NETWORK...
OH NO. YOU AREN'T GOING TO TELL ME SOME HORRIBLE STORY ABOUT YOU TWO?
NO! WE'VE ONLY EVER BEEN ROOMMATES. GRANTED, I HAVE SEEN HIM DO A LOT OF BAFFLINGLY STUPID THINGS, BUT HE'S MY FRIEND.
KKSSH
HE'S A GOOD GUY. AND SIMPLE. I WANT HIM TO BE HAPPY.

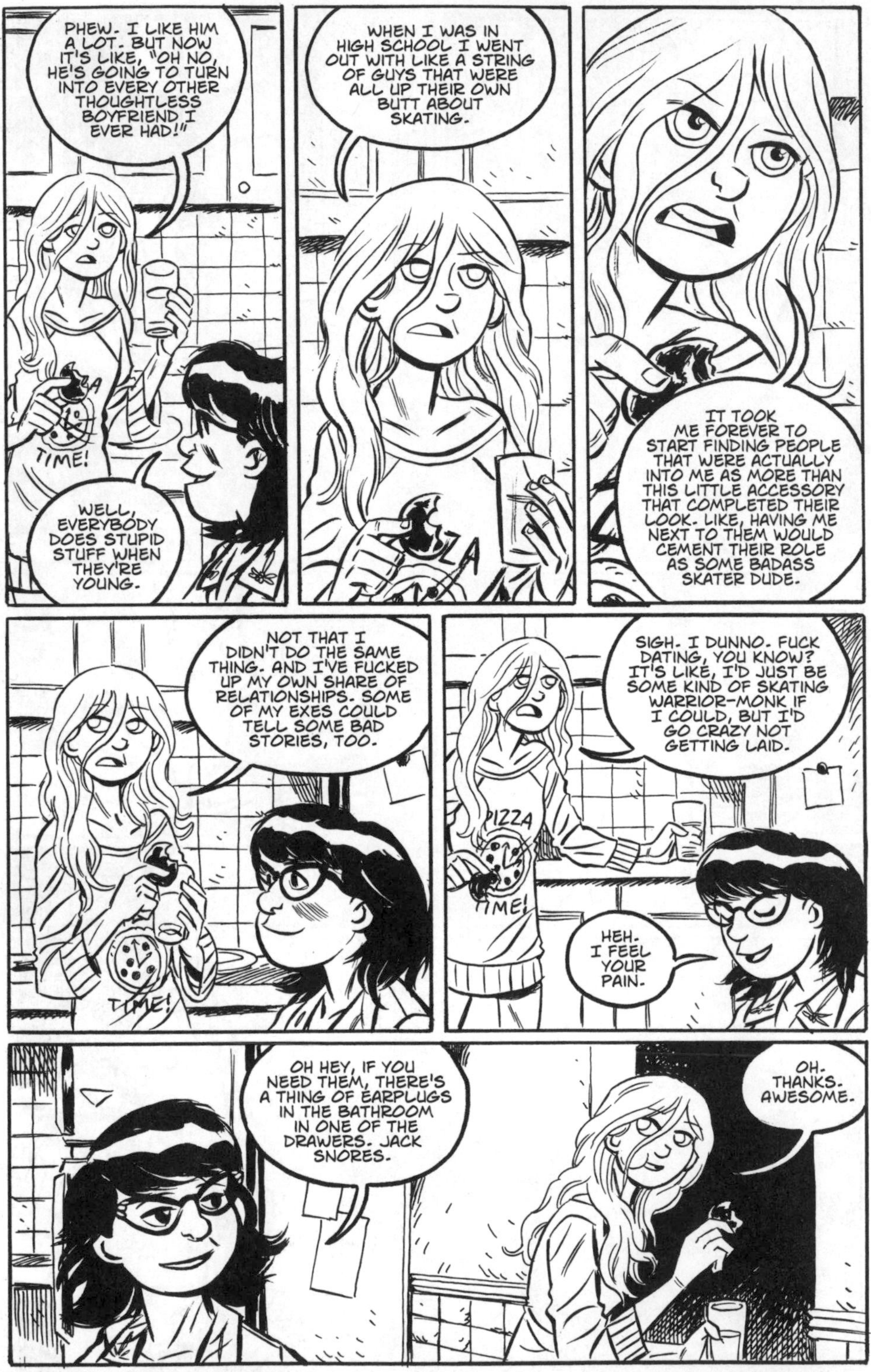
PHEW. I LIKE HIM A LOT. BUT NOW IT'S LIKE, "OH NO, HE'S GOING TO TURN INTO EVERY OTHER THOUGHTLESS BOYFRIEND I EVER HAD!"
PIZZA TIME!
WELL, EVERYBODY DOES STUPID STUFF WHEN THEY'RE YOUNG.
WHEN I WAS IN HIGH SCHOOL I WENT OUT WITH LIKE A STRING OF GUYS THAT WERE ALL UP THEIR OWN BUTT ABOUT SKATING.
IT TOOK ME FOREVER TO START FINDING PEOPLE THAT WERE ACTUALLY INTO ME AS MORE THAN THIS LITTLE ACCESSORY THAT COMPLETED THEIR LOOK. LIKE, HAVING ME NEXT TO THEM WOULD CEMENT THEIR ROLE AS SOME BADASS SKATER DUDE.
NOT THAT I DIDN'T DO THE SAME THING. AND I'VE FUCKED UP MY OWN SHARE OF RELATIONSHIPS. SOME OF MY EXES COULD TELL SOME BAD STORIES, TOO.
TIME!
SIGH. I DUNNO. FUCK DATING, YOU KNOW? IT'S LIKE, I'D JUST BE SOME KIND OF SKATING WARRIOR-MONK IF I COULD, BUT I'D GO CRAZY NOT GETTING LAID.
PIZZA TIME!
HEH. I FEEL YOUR PAIN.
OH HEY, IF YOU NEED THEM, THERE'S A THING OF EARPLUGS IN THE BATHROOM IN ONE OF THE DRAWERS. JACK SNORES.
OH. THANKS. AWESOME.

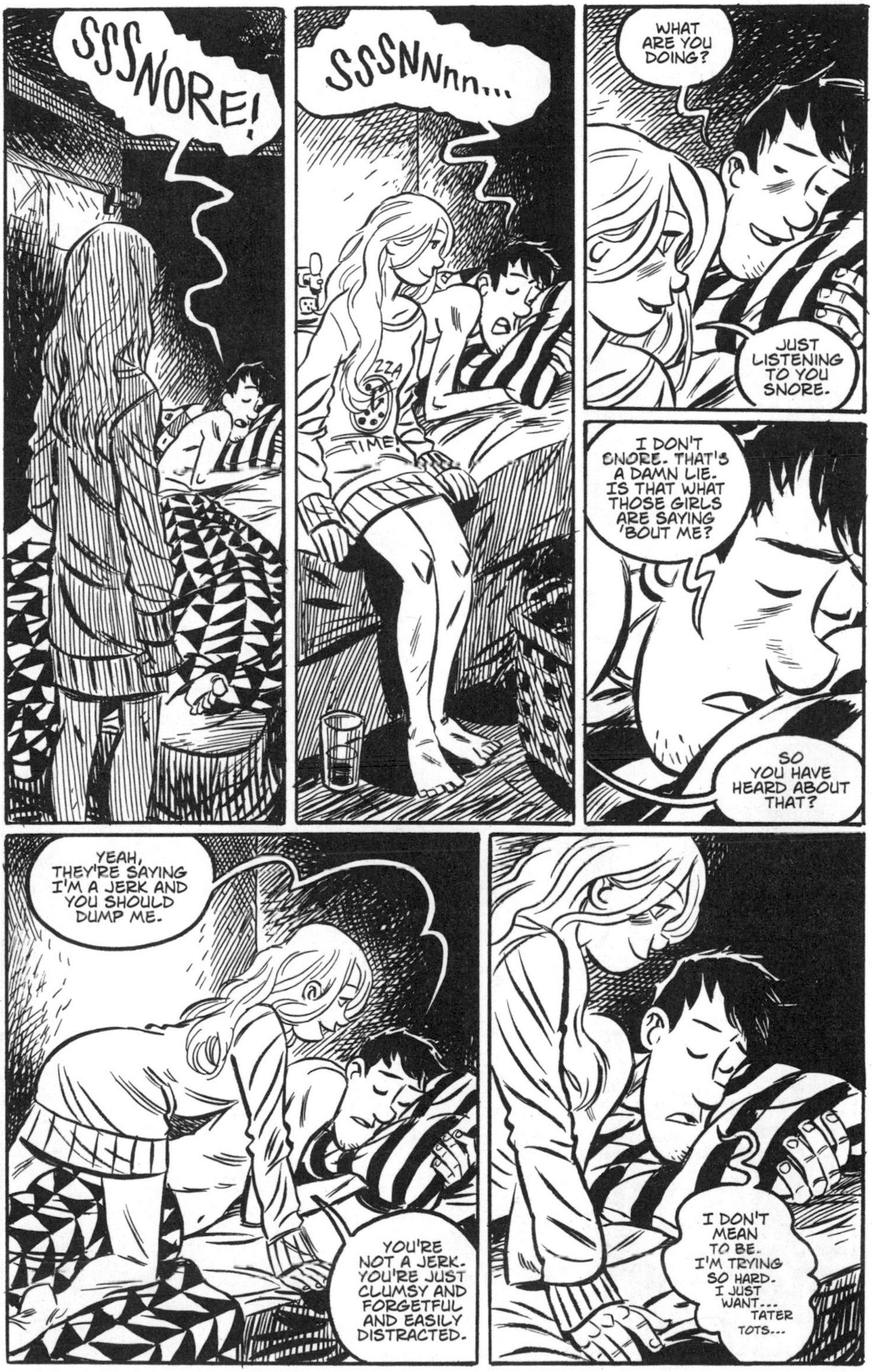
SSSNORE!
SSSNNnn...
ZZA
TIME
WHAT ARE YOU DOING?
JUST LISTENING TO YOU SNORE.
I DON'T SNORE. THAT'S A DAMN LIE. IS THAT WHAT THOSE GIRLS ARE SAYING 'BOUT ME?
SO YOU HAVE HEARD ABOUT THAT?
YEAH, THEY'RE SAYING I'M A JERK AND YOU SHOULD DUMP ME.
YOU'RE NOT A JERK. YOU'RE JUST CLUMSY AND FORGETFUL AND EASILY DISTRACTED.
I DON'T MEAN TO BE. I'M TRYING SO HARD. I JUST WANT... TATER TOTS...

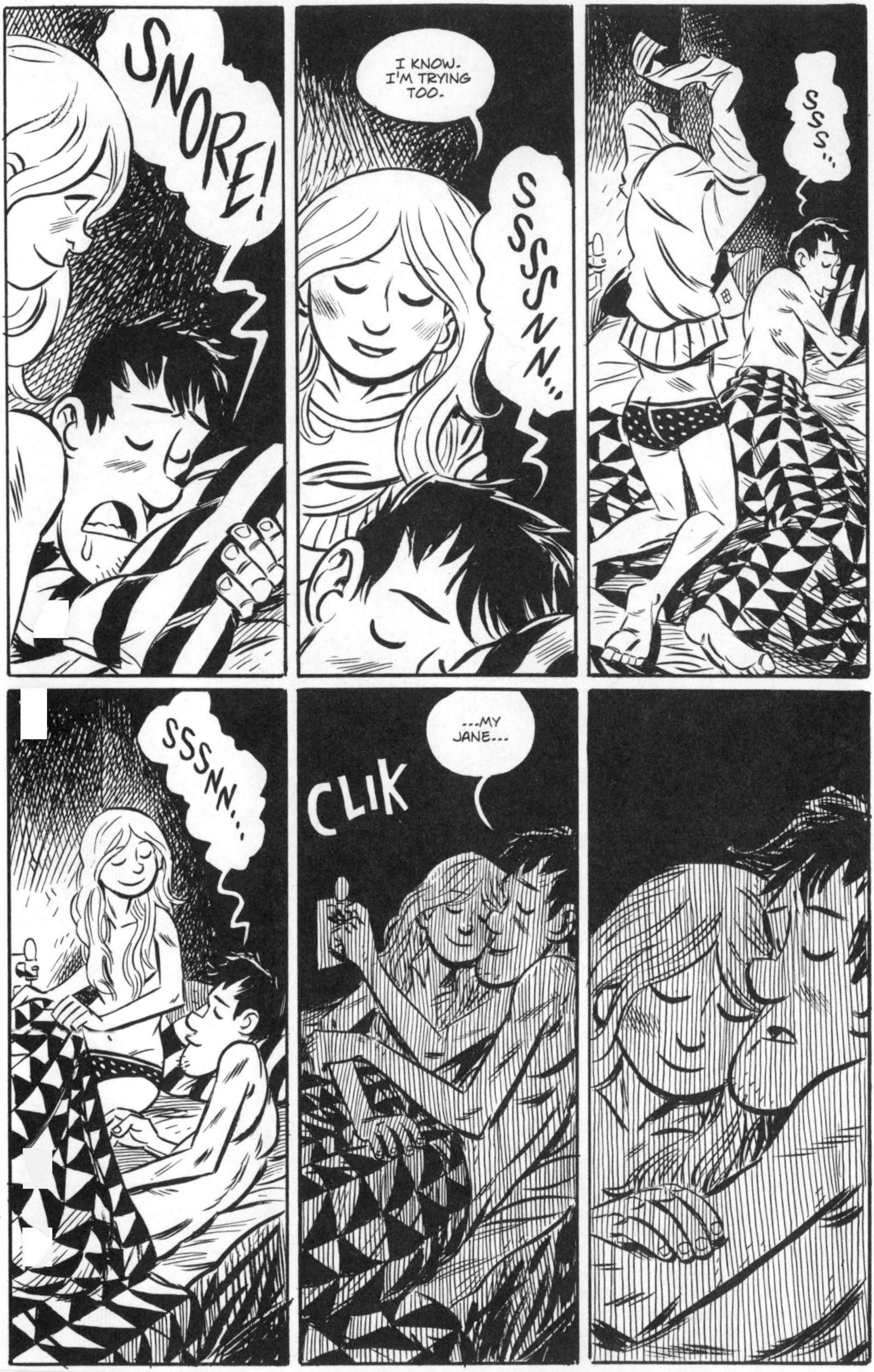
SNORE!
I KNOW. I'M TRYING TOO.
SSSSNN...
SSS...
SSSNN...
CLIK
...MY JANE...

CHAPTER SIX

"My Life with the Garbage Man"

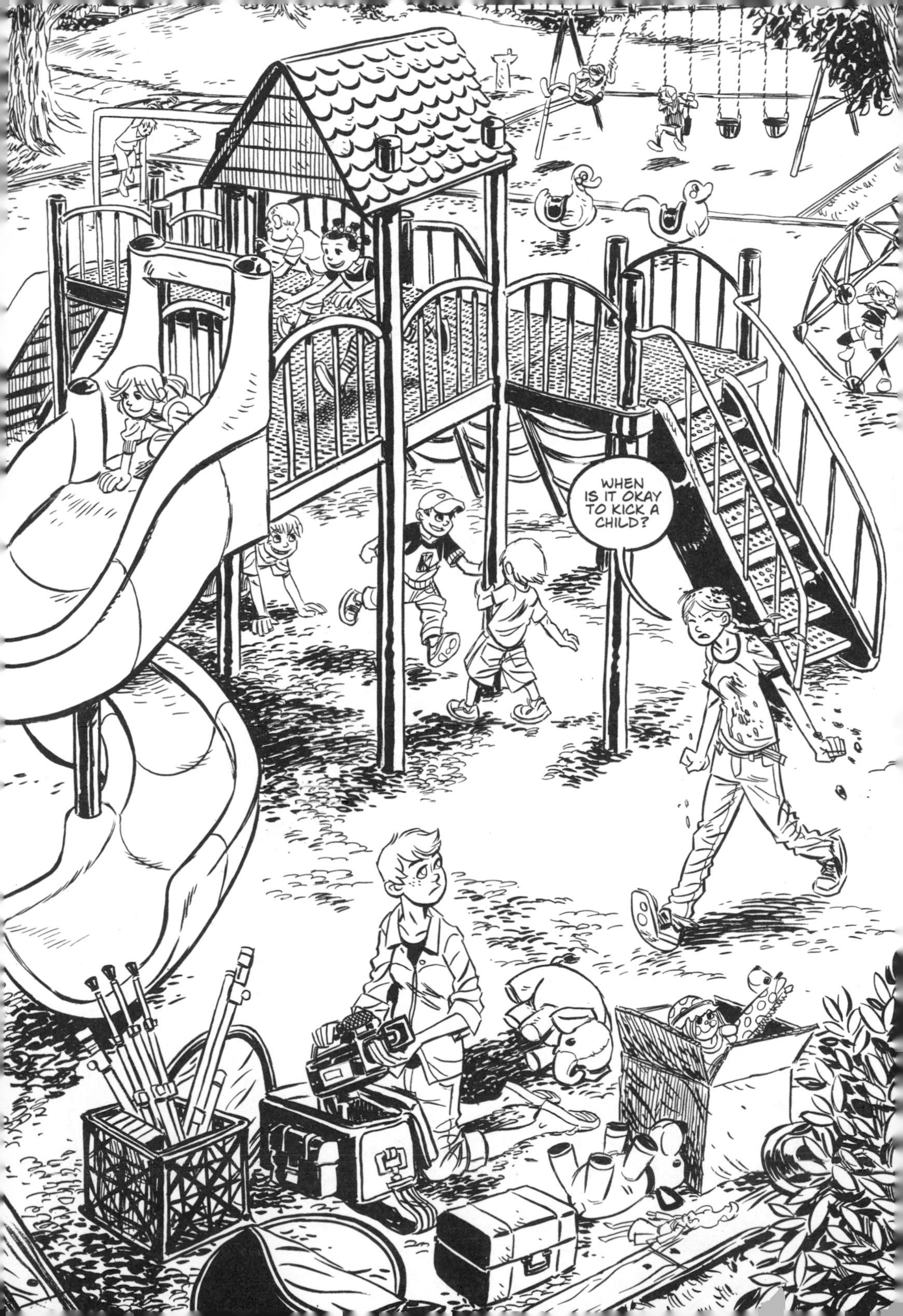
WHEN IS IT OKAY TO KICK A CHILD?

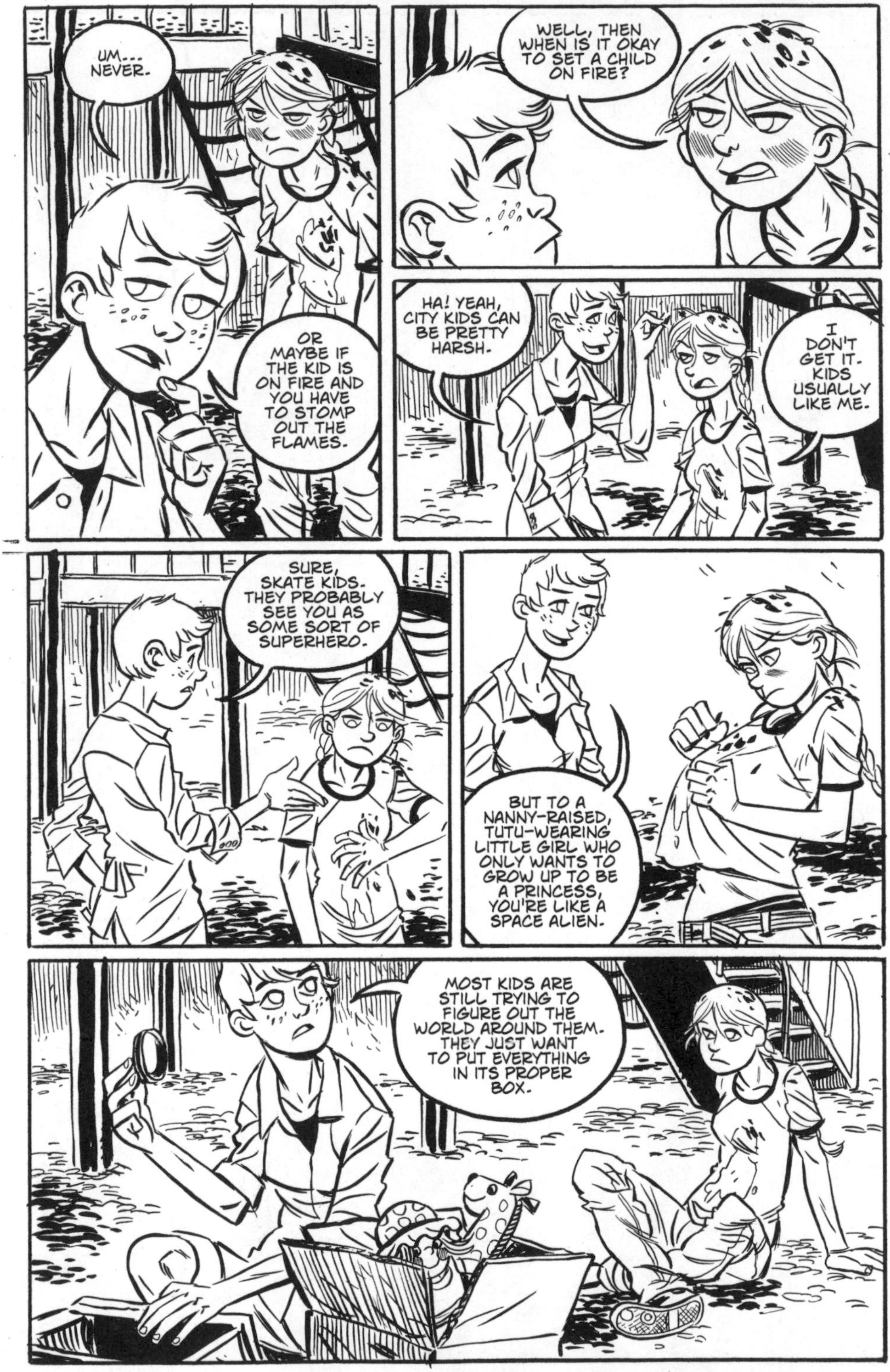
UM... NEVER.
OR MAYBE IF THE KID IS ON FIRE AND YOU HAVE TO STOMP OUT THE FLAMES.
WELL, THEN WHEN IS IT OKAY TO SET A CHILD ON FIRE?
I DON'T GET IT. KIDS USUALLY LIKE ME.
HA! YEAH, CITY KIDS CAN BE PRETTY HARSH.
SURE, SKATE KIDS. THEY PROBABLY SEE YOU AS SOME SORT OF SUPERHERO.
BUT TO A NANNY-RAISED, TUTU-WEARING LITTLE GIRL WHO ONLY WANTS TO GROW UP TO BE A PRINCESS, YOU'RE LIKE A SPACE ALIEN.
MOST KIDS ARE STILL TRYING TO FIGURE OUT THE WORLD AROUND THEM. THEY JUST WANT TO PUT EVERYTHING IN ITS PROPER BOX.

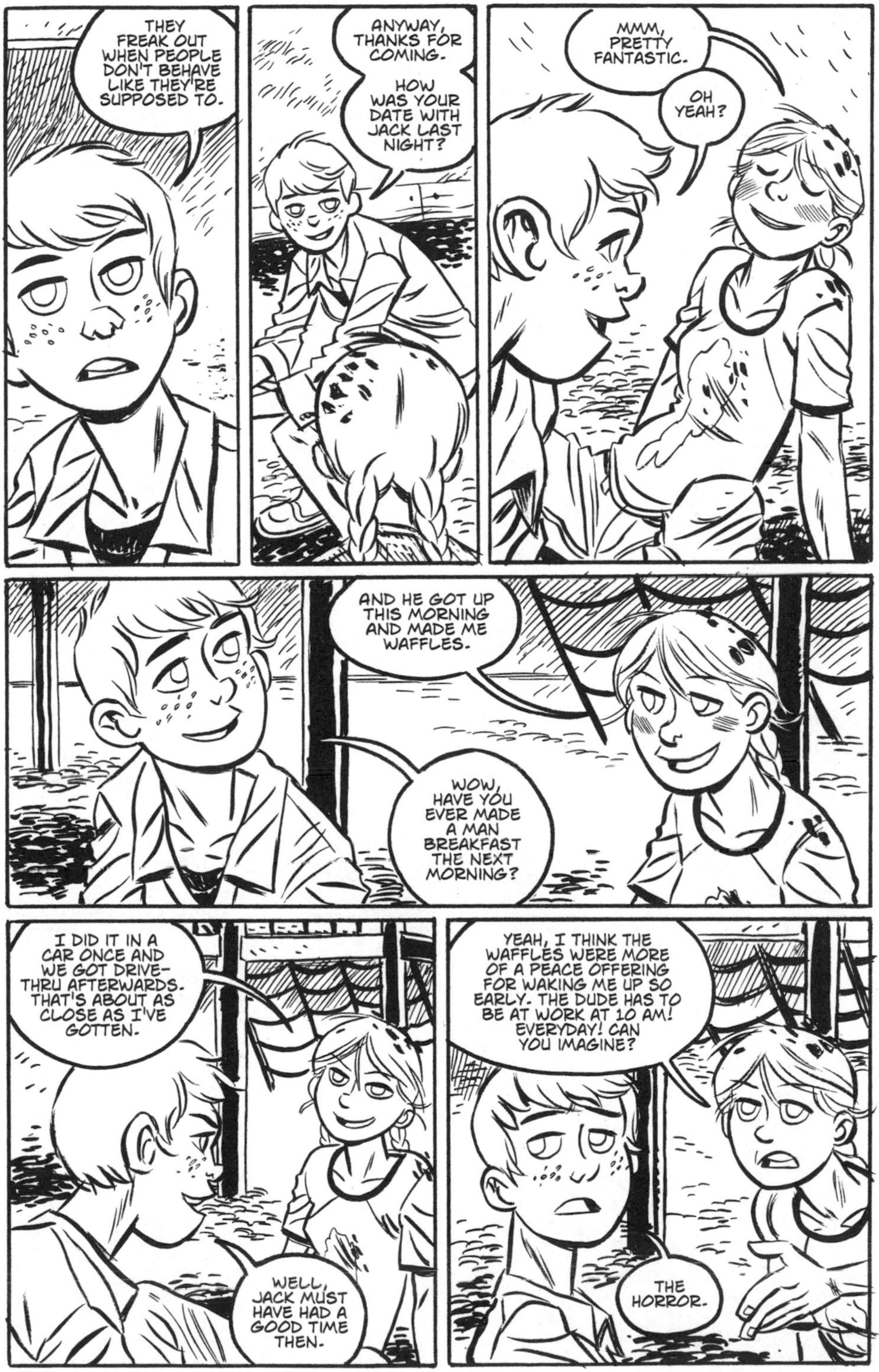
THEY FREAK OUT WHEN PEOPLE DON'T BEHAVE LIKE THEY'RE SUPPOSED TO.
ANYWAY, THANKS FOR COMING.
HOW WAS YOUR DATE WITH JACK LAST NIGHT?
MMM, PRETTY FANTASTIC.
OH YEAH?
AND HE GOT UP THIS MORNING AND MADE ME WAFFLES.
WOW, HAVE YOU EVER MADE A MAN BREAKFAST THE NEXT MORNING?
I DID IT IN A CAR ONCE AND WE GOT DRIVE-THRU AFTERWARDS. THAT'S ABOUT AS CLOSE AS I'VE GOTTEN.
WELL, JACK MUST HAVE HAD A GOOD TIME THEN.
YEAH, I THINK THE WAFFLES WERE MORE OF A PEACE OFFERING FOR WAKING ME UP SO EARLY. THE DUDE HAS TO BE AT WORK AT 10 AM! EVERYDAY! CAN YOU IMAGINE?
THE HORROR.

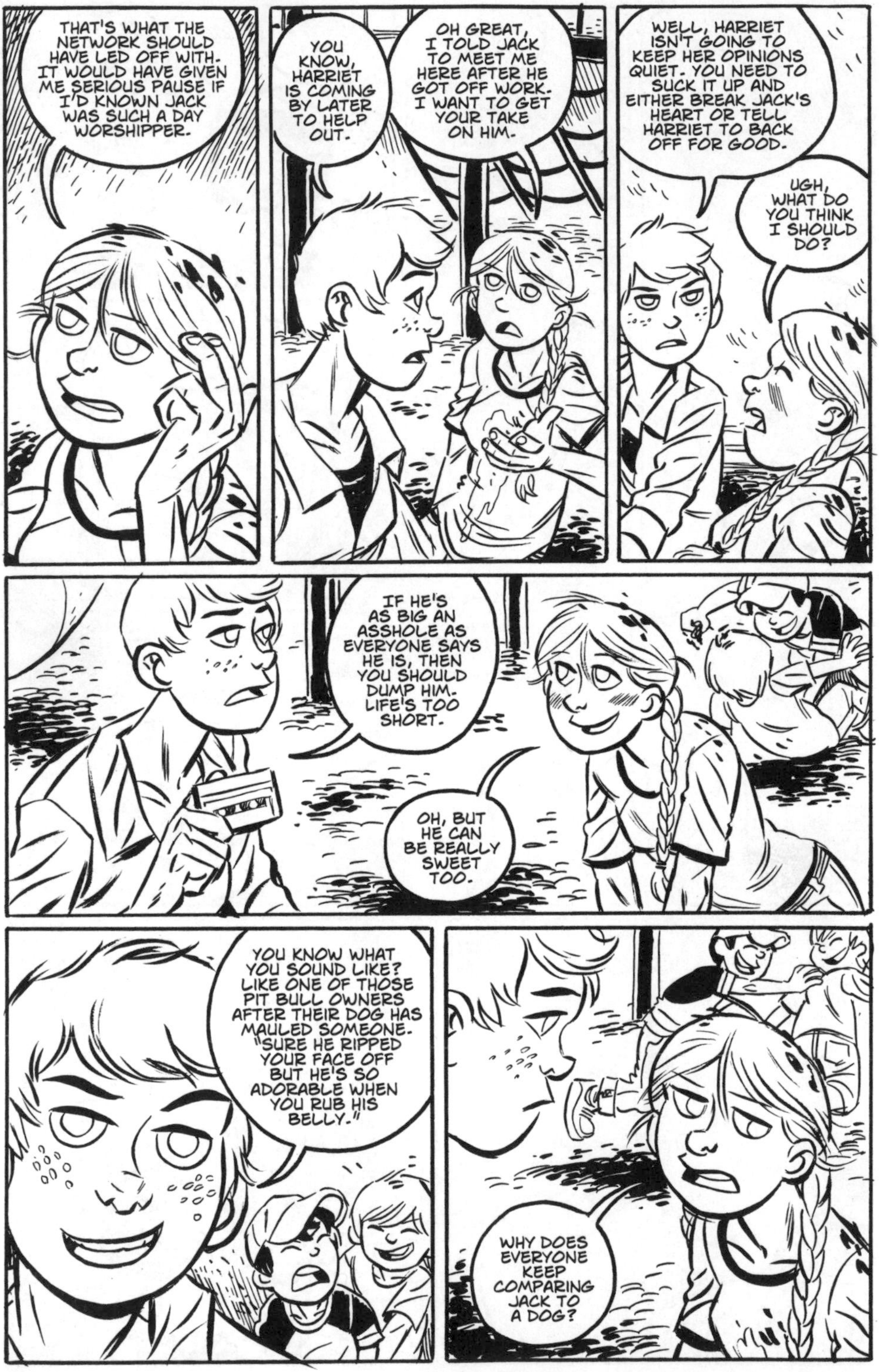
THAT'S WHAT THE NETWORK SHOULD HAVE LED OFF WITH. IT WOULD HAVE GIVEN ME SERIOUS PAUSE IF I'D KNOWN JACK WAS SUCH A DAY WORSHIPPER.
YOU KNOW, HARRIET IS COMING BY LATER TO HELP OUT.
OH GREAT, I TOLD JACK TO MEET ME HERE AFTER HE GOT OFF WORK. I WANT TO GET YOUR TAKE ON HIM.
WELL, HARRIET ISN'T GOING TO KEEP HER OPINIONS QUIET. YOU NEED TO SUCK IT UP AND EITHER BREAK JACK'S HEART OR TELL HARRIET TO BACK OFF FOR GOOD.
UGH, WHAT DO YOU THINK I SHOULD DO?
IF HE'S AS BIG AN ASSHOLE AS EVERYONE SAYS HE IS, THEN YOU SHOULD DUMP HIM. LIFE'S TOO SHORT.
OH, BUT HE CAN BE REALLY SWEET TOO.
YOU KNOW WHAT YOU SOUND LIKE? LIKE ONE OF THOSE PIT BULL OWNERS AFTER THEIR DOG HAS MAULED SOMEONE. "SURE HE RIPPED YOUR FACE OFF BUT HE'S SO ADORABLE WHEN YOU RUB HIS BELLY."
WHY DOES EVERYONE KEEP COMPARING JACK TO A DOG?

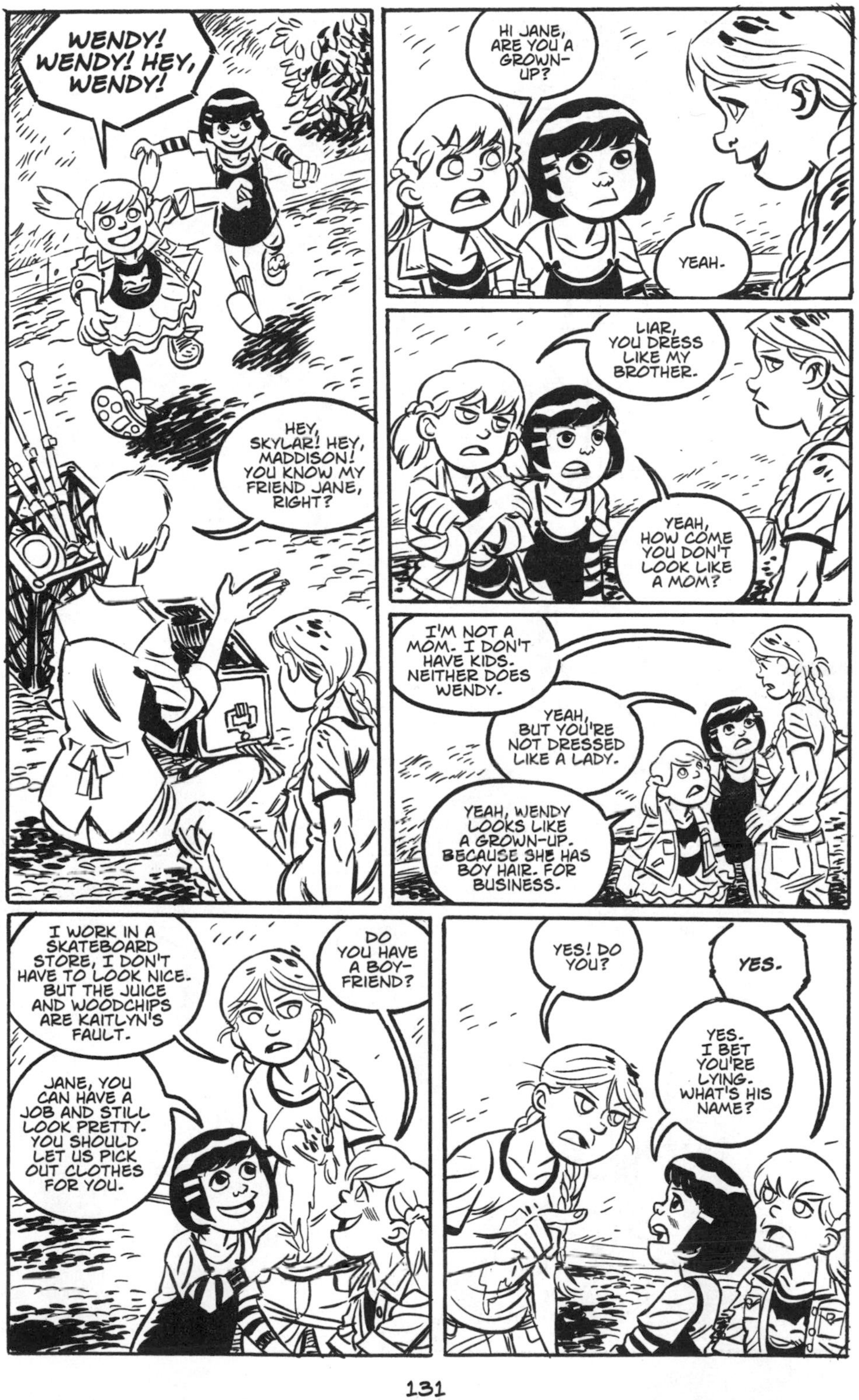
WENDY! WENDY! HEY, WENDY!
HEY, SKYLAR! HEY, MADDISON! YOU KNOW MY FRIEND JANE, RIGHT?
HI JANE, ARE YOU A GROWN-UP?
YEAH.
LIAR, YOU DRESS LIKE MY BROTHER.
YEAH, HOW COME YOU DON'T LOOK LIKE A MOM?
I'M NOT A MOM. I DON'T HAVE KIDS. NEITHER DOES WENDY.
YEAH, BUT YOU'RE NOT DRESSED LIKE A LADY.
YEAH, WENDY LOOKS LIKE A GROWN-UP. BECAUSE SHE HAS BOY HAIR. FOR BUSINESS.
I WORK IN A SKATEBOARD STORE, I DON'T HAVE TO LOOK NICE. BUT THE JUICE AND WOODCHIPS ARE KAITLYN'S FAULT.
DO YOU HAVE A BOY-FRIEND?
JANE, YOU CAN HAVE A JOB AND STILL LOOK PRETTY. YOU SHOULD LET US PICK OUT CLOTHES FOR YOU.
YES! DO YOU?
YES.
YES. I BET YOU'RE LYING. WHAT'S HIS NAME?

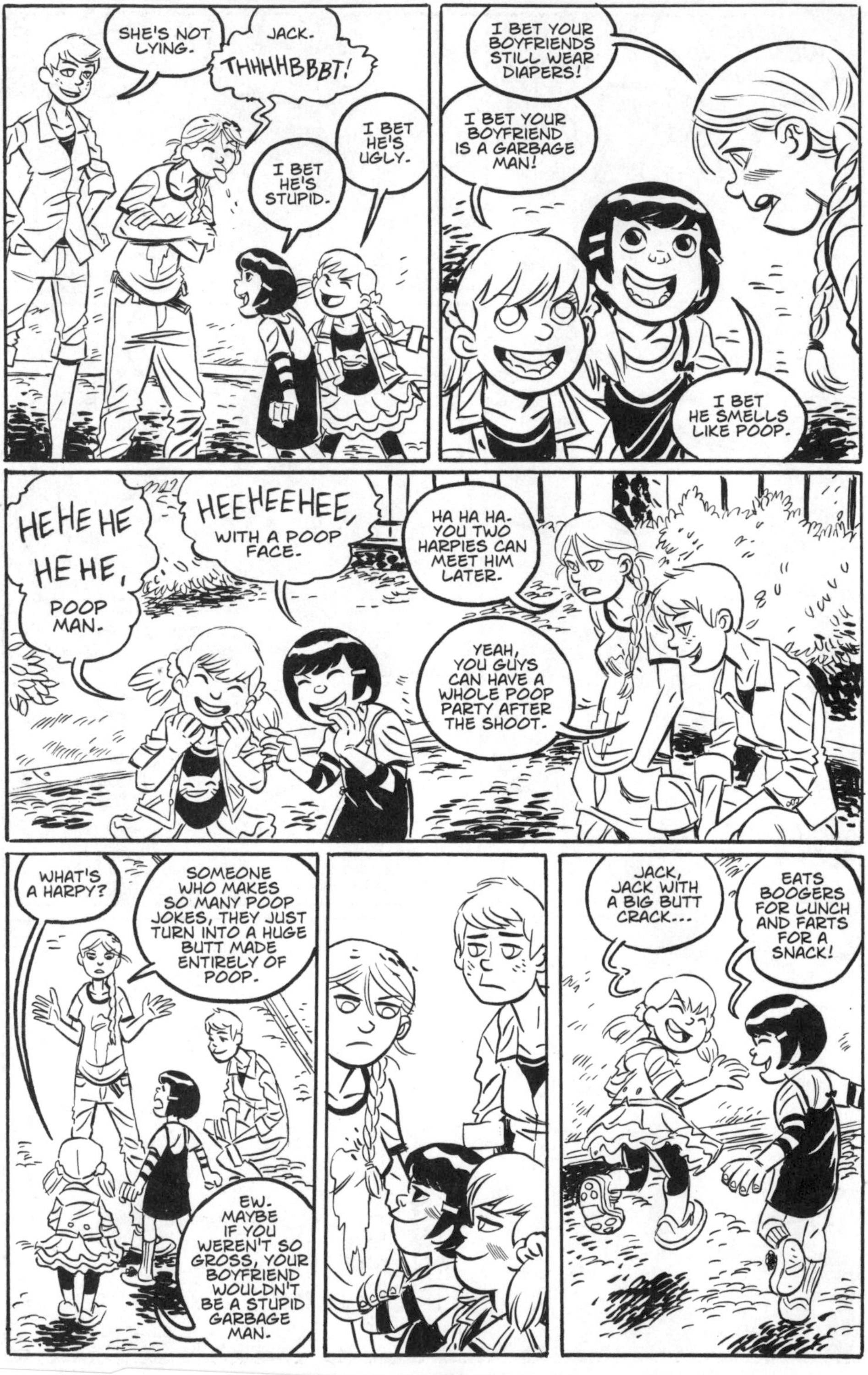
SHE'S NOT LYING.
JACK.
THHHHBBBT!
I BET HE'S STUPID.
I BET HE'S UGLY.
I BET YOUR BOYFRIENDS STILL WEAR DIAPERS!
I BET YOUR BOYFRIEND IS A GARBAGE MAN!
I BET HE SMELLS LIKE POOP.
HE HE HE HE HE, POOP MAN.
HEEHEEHEE, WITH A POOP FACE.
HA HA HA. YOU TWO HARPIES CAN MEET HIM LATER.
YEAH, YOU GUYS CAN HAVE A WHOLE POOP PARTY AFTER THE SHOOT.
WHAT'S A HARPY?
SOMEONE WHO MAKES SO MANY POOP JOKES, THEY JUST TURN INTO A HUGE BUTT MADE ENTIRELY OF POOP.
EW. MAYBE IF YOU WEREN'T SO GROSS, YOUR BOYFRIEND WOULDN'T BE A STUPID GARBAGE MAN.
JACK, JACK WITH A BIG BUTT CRACK...
EATS BOOGERS FOR LUNCH AND FARTS FOR A SNACK!

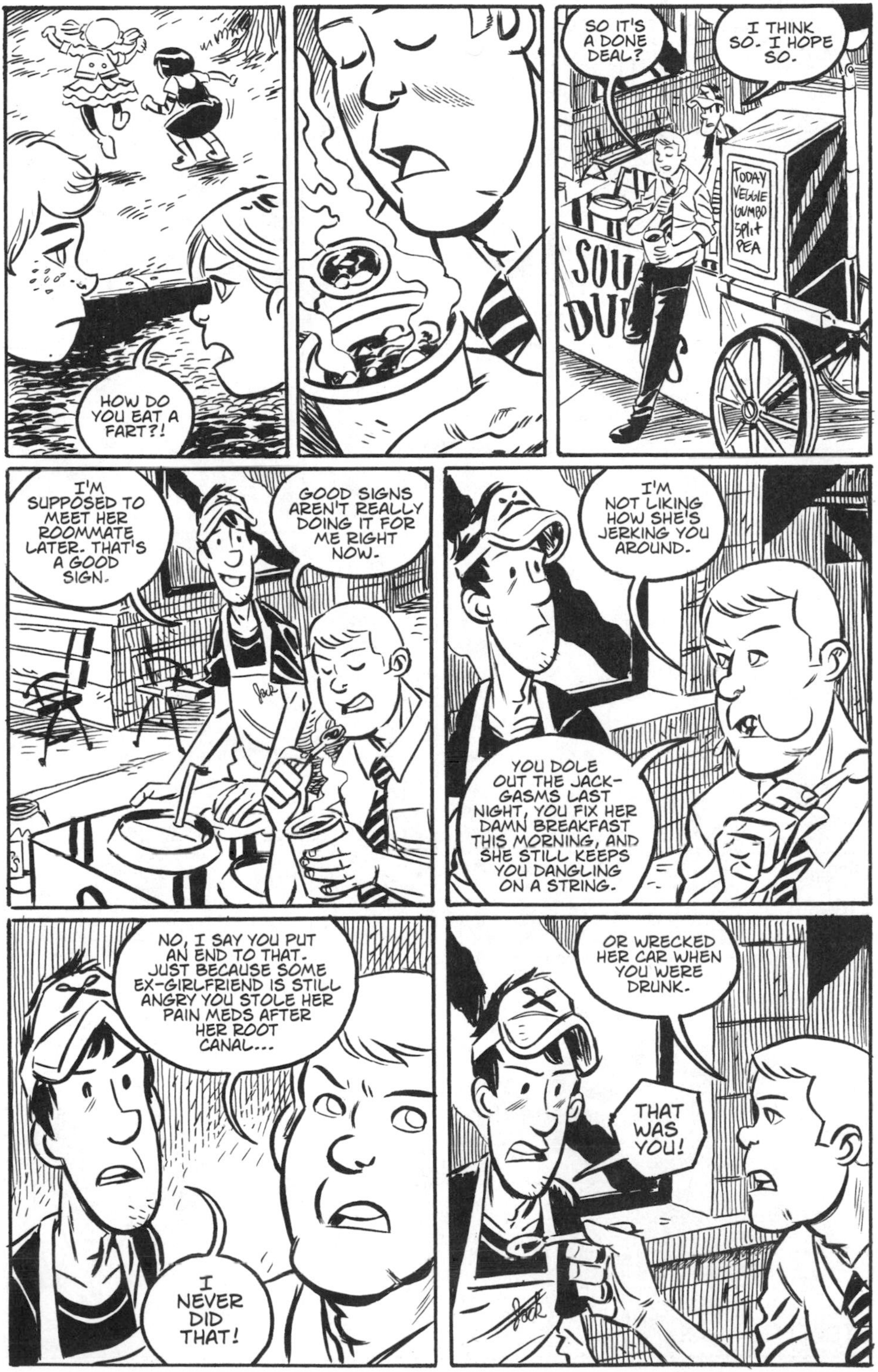
HOW DO YOU EAT A FART?!
SO IT'S A DONE DEAL?
I THINK SO. I HOPE SO.
TODAY VEGGIE GUMBO SPLIT PEA
I'M SUPPOSED TO MEET HER ROOMMATE LATER. THAT'S A GOOD SIGN.
GOOD SIGNS AREN'T REALLY DOING IT FOR ME RIGHT NOW.
I'M NOT LIKING HOW SHE'S JERKING YOU AROUND.
YOU DOLE OUT THE JACK-GASMS LAST NIGHT, YOU FIX HER DAMN BREAKFAST THIS MORNING, AND SHE STILL KEEPS YOU DANGLING ON A STRING.
NO, I SAY YOU PUT AN END TO THAT. JUST BECAUSE SOME EX-GIRLFRIEND IS STILL ANGRY YOU STOLE HER PAIN MEDS AFTER HER ROOT CANAL...
I NEVER DID THAT!
OR WRECKED HER CAR WHEN YOU WERE DRUNK.
THAT WAS YOU!

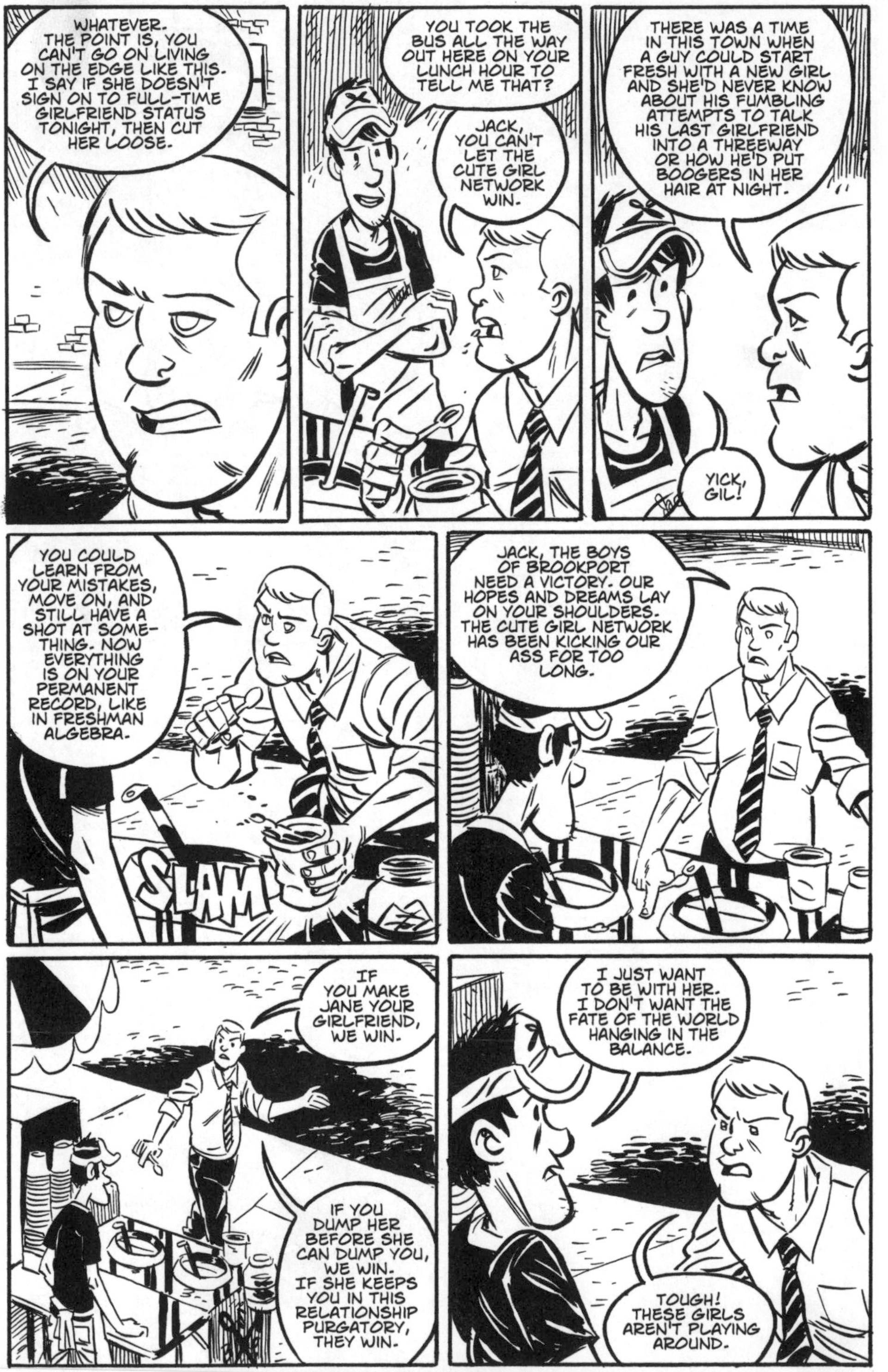

WHATEVER. THE POINT IS, YOU CAN'T GO ON LIVING ON THE EDGE LIKE THIS. I SAY IF SHE DOESN'T SIGN ON TO FULL-TIME GIRLFRIEND STATUS TONIGHT, THEN CUT HER LOOSE.
YOU TOOK THE BUS ALL THE WAY OUT HERE ON YOUR LUNCH HOUR TO TELL ME THAT?
JACK, YOU CAN'T LET THE CUTE GIRL NETWORK WIN.
THERE WAS A TIME IN THIS TOWN WHEN A GUY COULD START FRESH WITH A NEW GIRL AND SHE'D NEVER KNOW ABOUT HIS FUMBLING ATTEMPTS TO TALK HIS LAST GIRLFRIEND INTO A THREEWAY OR HOW HE'D PUT BOOGERS IN HER HAIR AT NIGHT.
YICK, GIL!
YOU COULD LEARN FROM YOUR MISTAKES, MOVE ON, AND STILL HAVE A SHOT AT SOME-THING. NOW EVERYTHING IS ON YOUR PERMANENT RECORD, LIKE IN FRESHMAN ALGEBRA.
SLAM
JACK, THE BOYS OF BROOKPORT NEED A VICTORY. OUR HOPES AND DREAMS LAY ON YOUR SHOULDERS. THE CUTE GIRL NETWORK HAS BEEN KICKING OUR ASS FOR TOO LONG.
IF YOU MAKE JANE YOUR GIRLFRIEND, WE WIN.
IF YOU DUMP HER BEFORE SHE CAN DUMP YOU, WE WIN. IF SHE KEEPS YOU IN THIS RELATIONSHIP PURGATORY, THEY WIN.
I JUST WANT TO BE WITH HER. I DON'T WANT THE FATE OF THE WORLD HANGING IN THE BALANCE.
TOUGH! THESE GIRLS AREN'T PLAYING AROUND.

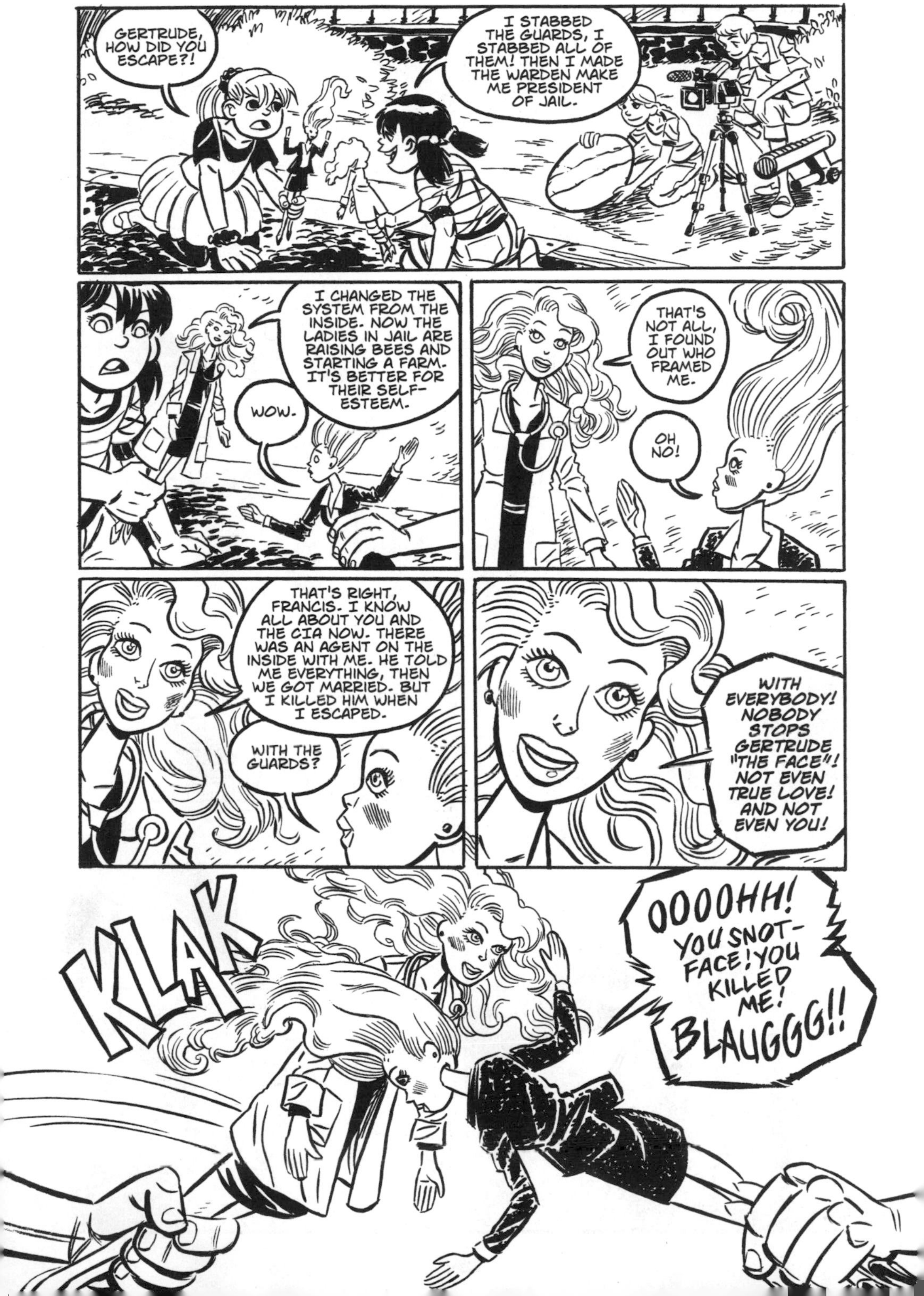
GERTRUDE, HOW DID YOU ESCAPE?!
I STABBED THE GUARDS, I STABBED ALL OF THEM! THEN I MADE THE WARDEN MAKE ME PRESIDENT OF JAIL.
I CHANGED THE SYSTEM FROM THE INSIDE. NOW THE LADIES IN JAIL ARE RAISING BEES AND STARTING A FARM. IT'S BETTER FOR THEIR SELF-ESTEEM.
WOW.
THAT'S NOT ALL, I FOUND OUT WHO FRAMED ME.
OH NO!
THAT'S RIGHT, FRANCIS. I KNOW ALL ABOUT YOU AND THE CIA NOW. THERE WAS AN AGENT ON THE INSIDE WITH ME. HE TOLD ME EVERYTHING, THEN WE GOT MARRIED. BUT I KILLED HIM WHEN I ESCAPED.
WITH THE GUARDS?
WITH EVERYBODY! NOBODY STOPS GERTRUDE "THE FACE"! NOT EVEN TRUE LOVE! AND NOT EVEN YOU!
KLAK
OOOOHH! YOU SNOT-FACE! YOU KILLED ME! BLAUGGG!!

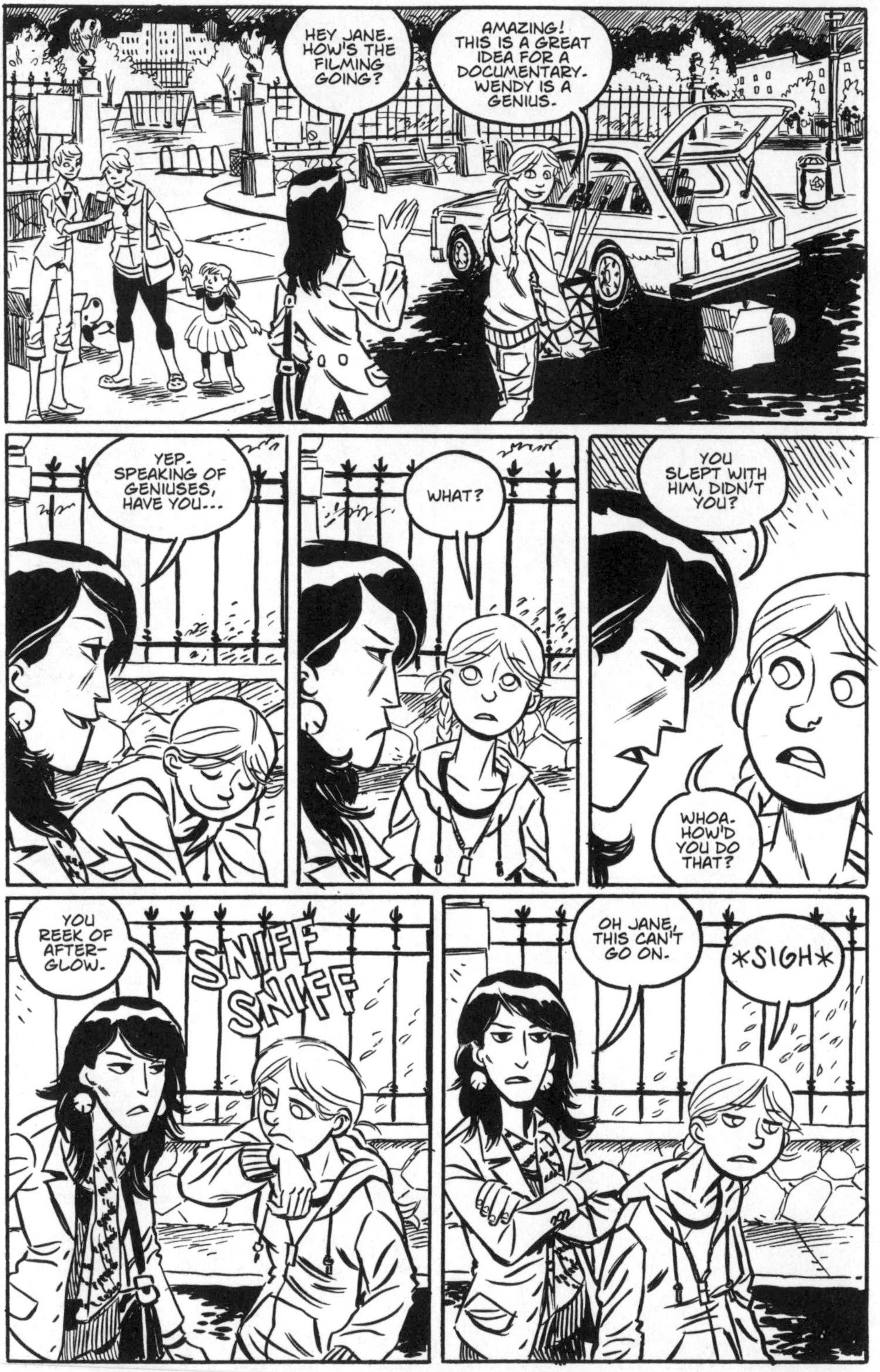
HEY JANE. HOW'S THE FILMING GOING?
AMAZING! THIS IS A GREAT IDEA FOR A DOCUMENTARY. WENDY IS A GENIUS.
YEP. SPEAKING OF GENIUSES, HAVE YOU...
WHAT?
YOU SLEPT WITH HIM, DIDN'T YOU?
WHOA. HOW'D YOU DO THAT?
YOU REEK OF AFTER-GLOW.
SNIFF SNIFF
OH JANE, THIS CAN'T GO ON.
SIGH

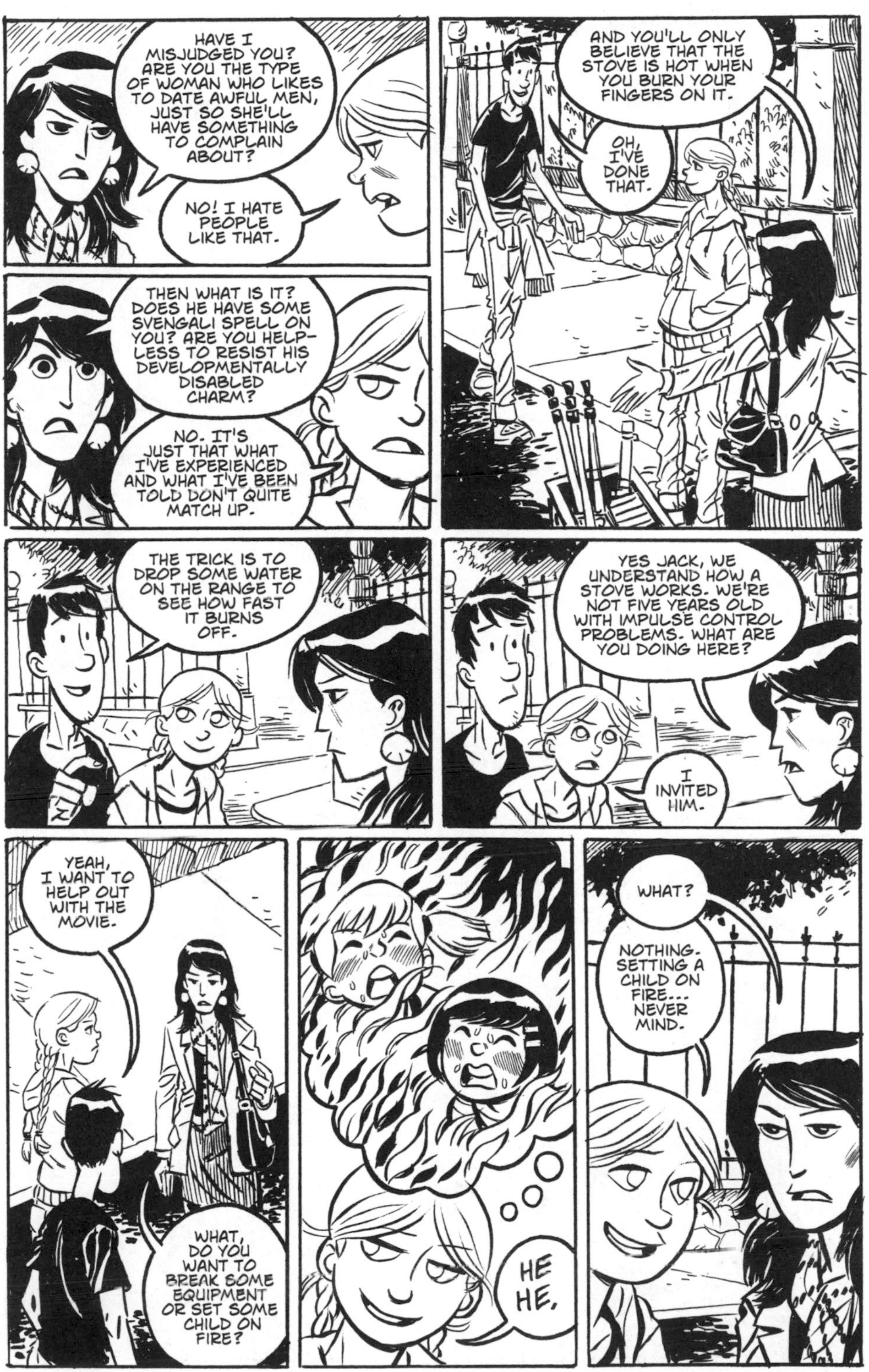
HAVE I MISJUDGED YOU? ARE YOU THE TYPE OF WOMAN WHO LIKES TO DATE AWFUL MEN, JUST SO SHE'LL HAVE SOMETHING TO COMPLAIN ABOUT?
NO! I HATE PEOPLE LIKE THAT.
AND YOU'LL ONLY BELIEVE THAT THE STOVE IS HOT WHEN YOU BURN YOUR FINGERS ON IT.
OH, I'VE DONE THAT.
THEN WHAT IS IT? DOES HE HAVE SOME SVENGALI SPELL ON YOU? ARE YOU HELP-LESS TO RESIST HIS DEVELOPMENTALLY DISABLED CHARM?
NO. IT'S JUST THAT WHAT I'VE EXPERIENCED AND WHAT I'VE BEEN TOLD DON'T QUITE MATCH UP.
THE TRICK IS TO DROP SOME WATER ON THE RANGE TO SEE HOW FAST IT BURNS OFF.
YES JACK, WE UNDERSTAND HOW A STOVE WORKS. WE'RE NOT FIVE YEARS OLD WITH IMPULSE CONTROL PROBLEMS. WHAT ARE YOU DOING HERE?
I INVITED HIM.
YEAH, I WANT TO HELP OUT WITH THE MOVIE.
WHAT, DO YOU WANT TO BREAK SOME EQUIPMENT OR SET SOME CHILD ON FIRE?
HE HE.
WHAT?
NOTHING. SETTING A CHILD ON FIRE... NEVER MIND.

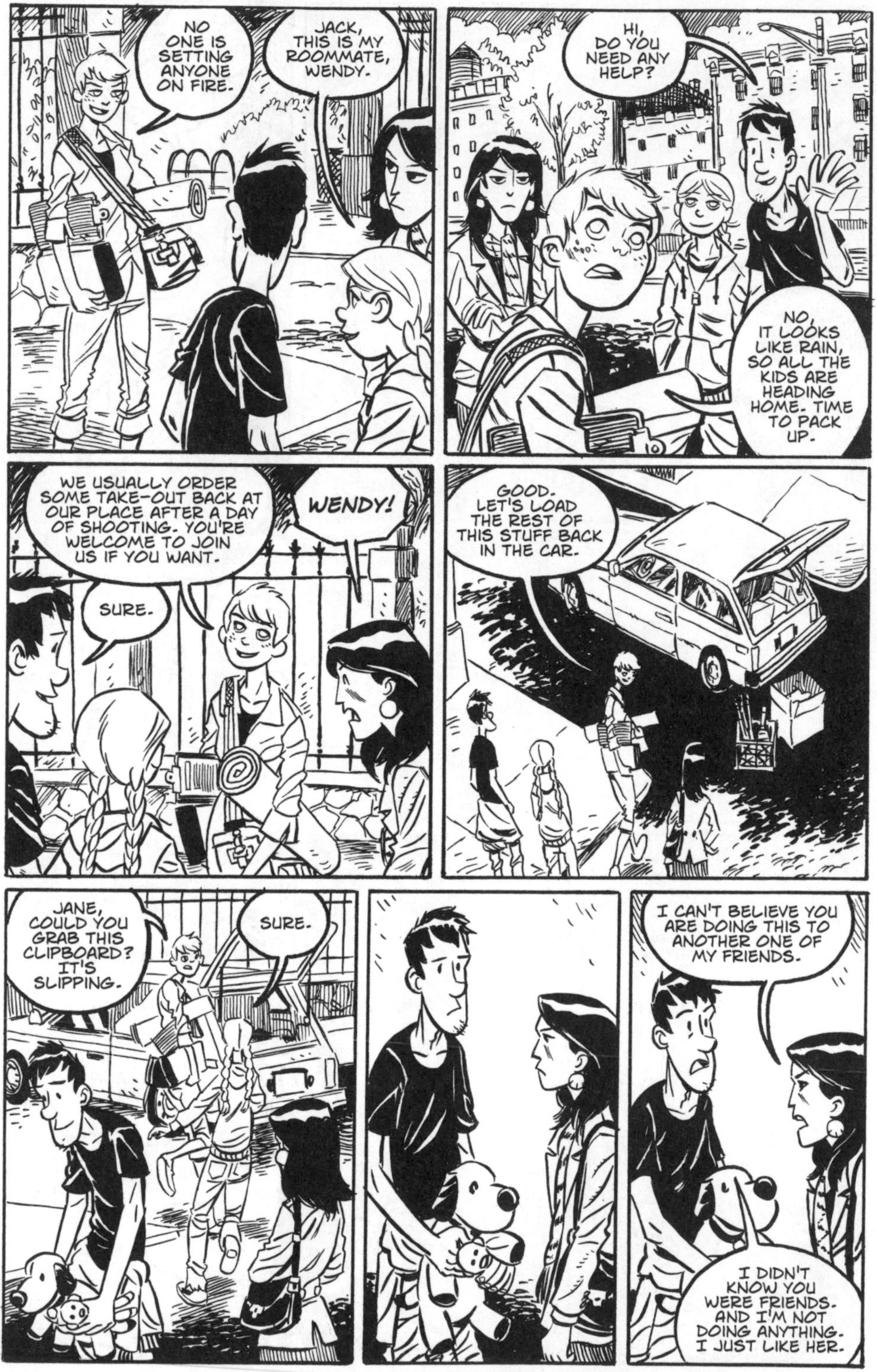
NO ONE IS SETTING ANYONE ON FIRE.
JACK, THIS IS MY ROOMMATE, WENDY.
HI, DO YOU NEED ANY HELP?
NO, IT LOOKS LIKE RAIN, SO ALL THE KIDS ARE HEADING HOME. TIME TO PACK UP.
WE USUALLY ORDER SOME TAKE-OUT BACK AT OUR PLACE AFTER A DAY OF SHOOTING. YOU'RE WELCOME TO JOIN US IF YOU WANT.
WENDY!
SURE.
GOOD. LET'S LOAD THE REST OF THIS STUFF BACK IN THE CAR.
JANE, COULD YOU GRAB THIS CLIPBOARD? IT'S SLIPPING.
SURE.
I CAN'T BELIEVE YOU ARE DOING THIS TO ANOTHER ONE OF MY FRIENDS.
I DIDN'T KNOW YOU WERE FRIENDS. AND I'M NOT DOING ANYTHING. I JUST LIKE HER.

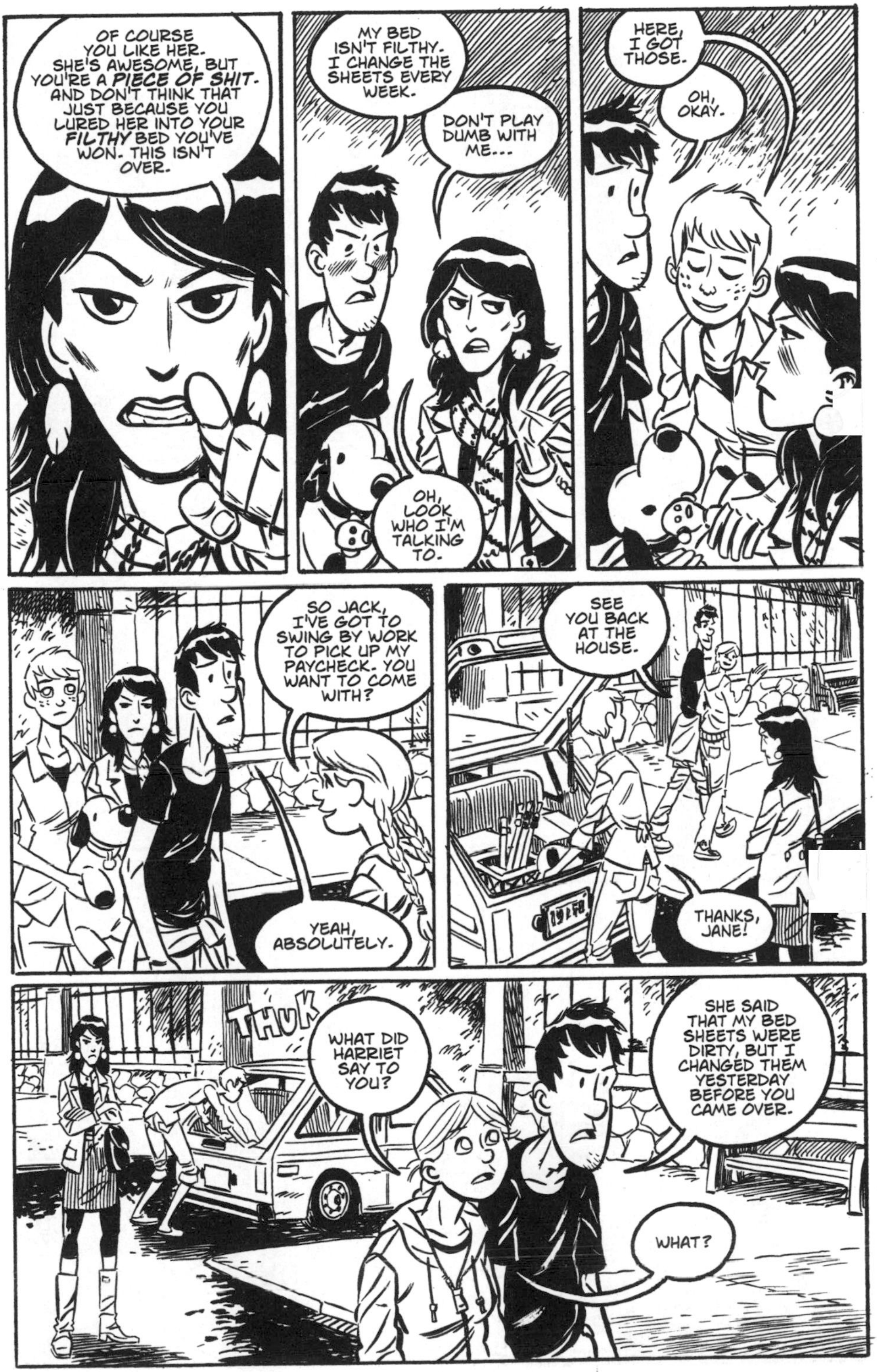
OF COURSE YOU LIKE HER. SHE'S AWESOME, BUT YOU'RE A PIECE OF SHIT. AND DON'T THINK THAT JUST BECAUSE YOU LURED HER INTO YOUR FILTHY BED YOU'VE WON. THIS ISN'T OVER.
MY BED ISN'T FILTHY. I CHANGE THE SHEETS EVERY WEEK.
DON'T PLAY DUMB WITH ME...
OH, LOOK WHO I'M TALKING TO.
HERE, I GOT THOSE.
OH, OKAY.
SO JACK, I'VE GOT TO SWING BY WORK TO PICK UP MY PAYCHECK. YOU WANT TO COME WITH?
YEAH, ABSOLUTELY.
SEE YOU BACK AT THE HOUSE.
THANKS, JANE!
THUK
WHAT DID HARRIET SAY TO YOU?
SHE SAID THAT MY BED SHEETS WERE DIRTY, BUT I CHANGED THEM YESTERDAY BEFORE YOU CAME OVER.
WHAT?

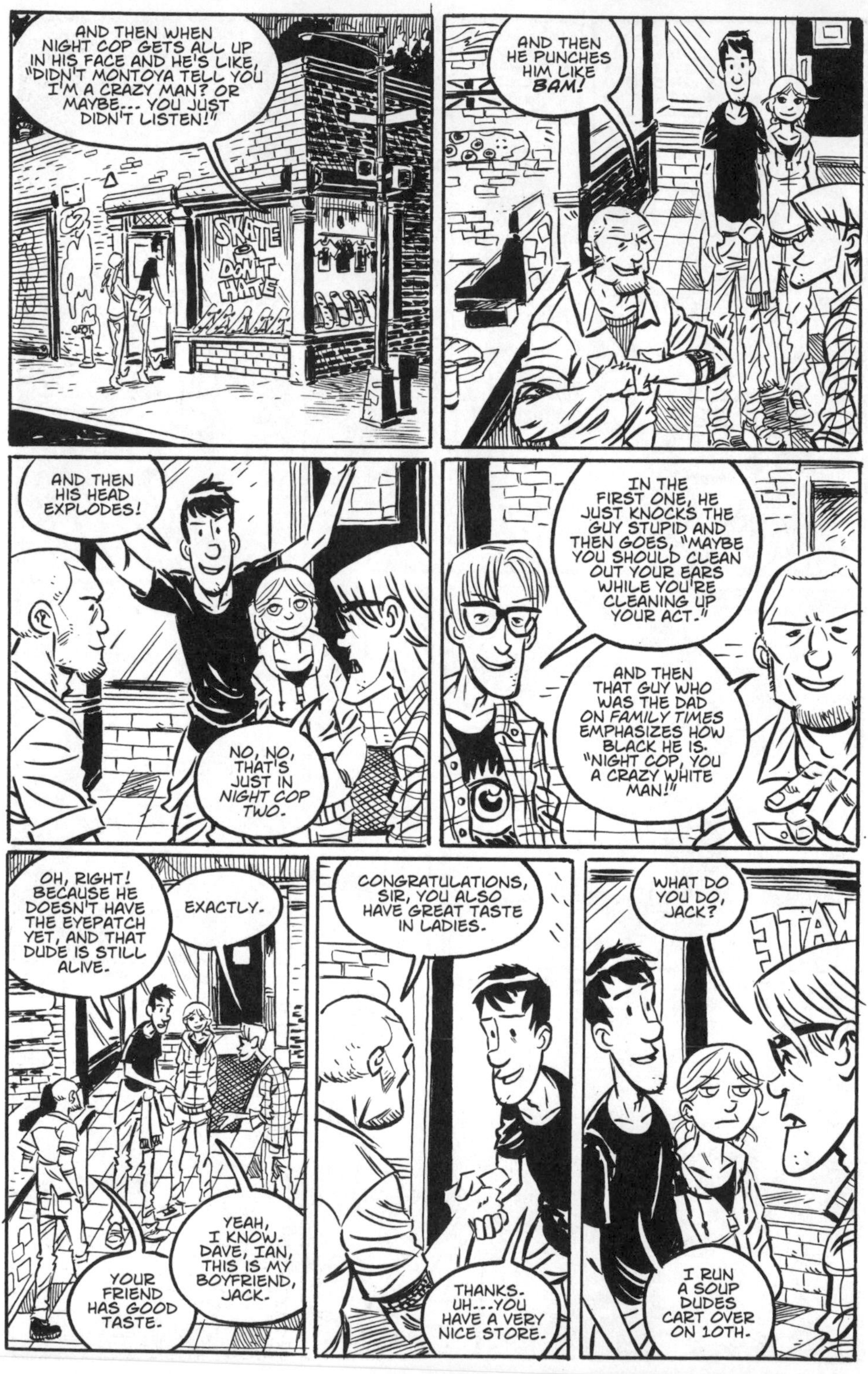
AND THEN WHEN NIGHT COP GETS ALL UP IN HIS FACE AND HE'S LIKE, "DIDN'T MONTOYA TELL YOU I'M A CRAZY MAN? OR MAYBE... YOU JUST DIDN'T LISTEN!"
SKATE DON'T HATE
AND THEN HE PUNCHES HIM LIKE *BAM!*
AND THEN HIS HEAD EXPLODES!
NO, NO, THAT'S JUST IN NIGHT COP TWO.
IN THE FIRST ONE, HE JUST KNOCKS THE GUY STUPID AND THEN GOES, "MAYBE YOU SHOULD CLEAN OUT YOUR EARS WHILE YOU'RE CLEANING UP YOUR ACT."
AND THEN THAT GUY WHO WAS THE DAD ON *FAMILY TIMES* EMPHASIZES HOW BLACK HE IS. "NIGHT COP, YOU A CRAZY WHITE MAN!"
OH, RIGHT! BECAUSE HE DOESN'T HAVE THE EYEPATCH YET, AND THAT DUDE IS STILL ALIVE.
EXACTLY.
YOUR FRIEND HAS GOOD TASTE.
YEAH, I KNOW. DAVE, IAN, THIS IS MY BOYFRIEND, JACK.
CONGRATULATIONS, SIR, YOU ALSO HAVE GREAT TASTE IN LADIES.
THANKS. UH...YOU HAVE A VERY NICE STORE.
WHAT DO YOU DO, JACK?
I RUN A SOUP DUDES CART OVER ON 10TH.

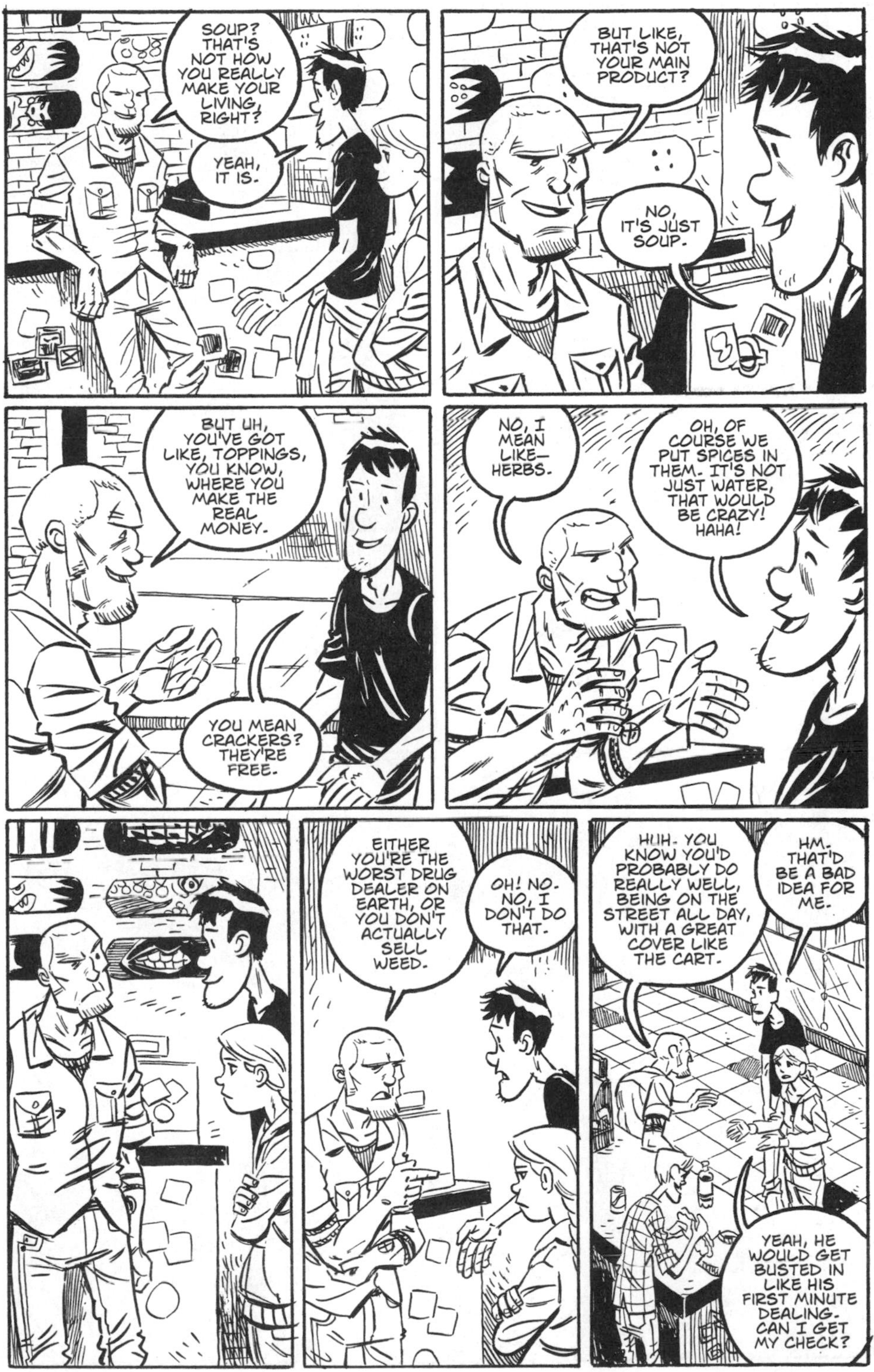
SOUP? THAT'S NOT HOW YOU REALLY MAKE YOUR LIVING, RIGHT?
YEAH, IT IS.
BUT LIKE, THAT'S NOT YOUR MAIN PRODUCT?
NO, IT'S JUST SOUP.
BUT UH, YOU'VE GOT LIKE, TOPPINGS, YOU KNOW, WHERE YOU MAKE THE REAL MONEY.
YOU MEAN CRACKERS? THEY'RE FREE.
NO, I MEAN LIKE— HERBS.
OH, OF COURSE WE PUT SPICES IN THEM. IT'S NOT JUST WATER, THAT WOULD BE CRAZY! HAHA!
EITHER YOU'RE THE WORST DRUG DEALER ON EARTH, OR YOU DON'T ACTUALLY SELL WEED.
OH! NO. NO, I DON'T DO THAT.
HUH. YOU KNOW YOU'D PROBABLY DO REALLY WELL, BEING ON THE STREET ALL DAY, WITH A GREAT COVER LIKE THE CART.
HM. THAT'D BE A BAD IDEA FOR ME.
YEAH, HE WOULD GET BUSTED IN LIKE HIS FIRST MINUTE DEALING. CAN I GET MY CHECK?

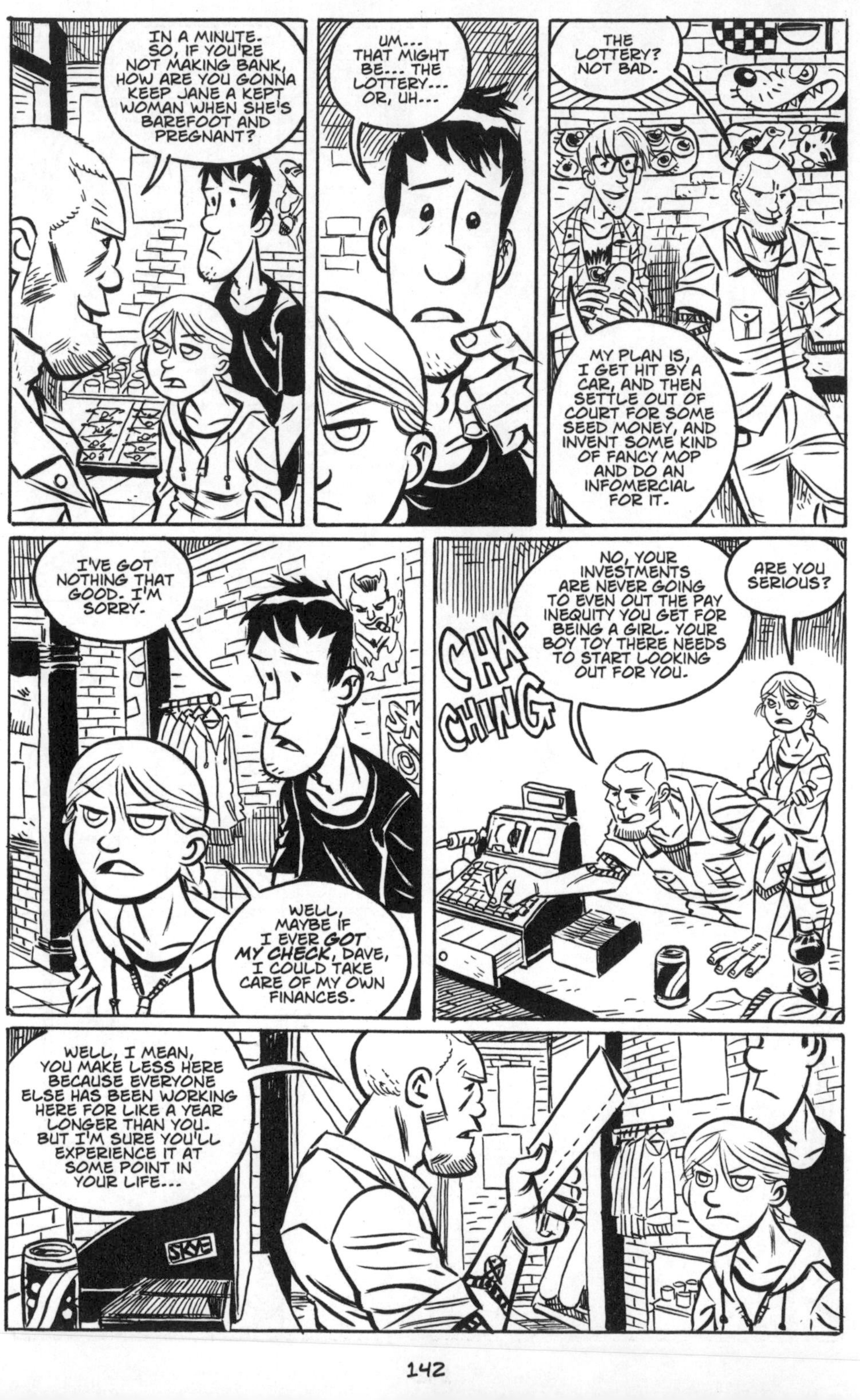
IN A MINUTE. SO, IF YOU'RE NOT MAKING BANK, HOW ARE YOU GONNA KEEP JANE A KEPT WOMAN WHEN SHE'S BAREFOOT AND PREGNANT?
UM... THAT MIGHT BE... THE LOTTERY... OR, UH...
THE LOTTERY? NOT BAD.
MY PLAN IS, I GET HIT BY A CAR, AND THEN SETTLE OUT OF COURT FOR SOME SEED MONEY, AND INVENT SOME KIND OF FANCY MOP AND DO AN INFOMERCIAL FOR IT.
I'VE GOT NOTHING THAT GOOD. I'M SORRY.
WELL, MAYBE IF I EVER **GOT MY CHECK**, DAVE, I COULD TAKE CARE OF MY OWN FINANCES.
CHA-CHING
NO, YOUR INVESTMENTS ARE NEVER GOING TO EVEN OUT THE PAY INEQUITY YOU GET FOR BEING A GIRL. YOUR BOY TOY THERE NEEDS TO START LOOKING OUT FOR YOU.
ARE YOU SERIOUS?
WELL, I MEAN, YOU MAKE LESS HERE BECAUSE EVERYONE ELSE HAS BEEN WORKING HERE FOR LIKE A YEAR LONGER THAN YOU. BUT I'M SURE YOU'LL EXPERIENCE IT AT SOME POINT IN YOUR LIFE...
SKYE

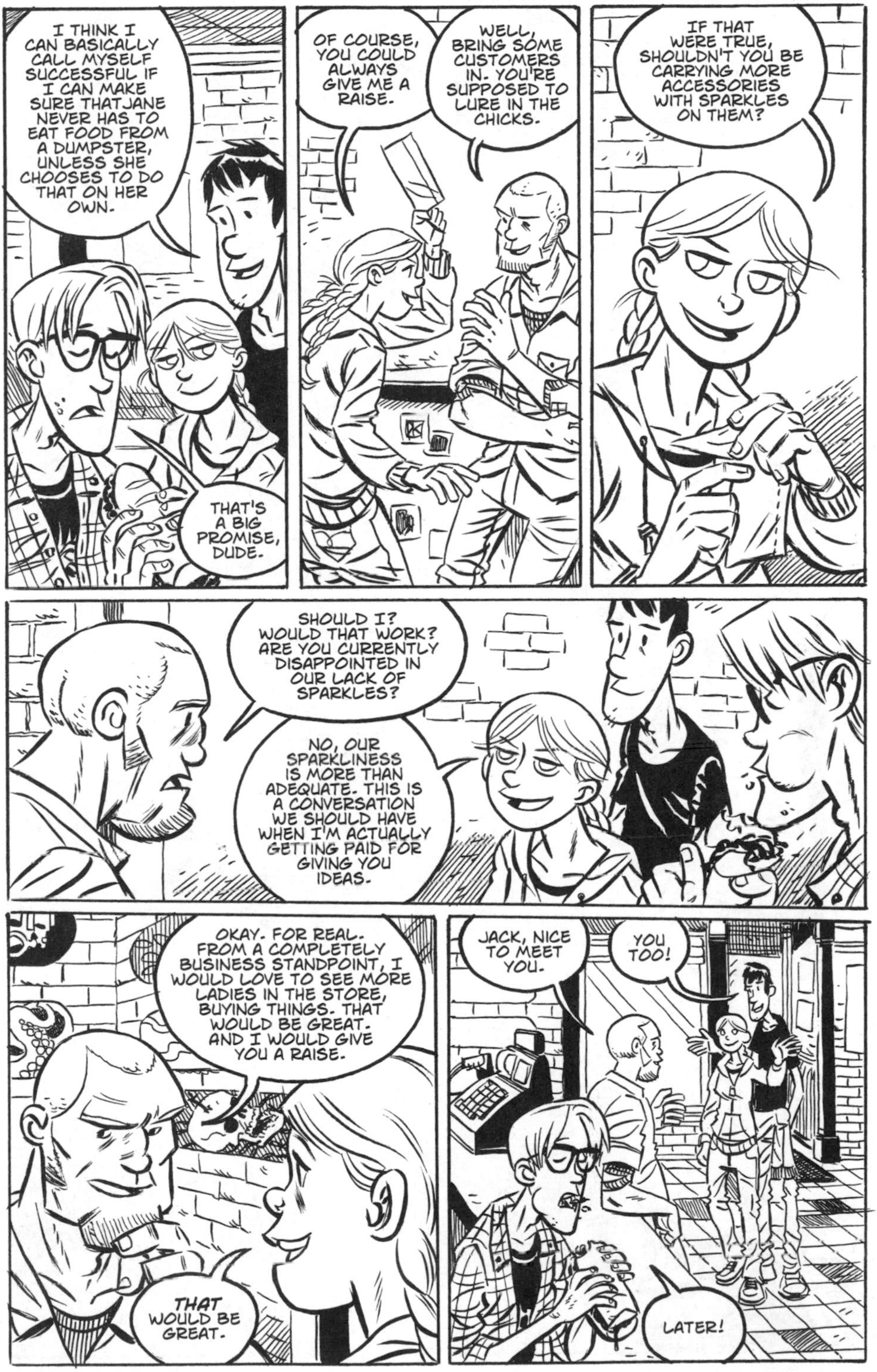
I THINK I CAN BASICALLY CALL MYSELF SUCCESSFUL IF I CAN MAKE SURE THATJANE NEVER HAS TO EAT FOOD FROM A DUMPSTER, UNLESS SHE CHOOSES TO DO THAT ON HER OWN.
THAT'S A BIG PROMISE, DUDE.
OF COURSE, YOU COULD ALWAYS GIVE ME A RAISE.
WELL, BRING SOME CUSTOMERS IN. YOU'RE SUPPOSED TO LURE IN THE CHICKS.
IF THAT WERE TRUE, SHOULDN'T YOU BE CARRYING MORE ACCESSORIES WITH SPARKLES ON THEM?
SHOULD I? WOULD THAT WORK? ARE YOU CURRENTLY DISAPPOINTED IN OUR LACK OF SPARKLES?
NO, OUR SPARKLINESS IS MORE THAN ADEQUATE. THIS IS A CONVERSATION WE SHOULD HAVE WHEN I'M ACTUALLY GETTING PAID FOR GIVING YOU IDEAS.
OKAY. FOR REAL. FROM A COMPLETELY BUSINESS STANDPOINT, I WOULD LOVE TO SEE MORE LADIES IN THE STORE, BUYING THINGS. THAT WOULD BE GREAT. AND I WOULD GIVE YOU A RAISE.
THAT WOULD BE GREAT.
JACK, NICE TO MEET YOU.
YOU TOO!
LATER!

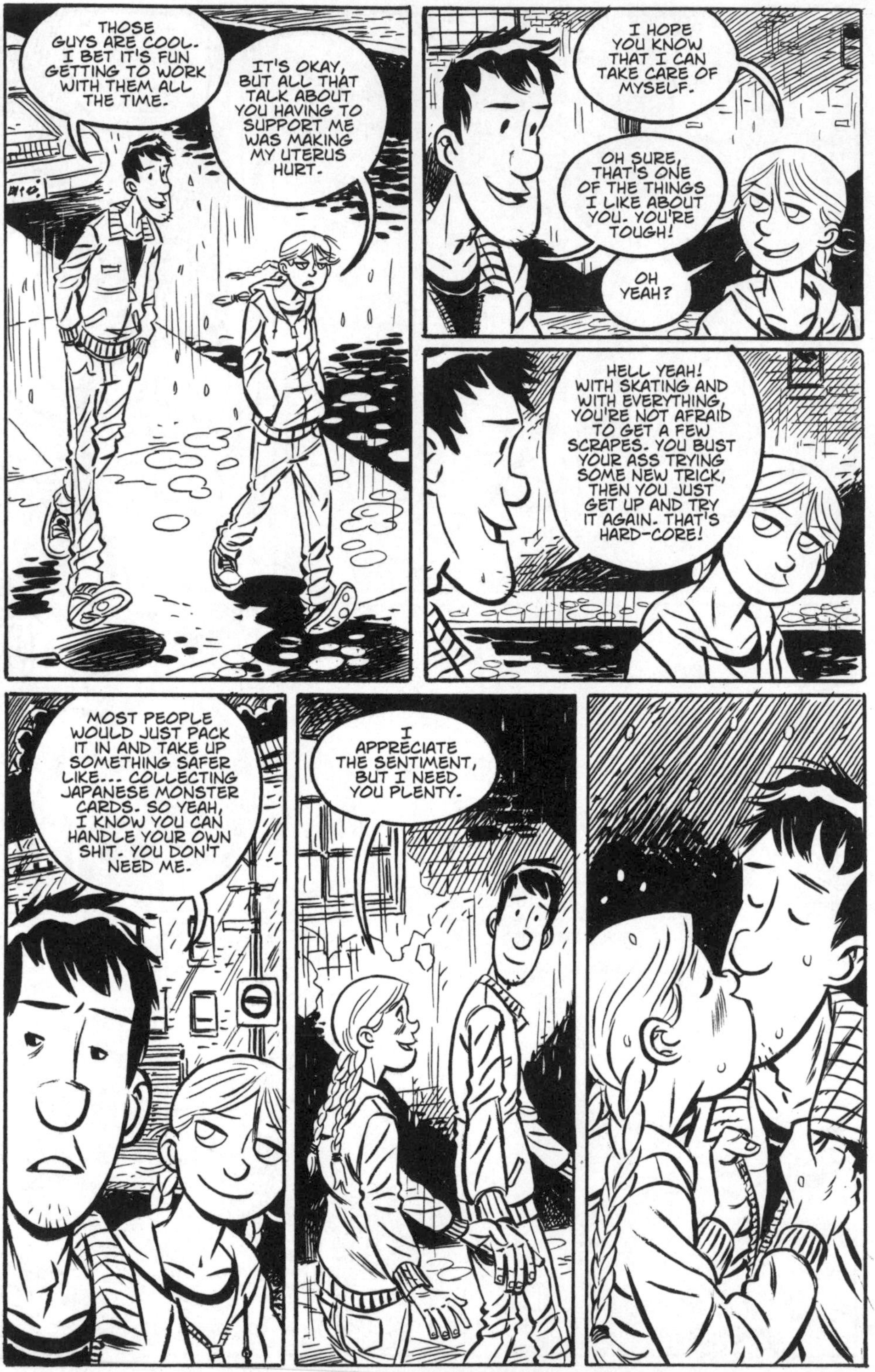
THOSE GUYS ARE COOL. I BET IT'S FUN GETTING TO WORK WITH THEM ALL THE TIME.
IT'S OKAY, BUT ALL THAT TALK ABOUT YOU HAVING TO SUPPORT ME WAS MAKING MY UTERUS HURT.
I HOPE YOU KNOW THAT I CAN TAKE CARE OF MYSELF.
OH SURE, THAT'S ONE OF THE THINGS I LIKE ABOUT YOU. YOU'RE TOUGH!
OH YEAH?
HELL YEAH! WITH SKATING AND WITH EVERYTHING, YOU'RE NOT AFRAID TO GET A FEW SCRAPES. YOU BUST YOUR ASS TRYING SOME NEW TRICK, THEN YOU JUST GET UP AND TRY IT AGAIN. THAT'S HARD-CORE!
MOST PEOPLE WOULD JUST PACK IT IN AND TAKE UP SOMETHING SAFER LIKE... COLLECTING JAPANESE MONSTER CARDS. SO YEAH, I KNOW YOU CAN HANDLE YOUR OWN SHIT. YOU DON'T NEED ME.
I APPRECIATE THE SENTIMENT, BUT I NEED YOU PLENTY.

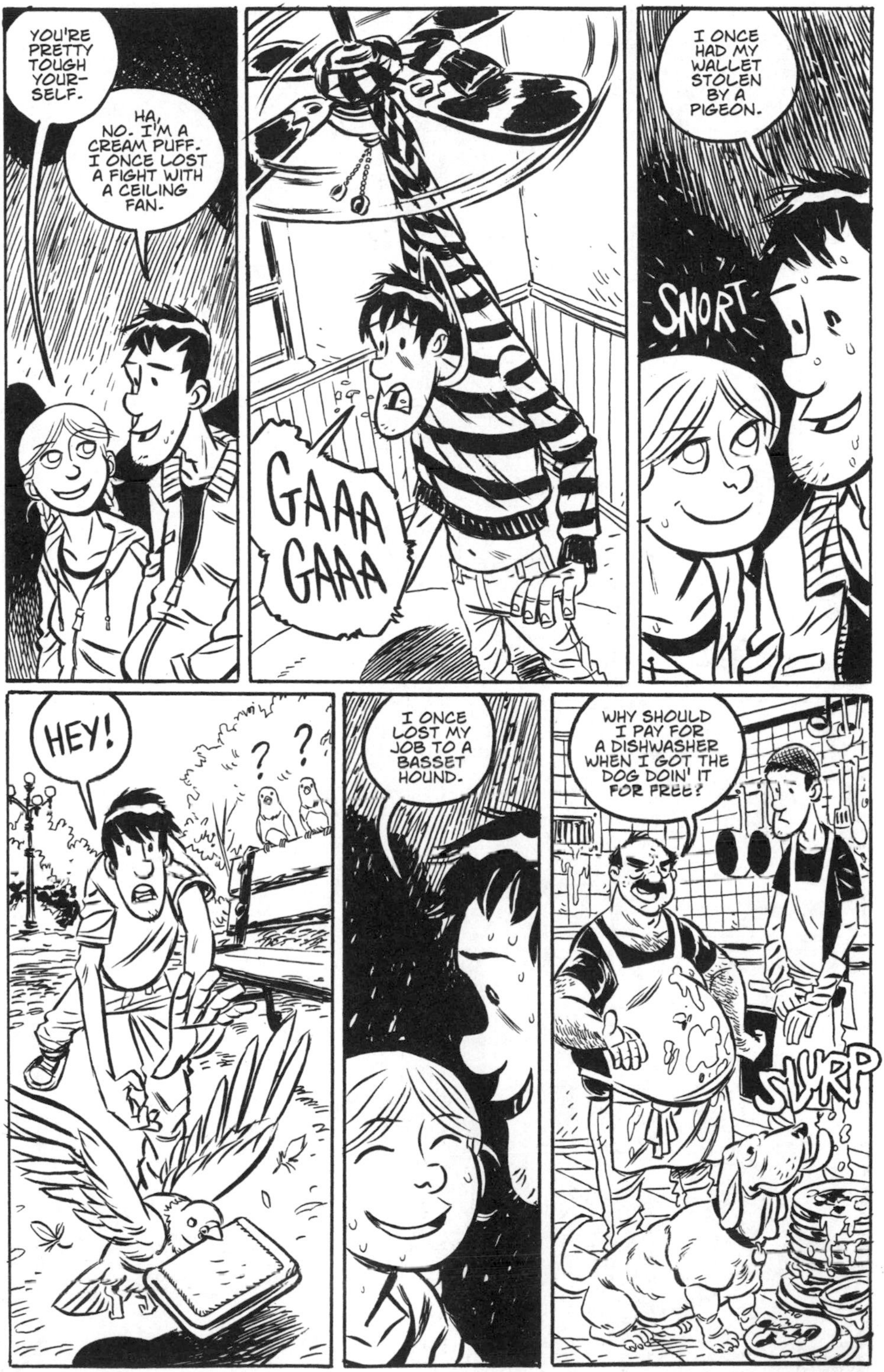
YOU'RE PRETTY TOUGH YOURSELF.
HA, NO. I'M A CREAM PUFF. I ONCE LOST A FIGHT WITH A CEILING FAN.
GAAA GAAA
I ONCE HAD MY WALLET STOLEN BY A PIGEON.
SNORT
HEY!
? ?
I ONCE LOST MY JOB TO A BASSET HOUND.
WHY SHOULD I PAY FOR A DISHWASHER WHEN I GOT THE DOG DOIN' IT FOR FREE?
SLURP

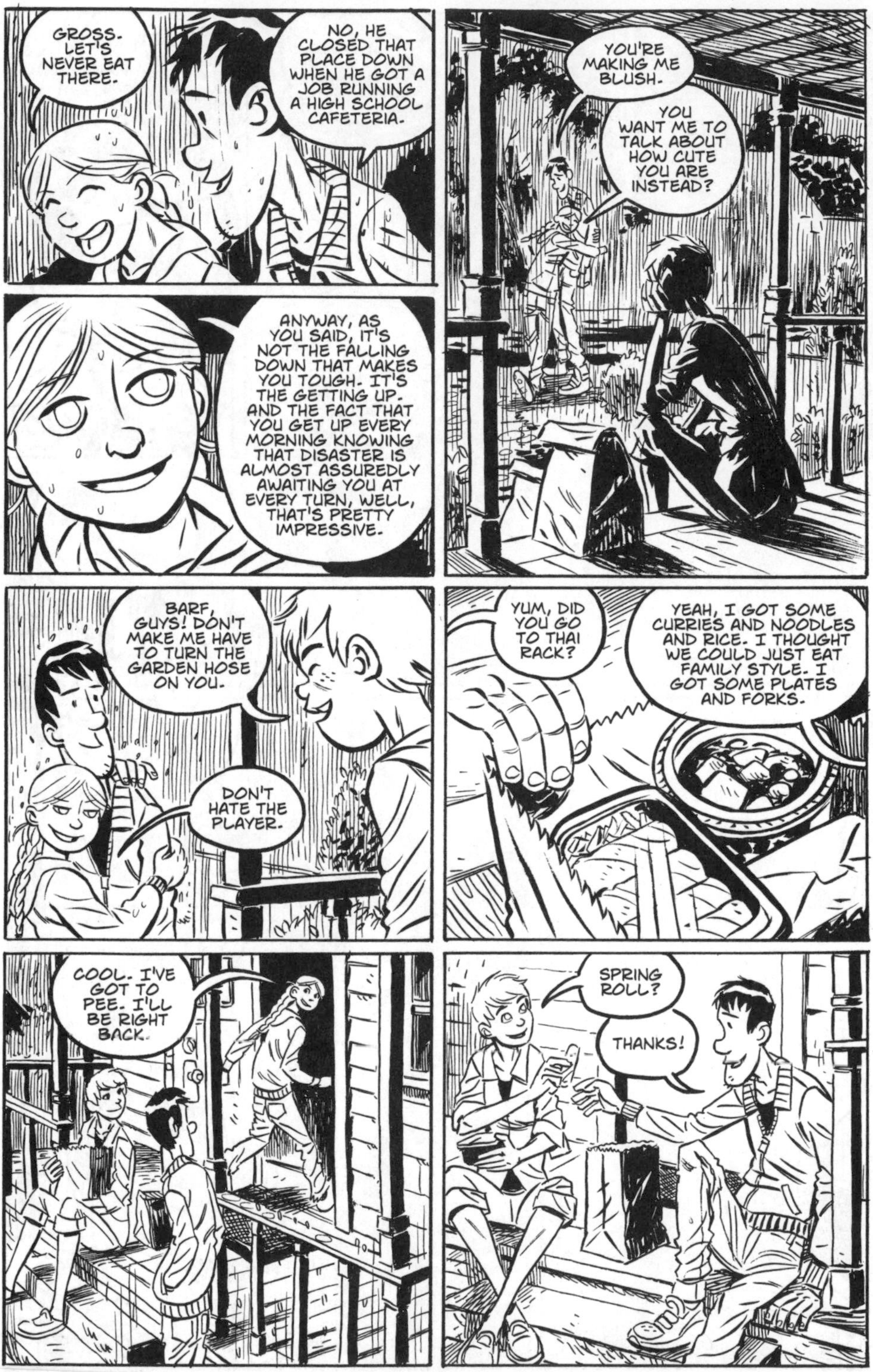
GROSS. LET'S NEVER EAT THERE.
NO, HE CLOSED THAT PLACE DOWN WHEN HE GOT A JOB RUNNING A HIGH SCHOOL CAFETERIA.
YOU'RE MAKING ME BLUSH.
YOU WANT ME TO TALK ABOUT HOW CUTE YOU ARE INSTEAD?
ANYWAY, AS YOU SAID, IT'S NOT THE FALLING DOWN THAT MAKES YOU TOUGH. IT'S THE GETTING UP. AND THE FACT THAT YOU GET UP EVERY MORNING KNOWING THAT DISASTER IS ALMOST ASSUREDLY AWAITING YOU AT EVERY TURN, WELL, THAT'S PRETTY IMPRESSIVE.
BARF, GUYS! DON'T MAKE ME HAVE TO TURN THE GARDEN HOSE ON YOU.
DON'T HATE THE PLAYER.
YUM, DID YOU GO TO THAI RACK?
YEAH, I GOT SOME CURRIES AND NOODLES AND RICE. I THOUGHT WE COULD JUST EAT FAMILY STYLE. I GOT SOME PLATES AND FORKS.
COOL. I'VE GOT TO PEE. I'LL BE RIGHT BACK.
SPRING ROLL?
THANKS!

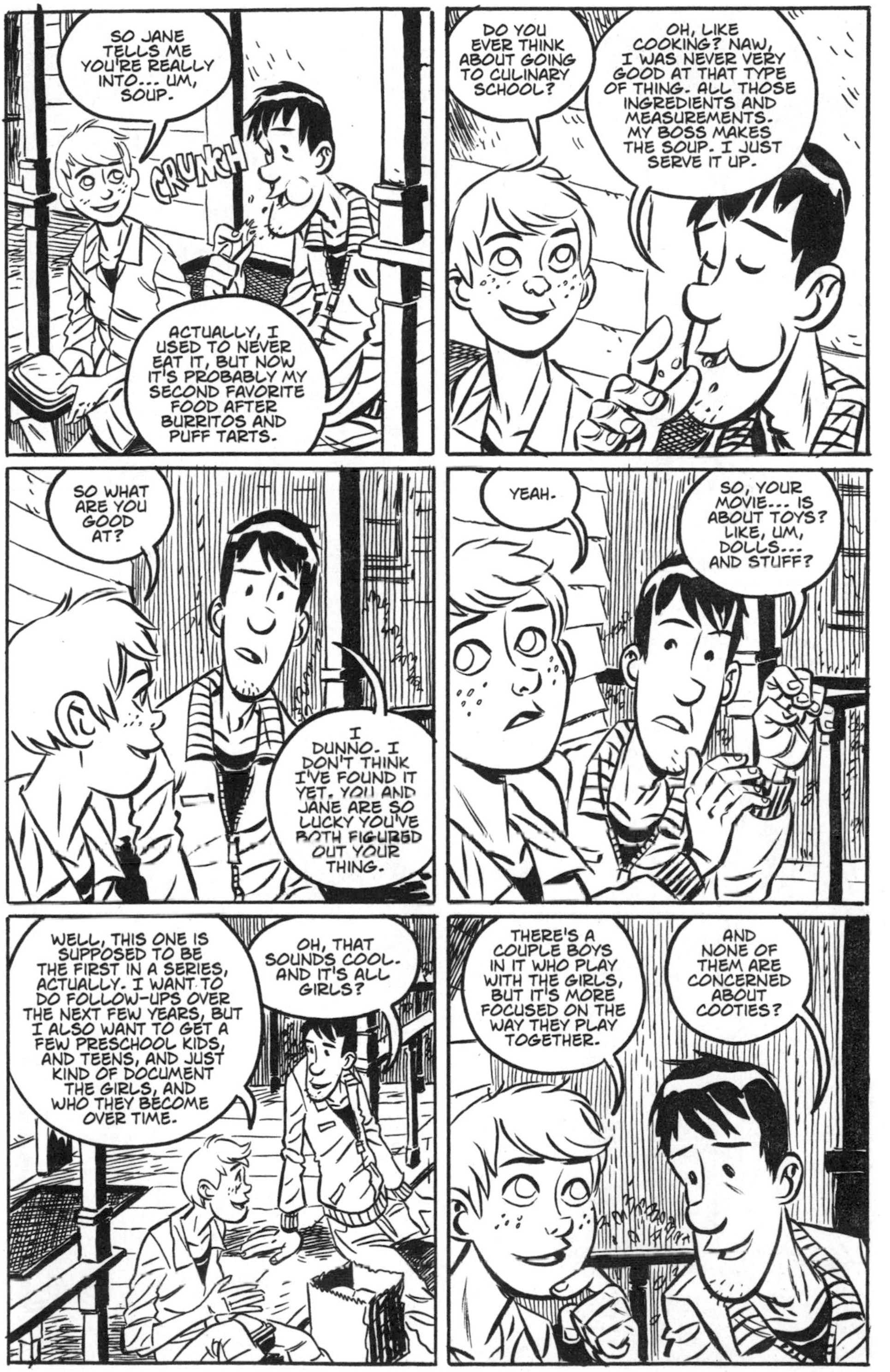
SO JANE TELLS ME YOU'RE REALLY INTO... UM, SOUP.
CRUNCH
ACTUALLY, I USED TO NEVER EAT IT, BUT NOW IT'S PROBABLY MY SECOND FAVORITE FOOD AFTER BURRITOS AND PUFF TARTS.
DO YOU EVER THINK ABOUT GOING TO CULINARY SCHOOL?
OH, LIKE COOKING? NAW, I WAS NEVER VERY GOOD AT THAT TYPE OF THING. ALL THOSE INGREDIENTS AND MEASUREMENTS. MY BOSS MAKES THE SOUP. I JUST SERVE IT UP.
SO WHAT ARE YOU GOOD AT?
I DUNNO. I DON'T THINK I'VE FOUND IT YET. YOU AND JANE ARE SO LUCKY YOU'VE BOTH FIGURED OUT YOUR THING.
YEAH.
SO, YOUR MOVIE... IS ABOUT TOYS? LIKE, UM, DOLLS... AND STUFF?
WELL, THIS ONE IS SUPPOSED TO BE THE FIRST IN A SERIES, ACTUALLY. I WANT TO DO FOLLOW-UPS OVER THE NEXT FEW YEARS, BUT I ALSO WANT TO GET A FEW PRESCHOOL KIDS, AND TEENS, AND JUST KIND OF DOCUMENT THE GIRLS, AND WHO THEY BECOME OVER TIME.
OH, THAT SOUNDS COOL. AND IT'S ALL GIRLS?
THERE'S A COUPLE BOYS IN IT WHO PLAY WITH THE GIRLS, BUT IT'S MORE FOCUSED ON THE WAY THEY PLAY TOGETHER.
AND NONE OF THEM ARE CONCERNED ABOUT COOTIES?

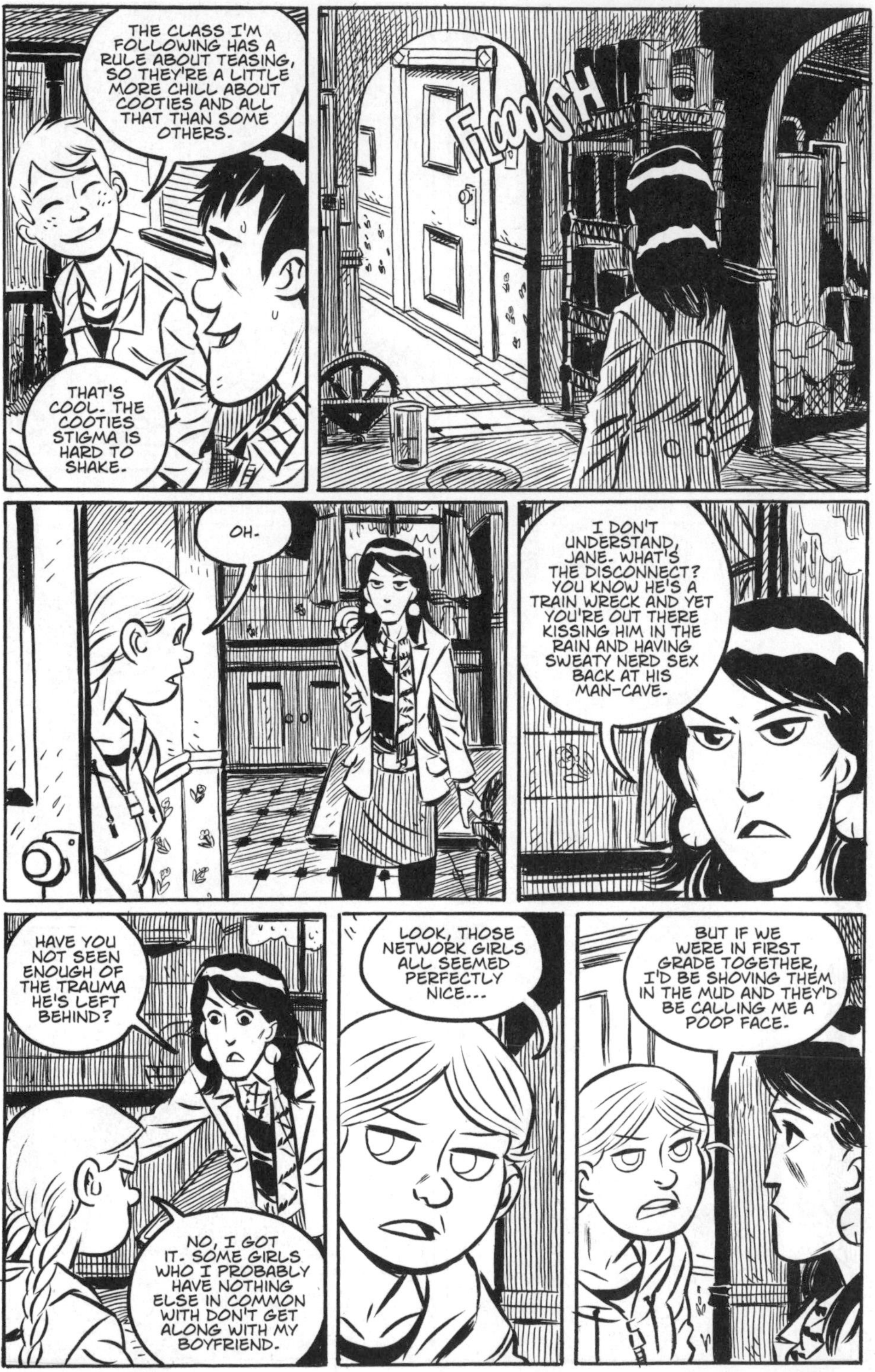
THE CLASS I'M FOLLOWING HAS A RULE ABOUT TEASING, SO THEY'RE A LITTLE MORE CHILL ABOUT COOTIES AND ALL THAT THAN SOME OTHERS.
THAT'S COOL. THE COOTIES STIGMA IS HARD TO SHAKE.
FLOOOSH
OH.
I DON'T UNDERSTAND, JANE. WHAT'S THE DISCONNECT? YOU KNOW HE'S A TRAIN WRECK AND YET YOU'RE OUT THERE KISSING HIM IN THE RAIN AND HAVING SWEATY NERD SEX BACK AT HIS MAN-CAVE.
HAVE YOU NOT SEEN ENOUGH OF THE TRAUMA HE'S LEFT BEHIND?
NO, I GOT IT. SOME GIRLS WHO I PROBABLY HAVE NOTHING ELSE IN COMMON WITH DON'T GET ALONG WITH MY BOYFRIEND.
LOOK, THOSE NETWORK GIRLS ALL SEEMED PERFECTLY NICE...
BUT IF WE WERE IN FIRST GRADE TOGETHER, I'D BE SHOVING THEM IN THE MUD AND THEY'D BE CALLING ME A POOP FACE.

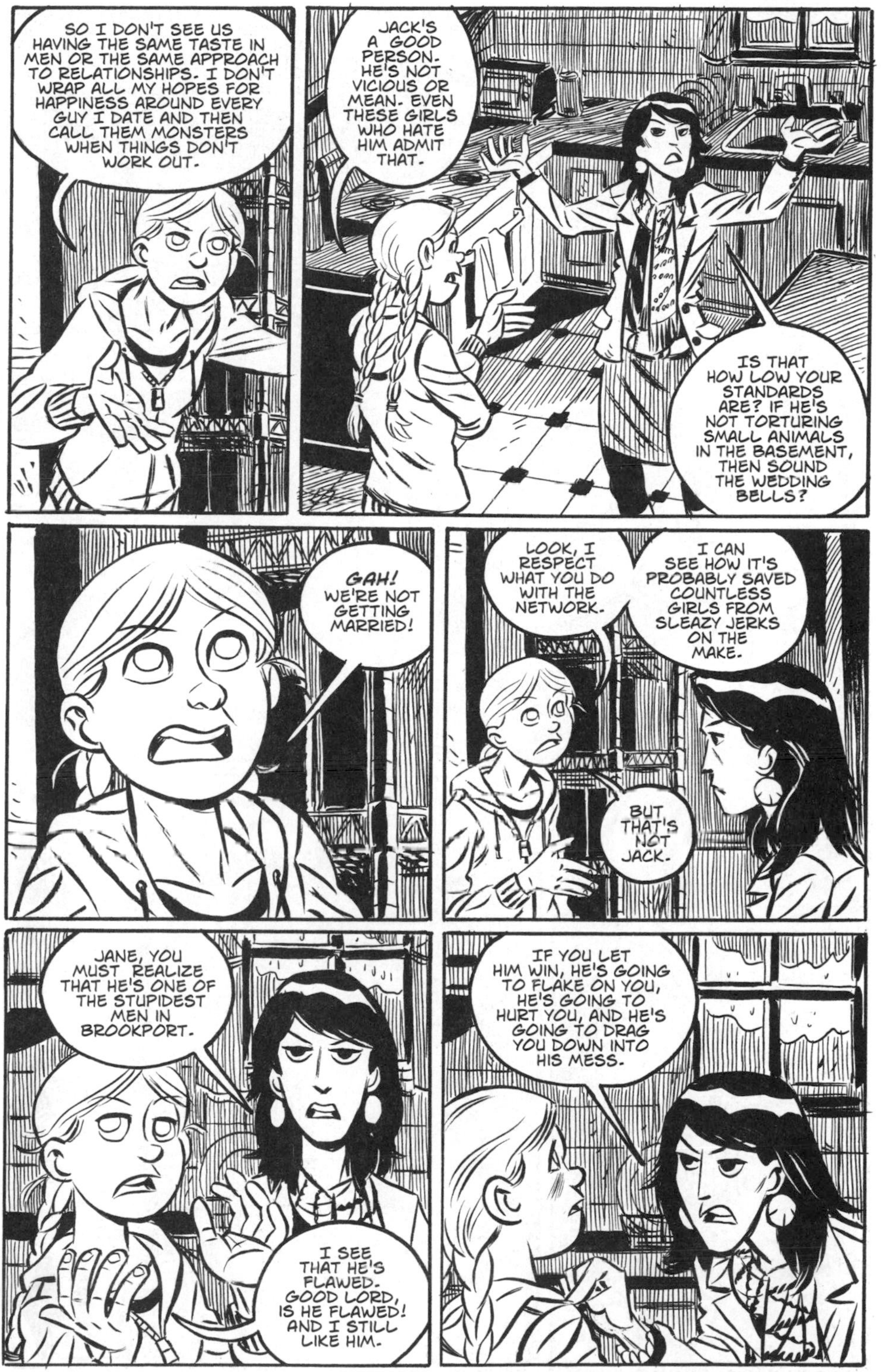
SO I DON'T SEE US HAVING THE SAME TASTE IN MEN OR THE SAME APPROACH TO RELATIONSHIPS. I DON'T WRAP ALL MY HOPES FOR HAPPINESS AROUND EVERY GUY I DATE AND THEN CALL THEM MONSTERS WHEN THINGS DON'T WORK OUT.
JACK'S A GOOD PERSON. HE'S NOT VICIOUS OR MEAN. EVEN THESE GIRLS WHO HATE HIM ADMIT THAT.
IS THAT HOW LOW YOUR STANDARDS ARE? IF HE'S NOT TORTURING SMALL ANIMALS IN THE BASEMENT, THEN SOUND THE WEDDING BELLS?
GAH! WE'RE NOT GETTING MARRIED!
LOOK, I RESPECT WHAT YOU DO WITH THE NETWORK.
I CAN SEE HOW IT'S PROBABLY SAVED COUNTLESS GIRLS FROM SLEAZY JERKS ON THE MAKE.
BUT THAT'S NOT JACK.
JANE, YOU MUST REALIZE THAT HE'S ONE OF THE STUPIDEST MEN IN BROOKPORT.
I SEE THAT HE'S FLAWED. GOOD LORD, IS HE FLAWED! AND I STILL LIKE HIM.
IF YOU LET HIM WIN, HE'S GOING TO FLAKE ON YOU, HE'S GOING TO HURT YOU, AND HE'S GOING TO DRAG YOU DOWN INTO HIS MESS.

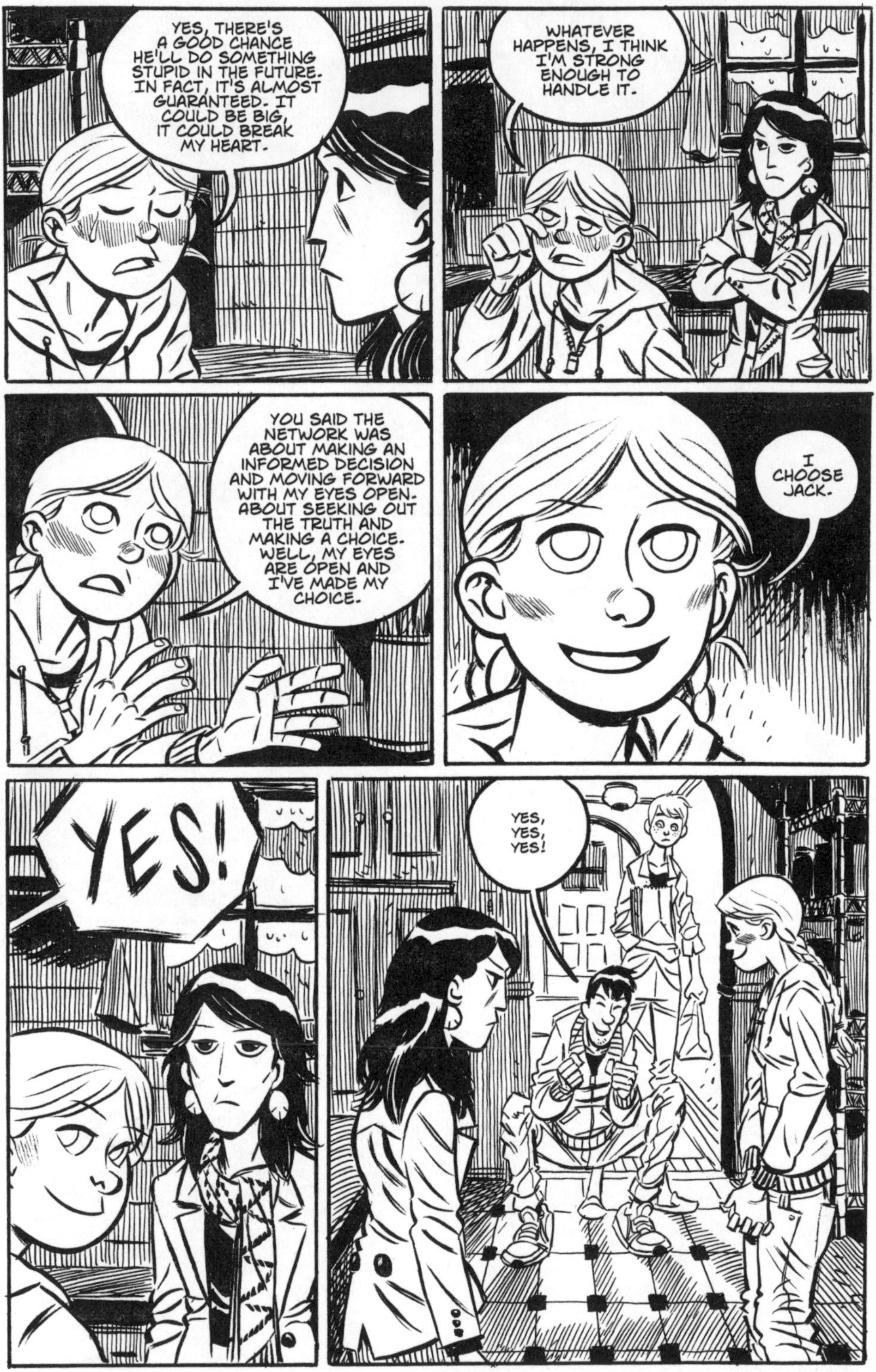
YES, THERE'S A GOOD CHANCE HE'LL DO SOMETHING STUPID IN THE FUTURE. IN FACT, IT'S ALMOST GUARANTEED. IT COULD BE BIG, IT COULD BREAK MY HEART.
WHATEVER HAPPENS, I THINK I'M STRONG ENOUGH TO HANDLE IT.
YOU SAID THE NETWORK WAS ABOUT MAKING AN INFORMED DECISION AND MOVING FORWARD WITH MY EYES OPEN. ABOUT SEEKING OUT THE TRUTH AND MAKING A CHOICE. WELL, MY EYES ARE OPEN AND I'VE MADE MY CHOICE.
I CHOOSE JACK.
YES!
YES, YES, YES!

CHAPTER SEVEN

"The Only Girl in Shredmore"

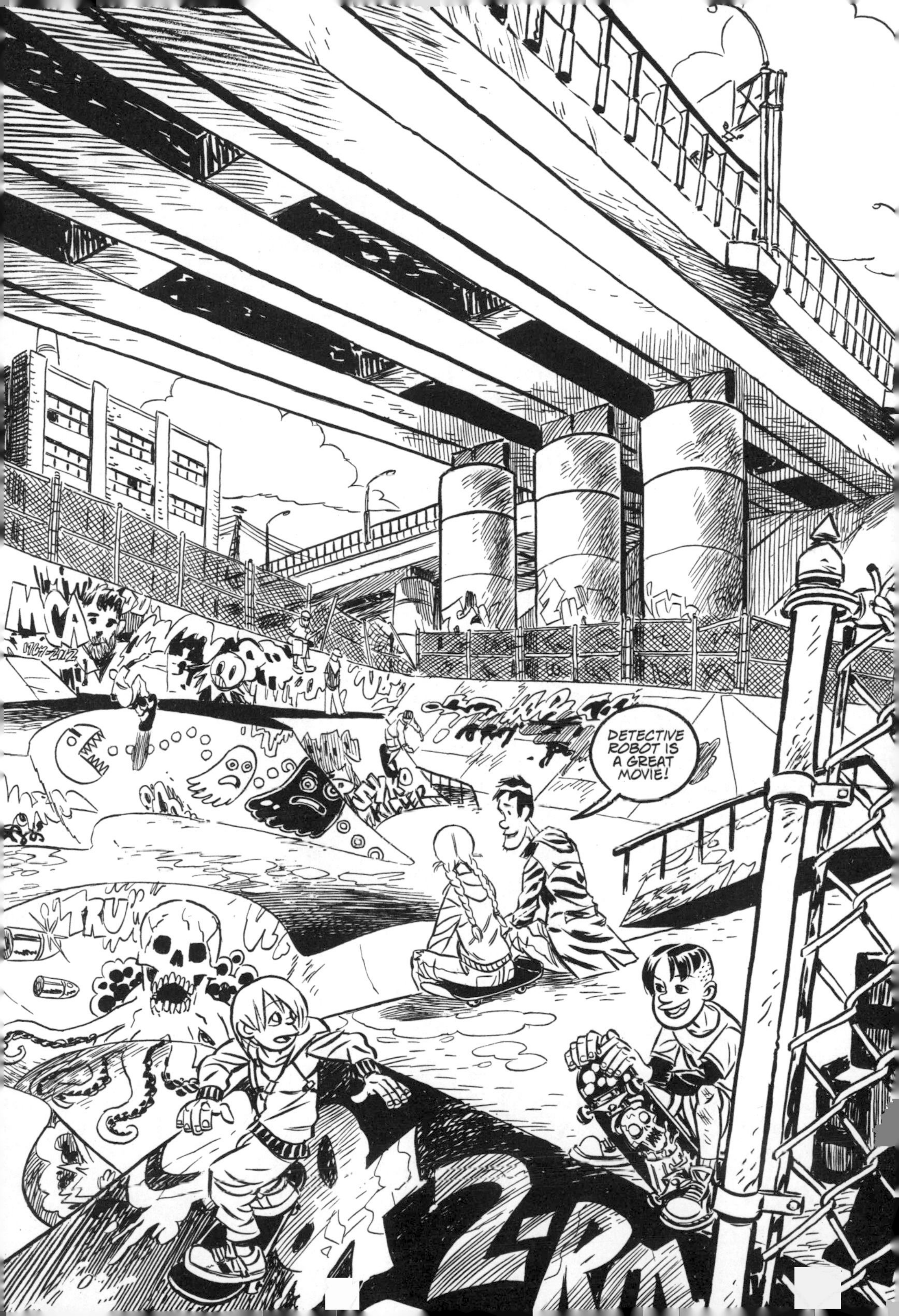
DETECTIVE ROBOT IS A GREAT MOVIE!

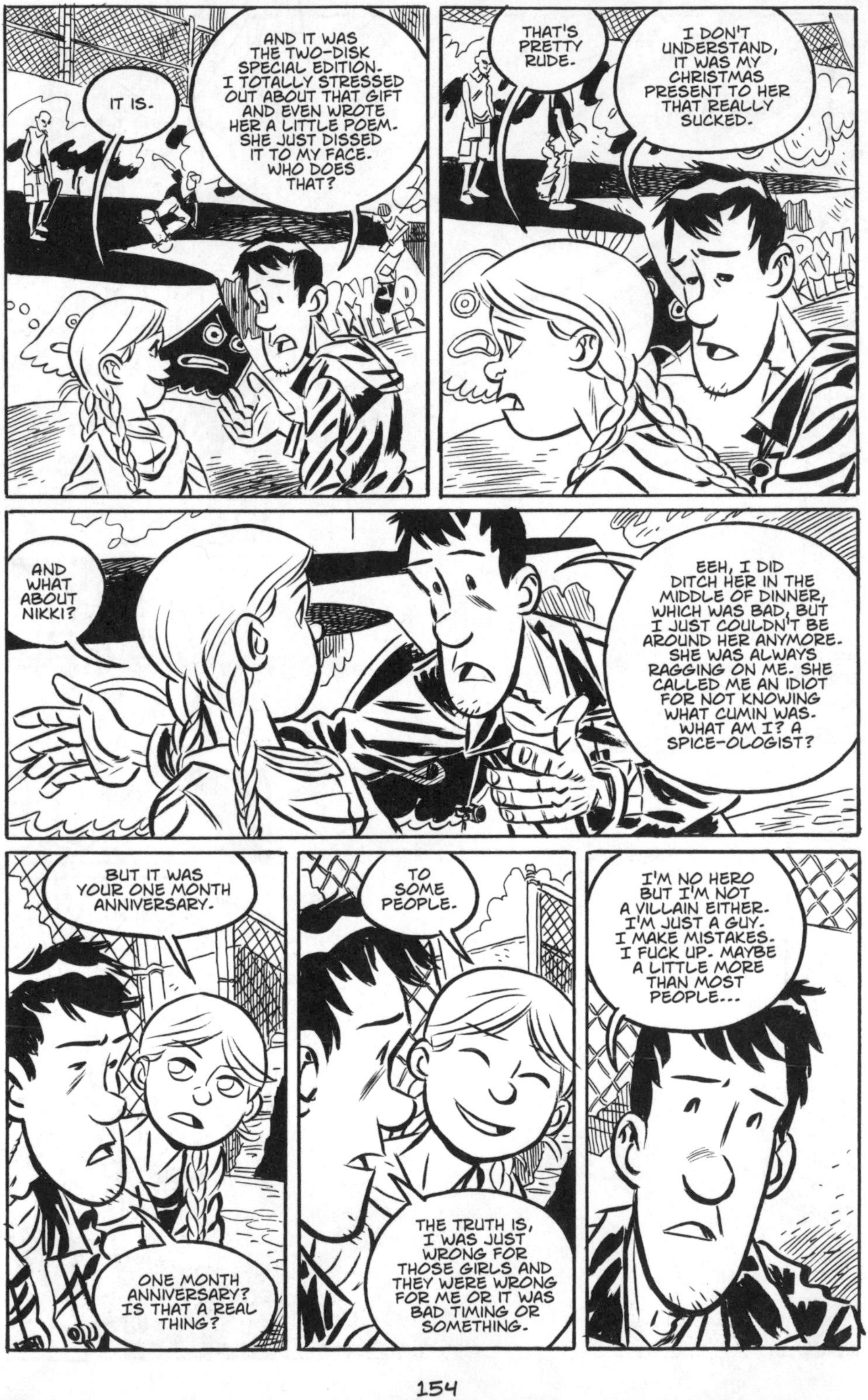
IT IS.
AND IT WAS THE TWO-DISK SPECIAL EDITION. I TOTALLY STRESSED OUT ABOUT THAT GIFT AND EVEN WROTE HER A LITTLE POEM. SHE JUST DISSED IT TO MY FACE. WHO DOES THAT?
KILLER
THAT'S PRETTY RUDE.
I DON'T UNDERSTAND, IT WAS MY CHRISTMAS PRESENT TO HER THAT REALLY SUCKED.
KILLER
AND WHAT ABOUT NIKKI?
EEH, I DID DITCH HER IN THE MIDDLE OF DINNER, WHICH WAS BAD, BUT I JUST COULDN'T BE AROUND HER ANYMORE. SHE WAS ALWAYS RAGGING ON ME. SHE CALLED ME AN IDIOT FOR NOT KNOWING WHAT CUMIN WAS. WHAT AM I? A SPICE-OLOGIST?
BUT IT WAS YOUR ONE MONTH ANNIVERSARY.
ONE MONTH ANNIVERSARY? IS THAT A REAL THING?
TO SOME PEOPLE.
THE TRUTH IS, I WAS JUST WRONG FOR THOSE GIRLS AND THEY WERE WRONG FOR ME OR IT WAS BAD TIMING OR SOMETHING.
I'M NO HERO BUT I'M NOT A VILLAIN EITHER. I'M JUST A GUY. I MAKE MISTAKES. I FUCK UP. MAYBE A LITTLE MORE THAN MOST PEOPLE...

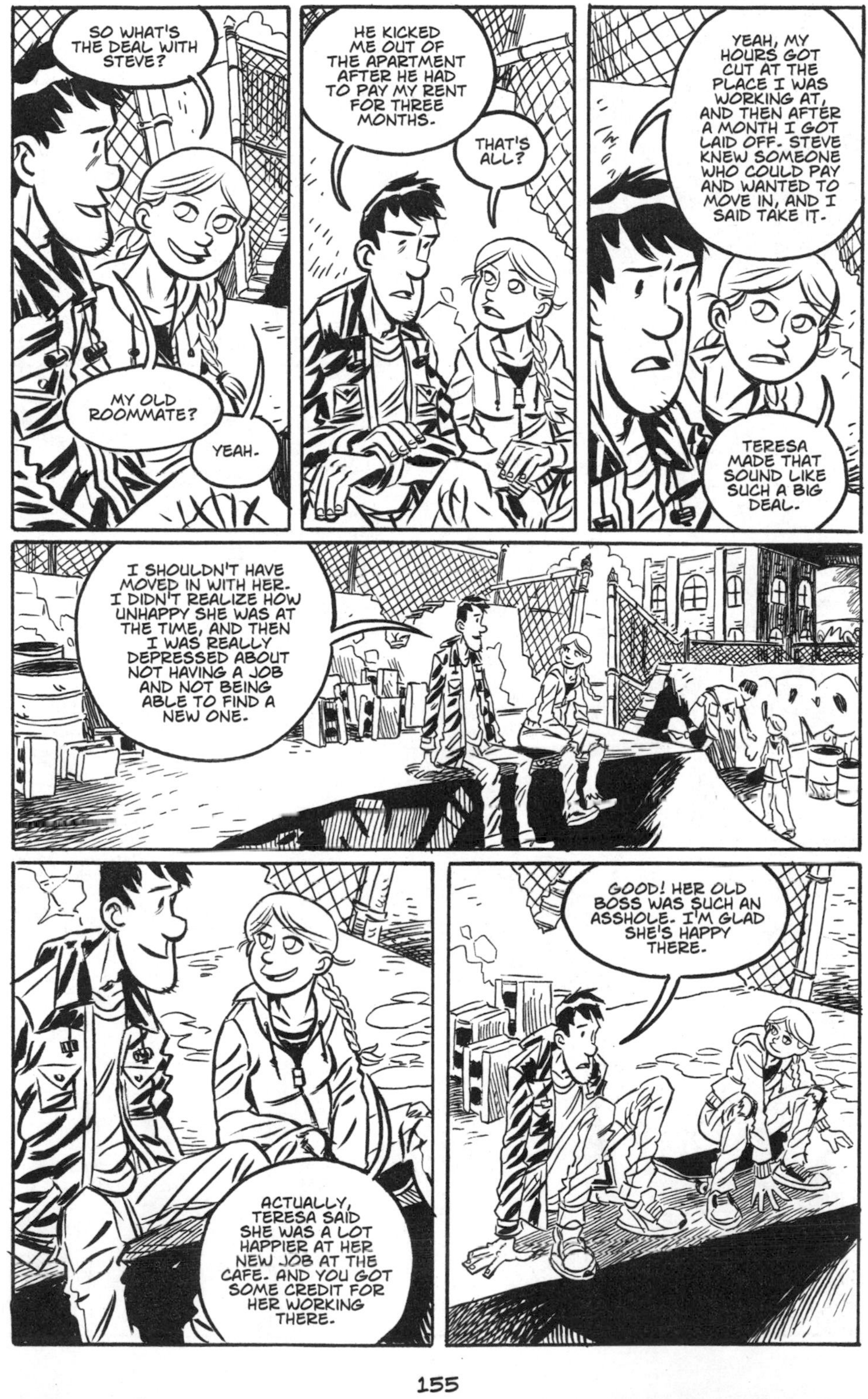

SO WHAT'S THE DEAL WITH STEVE?
MY OLD ROOMMATE?
YEAH.
HE KICKED ME OUT OF THE APARTMENT AFTER HE HAD TO PAY MY RENT FOR THREE MONTHS.
THAT'S ALL?
YEAH, MY HOURS GOT CUT AT THE PLACE I WAS WORKING AT, AND THEN AFTER A MONTH I GOT LAID OFF. STEVE KNEW SOMEONE WHO COULD PAY AND WANTED TO MOVE IN, AND I SAID TAKE IT.
TERESA MADE THAT SOUND LIKE SUCH A BIG DEAL.
I SHOULDN'T HAVE MOVED IN WITH HER. I DIDN'T REALIZE HOW UNHAPPY SHE WAS AT THE TIME, AND THEN I WAS REALLY DEPRESSED ABOUT NOT HAVING A JOB AND NOT BEING ABLE TO FIND A NEW ONE.
ACTUALLY, TERESA SAID SHE WAS A LOT HAPPIER AT HER NEW JOB AT THE CAFE. AND YOU GOT SOME CREDIT FOR HER WORKING THERE.
GOOD! HER OLD BOSS WAS SUCH AN ASSHOLE. I'M GLAD SHE'S HAPPY THERE.

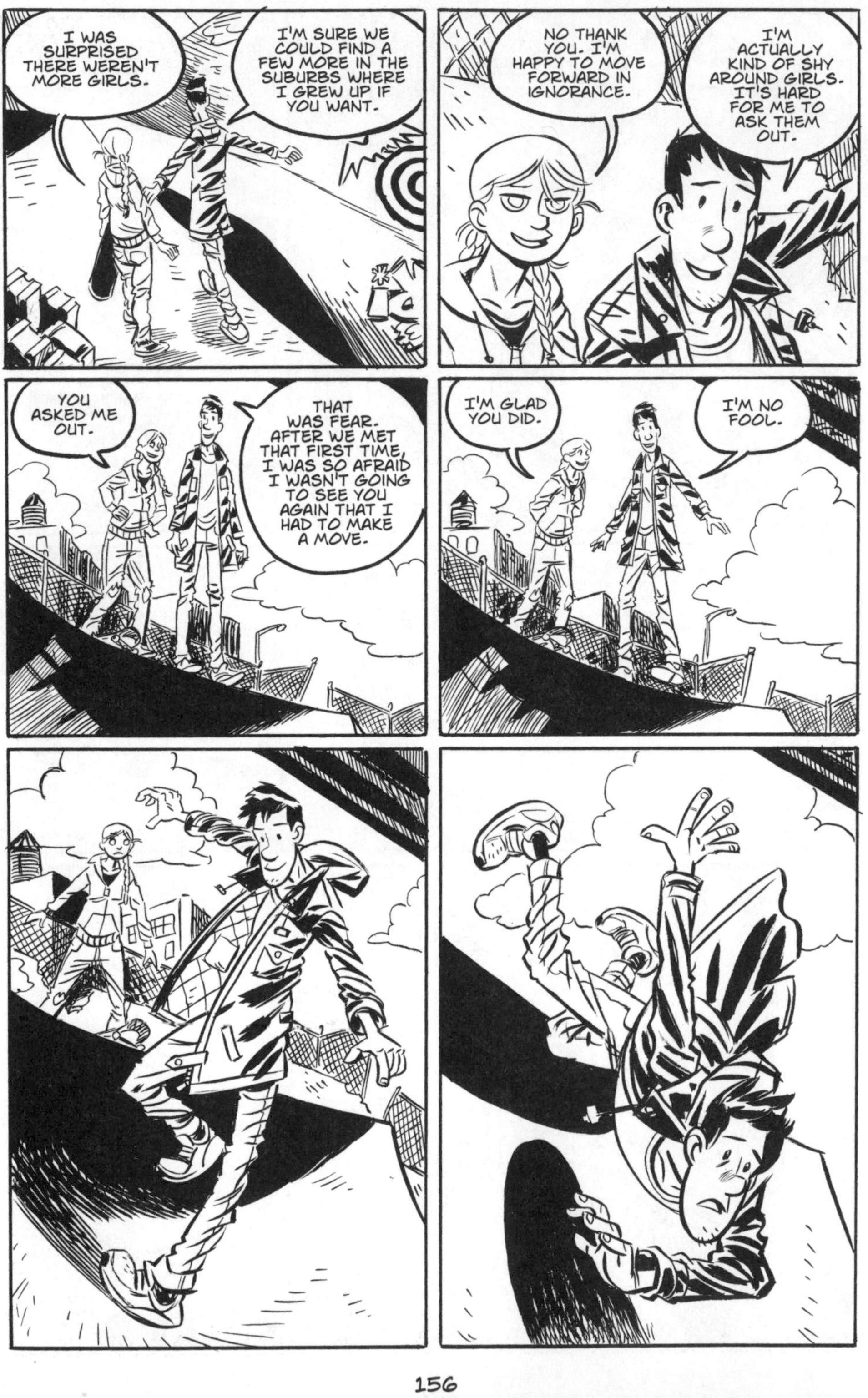

I WAS SURPRISED THERE WEREN'T MORE GIRLS.
I'M SURE WE COULD FIND A FEW MORE IN THE SUBURBS WHERE I GREW UP IF YOU WANT.
NO THANK YOU. I'M HAPPY TO MOVE FORWARD IN IGNORANCE.
I'M ACTUALLY KIND OF SHY AROUND GIRLS. IT'S HARD FOR ME TO ASK THEM OUT.
YOU ASKED ME OUT.
THAT WAS FEAR. AFTER WE MET THAT FIRST TIME, I WAS SO AFRAID I WASN'T GOING TO SEE YOU AGAIN THAT I HAD TO MAKE A MOVE.
I'M GLAD YOU DID.
I'M NO FOOL.

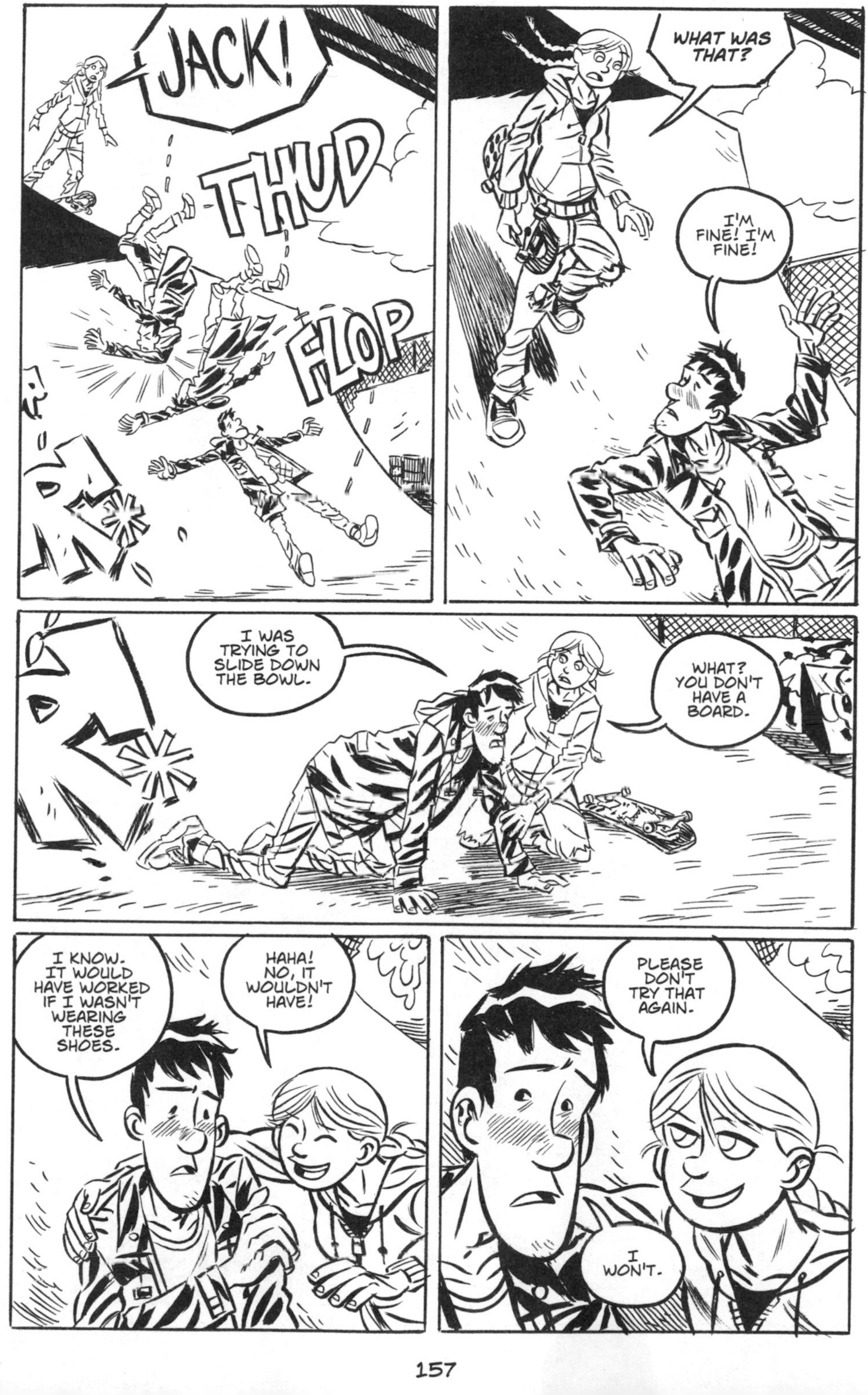
JACK!
THUD
FLOP
WHAT WAS THAT?
I'M FINE! I'M FINE!
I WAS TRYING TO SLIDE DOWN THE BOWL.
WHAT? YOU DON'T HAVE A BOARD.
I KNOW. IT WOULD HAVE WORKED IF I WASN'T WEARING THESE SHOES.
HAHA! NO, IT WOULDN'T HAVE!
PLEASE DON'T TRY THAT AGAIN.
I WON'T.

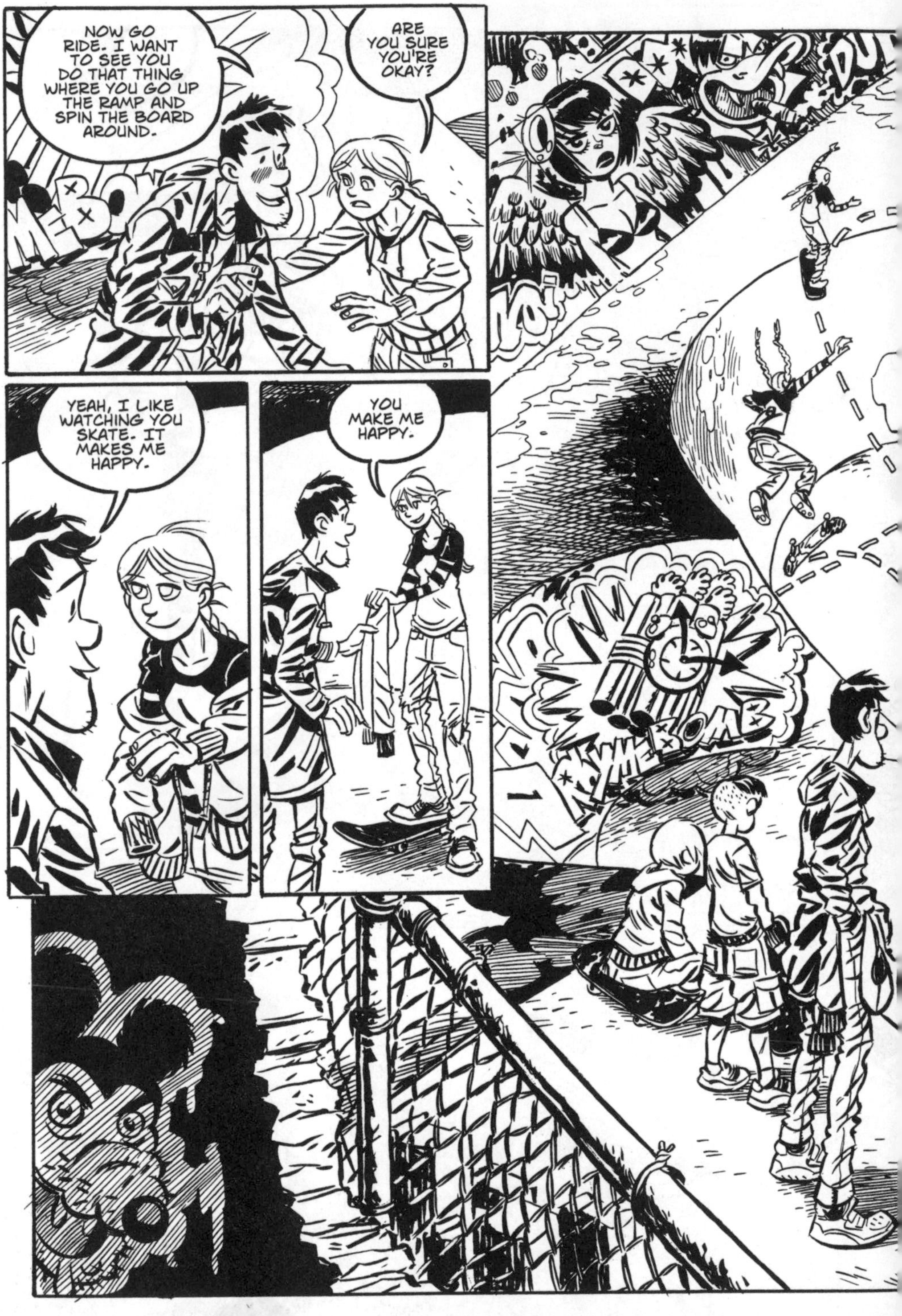
NOW GO RIDE. I WANT TO SEE YOU DO THAT THING WHERE YOU GO UP THE RAMP AND SPIN THE BOARD AROUND.
ARE YOU SURE YOU'RE OKAY?
YEAH, I LIKE WATCHING YOU SKATE. IT MAKES ME HAPPY.
YOU MAKE ME HAPPY.

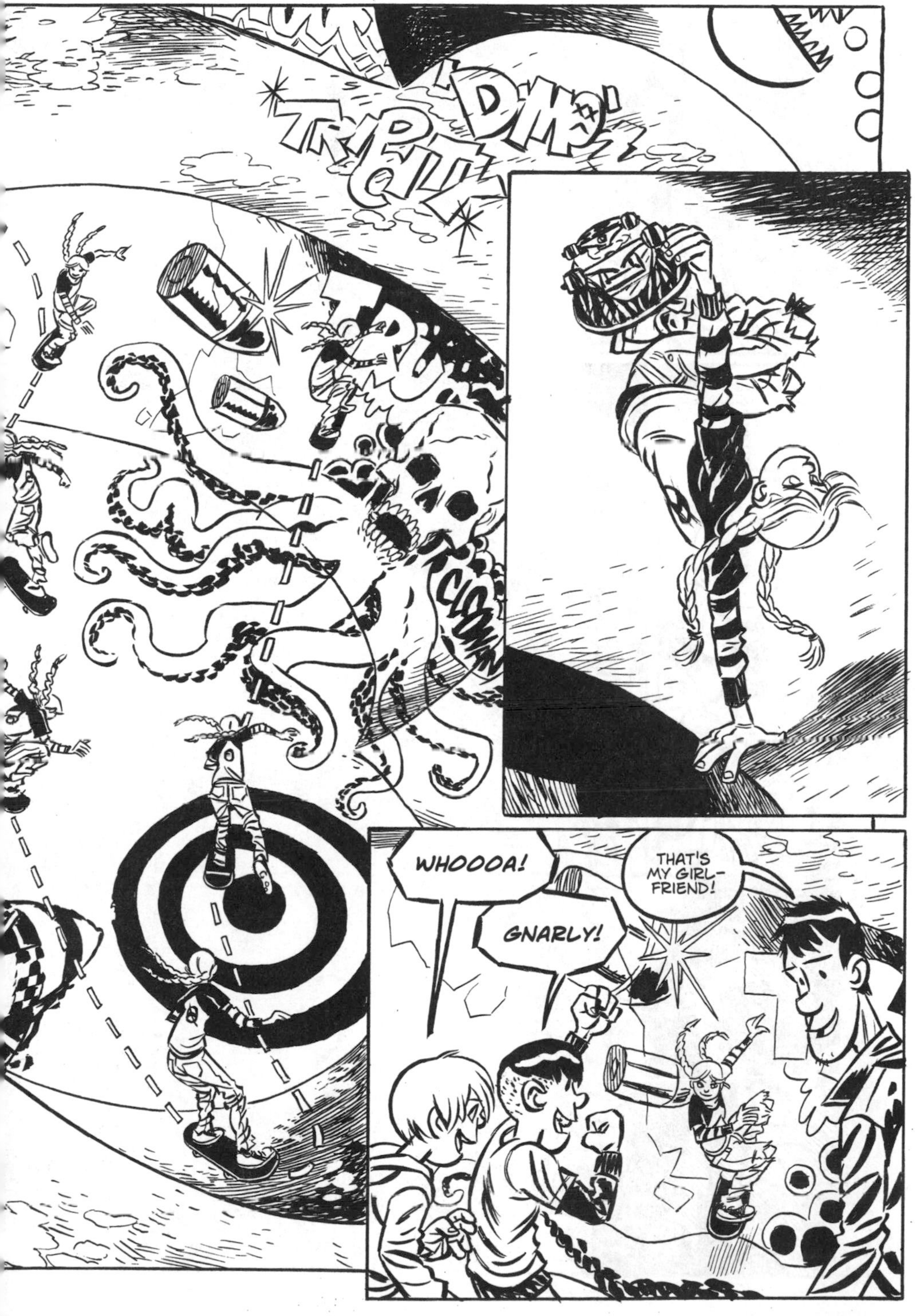
WHOOOA!
THAT'S MY GIRL-FRIEND!
GNARLY!

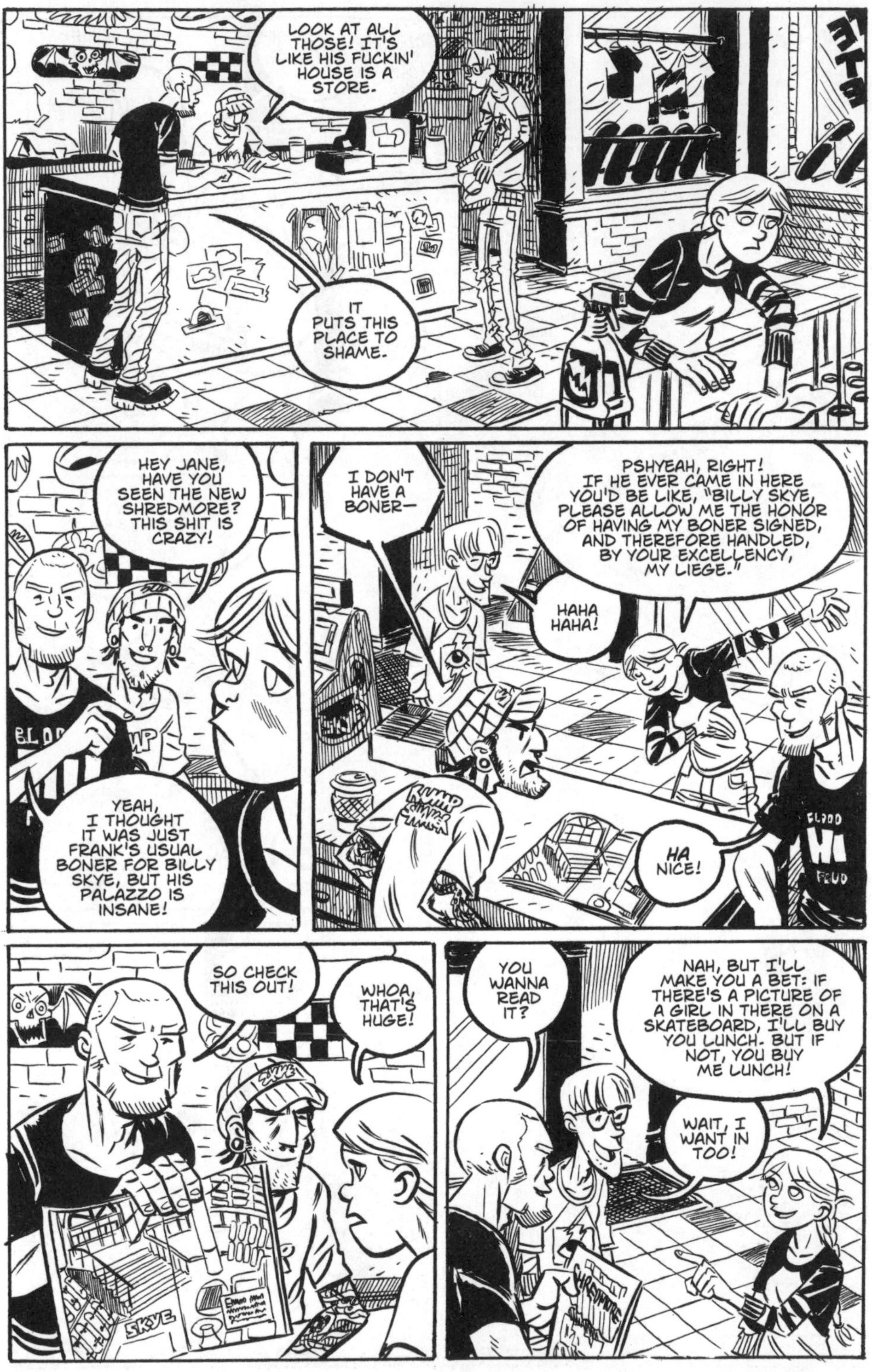
LOOK AT ALL THOSE! IT'S LIKE HIS FUCKIN' HOUSE IS A STORE.
IT PUTS THIS PLACE TO SHAME.
HEY JANE, HAVE YOU SEEN THE NEW SHREDMORE? THIS SHIT IS CRAZY!
YEAH, I THOUGHT IT WAS JUST FRANK'S USUAL BONER FOR BILLY SKYE, BUT HIS PALAZZO IS INSANE!
I DON'T HAVE A BONER—
PSHYEAH, RIGHT! IF HE EVER CAME IN HERE YOU'D BE LIKE, "BILLY SKYE, PLEASE ALLOW ME THE HONOR OF HAVING MY BONER SIGNED, AND THEREFORE HANDLED, BY YOUR EXCELLENCY, MY LIEGE."
HAHA HAHA!
HA NICE!
SO CHECK THIS OUT!
WHOA, THAT'S HUGE!
SKYE
YOU WANNA READ IT?
NAH, BUT I'LL MAKE YOU A BET: IF THERE'S A PICTURE OF A GIRL IN THERE ON A SKATEBOARD, I'LL BUY YOU LUNCH. BUT IF NOT, YOU BUY ME LUNCH!
WAIT, I WANT IN TOO!

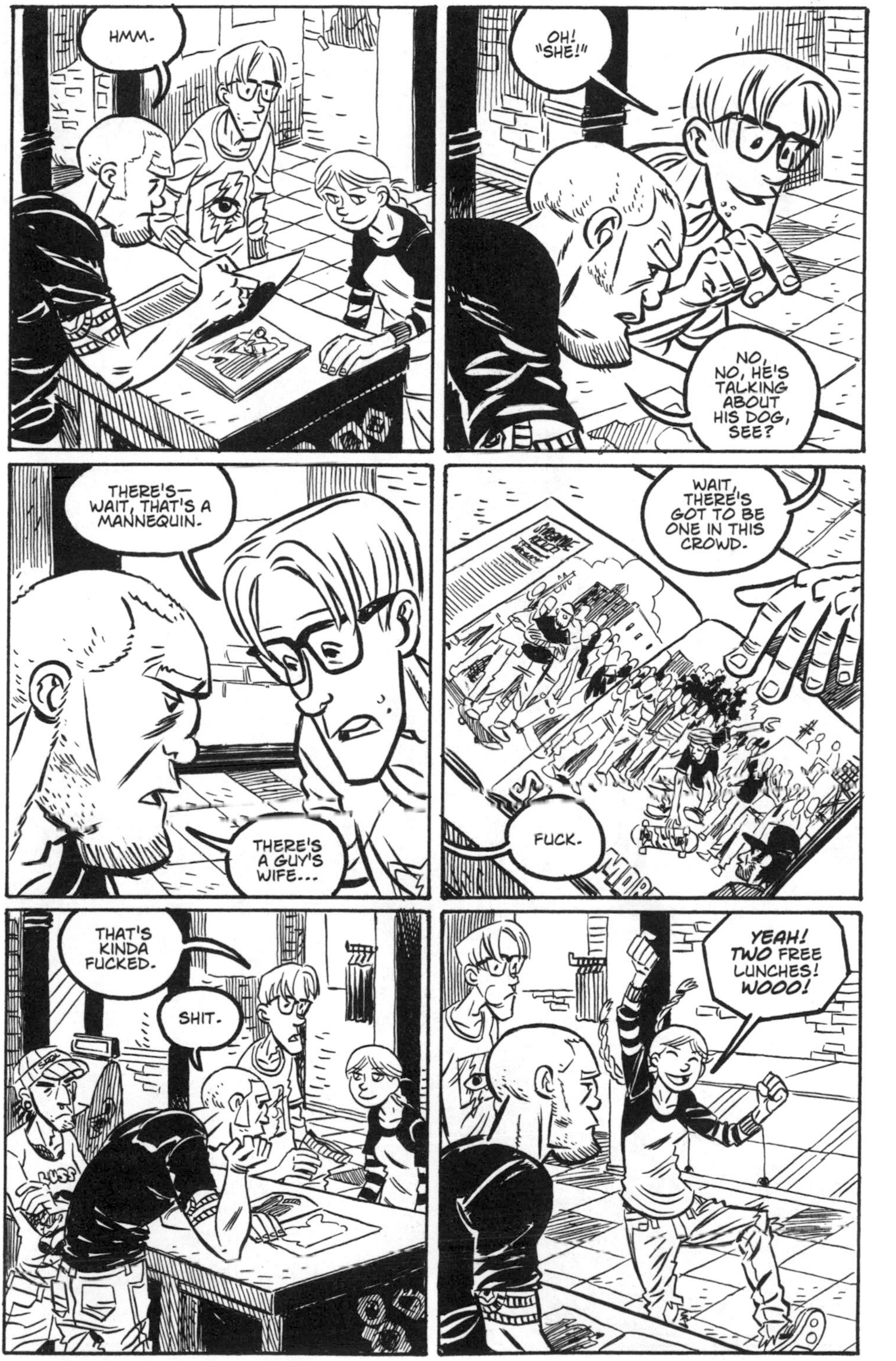
HMM.
OH! "SHE!"
NO, NO, HE'S TALKING ABOUT HIS DOG, SEE?
THERE'S— WAIT, THAT'S A MANNEQUIN.
THERE'S A GUY'S WIFE...
WAIT, THERE'S GOT TO BE ONE IN THIS CROWD.
FUCK.
THAT'S KINDA FUCKED.
SHIT.
YEAH! TWO FREE LUNCHES! WOOO!

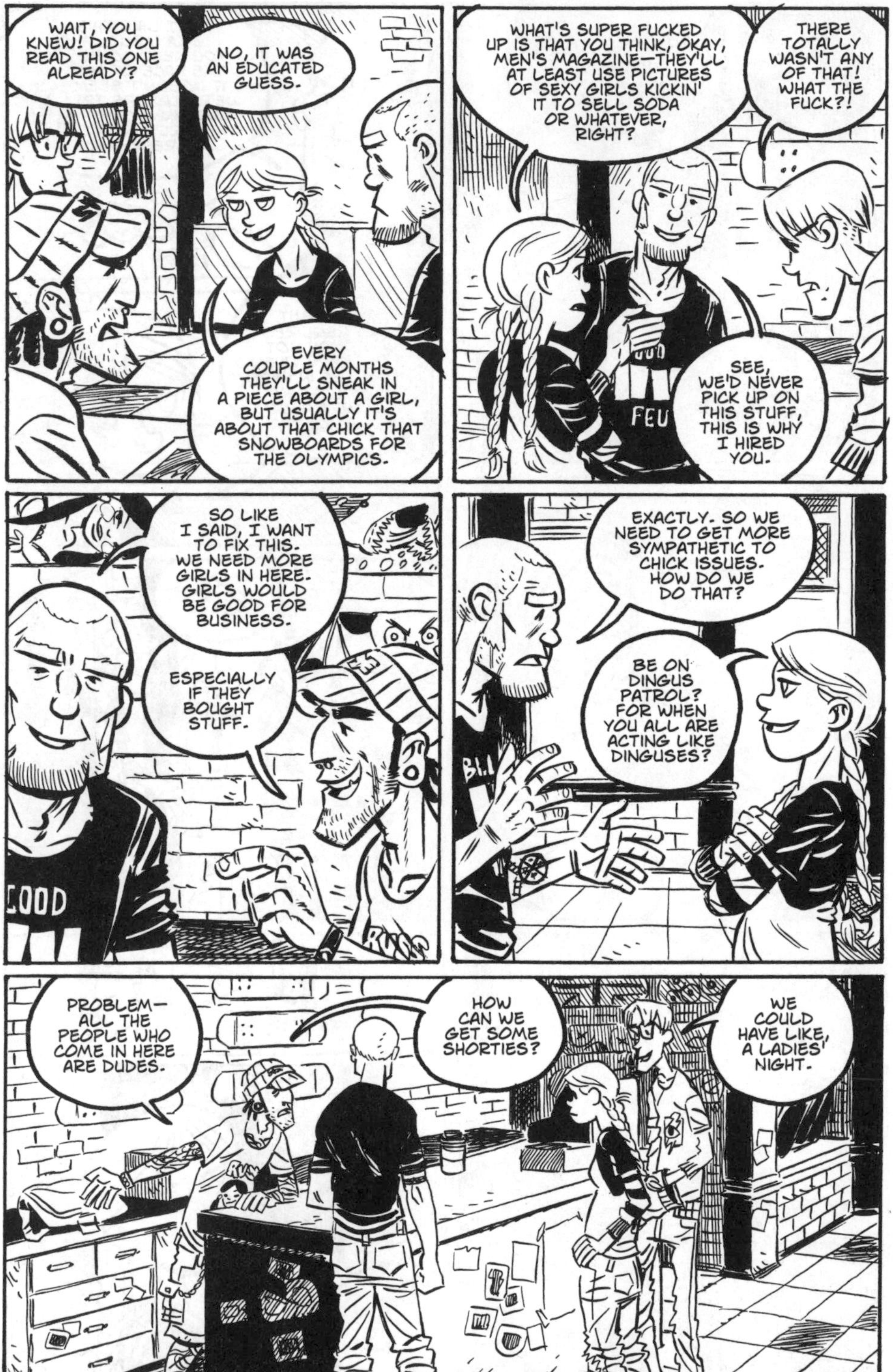
WAIT, YOU KNEW! DID YOU READ THIS ONE ALREADY?
NO, IT WAS AN EDUCATED GUESS.
EVERY COUPLE MONTHS THEY'LL SNEAK IN A PIECE ABOUT A GIRL, BUT USUALLY IT'S ABOUT THAT CHICK THAT SNOWBOARDS FOR THE OLYMPICS.
WHAT'S SUPER FUCKED UP IS THAT YOU THINK, OKAY, MEN'S MAGAZINE—THEY'LL AT LEAST USE PICTURES OF SEXY GIRLS KICKIN' IT TO SELL SODA OR WHATEVER, RIGHT?
THERE TOTALLY WASN'T ANY OF THAT! WHAT THE FUCK?!
SEE, WE'D NEVER PICK UP ON THIS STUFF, THIS IS WHY I HIRED YOU.
FEU
SO LIKE I SAID, I WANT TO FIX THIS. WE NEED MORE GIRLS IN HERE. GIRLS WOULD BE GOOD FOR BUSINESS.
ESPECIALLY IF THEY BOUGHT STUFF.
EXACTLY. SO WE NEED TO GET MORE SYMPATHETIC TO CHICK ISSUES. HOW DO WE DO THAT?
BE ON DINGUS PATROL? FOR WHEN YOU ALL ARE ACTING LIKE DINGUSES?
PROBLEM—ALL THE PEOPLE WHO COME IN HERE ARE DUDES.
HOW CAN WE GET SOME SHORTIES?
WE COULD HAVE LIKE, A LADIES' NIGHT.

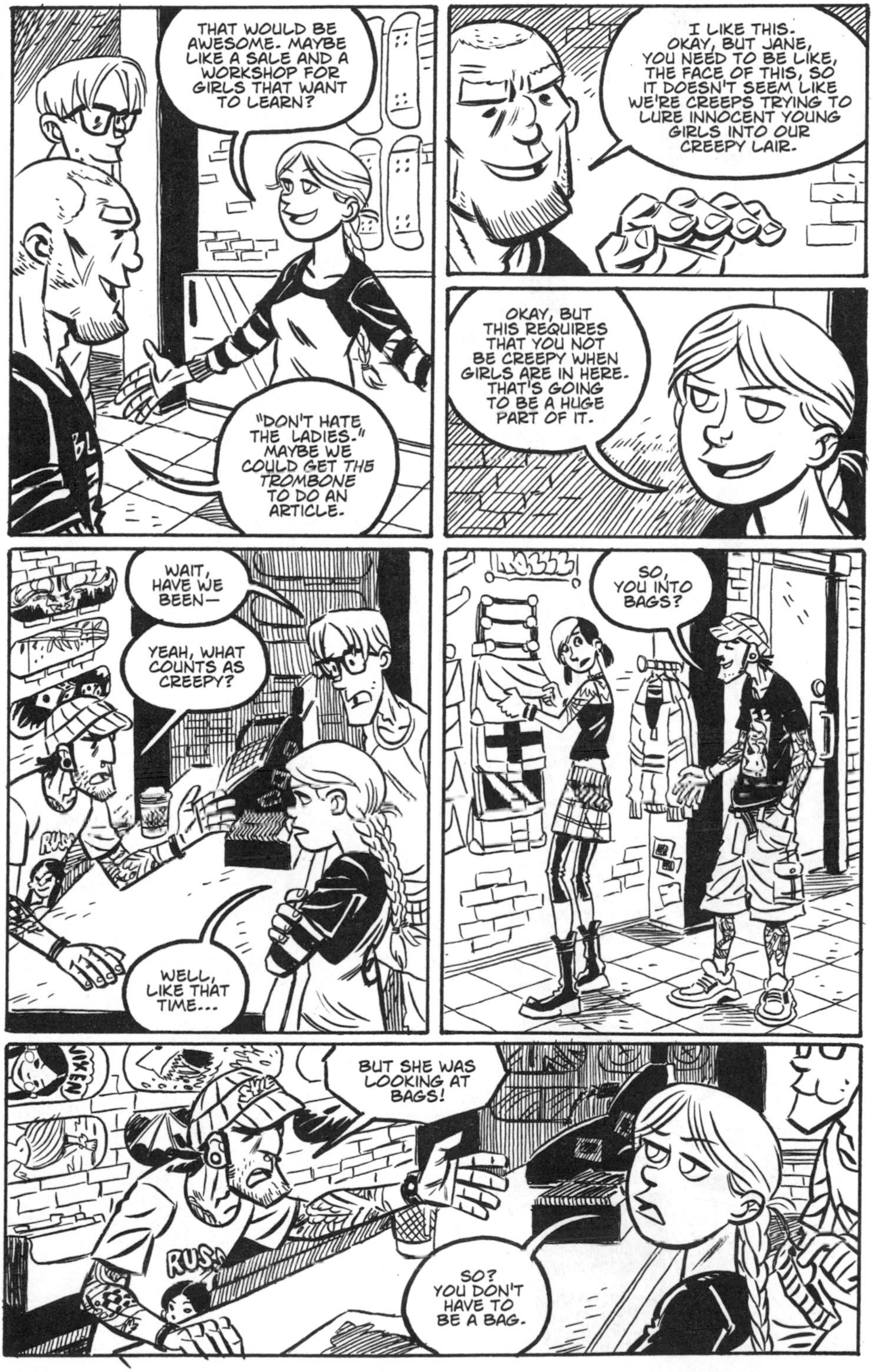
THAT WOULD BE AWESOME. MAYBE LIKE A SALE AND A WORKSHOP FOR GIRLS THAT WANT TO LEARN?
"DON'T HATE THE LADIES." MAYBE WE COULD GET THE *TROMBONE* TO DO AN ARTICLE.
I LIKE THIS. OKAY, BUT JANE, YOU NEED TO BE LIKE, THE FACE OF THIS, SO IT DOESN'T SEEM LIKE WE'RE CREEPS TRYING TO LURE INNOCENT YOUNG GIRLS INTO OUR CREEPY LAIR.
OKAY, BUT THIS REQUIRES THAT YOU NOT BE CREEPY WHEN GIRLS ARE IN HERE. THAT'S GOING TO BE A HUGE PART OF IT.
WAIT, HAVE WE BEEN—
YEAH, WHAT COUNTS AS CREEPY?
WELL, LIKE THAT TIME...
SO, YOU INTO BAGS?
BUT SHE WAS LOOKING AT BAGS!
SO? YOU DON'T HAVE TO BE A BAG.

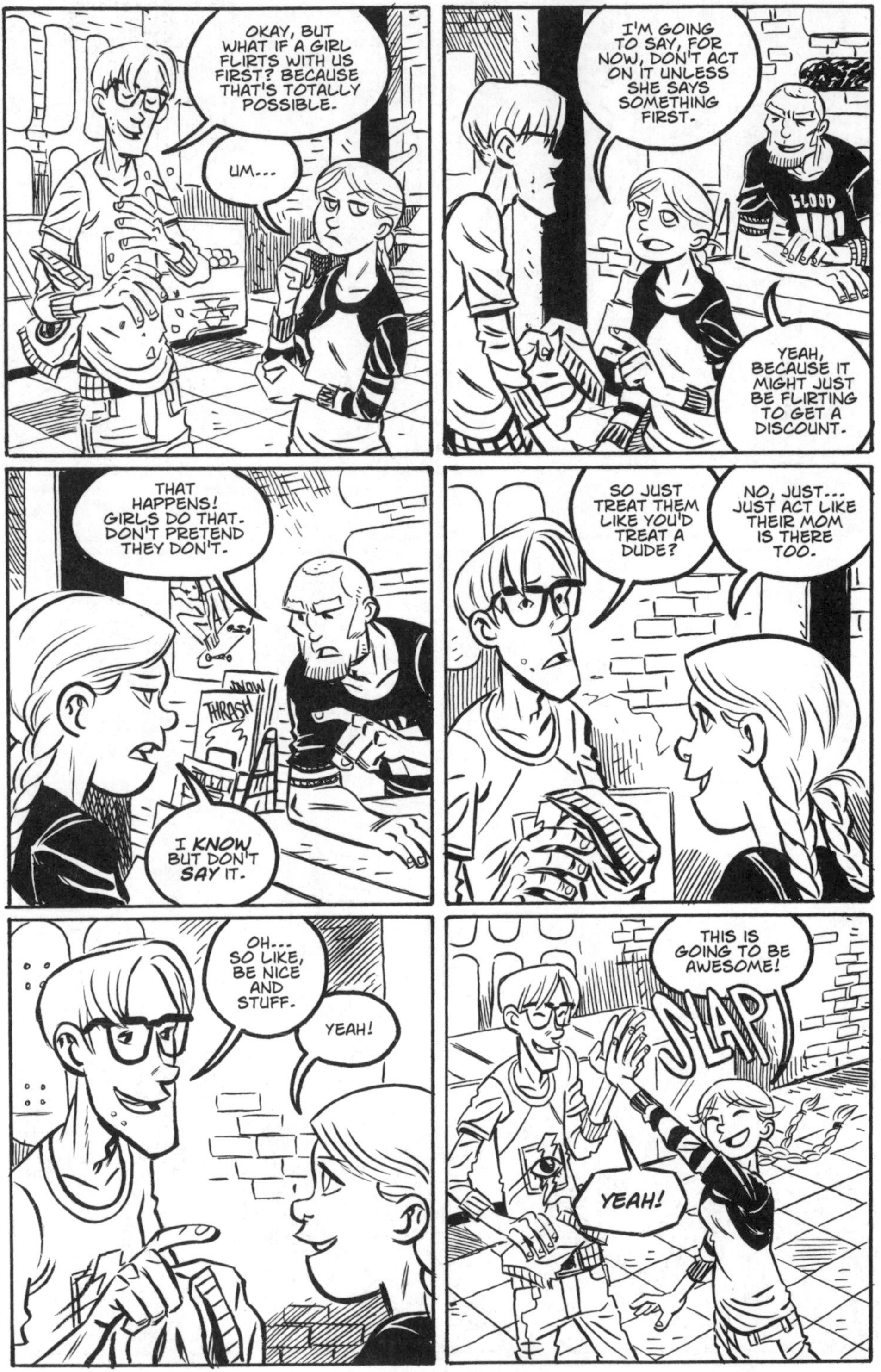
OKAY, BUT WHAT IF A GIRL FLIRTS WITH US FIRST? BECAUSE THAT'S TOTALLY POSSIBLE.
UM...
I'M GOING TO SAY, FOR NOW, DON'T ACT ON IT UNLESS SHE SAYS SOMETHING FIRST.
BLOOD
YEAH, BECAUSE IT MIGHT JUST BE FLIRTING TO GET A DISCOUNT.
THAT HAPPENS! GIRLS DO THAT. DON'T PRETEND THEY DON'T.
THRASH
I KNOW BUT DON'T SAY IT.
SO JUST TREAT THEM LIKE YOU'D TREAT A DUDE?
NO, JUST... JUST ACT LIKE THEIR MOM IS THERE TOO.
OH... SO LIKE, BE NICE AND STUFF.
YEAH!
THIS IS GOING TO BE AWESOME!
SLAP
YEAH!

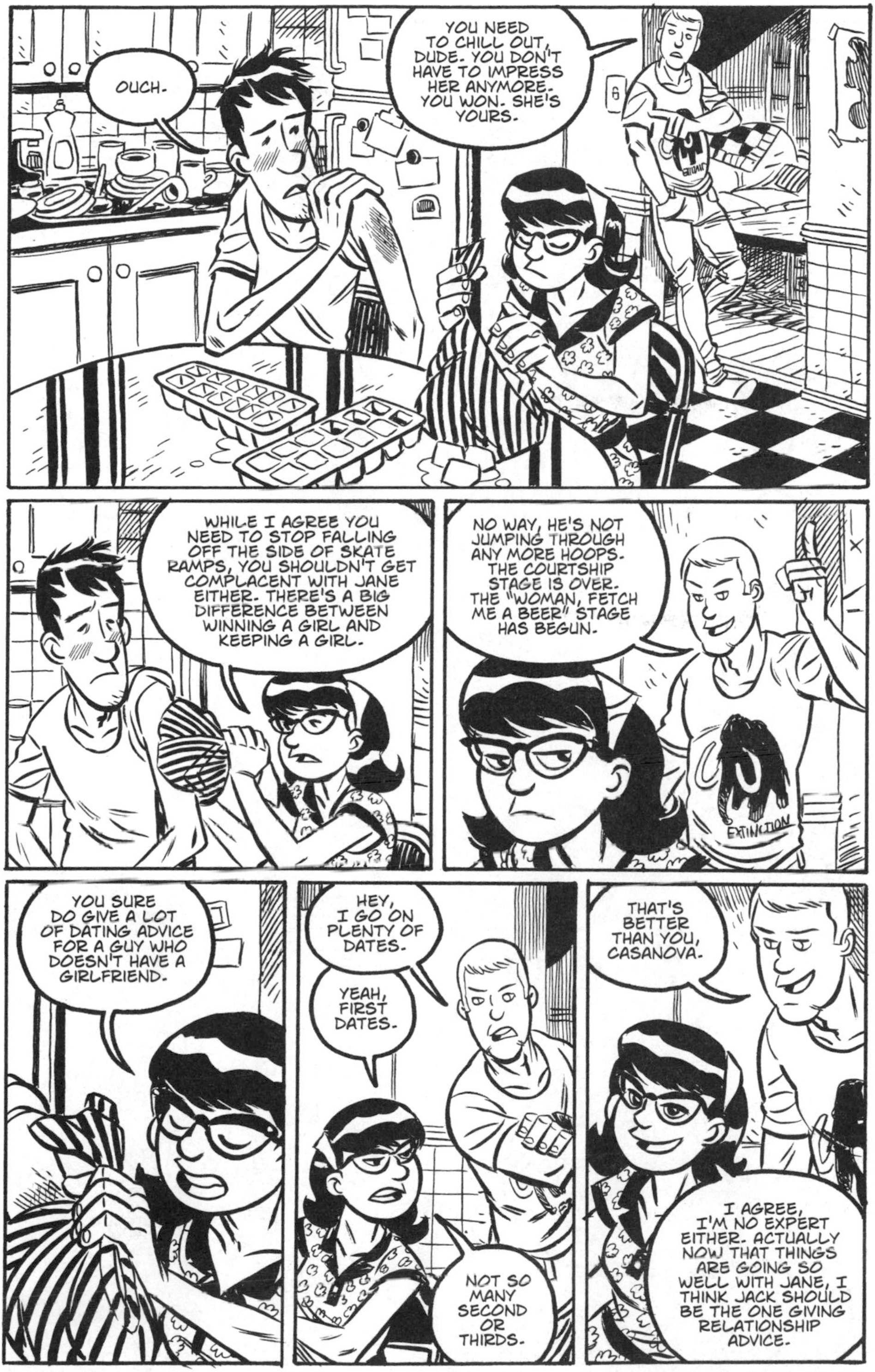
OUCH.
YOU NEED TO CHILL OUT, DUDE. YOU DON'T HAVE TO IMPRESS HER ANYMORE. YOU WON. SHE'S YOURS.
WHILE I AGREE YOU NEED TO STOP FALLING OFF THE SIDE OF SKATE RAMPS, YOU SHOULDN'T GET COMPLACENT WITH JANE EITHER. THERE'S A BIG DIFFERENCE BETWEEN WINNING A GIRL AND KEEPING A GIRL.
NO WAY, HE'S NOT JUMPING THROUGH ANY MORE HOOPS. THE COURTSHIP STAGE IS OVER. THE "WOMAN, FETCH ME A BEER" STAGE HAS BEGUN.
EXTINCTION
YOU SURE DO GIVE A LOT OF DATING ADVICE FOR A GUY WHO DOESN'T HAVE A GIRLFRIEND.
HEY, I GO ON PLENTY OF DATES.
YEAH, FIRST DATES.
NOT SO MANY SECOND OR THIRDS.
THAT'S BETTER THAN YOU, CASANOVA.
I AGREE, I'M NO EXPERT EITHER. ACTUALLY NOW THAT THINGS ARE GOING SO WELL WITH JANE, I THINK JACK SHOULD BE THE ONE GIVING RELATIONSHIP ADVICE.

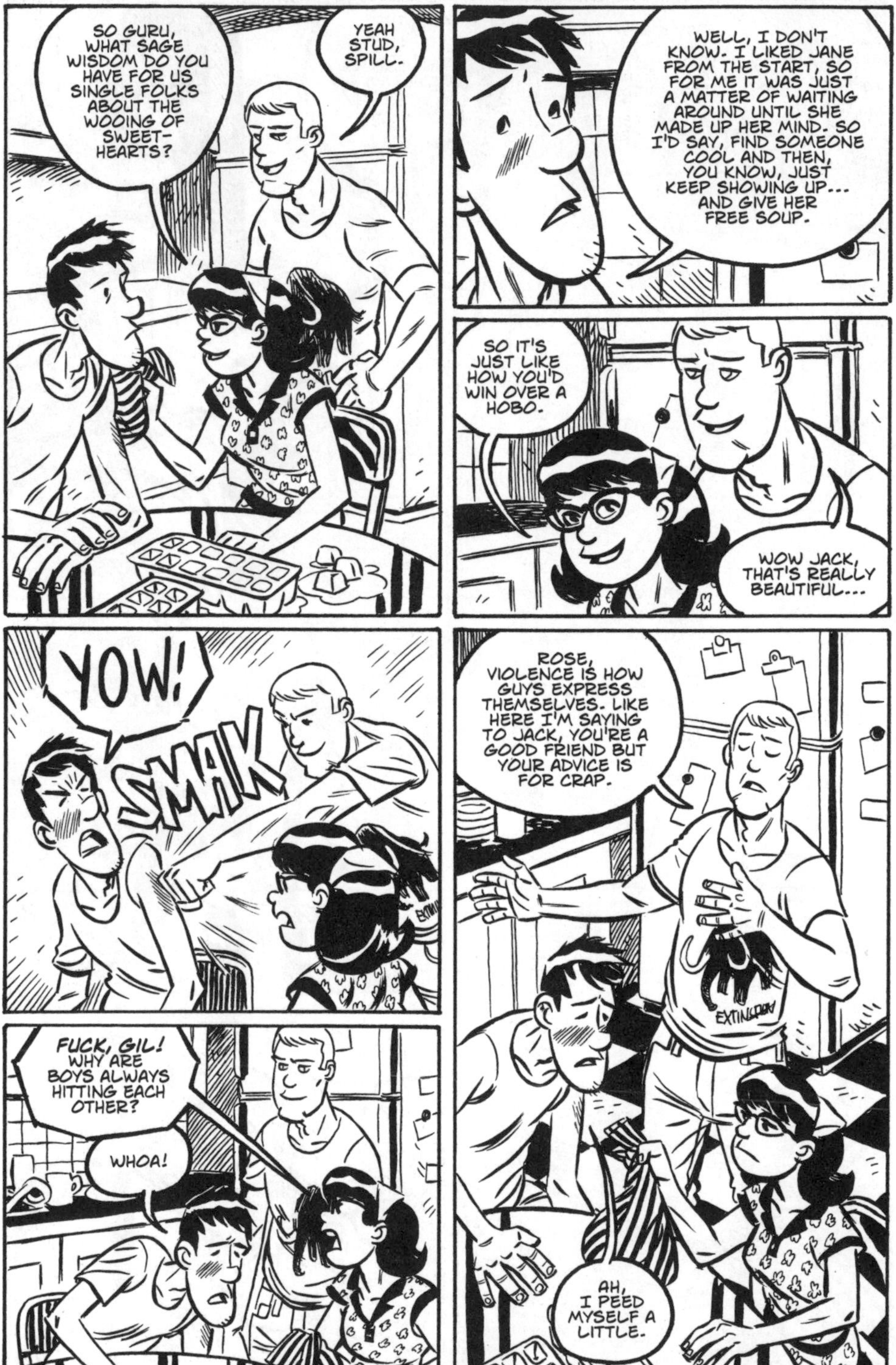
SO GURU, WHAT SAGE WISDOM DO YOU HAVE FOR US SINGLE FOLKS ABOUT THE WOOING OF SWEET-HEARTS?
YEAH STUD, SPILL.
WELL, I DON'T KNOW. I LIKED JANE FROM THE START, SO FOR ME IT WAS JUST A MATTER OF WAITING AROUND UNTIL SHE MADE UP HER MIND. SO I'D SAY, FIND SOMEONE COOL AND THEN, YOU KNOW, JUST KEEP SHOWING UP... AND GIVE HER FREE SOUP.
SO IT'S JUST LIKE HOW YOU'D WIN OVER A HOBO.
WOW JACK, THAT'S REALLY BEAUTIFUL...
YOW!
SMAK
FUCK, GIL! WHY ARE BOYS ALWAYS HITTING EACH OTHER?
WHOA!
ROSE, VIOLENCE IS HOW GUYS EXPRESS THEMSELVES. LIKE HERE I'M SAYING TO JACK, YOU'RE A GOOD FRIEND BUT YOUR ADVICE IS FOR CRAP.
AH, I PEED MYSELF A LITTLE.

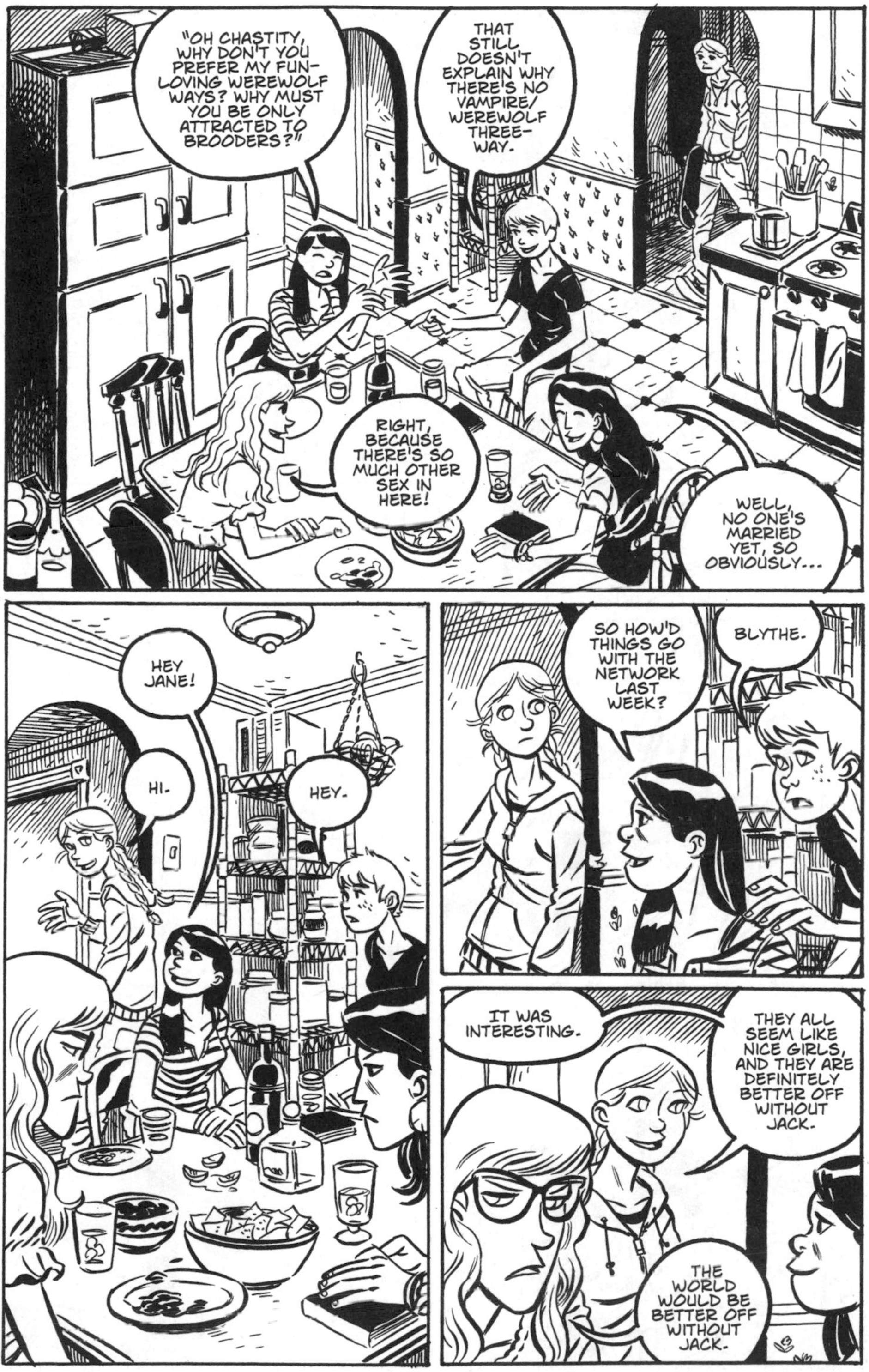
"OH CHASTITY, WHY DON'T YOU PREFER MY FUN-LOVING WEREWOLF WAYS? WHY MUST YOU BE ONLY ATTRACTED TO BROODERS?"
THAT STILL DOESN'T EXPLAIN WHY THERE'S NO VAMPIRE/ WEREWOLF THREE-WAY.
RIGHT, BECAUSE THERE'S SO MUCH OTHER SEX IN HERE!
WELL, NO ONE'S MARRIED YET, SO OBVIOUSLY...
HEY JANE!
HI.
HEY.
SO HOW'D THINGS GO WITH THE NETWORK LAST WEEK?
BLYTHE.
IT WAS INTERESTING.
THEY ALL SEEM LIKE NICE GIRLS, AND THEY ARE DEFINITELY BETTER OFF WITHOUT JACK.
THE WORLD WOULD BE BETTER OFF WITHOUT JACK.

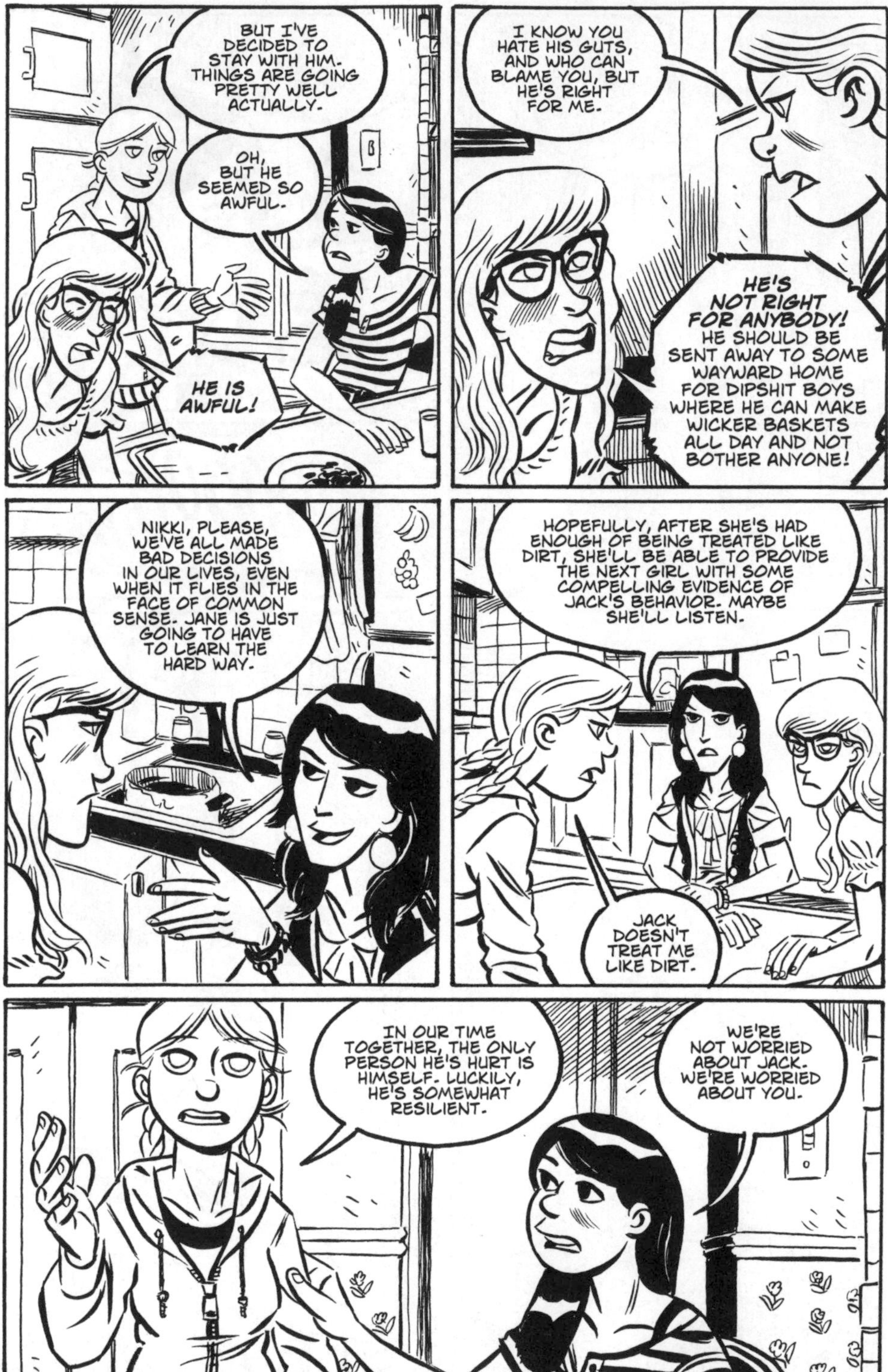
BUT I'VE DECIDED TO STAY WITH HIM. THINGS ARE GOING PRETTY WELL ACTUALLY.
OH, BUT HE SEEMED SO AWFUL.
HE IS AWFUL!
I KNOW YOU HATE HIS GUTS, AND WHO CAN BLAME YOU, BUT HE'S RIGHT FOR ME.
HE'S NOT RIGHT FOR ANYBODY! HE SHOULD BE SENT AWAY TO SOME WAYWARD HOME FOR DIPSHIT BOYS WHERE HE CAN MAKE WICKER BASKETS ALL DAY AND NOT BOTHER ANYONE!
NIKKI, PLEASE, WE'VE ALL MADE BAD DECISIONS IN OUR LIVES, EVEN WHEN IT FLIES IN THE FACE OF COMMON SENSE. JANE IS JUST GOING TO HAVE TO LEARN THE HARD WAY.
HOPEFULLY, AFTER SHE'S HAD ENOUGH OF BEING TREATED LIKE DIRT, SHE'LL BE ABLE TO PROVIDE THE NEXT GIRL WITH SOME COMPELLING EVIDENCE OF JACK'S BEHAVIOR. MAYBE SHE'LL LISTEN.
JACK DOESN'T TREAT ME LIKE DIRT.
IN OUR TIME TOGETHER, THE ONLY PERSON HE'S HURT IS HIMSELF. LUCKILY, HE'S SOMEWHAT RESILIENT.
WE'RE NOT WORRIED ABOUT JACK. WE'RE WORRIED ABOUT YOU.

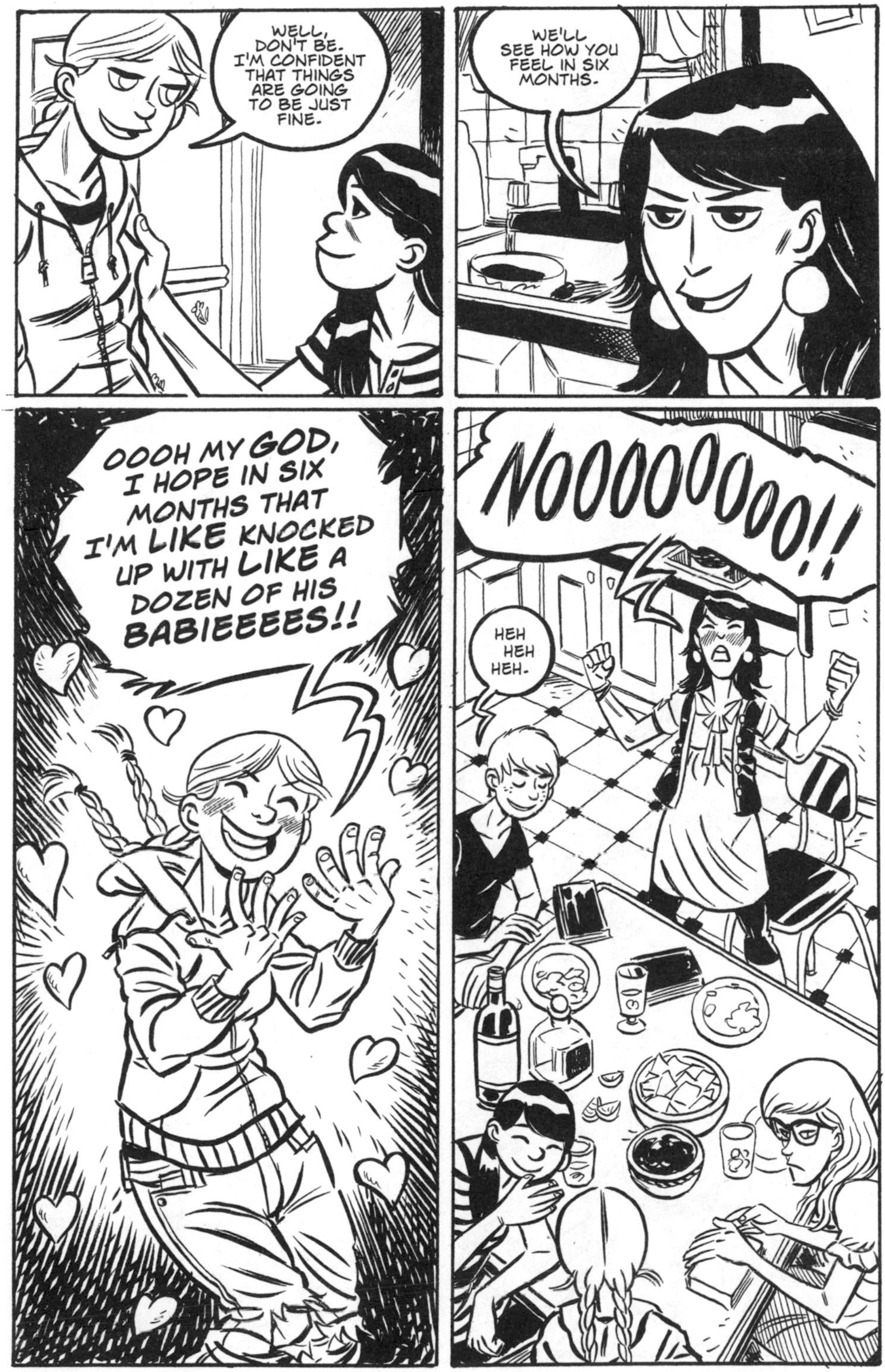
WELL, DON'T BE. I'M CONFIDENT THAT THINGS ARE GOING TO BE JUST FINE.
WE'LL SEE HOW YOU FEEL IN SIX MONTHS.
OOOH MY GOD, I HOPE IN SIX MONTHS THAT I'M LIKE KNOCKED UP WITH LIKE A DOZEN OF HIS BABIEEEEES!!
NOOOOOOOO!!
HEH HEH HEH.

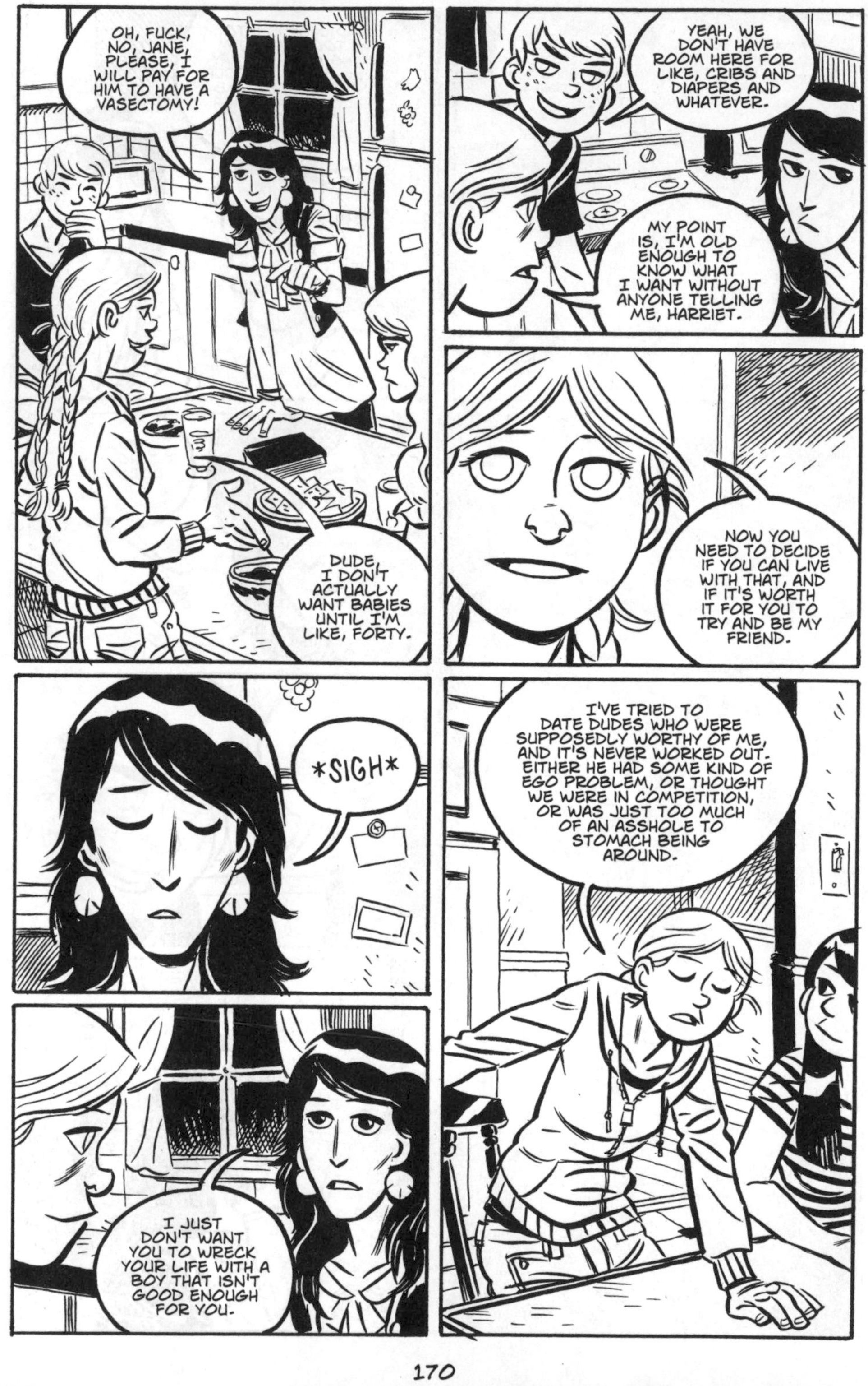
OH, FUCK, NO, JANE, PLEASE, I WILL PAY FOR HIM TO HAVE A VASECTOMY!
DUDE, I DON'T ACTUALLY WANT BABIES UNTIL I'M LIKE, FORTY.
YEAH, WE DON'T HAVE ROOM HERE FOR LIKE, CRIBS AND DIAPERS AND WHATEVER.
MY POINT IS, I'M OLD ENOUGH TO KNOW WHAT I WANT WITHOUT ANYONE TELLING ME, HARRIET.
NOW YOU NEED TO DECIDE IF YOU CAN LIVE WITH THAT, AND IF IT'S WORTH IT FOR YOU TO TRY AND BE MY FRIEND.
SIGH
I JUST DON'T WANT YOU TO WRECK YOUR LIFE WITH A BOY THAT ISN'T GOOD ENOUGH FOR YOU.
I'VE TRIED TO DATE DUDES WHO WERE SUPPOSEDLY WORTHY OF ME, AND IT'S NEVER WORKED OUT. EITHER HE HAD SOME KIND OF EGO PROBLEM, OR THOUGHT WE WERE IN COMPETITION, OR WAS JUST TOO MUCH OF AN ASSHOLE TO STOMACH BEING AROUND.

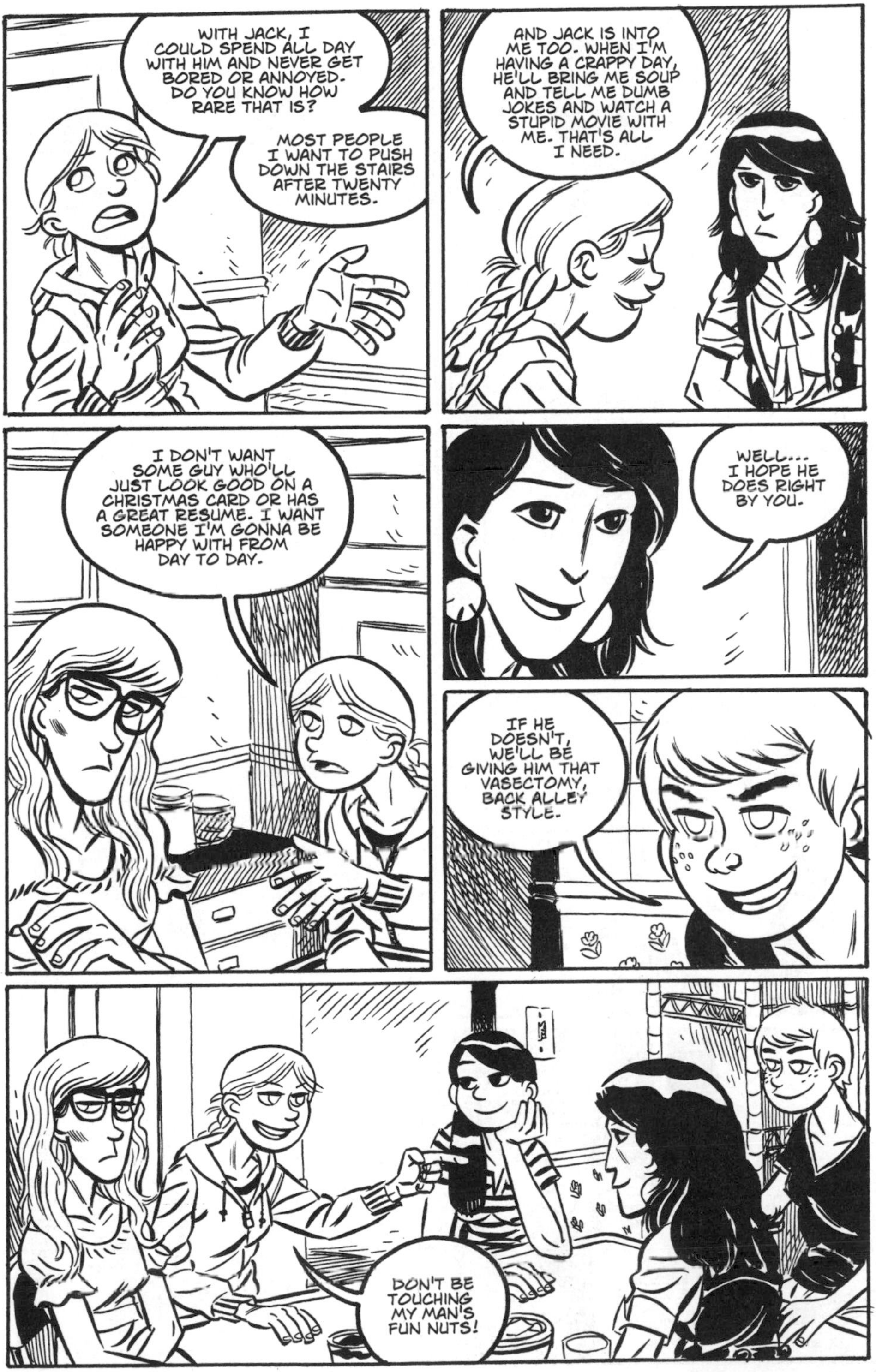
WITH JACK, I COULD SPEND ALL DAY WITH HIM AND NEVER GET BORED OR ANNOYED. DO YOU KNOW HOW RARE THAT IS?
MOST PEOPLE I WANT TO PUSH DOWN THE STAIRS AFTER TWENTY MINUTES.
AND JACK IS INTO ME TOO. WHEN I'M HAVING A CRAPPY DAY, HE'LL BRING ME SOUP AND TELL ME DUMB JOKES AND WATCH A STUPID MOVIE WITH ME. THAT'S ALL I NEED.
I DON'T WANT SOME GUY WHO'LL JUST LOOK GOOD ON A CHRISTMAS CARD OR HAS A GREAT RESUME. I WANT SOMEONE I'M GONNA BE HAPPY WITH FROM DAY TO DAY.
WELL... I HOPE HE DOES RIGHT BY YOU.
IF HE DOESN'T, WE'LL BE GIVING HIM THAT VASECTOMY, BACK ALLEY STYLE.
DON'T BE TOUCHING MY MAN'S FUN NUTS!

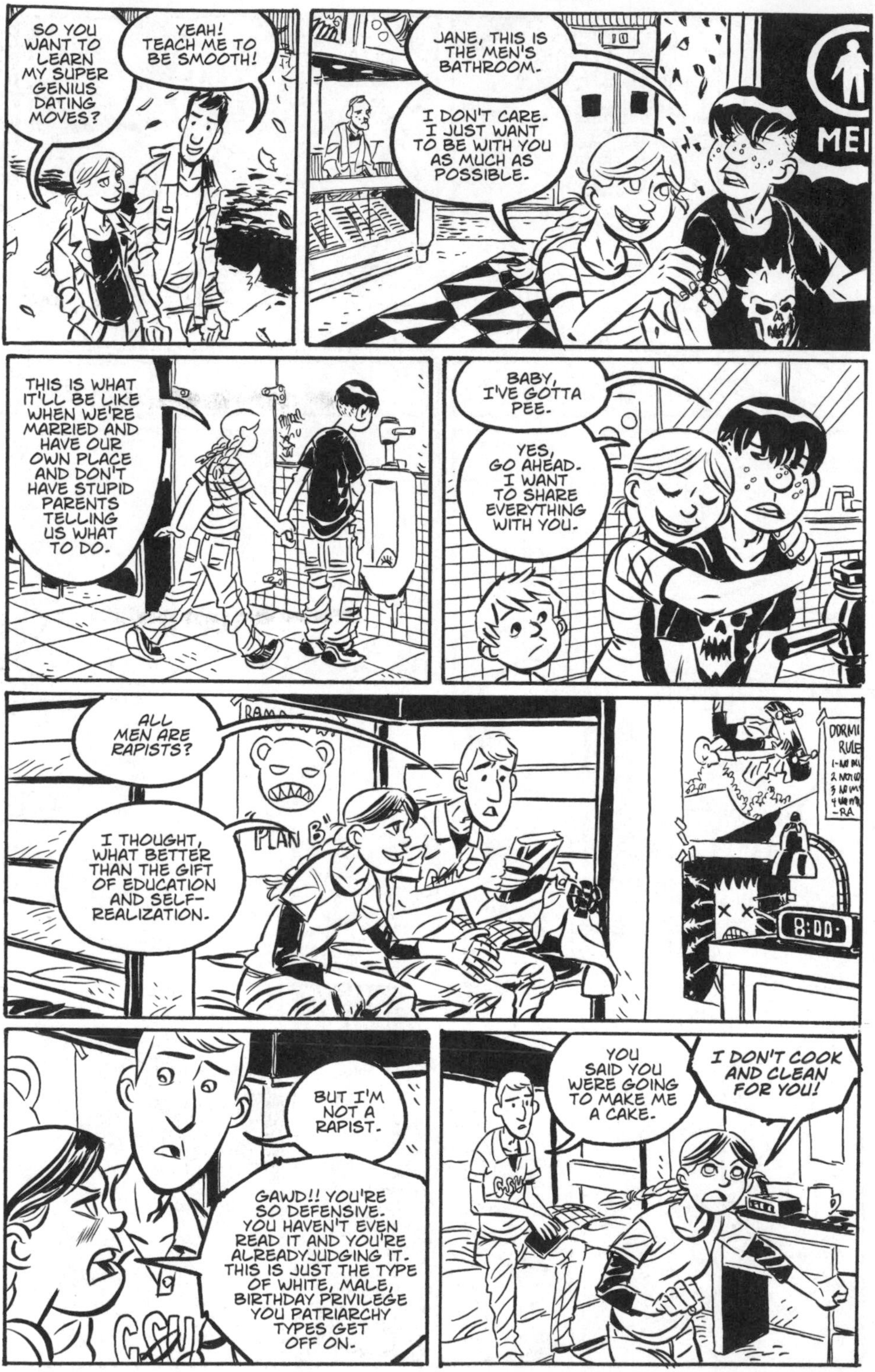
SO YOU WANT TO LEARN MY SUPER GENIUS DATING MOVES?
YEAH! TEACH ME TO BE SMOOTH!
JANE, THIS IS THE MEN'S BATHROOM.
I DON'T CARE. I JUST WANT TO BE WITH YOU AS MUCH AS POSSIBLE.
MEN
THIS IS WHAT IT'LL BE LIKE WHEN WE'RE MARRIED AND HAVE OUR OWN PLACE AND DON'T HAVE STUPID PARENTS TELLING US WHAT TO DO.
BABY, I'VE GOTTA PEE.
YES, GO AHEAD. I WANT TO SHARE EVERYTHING WITH YOU.
ALL MEN ARE RAPISTS?
I THOUGHT, WHAT BETTER THAN THE GIFT OF EDUCATION AND SELF-REALIZATION.
PLAN B
8:00
BUT I'M NOT A RAPIST.
GAWD!! YOU'RE SO DEFENSIVE. YOU HAVEN'T EVEN READ IT AND YOU'RE ALREADYJUDGING IT. THIS IS JUST THE TYPE OF WHITE, MALE, BIRTHDAY PRIVILEGE YOU PATRIARCHY TYPES GET OFF ON.
YOU SAID YOU WERE GOING TO MAKE ME A CAKE.
I DON'T COOK AND CLEAN FOR YOU!

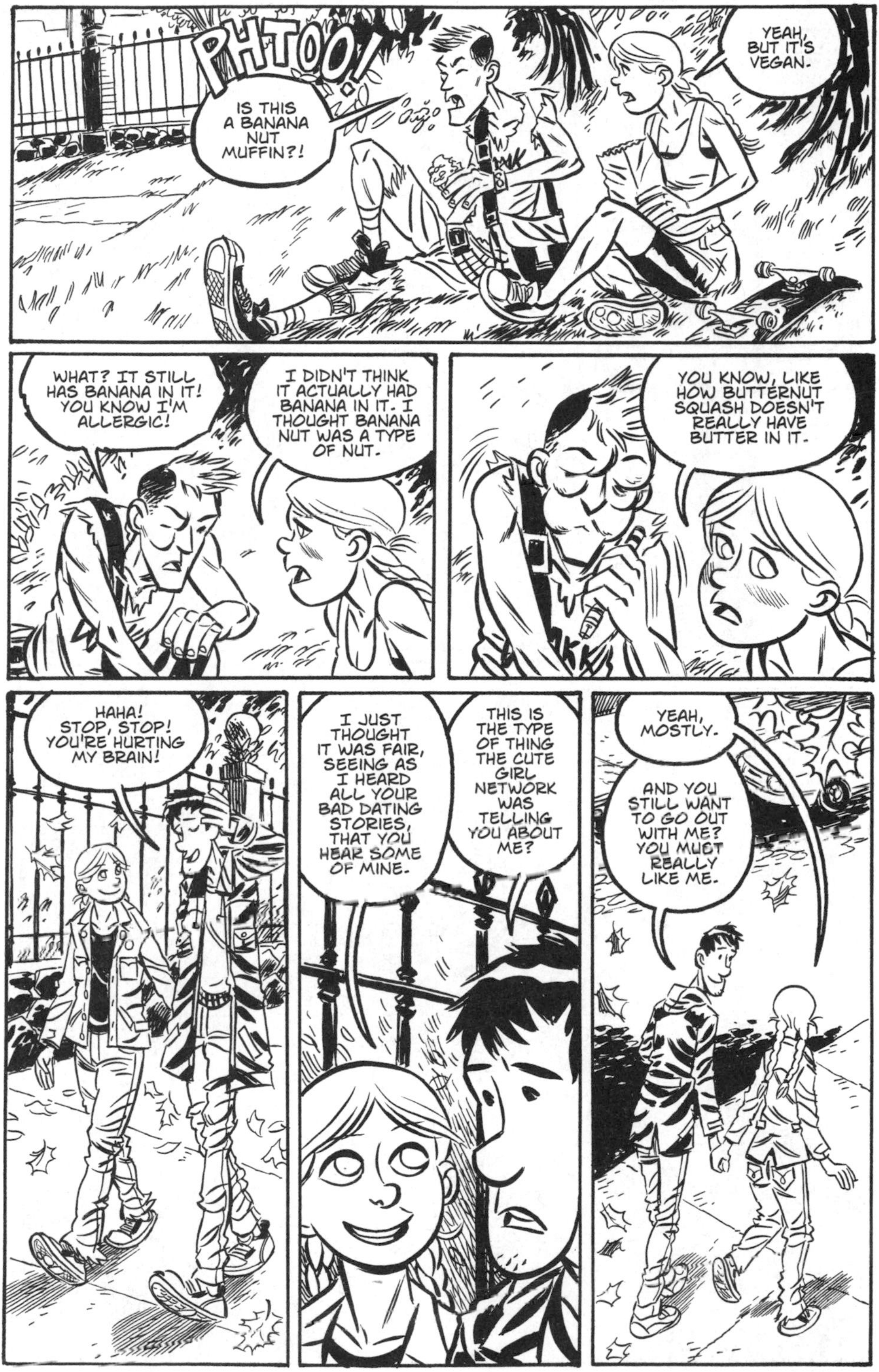
PHTOO!
IS THIS A BANANA NUT MUFFIN?!
YEAH, BUT IT'S VEGAN.
WHAT? IT STILL HAS BANANA IN IT! YOU KNOW I'M ALLERGIC!
I DIDN'T THINK IT ACTUALLY HAD BANANA IN IT. I THOUGHT BANANA NUT WAS A TYPE OF NUT.
YOU KNOW, LIKE HOW BUTTERNUT SQUASH DOESN'T REALLY HAVE BUTTER IN IT.
HAHA! STOP, STOP! YOU'RE HURTING MY BRAIN!
I JUST THOUGHT IT WAS FAIR, SEEING AS I HEARD ALL YOUR BAD DATING STORIES, THAT YOU HEAR SOME OF MINE.
THIS IS THE TYPE OF THING THE CUTE GIRL NETWORK WAS TELLING YOU ABOUT ME?
YEAH, MOSTLY.
AND YOU STILL WANT TO GO OUT WITH ME? YOU MUST REALLY LIKE ME.

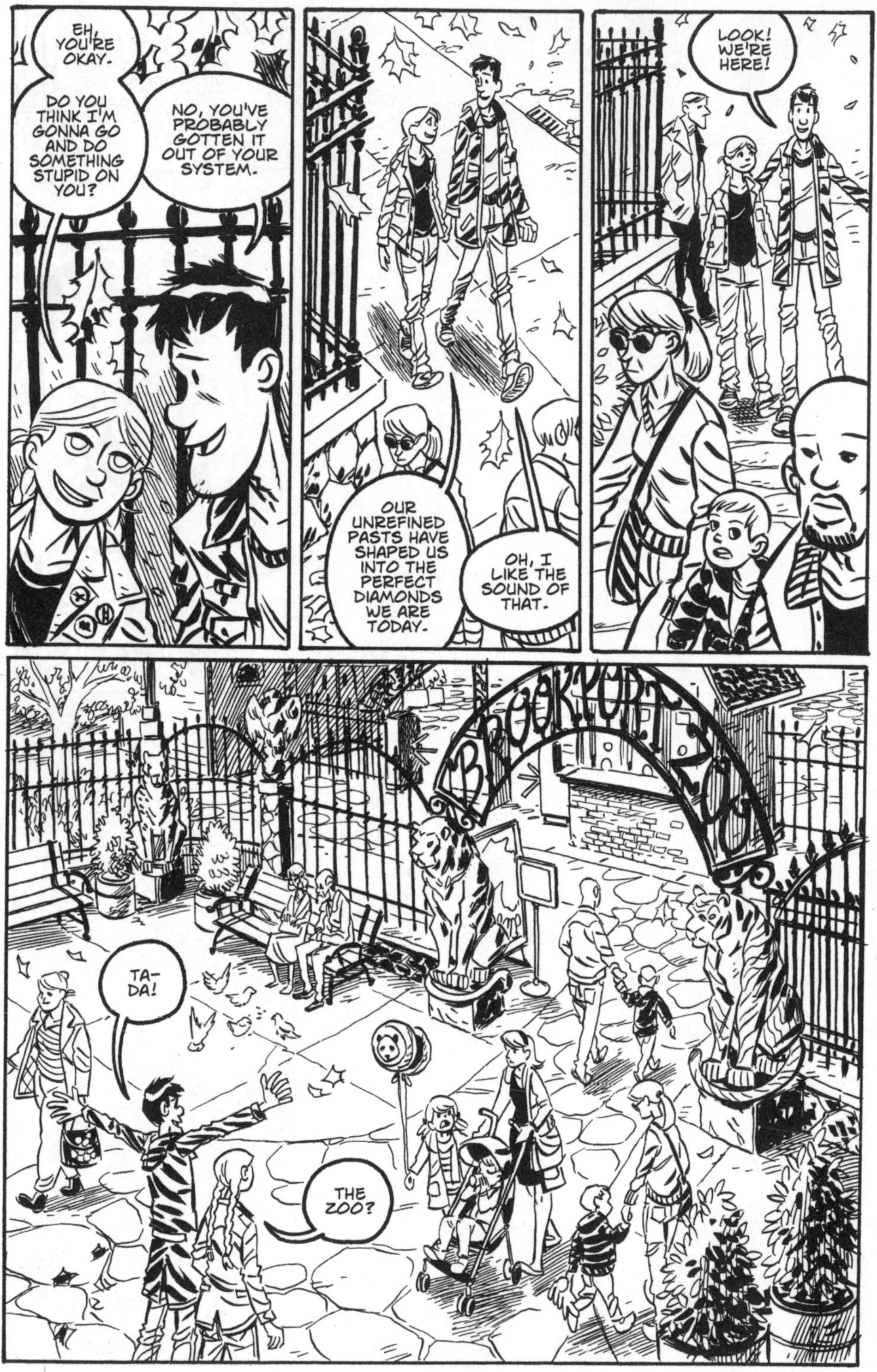
EH, YOU'RE OKAY.
DO YOU THINK I'M GONNA GO AND DO SOMETHING STUPID ON YOU?
NO, YOU'VE PROBABLY GOTTEN IT OUT OF YOUR SYSTEM.
OUR UNREFINED PASTS HAVE SHAPED US INTO THE PERFECT DIAMONDS WE ARE TODAY.
OH, I LIKE THE SOUND OF THAT.
LOOK! WE'RE HERE!
BROOKPORT ZOO
TA-DA!
THE ZOO?

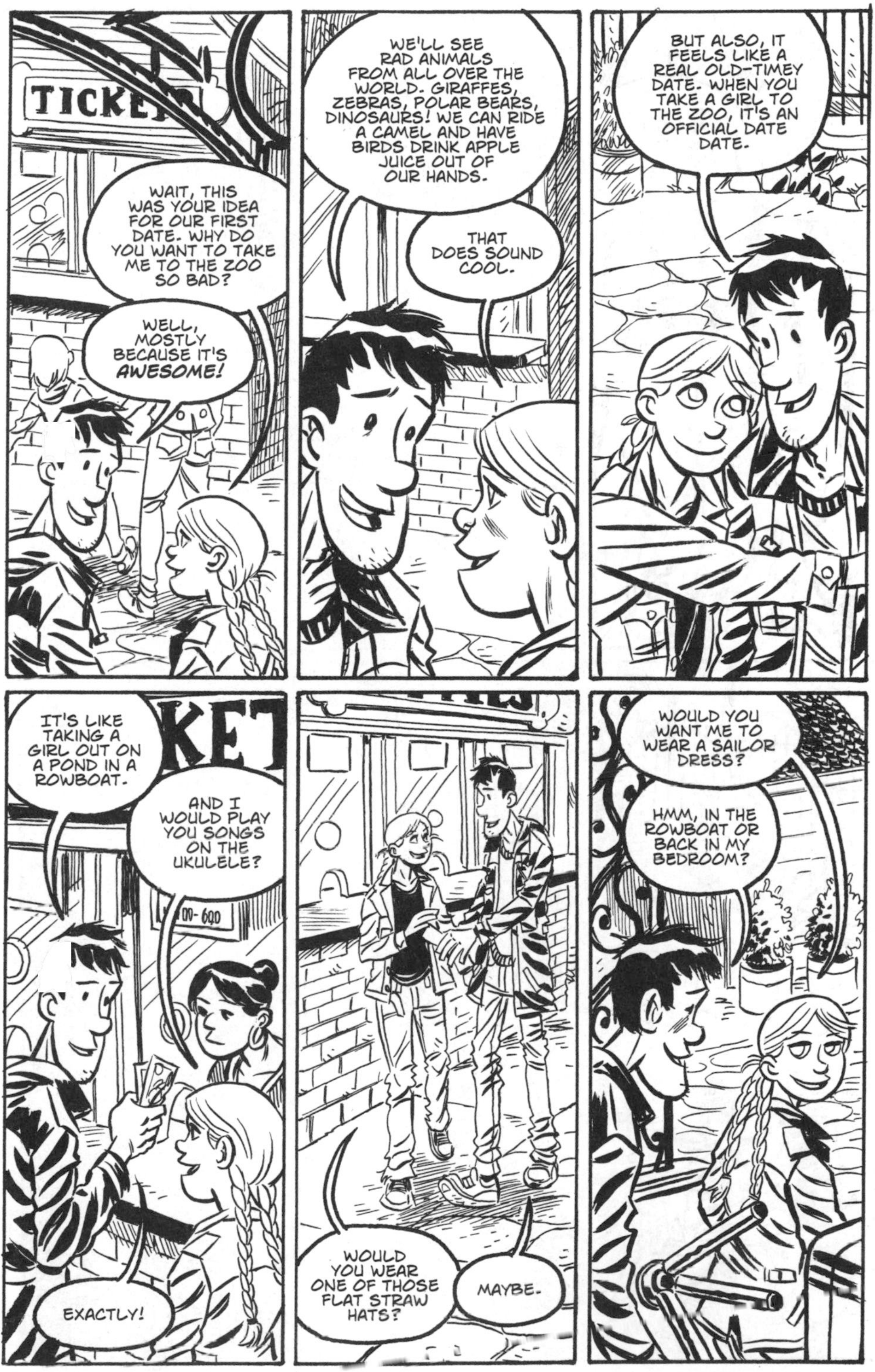
TICKETS
WAIT, THIS WAS YOUR IDEA FOR OUR FIRST DATE. WHY DO YOU WANT TO TAKE ME TO THE ZOO SO BAD?
WELL, MOSTLY BECAUSE IT'S **AWESOME!**
WE'LL SEE RAD ANIMALS FROM ALL OVER THE WORLD. GIRAFFES, ZEBRAS, POLAR BEARS, DINOSAURS! WE CAN RIDE A CAMEL AND HAVE BIRDS DRINK APPLE JUICE OUT OF OUR HANDS.
THAT DOES SOUND COOL.
BUT ALSO, IT FEELS LIKE A REAL OLD-TIMEY DATE. WHEN YOU TAKE A GIRL TO THE ZOO, IT'S AN OFFICIAL DATE DATE.
IT'S LIKE TAKING A GIRL OUT ON A POND IN A ROWBOAT.
AND I WOULD PLAY YOU SONGS ON THE UKULELE?
EXACTLY!
WOULD YOU WEAR ONE OF THOSE FLAT STRAW HATS?
MAYBE.
WOULD YOU WANT ME TO WEAR A SAILOR DRESS?
HMM, IN THE ROWBOAT OR BACK IN MY BEDROOM?

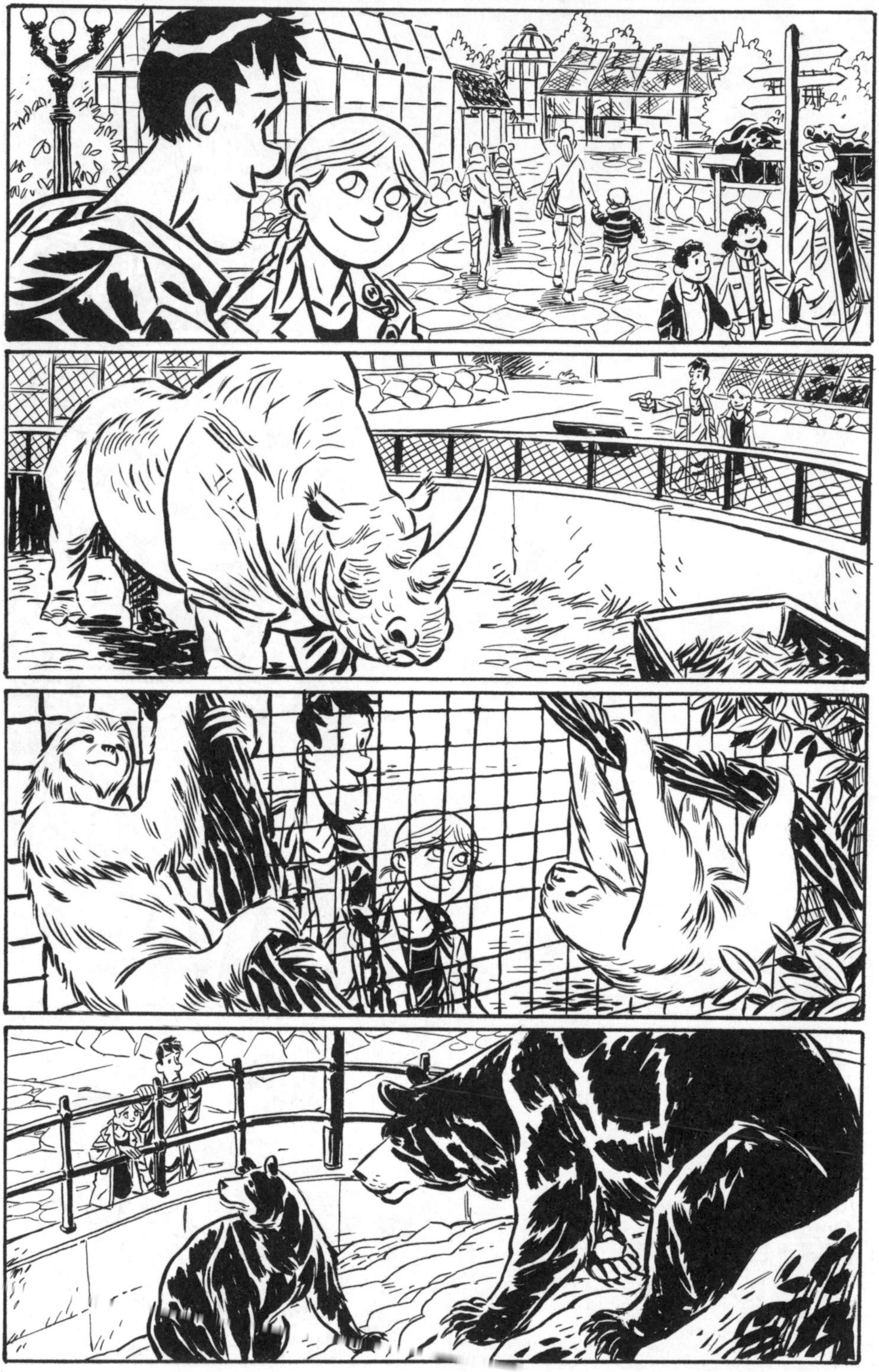

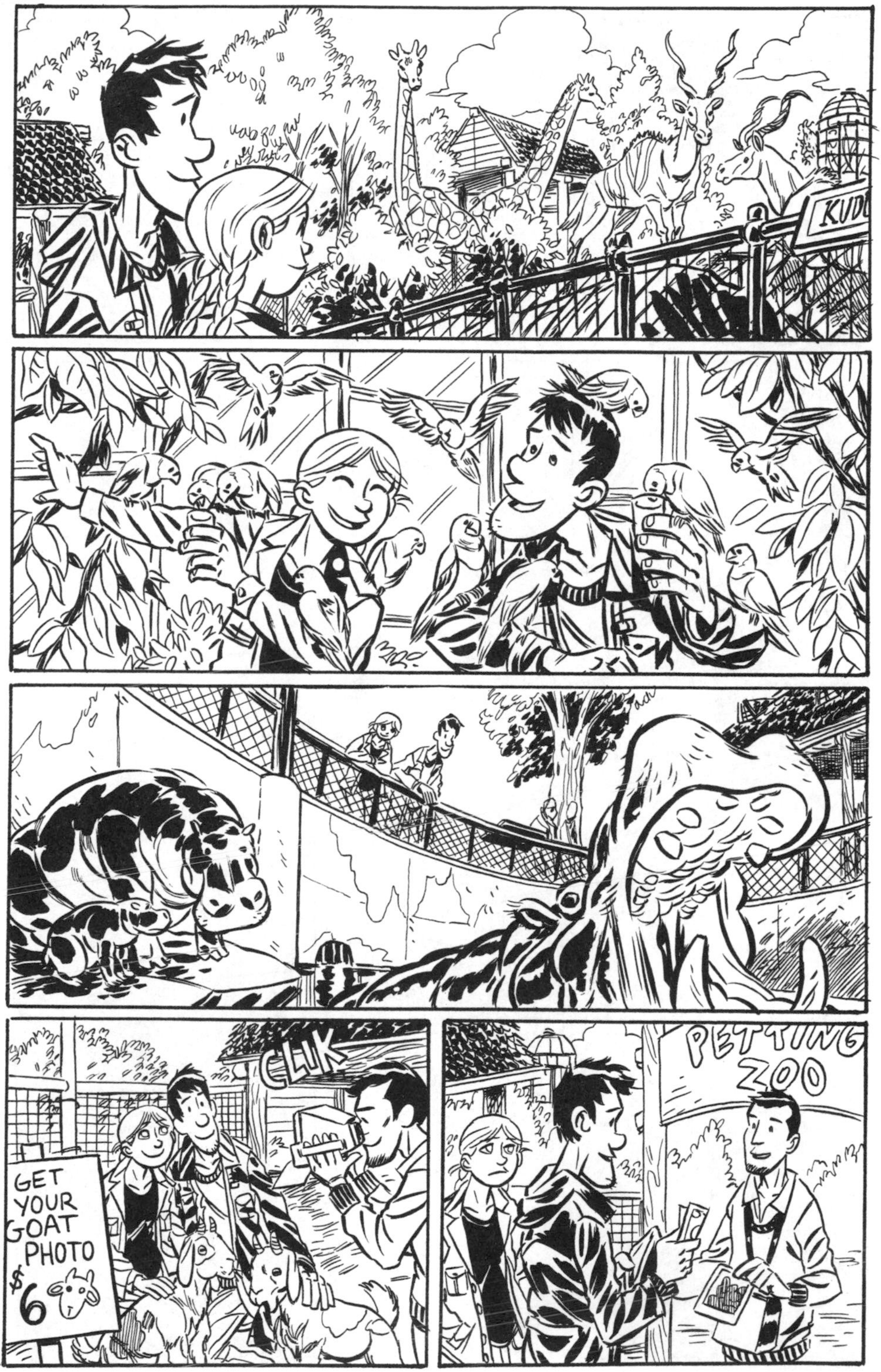
KUDU
CLIK
GET YOUR GOAT PHOTO $6
PETTING ZOO

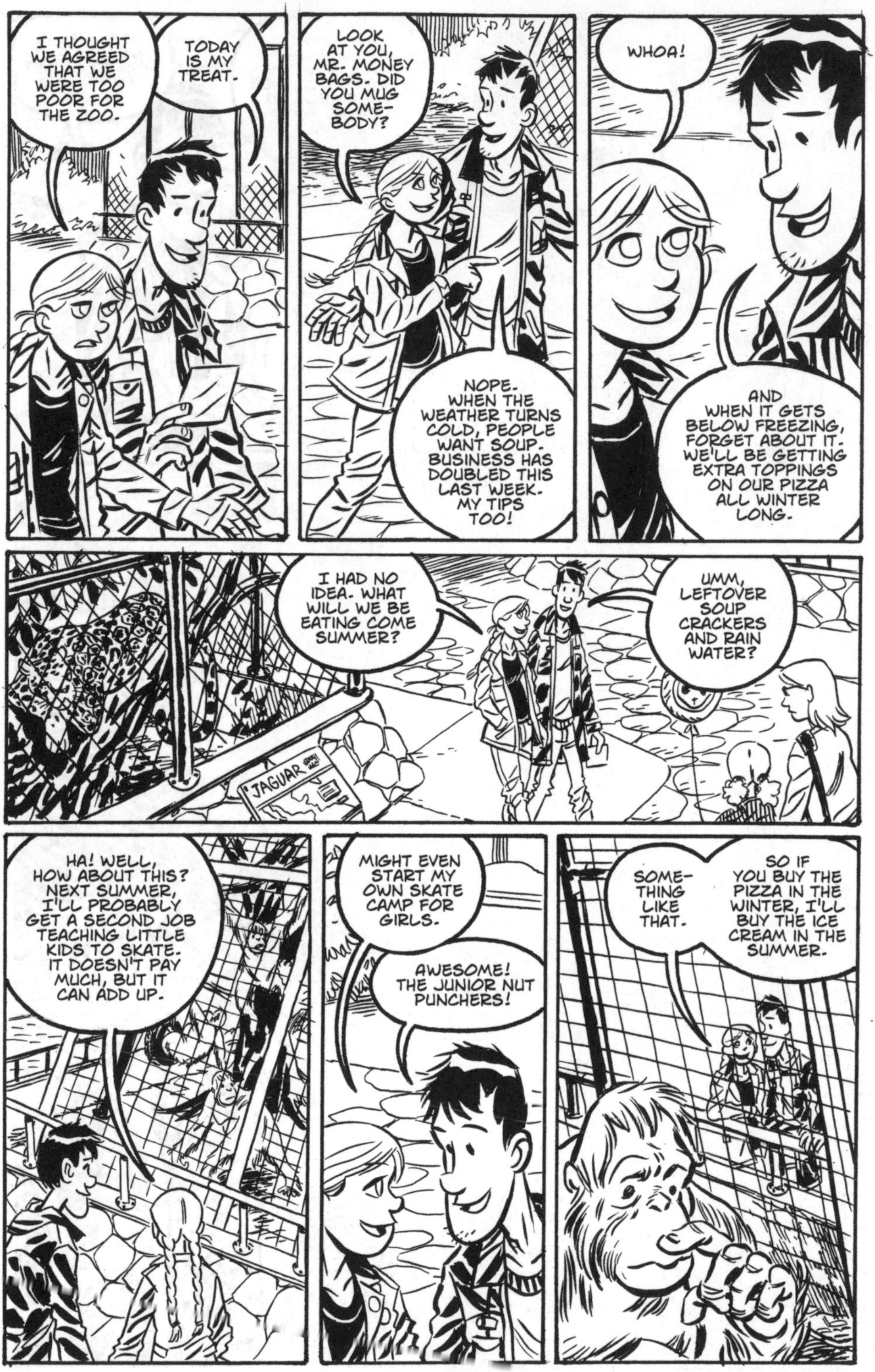
I THOUGHT WE AGREED THAT WE WERE TOO POOR FOR THE ZOO.
TODAY IS MY TREAT.
LOOK AT YOU, MR. MONEY BAGS. DID YOU MUG SOMEBODY?
NOPE. WHEN THE WEATHER TURNS COLD, PEOPLE WANT SOUP. BUSINESS HAS DOUBLED THIS LAST WEEK. MY TIPS TOO!
WHOA!
AND WHEN IT GETS BELOW FREEZING, FORGET ABOUT IT. WE'LL BE GETTING EXTRA TOPPINGS ON OUR PIZZA ALL WINTER LONG.
I HAD NO IDEA. WHAT WILL WE BE EATING COME SUMMER?
UMM, LEFTOVER SOUP CRACKERS AND RAIN WATER?
JAGUAR
HA! WELL, HOW ABOUT THIS? NEXT SUMMER, I'LL PROBABLY GET A SECOND JOB TEACHING LITTLE KIDS TO SKATE. IT DOESN'T PAY MUCH, BUT IT CAN ADD UP.
MIGHT EVEN START MY OWN SKATE CAMP FOR GIRLS.
AWESOME! THE JUNIOR NUT PUNCHERS!
SO IF YOU BUY THE PIZZA IN THE WINTER, I'LL BUY THE ICE CREAM IN THE SUMMER.
SOME-THING LIKE THAT.

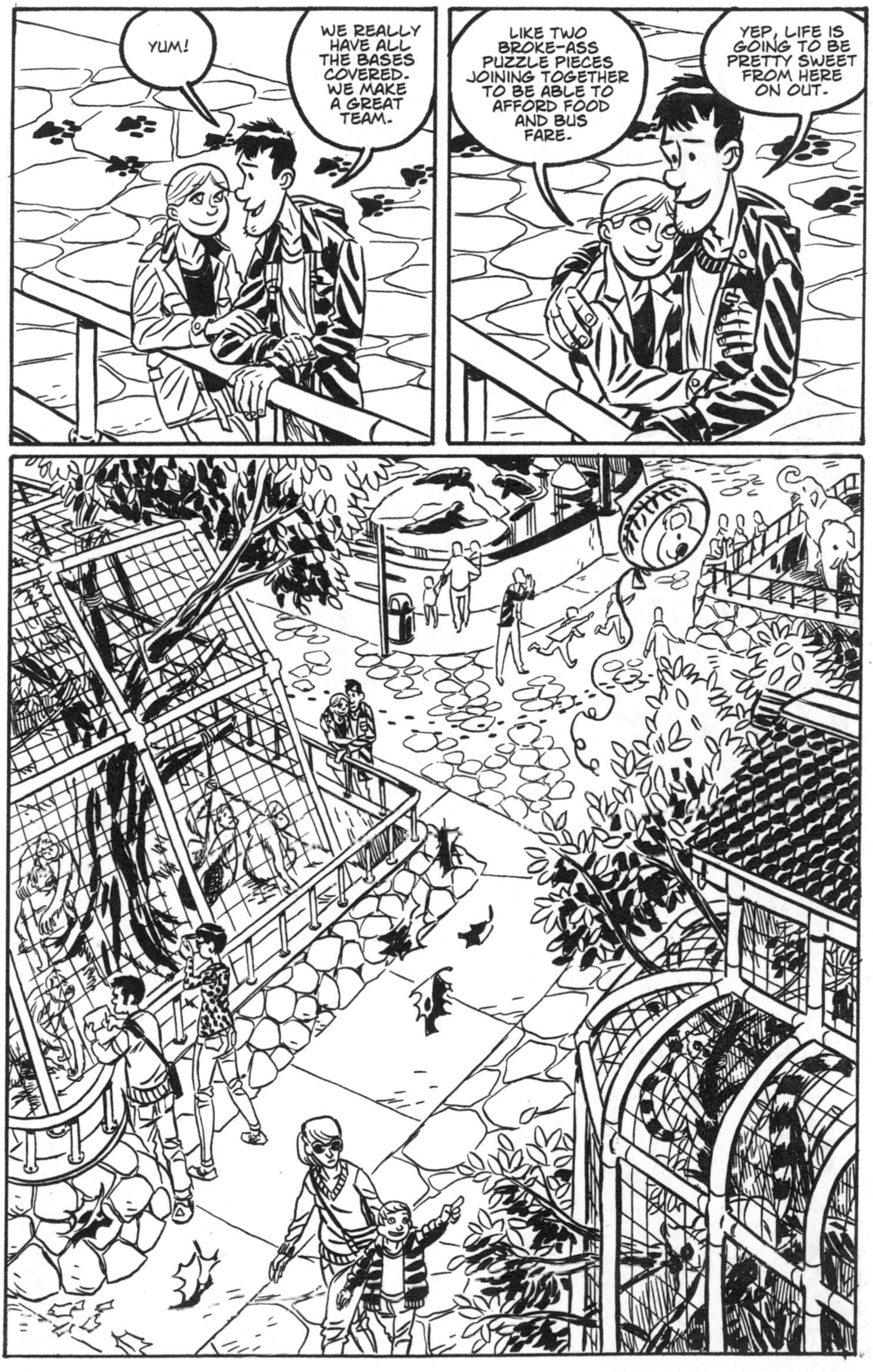
YUM!
WE REALLY HAVE ALL THE BASES COVERED. WE MAKE A GREAT TEAM.
LIKE TWO BROKE-ASS PUZZLE PIECES JOINING TOGETHER TO BE ABLE TO AFFORD FOOD AND BUS FARE.
YEP, LIFE IS GOING TO BE PRETTY SWEET FROM HERE ON OUT.

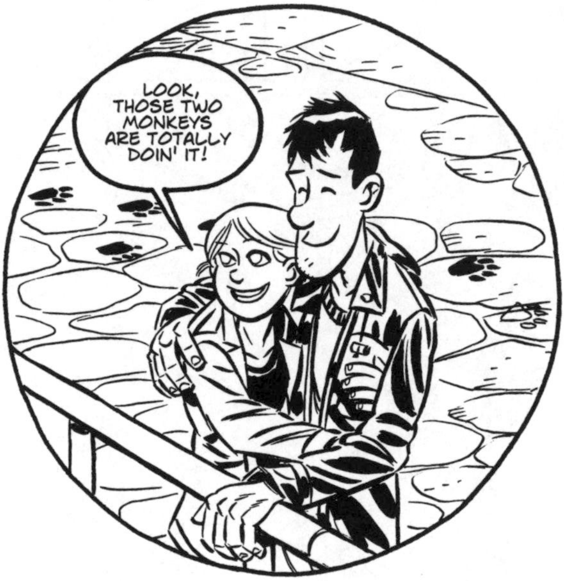
LOOK, THOSE TWO MONKEYS ARE TOTALLY DOIN' IT!

~FIN~

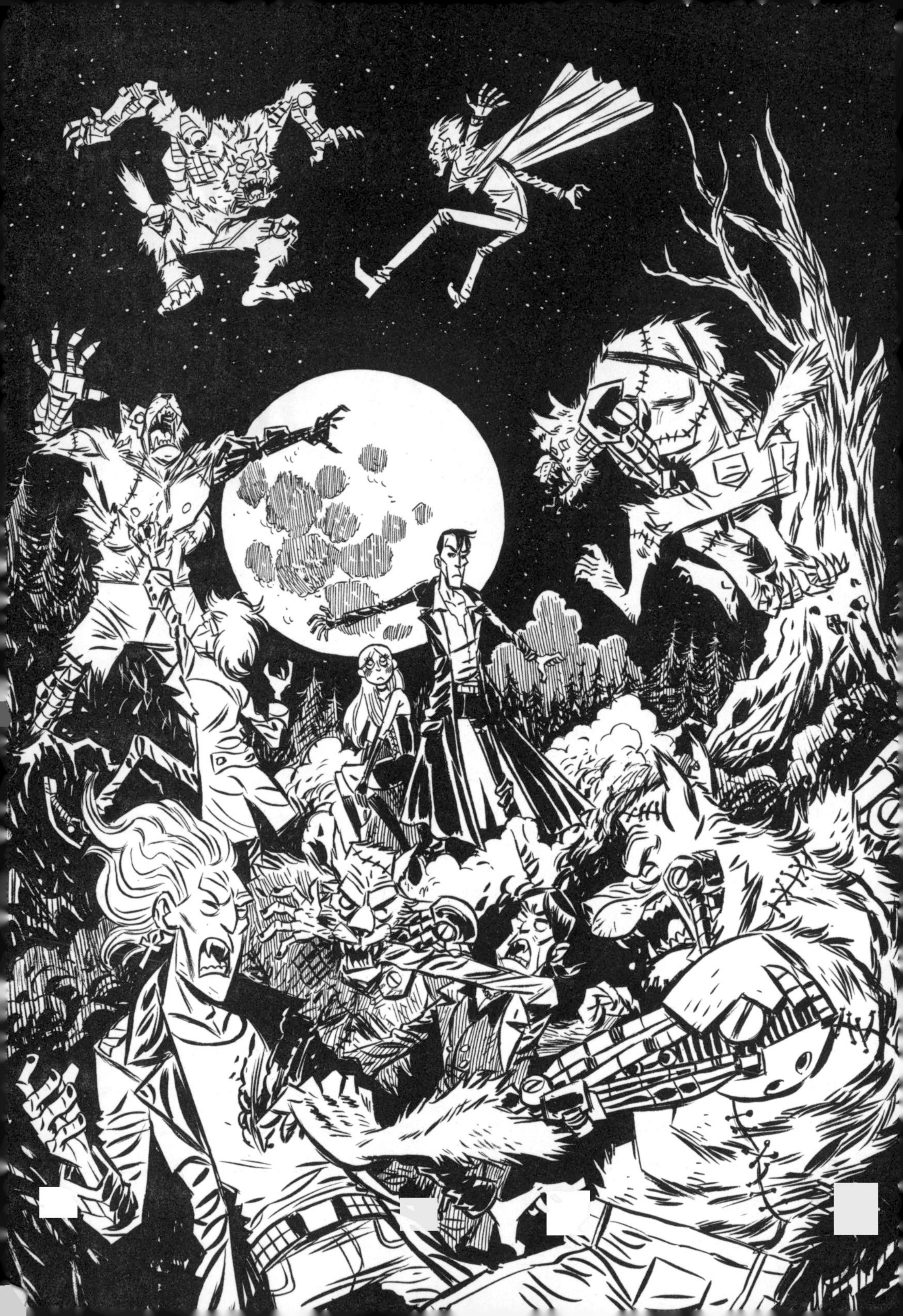

Chapter 36

A HEART AS HUNGRY AS A WOLFKENBORG

Caleb stood guard in front of Chastity, prepared to strike any of the Wolfkenborgs who attempted to come near her.

"Chastity," he said austerely as he glanced down at her with calmness, "these Wolfkenborg rival us in strength and are aided by their robot skeletons. But I will never, ever, EVER let anything happen to you."

Caleb snapped his bangs out of his eyes, pale skin glittering in the full moon's light. Chastity watched his every move intently, memorizing Caleb's actions and loving every molecule of his being. Sure, he had turned down her invitation to go to the mall and make fun of other humans with her because of vague "vampyr problems," but it was a mistake he would never make again. Since D'Jeffrey had taken her to the top floor of the Galleria and assessed which jeans best complimented her figure and which were cut all wrong for her perfect human teenage body, Caleb's jealousy had been inflamed to insane depths. He knew that he could no longer be apart from Chastity for more than a few hours or some other male would get all up in her shit. Because Chastity was a special flower, a beautiful orchid in a sea of common, disgusting daisies, and yeah, maybe it wasn't a beauty that the football team was into, per se, but it was there, and it was undeniable.

Chastity worried her presence was too dangerous among these monster-men. It was tough for the other vampyr to not hit on Chastity in front of Caleb, because their vampyr powers amplified the intensity of everything. But they fought alongside their bro, each sexy in their own way. Dante, the intellectual with impeccable style, like some kind of sexy British spy; Paolo and Andre, the twins, so very blond and pale; and Skip, the funny one, who Chastity didn't actually find all that funny but would still think about making out with if there was some tragedy where all the other vampyr were dead.

Suddenly, one of D'Jeffrey's muscular brethren Wolfkenborg leapt directly at Caleb, but Caleb's awesome vampyr sensitivity picked up on the movement before the other boy left the ground. Caleb struck off the boy's head with his palm, and it sailed across the grassy knoll, landing under a cedar. "How ironic," thought Chastity, "that these immortal tribes would battle under evergreens." The body slumped to the ground, but Chastity could already see the robot spider legs emerging from the boy's neck to reassemble itself. Caleb lifted the boy's body with one hand, as though it were as light as a pillow and not a hulking young male with a rippling torso and crazy abs. He tossed the body high into the air and it landed somewhere in the trees in the distance.

"Why don't you go do . . . whatever it is that wolves do . . . somewhere else?" Caleb sneered at the head.

The corners of Chastity's perfect mouth moved slightly higher, and Caleb sensed the movement. His cold heart pounded, thrilled to amuse his lady love so much.

"Chastity," he said coolly, so as not to enflame his passion, "when this is over, I want to take you far away from here and just look into your eyes for a week."

"I guess that'd be pretty cool," she replied, trying not to reveal how awesome she thought that would be, lest Caleb lose control of himself. It was so hard to hide her super deep feelings from him now, for she ached for his touch, and though they were all monsters, these teenaged-looking boys were all kinds of hotness, glistening with either sweat or a weird sheen to their supernatural skin. And they all cared enough about Chastity to fight each other night after night, regenerating for hours, filling the air with the scent of manimal.

Maybe tonight would be the night the boys all made out together, thought Chastity.

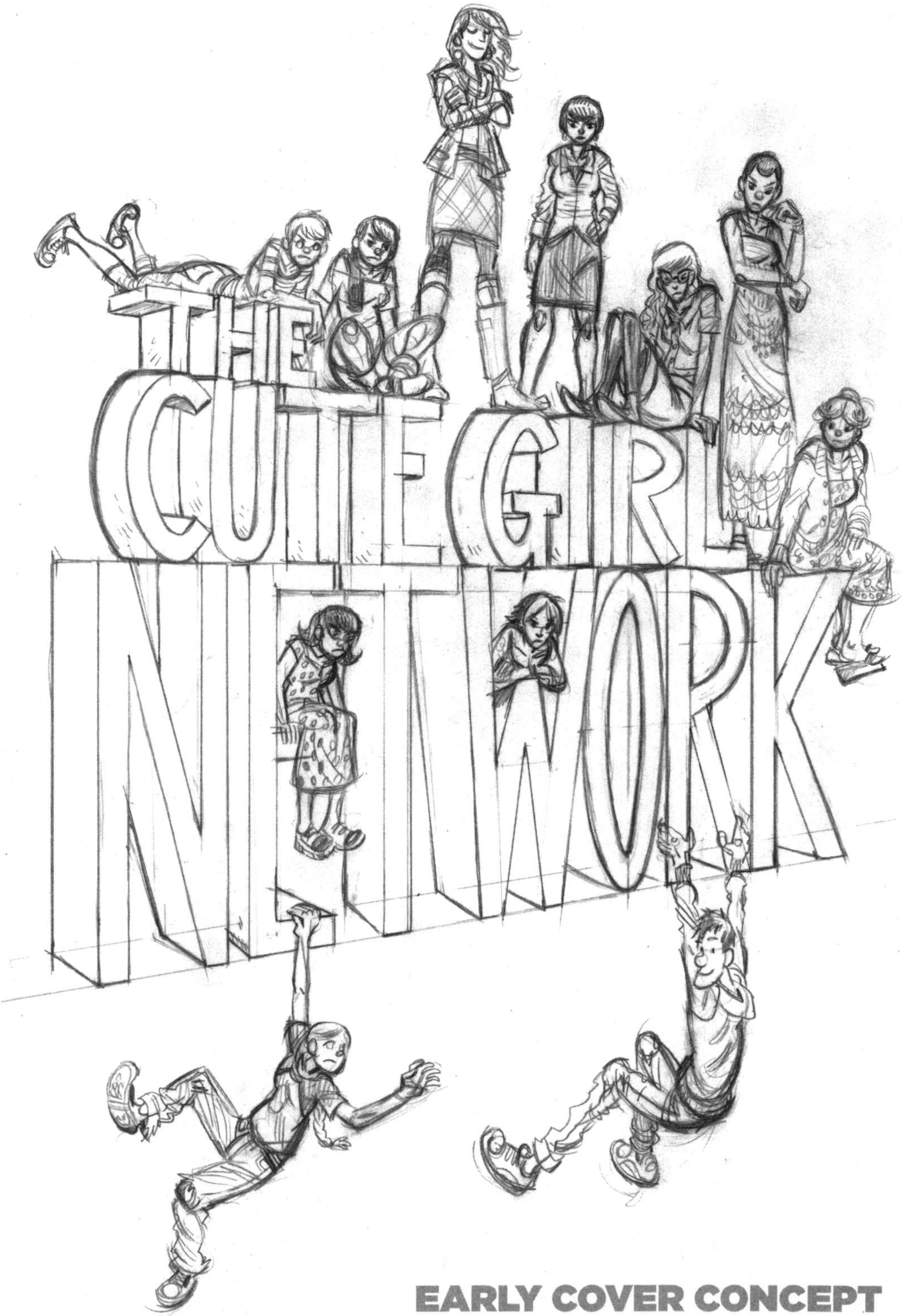
THE
CUTE GIRL
NETWORK

EARLY COVER CONCEPT

JANE'S BOARD

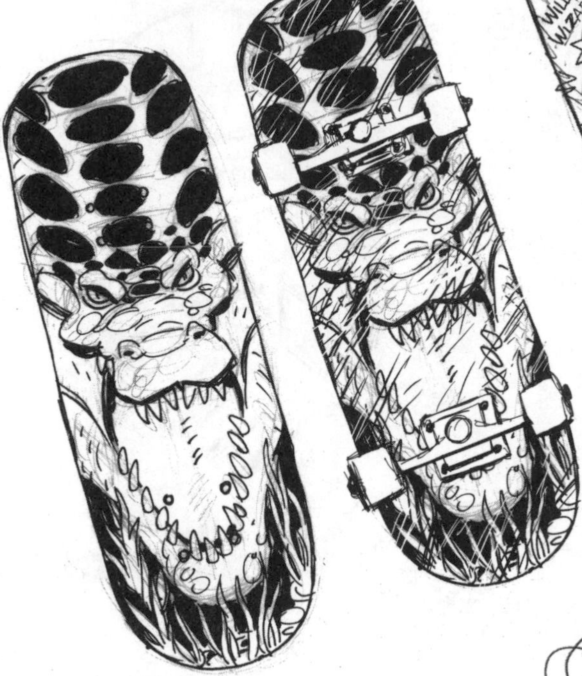

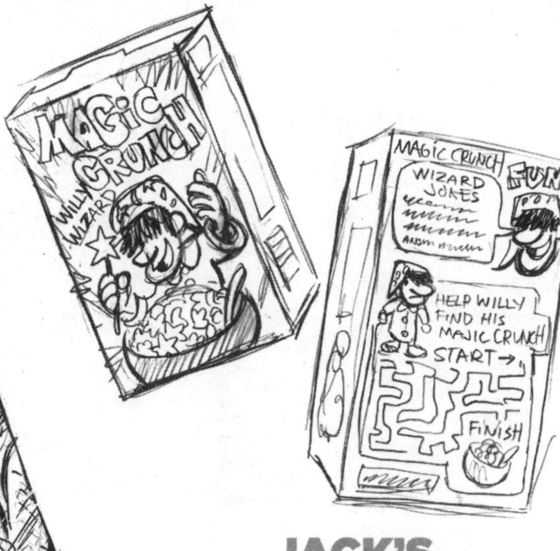
MAGIC CRUNCH
WILLY WIZARD
MAGIC CRUNCH
FUN
WIZARD JOKES
HELP WILLY FIND HIS MAJIC CRUNCH
START→
FINISH

JACK'S FAVORITE CEREAL

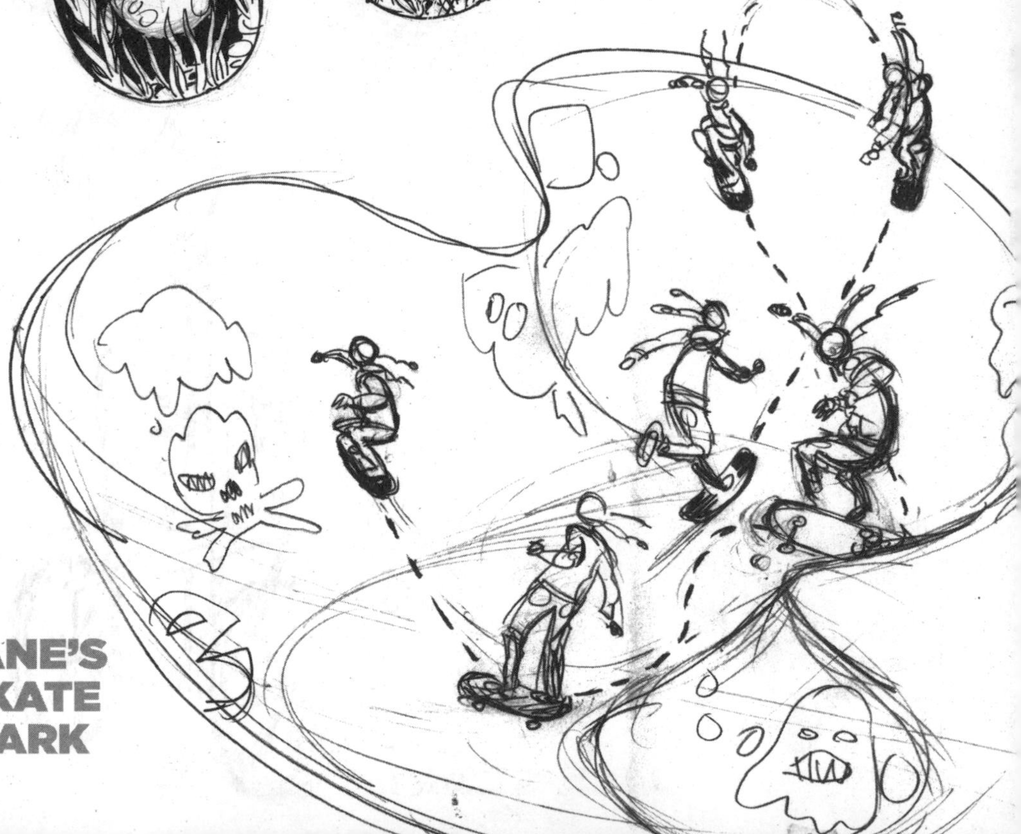

JANE'S SKATE PARK

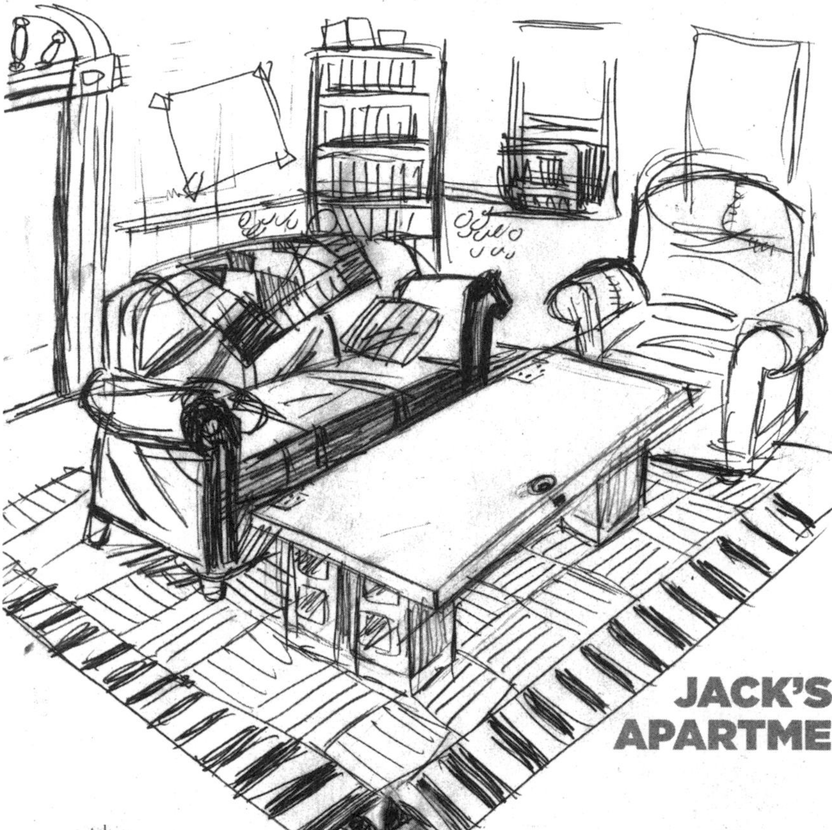

JACK'S APARTMENT

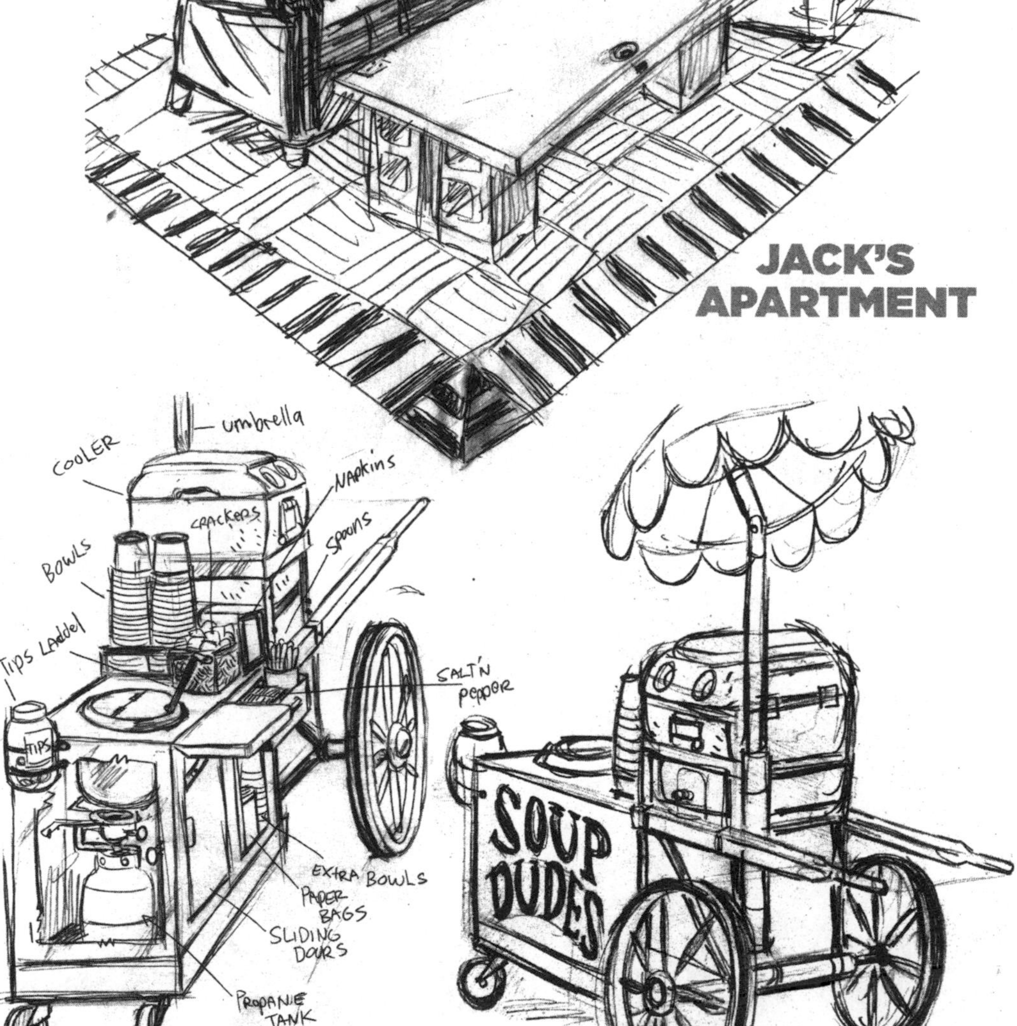

umbrella
COOLER
Napkins
Crackers
BOWLS
Spoons
Tips Laddel
Salt'n Pepoor
TIPS
EXTRA BOWLS
PAPER BAGS
SLIDING DOOR'S
PROPANIE TANK
SOUP DUDES

JACK'S CART

GREG MEANS is a writer, editor, and librarian from Portland, Oregon. He runs the micropublishing house Tugboat Press and edits the comic book anthologies Papercutter and Runner Runner. *The Cute Girl Network* is his first graphic novel.

MK REED is the author of *Americus* (drawn by Jonathan Hill) and the web comic *About A Bull*. She lives in Brooklyn with her very tall husband. Find her online at mkreed.com and on twitter @yesthatmkreed.

JOE FLOOD is an illustrator and comic book artist. He adapted the fantasy world of Stan Nicholls for the graphic novel, *Orcs: Forged for War*. Joe is thirty-three and lived in Brooklyn for nine years in preparation for this book.